Peter Norton's
Inside
OS/2

Peter Norton's
Inside
OS/2

Robert Lafore
and
Peter Norton

Brady Books • New York

Simon & Schuster, Inc.
Gulf + Western Building
One Gulf + Western Plaza
New York, NY 10023

Distributed by Prentice Hall Trade

Manufactured in the United States of America

10 9 8 7 6 5 4 3 2 1

Library of Congress Cataloging-in-Publication Data

Lafore, Robert (Robert W.)
    Peter Norton's Inside OS/2 / by Robert Lafore and Peter Norton.
        p.   cm.
    Includes index.
    ISBN 0-13-467895-8   : $24.95
    1. OS/2 (Computer operating system) I. Norton, Peter, 1943-   .
II. Title.   III. Title: Inside OS/2.
QA76.76.063L33 1988
005.4'469--dc19   88-25066
                                                      CIP

Don't waste any more time.

Don't key in another example from this book. You can order a two-diskette package of the source (.C) files and the executable (.exe) files for all the example programs in this book. You can use these files:

- to modify and experiment with already existing programs;
- to see what a program does without having to compile it;
- and to check the operation of your system.

Send this form in today with a check for $40.00 or credit card information to the address below. Be sure to choose the type of diskette you need.

Check One:

☐   Two 3.5" diskettes for Inside OS/2
☐   Two 5.25" high-density diskettes for Inside OS/2

Payment:

☐   Check Enclosed
☐   Charge to my credit card
     ☐   MasterCard
     ☐   VISA

Account Number _____ Expiration Date _____

Signature as it appears on card _____

Your Name _____
Address _____
City _____ State _____ Zip _____

Send to:

MicroService
Simon & Schuster Inc.
200 Old Tappan Road
Old Tappan, NJ 07675

Please allow 4-5 weeks for delivery.
For more information call 1 (800) 624-0023 (national) or 1 (800) 624-0024 (New Jersey).

This book is dedicated to Miss Joanie, with love.

RL

Acknowledgements

The authors want to thank our past and present editors at Brady Books: Janice Mandel, who talked us into this project, and Milissa Koloski, whose competence and unfailing good humor were essential to its completion. We are also grateful to Dan Rollins of Flambeaux Software, and Andy Reddig of TEK Microsystems, for their painstaking and expert technical edits. Mia McCroskey and Geraldine Ivins in the Brady production department burned the midnight oil to give the book its physical form.

Last but not least, we want to acknowledge the contribution of Microsoft Corporation in general and Marty Taucher in particular, for providing the various versions of OS/2 (starting when it was called 286DOS), without which this would be a book about Algol.

Limits of Liability and Disclaimer of Warranty

Trademarks

Contents

Table of Contents

Introduction

This book shows you how to program in OS/2. It is an easy step-by-step tutorial, starting simply and working up gradually to more complex topics. We use working C-language program examples to illustrate the concepts. Our goal is to make it easy for you to open the door to a whole new world of programming.

Do you remember when you wrote your first BASIC or Pascal program, and the excitement you felt when it functioned as you intended? Learning to program in OS/2 offers the same sense of discovery. Before OS/2, such features as multitasking and inter-process communication were available only to mainframe and mini-computer programmers (and to a limited extent on Unix-based systems such as Xenix). Now any programmer with a personal computer has access to some of the most powerful software capabilities available anywhere.

But how hard is it to apply these new techniques? A considerable mystique has grown up around OS/2 programming. There are even those who say it is impossible for ordinary programmers, without months or years of specialized training, to write serious programs for OS/2. This is emphatically not true. In a reasonably short period of time, the average programmer can become proficient in this new environment.

Why Should You Learn to Program in OS/2?

The OS/2 operating system is the heir to MS-DOS: it will become the dominant operating system in the years ahead, and will be the standard system well through the 1990s. Why? Because it solves problems endemic to MS-DOS.

First, OS/2 transcends the 640K memory barrier, so that programs and data can be far larger than under MS-DOS. There is a 16 Megabyte limit on the amount of memory the 80286 chip can address, but OS/2 permits virtual memory management, allowing programs larger than this to run. In the future, even this 16 megabyte limit will disappear as versions of OS/2 for the 80386 became available.

OS/2 also permits many programs to reside in memory at the same time, in an organized way that prevents them from interfering with each other. This eliminates the problems MS-DOS users faced when trying to use multiple TSR (Terminate and Stay Resident) programs. Moreover, under OS/2, programs can not only reside in memory simultaneously, they can also run simultaneously. In effect, this enables your computer to do several things at the same time: calculating a large spreadsheet while you type a letter, for example.

Not only can you run several programs at once, but each program can be doing several things at the same time: writing to the disk while getting keyboard input, for instance. This can result in programs that accomplish their jobs faster than is possible under the old single tasking system.

OS/2 provides a consistent and powerful programmer interface, a great improvement over the limitations of the "Int 21" interface of MS-DOS, which was awkward or impossible to access from higher-level languages, and had other problems as well. Many tasks, such as writing TSR-type programs, are greatly simplified in OS/2. And OS/2 offers many new possibilities, such as multitasking and sophisticated memory management.

Whom This Book Is For

This book is for anyone who is interested in learning how to program in OS/2. This includes professional programmers, students, hackers, and the merely curious. It is *not* just for the super-professional who dreams in assembly language and designs operating systems before breakfast. We make very few assumptions about our reader's prior experience. It's nice if you have programmed in the MS-DOS world, but not essential.

The C Language

To understand this book you must know how to program in the C language. C is the language of choice for MS-DOS programming, and with OS/2 it will continue to dominate. The major higher-level language development tools available for OS/2 are C compilers.

The DOS User Interface

Of course you should also have some acquaintance with MS-DOS as a user, and know how to list files, execute programs, and move around the directory structure. You don't need any particular training using OS/2, since from a user's perspective the OS/2 kernel commands are much the same as those in MS-DOS.

Assembly Language

It is not necessary to know assembly language to read this book. The OS/2 programmer's interface allows easy access to the operating system functions from higher-level languages as well as from assembler. All the program examples in this book are in C; there is almost no assembly language code.

The Equipment You'll Need to Use This Book

In brief, you'll need a computer capable of running OS/2, a copy of OS/2 itself, a C compiler capable of generating protected mode programs, and at least some parts of a development system. Let's look at these requirements in more detail.

Hardware

The IBM-PC AT will run the IBM version of OS/2, as will PS/2 models 50 and above. Many—but not all—AT clones will run either the Microsoft version of OS/2, or their manufacturer's version. The basic requirement is an 80286 or 80386 CPU. However, some computers, even though they are based on these chips and run MS-DOS, have hardware incompatibilities that prevent them from running OS/2. Computers based on 8088 and 8086 chips (such as the IBM-PC and XT and their clones) cannot run OS/2 at all.

You can actually run the OS/2 kernel with as little as 1 megabyte of memory. However, a more practical minimum is 1.6 megabytes (640K base memory and another megabyte above the 1M boundary). Two megabytes is adequate for the example programs in this book. Of course, if you intend to run many large programs at the same time, you may need additional memory.

If you are using the Presentation Manager you will definitely need more memory; consult the documentation for the latest recommendations.

A hard disk is a necessity for OS/2 systems. A 20 megabyte capacity is adequate. You'll also need a high-density floppy drive, either a 5 1/4 inch or a 3 1/2 inch, to load OS/2 and other files.

Either a monochrome or color monitor will work with OS/2, with the appropriate monochrome, CGA, EGA, or VGA adaptor. Not all third party graphics adaptors will work with OS/2; check them for compatibility before buying.

Printers are in general compatible with OS/2.

The Operating System

The examples in this book were written in OS/2 version 1.0, but they should be compatible with version 1.1 as well. We'll assume that you have OS/2 installed and running on your system.

Your system should come with a variety of files, including DOSCALLS.LIB, which contains the executable code for the API functions.

The C Compiler

The book is based on C language examples, so you should have a C compiler to turn them into executable programs. At this writing the Microsoft C Optimizing Compiler and a similar offering from IBM are the major products available. The examples in this book were created with version 5.10 of the Microsoft compiler. Doubtless other manufacturers will offer competing products in the near future. The compiler must be designed to produce code that will run in protected mode. Older compilers, designed for MS-DOS, won't work.

You'll need an editor to generate source files. If you do your editing in protected mode, which is somewhat more convenient, you'll need an editor written for this mode. One provided by Microsoft, called MEP, works well. You can also use your favorite old-style MS-DOS editor in the real-mode compatibility box. Most editors will run in the box, and you can quickly toggle back and forth between the editor in real mode and the compiler in protected mode.

OS/2 Development Systems

Microsoft and IBM offer development systems for writing OS/2 programs. These kits contain documentation, header files, and utility programs. This book is based on the Microsoft Programmer's Toolkit, which works with version 1.0 of OS/2. The development kits currently available are expensive, although their prices are expected to fall in the near future. What are the essential ingredients of these development kits?

In this book we describe many of the Application Program Interface (API) functions built into OS/2. These descriptions are probably adequate for learning about OS/2. However, for more information, and to develop your own programs, you'll need the more complete descriptions in the programmer's reference or technical reference provided with the development kits. An alternative is a reference book from a third party; these are already beginning to appear in bookstores. The development kits provide other documentation as well, but the description of the API functions is the most critical.

Second, you'll need the header files that provide prototypes for the API functions. (We discuss these files in detail in Chapter 2.) It is possible to write your own prototypes into each program. This is less convenient, but if the only reason you need a development kit is to buy the header files, it's worth considering. It's also possible that third party manufacturers will make header files available.

Finally there are various utility programs that are helpful in OS/2 program development. The only one used in this book is IMPLIB.EXE, which is used in the creation of dynamic link libraries (DLLs). However, there are other ways to create DLLs, as we'll see in Chapter 14.

Thus, while it is convenient to have an OS/2 development kit when using this book, it is not essential if you can piece together its key ingredients from other sources.

What's in This Book

The Applications Program Interface consists of more than 200 "system calls" or functions built into OS/2. Learning to program in OS/2 is largely a matter of learning how these functions work and the concepts underlying them. This book discusses the major API functions. A few API function calls, and the concepts they embody, are beyond the scope of this book.

Examples

This book uses working programming examples to demonstrate the various system calls. We recommend that you type in the example programs, experiment with them, and use them as a base for creating your own programs. The best way to learn anything is to actually do it. A disk containing the source code for the examples is also available with the coupon appearing in the front of the book.

Our programming examples are not meant to be full-scale applications. We feel that, in general, examples should be as compact as possible while still demonstrating the topic under discussion. Programming examples dozens of pages long obscure with their own complexity the points they intend to demonstrate.

How This Book Is Organized

Chapter 1 is a brief introduction to operating systems in general, and the OS/2 system in particular. Since there are so many new ideas in OS/2, it's important to see how they relate to what has gone before. We focus here on how features such as multitasking have evolved over the years.

The next chapter discusses how to set up the environment for program development. It then introduces you to the API, and gets you started writing your first simple OS/2 programs.

In the third chapter we start our serious exploration of the API, with system calls which put data on the screen and read it from the keyboard. This material will consolidate your understanding of the API before we attack the heart of OS/2 programming: multitasking.

There are actually two levels of multitasking available to programmers in OS/2: processes and threads. We'll cover these separately, in Chapters 4 and 5. In Chapter 6 we'll look at the principle method of interprocess synchronization: semaphores.

In Chapters 7 through 9 we'll explore the file system. Chapter 7 describes the API functions that handle directories, Chapter 8 covers reading and writing files, and Chapter 9 shows how to increase program efficiency by performing disk I/O at the same time as other activities. Chapter 10 covers memory allocation, an important topic in a multitasking environment, and Chapter 11 describes the three methods of interprocess communication: shared memory, pipes, and queues.

Chapter 12 covers device monitors, which give an OS/2 program the ability to act like an MS-DOS TSR; and signals, which are events such as the user pressing [Ctrl] [c]. Chapter 13 shows how to use the mouse in OS/2 and also how to write graphics images to the screen. Chapter 14 explores dynamic linking, a system of library files that are loaded into memory at run time.

The Presentation Manager

This book focuses on the OS/2 kernel. However, OS/2, in its full implementation, consists of two parts: the kernel and the Presentation Manager (PM). The PM is the Windows-like user interface included in release 1.1 of OS/2. PM programming is not covered in this book: it is a complex topic, and requires a book (or more) in itself. However, if you intend to learn PM programming, OS/2 kernel programming is an important first step, as the kernel underlies the PM.

Don't feel that you need to learn how to program under the Presentation Manager to be an OS/2 programmer. Many applications will have no need for the PM's sophisticated user interface. If you don't need menus, windows, and other complex graphics capabilities, then you can write applications using the character mode I/O functions included in the OS/2 kernel and described in this book. Such applications can run either with or without the Presentation Manager, and they will be easier and faster to create than full-scale PM applications.

A Tutorial, Not a Reference

This book is not intended as an all-inclusive reference or encyclopedia of OS/2 functions. It is an introduction to OS/2 programming, intended to make the learning process easy. The manuals that accompany OS/2 provide details on the complete range of API capabilities. (Or, see Brady's Advanced Programmer's Guide to OS/2.)

Typographical Conventions

This book uses two different fonts: a normal proportional font for text; and a monospaced font for program listings, examples of program output, and examples of program lines. Thus text you normally see on the computer screen appears in the monospaced font.

In the text (but not in the monospaced material) the following conventions are used to represent the various programming constructs used in C and OS/2.

Keywords in the C language, such as **if, while,** and **far**, are in bold. Also in bold are variable names from C programs: **temp**, **ByteCount**. Many of these words have uses in English as well as in C; using bold for the C versions helps to clarify which usage is intended.

OS/2 API functions are shown in both upper and lower case with the parentheses included; e.g., DosSleep(), and VioWrt-CharStrAttr(). C library functions are in lowercase, with the parentheses included: printf(), exit().

Operating system utility programs, like FORMAT and CHKDSK are in all upper case, as are other system and C language files like STDIO.H and OS2.H. The names of example programs in the book are in lowercase with the .C file extension included: sleep.c, horsrace.c, or setvio.exe. Where file extensions are referred to by themselves they are in all uppercase, as in .EXE and .DLL.

Keyboard keys referred to in the text are surrounded by brackets, as in [Enter], [F1], [PgUp], [C], and [Esc].

New terms are italicized when first introduced.

Doctor Livingston, I Presume

Learning to program in a completely new environment is a challenging adventure. Like Africa in the early nineteenth century, OS/2 is at this point largely unexplored. Most of the important and innovative programs that make use of these capabilities remain to be written. Perhaps you will be one of the pioneers, hacking out undiscovered territory from the vast range of possibilities embodied in OS/2. If so, we hope this book contributes in some small measure to your success.

Chapter 1

In this chapter we take a brief look at how operating systems have evolved over the years, and where OS/2 fits into this family tree. We'll also examine OS/2's features, and discuss how a programmer can use them to provide increased power and flexibility to the user.

It is not our intention in this book to dwell on abstract ideas; we prefer actual examples. In fact very soon—in the next chapter—we'll look at our first real live OS/2 programs. However, OS/2 and many of its features are so new that some background, and an overview of OS/2's capabilities from a programmer's perspective, will be helpful before we move on to the details. To return to our earlier analogy, it's useful to have an aerial view of the jungle before we land and start chopping our way through the vines and swatting at tze-tze flies.

A Very Brief History of Operating Systems

In this section we'll examine the evolution of operating systems. Our intent is not to provide a detailed history of operating systems, but rather to put OS/2 in perspective by reviewing the sorts of problems operating systems were designed to solve. We'll see how OS/2 fits into this picture.

Two Sides of the Coin

Operating systems present two faces to the world; one seen by the user, the other by the programmer.

The user sees the file and program management aspects of the system. Users command the operating system to list, copy, erase, and perform other file-related activities. They also command the execution of programs.

Programmers, on the other hand, see a set of utility functions that they can call from their programs. These utility functions place characters on the screen, read files, and perform countless other tasks for which programmers would otherwise need to write complex routines. How did these two faces of the operating system develop?

The No-System System

On the earliest computers there was no such thing as an operating system. These machines were room-size devices constructed of unreliable vacuum tubes. Programs, written in machine language, ran on the "bare" machine with no intermediating system software. Users brought their programs to the computer in the form of a deck of punched cards (or on the earliest machines as a hard-wired plug board), loaded the program, ran it, and carried off a printout containing the output. Then the next user loaded a program. In a sense the human programmers were the operating system, since they controlled all details of machine operation.

Early machines were not consumer products. Programmers had to write all the I/O routines for their programs. Sending a character to a printer, for example, required many detailed machine instructions, since there were no routines built into the computer. If it wasn't in your program, it wasn't there at all. There was also no memory management. Each user program had access to the entire memory space—the program took what it needed, and the rest was idle. Booting the system involved loading a routine, in binary, into memory using switches on the front panel, a time-consuming task.

Batch Processing Systems

In the mid-1950's, computers started to use transistors. This made them more reliable and they changed from a government-sponsored curiosity into a commercial product. However, they were still expensive, typically costing millions of dollars. And, using them was laborious. One user at a time (or the computer operator) loaded a program in the form of punched cards, waited for it to execute, and waited some more for it to print out the results, before the next program could be loaded. Computer owners soon saw that this was a highly inefficient use of very expensive equipment.

The problem is one all operating systems must attempt to solve: in general, input and output of data (I/O) takes time but does not fully engage the computing ability of the Central Processing Unit (CPU). A computer waiting for I/O to take place is mostly sitting idle, a wasted resource.

The first solution to the problem of keeping the CPU busy was a simple *batch* system. In this approach the punched cards for *many* programs were read by a smaller computer onto magnetic tape. The CPU processed the programs on the entire tape one after the other with the output going to a second reel of magnetic tape. Since magnetic tape drives were faster than card readers and printers, throughput was improved. The problem of wasted CPU time during I/O was dealt with by speeding up the I/O process.

The operating system consisted of commands placed between the jobs being read into the machine, and a batch monitor, resident in memory, to interpret the commands. (An example was IBM's JCL, for Job Control Language.)

Multiprogramming

However, there was still room for improvement. The expensive CPU was largely idle while data was being read or written, even though the I/O process had been speeded up. So another solution was devised: put more than one program in memory at the same time. Memory was partitioned, with each program placed in a separate partition. Now while I/O was taking place for one program, a second program could be computing, as shown in Figure 1-1. This approach, in which several programs share memory and alternate CPU usage among them, is called *multiprogramming*.

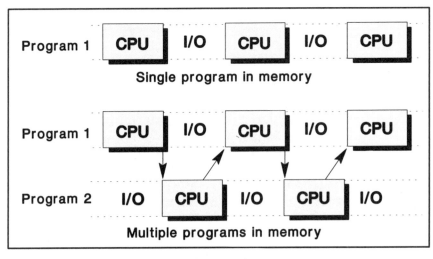

Figure 1-1
Multiprogramming Versus Sequential Programming

The situation shown in Figure 1-1 is somewhat idealized, since I/O time is assumed to be equal to processing time, a situation which leads to 100 percent utilization of the CPU by the two programs. In most situations the programs will not be so cooperative. However, by running more than two programs at the same time the CPU can be usefully employed a very high percentage of the time.

Of course multiprogramming required a more sophisticated operating system to keep track of which program was where, and help prevent (along with the hardware) one program from interfering with another.

Memory management on early multiprogramming systems could be fairly simple in that each program occupied only one partition in memory, and remained there until it was finished and unloaded.

However, there was always the problem that some programs were too big to fit in a given partition, or even too big to fit in the entire memory. Programs could be split into *overlays*—essentially separate programs that called each other—but this placed the burden on each programmer to divide the program up into appropriate-size sections.

A better solution was *virtual memory*, in which the memory space available looked bigger to each program than it actually was. A program could be divided into *pages* (usually equal-size sections of memory). Those pages in a program which were active (code being executed or data being accessed) were kept in RAM memory, while those which had not been used for a while were swapped out to a high-speed disk. This process was handled entirely by the operating system, and was invisible to the programmer, who could write programs that occupied a larger amount of memory than was physically available.

Designers also realized that it was inefficient for each user to create I/O routines from scratch. After all, the operating system already had routines of its own to write characters to the screen and perform other I/O tasks. It was logical for other programs to simply make use of these routines rather than replicating them in each program. Thus was born the idea of system functions or *system calls*, which are still a feature of most operating systems.

Time-Sharing Systems

Although multiprogramming kept the expensive CPU operating most of the time, it did nothing to help another problem: long turnaround time. A programmer would typically bring a program—in the form of a deck of punched cards—to the computer room and submit it to an operator. It would then wait its turn to run, which might be hours. Finally the programmer could pick up the printed output from the computer room, and see what had happened. There might be time for only two or three such runs per day, so debugging was a long process. (It's amazing that any software was ever written.)

The solution to the problem of long turnaround time was time-sharing. With time-sharing, a number of terminals are connected to the same CPU and each receives a series of small slices of CPU time. Since humans are generally much slower than the CPU, one user hardly notices that several others have been serviced between the typing of the "l" and the "s" in "ls". The result was an interactive system, in which the computer appeared to respond (at least in theory) almost instantly to user input.

The first widely used time-sharing system was Unix, which has since achieved wide distribution and been ported to a variety of different machines.

In a time-sharing environment the operating system has different priorities than in a batch system. It is still a multiprogramming system, but rather than optimizing CPU utilization and throughput, emphasis is placed on minimizing response time. This allows a user to type normally and see the results of executed programs in a reasonable length of time. When there are too many users on the system the response time is degraded and the users grow mutinous. The system must also attempt to treat all users fairly, with each one getting an equal share of CPU time.

The task of allocating CPU time in a time-sharing system is much more complicated than in a batch system. It is handled by a special part of the operating system called the *scheduler*. The assumptions programmed into the scheduler are important factors in the operating characteristics of the system. In a time-sharing system, each program runs for a short time: it is said that a program receives a *time slice*. When one program's time slice is over, another program starts to operate, even though the first program has not finished executing. This is called a *preemptive* system, since the scheduler switches off the process without asking: each process "preempts" or replaces another.

Notice that when we speak of two programs running at the same time in a time-sharing system we don't really mean *exactly* at the same time, since the CPU allots a time slice to only one user at a given time. To the users it appears that many programs are running at the same time (concurrently), but in reality the CPU runs user A's program for a few milliseconds, then user B's program, and so on for several or a dozen users. It then returns to give user A another time slice. It is only the rapidity of this round-robin switching of CPU time that provides the illusion of concurrency to the users.

A time-sharing operating system must also manage *resources*. As in the real world, resources are those things that are in short supply; that is, shared by a number of users. Examples of resources are printers and memory. The operating system maintains order, ensuring that user programs take turns at the printer, and allots memory as fairly and efficiently as possible.

The methods for dealing with memory are somewhat complicated. One common approach is to divide each user's program into *segments*. Segments are similar to pages—they divide a program into smaller pieces. However, while pages are of a fixed size, segments are usually different sizes. Segments can correspond to logical parts of the program: for example, one segment for the code, one segment for data, and one for the stack. The segments can be swapped in and out of memory as needed. They can also be protected, so that only one program can access them. Or, they can be shared, making a group of data available to many users.

Because they have multiple users, time-sharing systems introduce additional complexities. Security must be provided, so a user cannot inadvertently (or maliciously) alter another's programs or data, or disrupt the system itself. A system able to do some simple bookkeeping is desirable. It may track, for example, how long particular users were logged onto the system, so they or their department can be charged appropriately for computer time.

Single-Task Personal Computers

In the 1970s large-scale integration (LSI) chip fabrication technology lowered the cost, and size, of a single transistor to the point where personal computers became practical. This caused a return to the one-program, one-user situation of the early days of computing, except that now the computer was affordable by private individuals as well as large institutions. Early mass market personal computers included the IMSAI 8080, the Radio Shack TRS-80 Model I, the Apple II, and later, the IBM PC.

Operating systems on personal computers could be quite simple. They needed to deal with the operation of only one program at a time, so their primary roles were file management and providing a set of utilities to the programmer. This was usually an assembly language programmer, since early machines had no facility for a higher-level language (usually BASIC) to access the system calls built into the operating system. The early operating systems on Intel-based computers were CP/M and—with the introduction of the IBM PC—MS-DOS. MS-DOS has served admirably for more than half a decade, a long time in the computer world.

However, it has become increasingly clear that a single-tasking personal computer system is not the final answer. An operating system which can only load and run one program into memory limits a user's productivity in several ways. (We'll see examples in the next section.)

Developers have tried to provide a limited form of multiprogramming in MS-DOS by using TSRs (Terminate and Stay Resident programs), but this solution is far from perfect. For one thing, TSRs do not perform real multitasking: if you bring up a TSR to your screen, the program you were working on before will stop running. For another, TSRs tend to conflict with one another, since the architecture of MS-DOS was not created with TSRs in mind.

Of course, there are other limitations to MS-DOS as well; we'll look at these, and at OS/2's improvements, later in the chapter.

Multitasking Single-User Personal Computers

The term *multitasking* is similar to multiprogramming. Both refer to systems in which several programs can reside in memory at the same time, and execute concurrently. However, "task" does not mean quite the same thing as "program," as we'll see when we look at processes and threads later on.

Several products other than OS/2 attempt to transcend the limitations of MS-DOS. It is possible to run versions of multitasking, multi-user operating systems on personal computers using systems such as Unix and Xenix. But these really use the personal computer as a minicomputer to create a time-sharing system, bringing with them all the overhead of a multi-user environment. Such systems are not optimized for a single-user situation.

There is also a user-related problem in the upgrade of an MS-DOS personal computer to Unix. MS-DOS users don't want to learn a completely new set of commands to obtain multitasking and other improvements over MS-DOS. What is needed is a system designed specifically for personal computers, which is as compatible as possible with MS-DOS.

Several companies offer operating systems that embody some features of a multitasking system, such as DESQView from Quarter-Deck Office Systems, Windows from Microsoft, and PC-MOS from The Software Link. However, these systems do not offer the capabilities and features of OS/2, and they lack OS/2's wide acceptance, due to its backing by IBM and Microsoft.

OS/2 is thus the first major single-user, multitasking operating system developed specifically for personal computers. What are the goals of such a system, and how do they differ from those of batch processing, time-sharing, and single user systems that have gone before?

OS/2 Features

In this section we'll look at OS/2's features, and see how this system attempts to solve the various design problems of earlier systems. Our focus will be on those features that affect programming in OS/2.

Multitasking

The ability to run two or more programs at the same time is undoubtedly OS/2's most interesting feature. Typically, one program runs in the foreground, interacting with the user. At the same time, others are running unseen in the background. In addition, as we'll see, parts of the same program can also run concurrently.

The scheduler determines which of several tasks should receive CPU time. What are the design goals of the OS/2 scheduler? A batch-processing system attempts to maximize CPU utilization and throughput, while a time-sharing system tries to maximize response time and provide a fair distribution of time among different users. OS/2 attempts to optimize response time for the foreground process seen by the user, and at the same time provide a fair distribution of computing time among various background processes. It does this with what is called a "priority based, preemptive, time-sliced" scheduler.

The scheduler is *priority-based* in that different tasks are assigned different priorities: the higher a task's priority, the more often it will run. There are three main priority classes: time-critical, normal, and idle-time. Programs usually run at the normal priority class. Within each class, OS/2 assigns one of 32 priority levels. The foreground task has the highest priority; other tasks are given lower priorities. The operating system can change the priority of a task while it is running: normally, if a task has not run for a while its priority is raised.

For most applications, a programmer does not need to be concerned with priorities. However, in some situations it is necessary for a task to change its own priority; OS/2 provides system calls for this purpose.

The scheduler is called "preemptive" because (as we noted earlier) it will interrupt a program before it is finished, in order to run another program. It is called "time-sliced" because it divides time into equal-length slices, and allots the slices to different tasks on the basis of their priority.

Kinds of Multitasking

OS/2 actually provides for three separate kinds of multitasking. Different *screen groups* can run at the same time, different *processes* can run at the same time, and different *threads* can run at the same time. Let's look at each of these.

Screen Groups

Screen groups (which are also called "sessions") constitute a form of OS/2 multitasking accessible to the user, not just to the programmer. In essence a screen group is a virtual computer: it has its own screen image and its own "imaginary" keyboard (and mouse, if one is installed). We assume you've experimented with screen groups, running one program in one screen group and another in a second, and have switched from one to another using the [Ctrl] [Esc] keys to call up OS/2's Session Manager, or toggled directly between running programs with the [Alt] [Esc] keys. You might, for instance, try copying a directory full of files in one screen group, while using your word processor in another. Switching from one screen group to another is as close as OS/2 can come to switching to a completely separate computer.

The screen group currently using the video screen and keyboard is the "foreground" session; the others are called (not surprisingly) "background" sessions.

Of course, different screen groups must still compete for resources. Those running in the background cannot (usually) access the screen until the user brings them to the foreground. Programs running in separate screen groups cannot simultaneously access the same peripheral device or part of memory. However, as far as the user, and the programmer, are concerned, applications operating in different screen groups can *act* as if they own the entire computer. OS/2 makes sure they don't interfere with one another.

Starting One Session from Another

It is possible to start one screen group from another, without invoking the session manager. This is done using the command START. Suppose, for instance, you want to run the CHKDSK program in the background, and see the results when you are through. At the same time, you want to look through some directories with the DIR command. You can run the CHKDSK program in the background by typing:

```
C>start "CHECK" chkdsk a:
```

This starts a new screen group (session). The new session is given the name "CHECK" (or whatever name you typed in quotes). This name appears in the session manager's list. As soon as the new screen group comes into existence, it starts to execute the chkdsk a: command.

When you're done in the current screen group, change to the new one by calling up the session manager with [Ctrl] [Esc]. Select the entry "CHECK" from the list of sessions. The results of the operation will be on that session's screen.

Processes

The second form of OS/2 multitasking is the *process*. From a programmer's perspective, a process is similar to a program (although there is a distinction, as we'll see). One process can cause the execution of another; the first process is called the parent, and the second, the child. Child processes are a familiar aspect of Unix programming. They are different from overlays, mentioned earlier, in that both the parent and the child processes can exist in memory at the same time, and can continue to execute concurrently. Later in this chapter we'll see situations where child processes might be used.

There is a difference in this context between the words "program" and "process." A *program* is essentially an .EXE file (or perhaps more than one .EXE file). It is nothing more than the executable code, which may reside in memory, on a hard disk, or even on a floppy locked away in a drawer. A *process*, on the other hand, is an instance of a program actually being executed. The process is the executable code, plus the resources the process is using, such as memory, files, and I/O devices. One might say that the program is an inert body, while the process is the body which has been brought to life. To clarify the distinction, realize that the same program, or section of code, can be executed by two or more processes at the same time. If the code is written properly there is no reason either process will know another is executing the same code.

Starting a Background Process

When you run a program, by typing DIR for example, you start a process. In the simplest case this process runs in the foreground. For instance, if you type

```
C>dir >PRN
```

the contents of your directory will be sent to the printer.

However, while printing is going on, your screen is frozen; you can't do any other computing. You could have performed the printing in a different screen group, using the session manager as we saw earlier. But there is another way: a process can be executed in the background. This process will not have its own screen, so we will not be able to see the output, but in the present example that doesn't matter.

To start a process in the background, type "DETACH" followed by the program name (and any parameters the program needs). To print the directory in the background, type:

```
C>detach dir >PRN
```

The system prints a message like:

```
C>Process ID is 10
```

Each process has its own unique ID number. The numbers are assigned in sequence. After this message appears, you'll get back control of the keyboard, while the printing process continues running in the background.

Several different programs can be launched in the background at the same time. Also, multiple versions of the same program can run simultaneously. You could, for instance, sort two different files at the same time, using the SORT command.

Remember that a process running in the background does not (usually) have access to the screen or keyboard. Thus if something goes wrong (for instance, in this example the printer might not be turned on) you will never find out about it. It is possible to write an application which can "break through" to the foreground if necessary; we'll see how this is done later on.

It's also important that an application running in the background be able to terminate itself. If it hangs up for any reason, it will hang forever, since there is no way for the user to terminate it externally. Even exiting from an entire screen group doesn't kill it; the process continues to run in the background, as an "orphan".

Threads

The third kind of multitasking in OS/2 involves *threads*. A C programmer can think of a thread as a function; one which can run at the same time as other functions in the program. A thread in a program listing looks very much like a function, and in many ways behaves like one. When a process is first started it consists of a single thread. It can then start new threads using an API call. These threads can then execute concurrently with the first one.

Threads are useful for avoiding wasted CPU time while waiting for I/O. One thread is assigned to wait for the I/O, while another continues with computation or other activities. However, there are many other uses for threads.

Figure 1-2 shows the relationship of screen groups, processes, and threads. Each screen group can contain one or more running processes, and each process can contain one or more running threads.

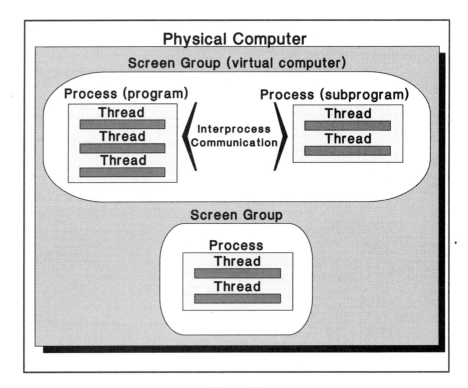

Figure 1-2
Screen Groups, Processes, and Threads

We'll return to the ideas of processes and threads in this chapter, and in later chapters, where we'll supply many examples of each.

Interprocess Synchronization

When more than one process or thread is running at the same time, the possibility arises that two such entities (we'll call them *tasks*) will start to interfere with each other. For instance, suppose two tasks have access to a buffer full of data, and one must fill the buffer before the other reads it. If the tasks are not properly synchronized, the first one might read the contents of the buffer before the other finishes writing, with the unfortunate results you might expect.

To prevent such problems OS/2 makes available a synchronization device called a *semaphore*. As its name implies, a semaphore holds up a task at a particular spot until another task changes the semaphore to indicate that a resource can be accessed. There are two kinds of semaphore, RAM semaphores, used mostly between threads, and system semaphores, usually used between processes.

Semaphores are an important part of OS/2 programming, and are discussed in detail in Chapter 6.

Interprocess Communication

Threads, which are similar to C functions, can communicate in some of the ways normal functions do: most importantly by using global variables. Separate processes, on the other hand, since they are in effect separate programs, require a different approach if they are to communicate. OS/2 has a particularly rich assortment of such interprocess communication facilities, including shared memory, pipes, and queues.

Shared memory is simply a segment of memory which is known to two or more separate processes; each can read or write to it. One process uses an API call to create a segment of shared memory. Other processes use other calls to find out where the memory is so they can access it.

Pipes are, at least to the programmer, similar to files. One process writes data to the pipe, where it is available for another process to read. However, the data sent to a pipe actually remains in memory, making them faster than files.

Queues are a more complex facility in which many messages, which can be quite large, can be stored and retrieved in various ways by different processes.

We'll look at all these techniques in the chapter on interprocess communication.

Memory Management

A problem specific to the MS-DOS operating system is the limitation on the amount of memory that can be addressed by programs: 640K. This limitation is the result of the 8088 or 8086 chip used on the IBM PC and XT: the chip can address only 1 megabyte. Available memory is further reduced because addresses between 640K and 1M are needed for graphics memory and the ROM BIOS. The 80286 and 80386 chips permit addressing much larger amounts of memory, but MS-DOS cannot take advantage of it.

Attempts to get around the MS-DOS 640K memory limitation have been devised, such as the EMS and EEMS memory standards and their extensions. These involve opening a sort of "window" on additional memory, but the process is complex and inefficient.

OS/2 eliminates the 640K memory limitation. The present version of OS/2 is designed for the 80286 chip, and permits directly addressing up to the 16 megabyte limit of physical memory imposed by this chip.

In fact, even this 16 megabyte limit is not absolute. Under OS/2 memory management, programs and their data can actually be larger than available physical memory. As described earlier, applications are divided into segments, and if there is not enough space in RAM for a complete application, OS/2 swaps some segments out of memory to the disk, while those actually being used remain. In many instances, the programmer can ignore the actual physical memory limit in the machine.

In theory, the programmer can address up to one gigabyte (1 megabyte times 1024) using virtual memory. However, in practice the amount of available virtual memory is limited by the free space on the hard disk. The parts of the program not in memory are swapped into a special file on the disk called the swap file. An application (or a group of applications running concurrently) must not be larger than available RAM plus the space available for the swap file.

Once a program is running, the operating system takes care of swapping the appropriate segments in and out of memory. When there is not enough memory for all the tasks currently running, the system looks for those memory segments which have not been referenced for a long time and saves them on the disk. This is called the *LRU* algorithm (for "Least Recently Used").

The 80286 hardware translates references to virtual addresses into physical addresses. Each executing process is assigned a *descriptor table*, which lists information about the segments it is using, such as their location and length. The operating system updates these tables to reflect the process currently loaded, and the hardware uses them to translate a reference to a virtual address into a physical memory address. If the address accessed is not in memory, the appropriate segment is loaded from disk into memory.

This activity is invisible to the programmer, who does not (usually) need to know whether a given segment is in memory or on the disk.

In C, the compiler sets up the segments needed for the program code, for the stack, and for the variables defined in the program. However, the programmer may want to create other segments to hold data which can be swapped in and out independent of the program itself, which can be shared by different processes, and which can be freed when no longer needed. The OS/2 API provides an extensive collection of functions for creating, using and freeing segments. We'll look at these in Chapter 10, which covers memory.

Future versions of OS/2 will make use of the capabilities unique to the 80386 chip, which permits directly addressing 4 gigabytes of physical memory and up to 64 terabytes of virtual memory (a terabyte is 1024 gigabytes). The current version of OS/2 runs on a 80386 machine, buts treats it only as a fast version of an 80286.

Programmer Interface

How does a programmer access the routines built into the operating system? In MS-DOS this was largely handled using a method called "INT 21," where a program called software interrupt number 21 hex, which then dispatched the program to the appropriate routine, depending on the contents of the AX register.   This system was inaccessible to higher-level languages unless they incorporated special library functions to load the CPU registers appropriately and transfer control to the interrupt. The process was clumsy and inefficient, since a programmer had to place values in variables representing the system registers, and the library function then had to take these values from the variables and transfer them to the registers prior to making the INT 21 call.

By contrast, OS/2 uses a very clean approach to access the system functions. Instead of using software interrupts, functions are accessed by calling them directly. Parameters need no longer be placed in registers, but are pushed onto the stack as they are in other function calls (although using the Pascal convention to specify which parameter comes first, as we'll see in the next chapter). Calls can be made directly from higher-level languages even more easily than from assembly language, and the process is faster and more efficient than under MS-DOS.

These system calls and the way they are accessed are called the "API", for Application Program Interface. There are over 200 API calls. They perform I/O, control processes, manage interprocess communication, and perform many other tasks. Exploring these functions is the main focus of this book.

Hardware Access

In MS-DOS it is usual for routines to access hardware directly, without going through the operating system. Calls are made to the ROM BIOS or data is sent directly to and from I/O ports. This is not the case in OS/2. Since several processes may try to access the same hardware at the same time, the operating system must oversee requests for each device, to ensure that one process doesn't interfere with another. This situation is shown in Figure 1-3.

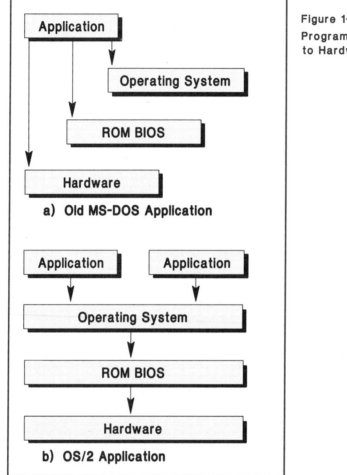

Figure 1-3
Program Access
to Hardware

a) Old MS-DOS Application

b) OS/2 Application

Fortunately, OS/2 provides very efficient routines for accessing the peripherals, so there is little performance degradation when compared with direct access.

Compatibility Mode

Once you install OS/2 in your system, can you run your old MS-DOS programs? Yes, backward compatibility is an important element in the OS/2 design. OS/2 provides for MS-DOS programs with something called variously the "compatibility box," "real mode box," or "3.x box." This so-called box, which is really one of two modes of OS/2 operation, permits one old MS-DOS style program to share the computer with a number of new programs written specifically for OS/2. MS-DOS programs run in *real* mode (the mode of the 80286 chip which emulates the older 8088 and 8086 chips), while programs running in the "normal" OS/2 environment are called *protected* mode programs, since in this mode one program's memory and resources are protected from other programs.

Most programs which run under MS-DOS will run in the compatibility box. A few, however, which are not "well-behaved" will not.

Family API

Writing a program which runs both under MS-DOS and under OS/2 protected mode (without using the compatibility box) would save having to develop two versions of a program intended to work in both environments. Microsoft has provided for this situation with something called "Family API." The "Family" here includes three possible environments: MS-DOS, the OS/2 compatibility box, and OS/2 protected mode.

A family API program is written using a subset of the OS/2 API calls. This permits compatibility with the three environments, but limits what the program can do. It cannot (since it must run in MS-DOS) engage in multitasking, and it cannot use interprocess communication or various other advanced features of OS/2.

Since this book focuses on the new features of OS/2, we will not have much to say about family API. For a discussion of this topic, and on the subject of converting existing programs to run under OS/2, see *Converting Applications to OS/2* (Brady Books, 1988).

Device Monitors

In a MS-DOS "memory resident," or TSR program, a programmer usually needs to trap or intercept the stream of characters typed at the keyboard before they reach the foreground program. In this way, when a specific key (a "hot key") is typed, the program can then branch to the TSR program. Arranging for this interception is quite complicated, and involves altering interrupt vectors and performing other acts with potentially troublesome repercussions.

OS/2 has systematized the interception of data intended for various I/O devices. A program, via an API function, asks the operating system to install a system routine called a "device monitor." This monitor routine then intercepts the stream of characters going to the device, so the program can monitor them and take action if appropriate.

Many different programs can install these monitors at the same time, and the operating system ensures that they don't interfere with each other. We'll show examples of device monitors in Chapter 12.

Dynamic Linking

OS/2 permits routines to be dynamically linked to a program at run time, rather than at link time. This helps with memory management, since a dynamically linked routine does not need to be loaded into memory along with the main program. It can be loaded later, when it is needed, and discarded after use, thus freeing memory space. Memory usage is further optimized because different programs can share the same Dynalink routines. We cover dynamic linking in Chapter 14.

Protection Rings

80286 and 80386 hardware permits programs to run at several different protection levels. Programs can access code running at lower levels (higher numbers), but programs at lower levels can't access those at higher levels. The OS/2 kernel occupies the highest level, ring 0, while applications occupy the lowest level, ring 3. Figure 1-4 illustrates this.

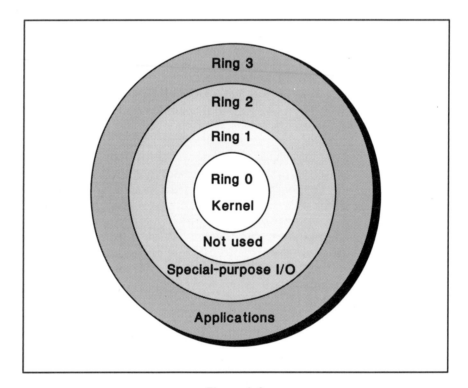

Figure 1-4
Protection Rings

In general, applications are written to operate entirely in ring 3. It is possible to write device drivers that make use of ring 2, but we will not be concerned with that possibility in this book, since the process is quite complicated.

Memory Organization

In OS/2 the operating system occupies two distinct areas of memory. The first is in low memory starting shortly above 0K, and the second starts at 1M (1024K), as shown in Figure 1-5.

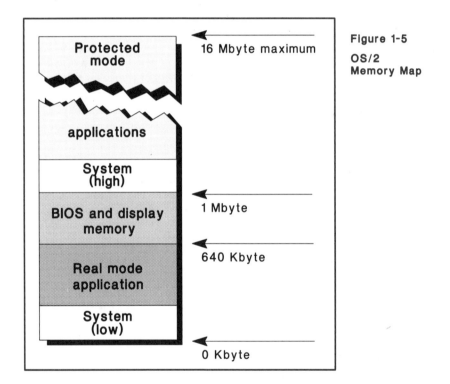

Protected mode

applications

System (high)

BIOS and display memory

Real mode application

System (low)

16 Mbyte maximum

1 Mbyte

640 Kbyte

0 Kbyte

Figure 1-5
OS/2
Memory Map

The operating system is split so that it doesn't occupy too much space below 640K, since only this space can be used for the compatibility box.

Application programs running in protected mode typically occupy the space above the high end of the operating system. However, OS/2 offers the user the option of removing the compatibility box and using this memory for protected mode programs as well. This option is selected using the config.sys file, as we'll see in the next chapter.

The programmer's approach to memory is quite different in OS/2 than in MS-DOS. In MS-DOS it is usual to assume a program and its data always occupy the same memory addresses, once loaded, leaving the balance of memory free. A program can thus modify its own code and directly address absolute memory locations. In OS/2, however, a program or its data may be swapped out to the disk, and written back into memory at a different place, while it is running. Also, parts of memory not occupied by a program may contain other programs, so there is no free memory other than that obtained specifically from the operating system. Thus programmers must play by the rules to a greater extent, and make fewer assumptions about where things are in memory than they could in MS-DOS.

Error Handling

An important OS/2 design goal is a consistent, easy-to-use way of returning errors from operating functions to a program. The return value of every OS/2 function is the same: a value of 0 if no error, and a positive code number if there is an error. All functions use the same list of error numbers, thus simplifying error analysis. The error number is returned in the AX register; for C programmers the function itself returns the error number, which can be conveniently analyzed by the program.

What Can a Programmer Do with OS/2?

Now that we've looked at some of OS/2's features, let's briefly discuss some of the ways you can put these features to use in your own programs.

Independent Programs

Although not directly relevant to programming, one of OS/2's advantages is that independent programs can be run at the same time by starting a new screen group (or by starting more than one application from the Presentation Manager). There are many times when running two or more programs at the same time is advantageous.

As we noted earlier, you may be running a spreadsheet which requires several minutes for a recalculation; during this time you can start up your word processor and write a memo (or switch back to edit a memo already started). You may be downloading a long file from CompuServe at the same time; while this is happening you can continue typing your memo, or go to examine the results of the spreadsheet recalculation.

These and similar activities all profit from running several programs at the same time, in different screen groups selected from the session manager, or as different Presentation Manager tasks. However, such examples don't involve the creation of new programs.

Separate Threads

For the programmer, perhaps the most obvious way to make use of OS/2's new features is to employ programs with separate threads. This enables a program to do more than one thing at once.

For instance, on startup, your program can read initialization data from the disk at the same time it prints a message to the user. Or, if you're writing a word processing program, one thread can calculate how to reformat the page, while another receives the typed text from the user at the keyboard, and a third waits for a disk access to finish.

What is the advantage of this sort of multitasking? In general, the program will run more quickly than before. Instead of waiting until the user has finished typing a message, the program uses one thread to wait for the user, and at the same time carries out other tasks with other threads, such as calculations or disk I/O. We'll show examples of such speed improvements later on.

There are also situations where, although there is no speed advantage, threads make it easier to conceptualize a problem or write a particular kind of routine. For instance, in a game program involving multiple ghosts that chase an icon representing the user around a maze, each ghost can be created and managed by a separate thread. Once a thread is started, it maintains an independent identity which fits perfectly with the operation of independent entities like ghosts, enemy spacecraft, and various other more serious kinds of data structures.

Different threads can also conserve memory. If many threads are doing the same thing at the same time, they can all use the same code; it is not necessary to have separate code for each thread.

Separate Processes

Separate processes are appropriate when two or more major activities are taking place simultaneously. For instance, in an integrated program involving a spreadsheet, database, and word processor, it might be desirable to have all three activities running at the same time. Rather than being independent applications, all would be related, perhaps child processes of a single control program. In this way the processes could coordinate their activities and share data. For instance, sales figures in a memo could be automatically updated as a result of changes in a spreadsheet.

Separate processes can also be used to save memory. An application may have an extensive "help" facility; to conserve memory the process that controls the help function may be kept on disk, as a separate file, until called from the main program.

"Memory Resident" Programs

It is convenient for certain utility programs to exist in memory at the same time as other, more major programs. Most users have their own favorite TSR utilities, which change the operation of certain keystrokes, pop a calculator onto the screen, and perform a wide variety of other helpful activities.

OS/2 makes it easier to write such utilities. They can also be more powerful than those in MS-DOS.

A TSR-type program in OS/2 can actively carry out tasks while the main program is running, rather than simply waiting for hot keys to be struck. For instance, a spelling-checker utility, activated by pressing a hot key, could consult a dictionary while the user continues to type text into a word-processor.

In MS-DOS the number of TSRs that could be used at once was restricted by the available memory; in OS/2 more memory is available, so a larger number of more powerful TSRs can be loaded into memory at the same time. The problem of interference between TSRs is also eliminated. The system treats TSRs like any other program running in a multitasking environment, and device monitors systematize the use of hot-keys.

The Best Is Yet to Come

This discussion has given only a hint of the ways OS/2 can be put to use. As we noted earlier, the major applications for OS/2 are waiting to be written. There are without a doubt new and astonishing ways to use multitasking, and OS/2's other features, that no one has yet discovered.

Summary

In this chapter we've traced the history of operating systems, showing the origin of multiprogramming and time-sharing operating systems, and how these relate to OS/2. We examined the general features of OS/2 from a programmer's perspective, and discussed some of the ways these features can be used to provide added functionality in applications.

In the next chapter we'll be much more specific. We'll discuss the various files needed to develop C language OS/2 applications, and we'll put the system to work by creating programs that demonstrate some simple API functions.

GETTING STARTED

In this chapter we'll discuss setting up your operating system environment so you can develop C language OS/2 programs, and then introduce you to some simple API functions to give you a feel for what these functions look like and how they operate.

Setting Up the OS/2 Environment

In this section we briefly discuss some aspects of the way OS/2 is set up for program development. Our intent here is not to provide detailed, step-by-step instructions for setting up your system; the manuals accompanying your system do that, and an automated installation program handles most of the details of configuring the system. Rather, we want to provide an overview of the directories and files needed for developing programs, and explain some aspects of the system which might otherwise seem obscure.

The details described here may vary somewhat from one manufacturer's version of OS/2 to another, so for exact filenames and other specifics, consult the documentation for your particular system. Our comments are based on Microsoft's version of OS/2 1.0.

Dual Boot

Some versions of OS/2 let you configure your system with the option of booting up in either OS/2 or MS-DOS. (This isn't MS-DOS in the compatibility box, but the genuine old MS-DOS.)

There are several reasons to retain the ability to run MS-DOS. One is that a few MS-DOS programs won't run in the compatibility box. Of course, if you have two computers you can keep MS-DOS in one and install OS/2 in the other, thus preserving complete flexibility. However, if you have only one machine, the next best thing is the dual boot option.

Select dual boot from the install program. Once the system is installed, you then select either MS-DOS or OS/2 each time you boot up the system. Switching between the two operating systems by rebooting in this way is not nearly as convenient as switching to and from the compatibility box, which takes less than a second, but it is useful if you want to keep your old MS-DOS system working exactly the way it always did.

System Files

OS/2 consists of a large number of files of different types, considerably more than are in MS-DOS. The system directory and file structure can be created either using the automated initialization program included with OS/2, or by hand, following the instructions in the setup guide.

There are many ways to arrange the directories used in the OS/2 system. The particular arrangement may vary, depending on the installation program used and the desires of the person configuring the system, so we won't attempt to describe the exact OS/2 directory structure here. We will describe, in general terms, the files used in the system.

Basic System Files: These form the heart of the operating system. They include the files OS2BIO.COM and OS2DOS.COM, and the command processor programs COMMAND.COM, which works in the compatibility box, and COM.EXE, which works in protected mode. These files correspond to the IBMBIOS.COM, IBMDOS.COM, and COMMAND.COM files in MS-DOS. The session manager SHELL.EXE allows you to switch between programs, and between real and protected mode. It is invoked with [Ctrl] [Esc].

When OS/2 is installed, these system files are typically copied to the root directory of the disk used to boot the system.

Utility Programs: OS/2 uses most of the same utilities as MS-DOS, modified to take advantage of OS/2's capabilities. For example, the OS/2 DISKCOPY program can use more than 640K of memory, so an entire high-capacity diskette can be stored in memory at once, and copied without repeatedly swapping the disks. Other familiar utilities such as FORMAT, EDLIN, SORT, and XCOPY are also present. In most instances the old MS-DOS versions of these utilities will not work in protected mode.

Dynamic Link Files have .DLL extensions. They are parts of the operating system which are loaded and linked with a program only as needed. For instance, KBDCALLS.DLL is loaded at run time, when the system determines, using information left by the linker, that an application calls a keyboard API function. Most of these files are necessary for running applications.

Code Page Files support code page functions to reconfigure the system for different countries. This permits different keyboard configurations, date and money formats, and so on. These files use the .DCP extension.

Device Drivers have the .SYS extension. There are drivers for the screen, keyboard, and other peripherals. These drivers are specially written to operate in a multitasking environment. The old MS-DOS drivers won't work. If two or more tasks request service from a driver at the same time, one must be given access, while the others are put in a queue and permitted to use the device only after the first is finished. This requires more complicated code than do MS-DOS drivers.

Development Tools: Various files contain the programs used for software development. These include the C compiler/linker, the MAKE, LINK, LIB utilities, and versions of the CodeView debugger for real and protected mode.

The INCLUDE and LIB Directories: As in other versions of C, the INCLUDE directory contains various header files, such as STDIO.H.

The function prototypes for the API functions are contained in a hierarchy of files with the .H extension. These are important files when working with the OS/2 API, as we'll discuss later.

The LIB directory contains the .LIB and .OBJ files that the compiler uses to add library routines and run-time routines to C programs. This provides for different memory models and different kinds of floating point support. When the system is first installed these library files are built for the appropriate models.

Only the needed libraries are built, since they are quite large. For instance, if your system does not have a math coprocessor chip installed, the libraries for this option are not installed. Compiler command-line options determine which of these installed libraries are used for a particular job.

The Swap File: If you're going to run with segment swapping enabled, another file is necessary: the swap file. This is the storage area for segments which "overflow" from memory when the running programs and data will no longer fit in available RAM. The system creates this file automatically when it needs it, then expands it as the amount of information to be swapped out of memory changes. The file is called SWAPPER.DAT.

The swap file can grow quite large. If you have a program that needs a megabyte of data storage and the system needs to swap it out of memory to run another program, then you'll need a megabyte of storage in SWAPPER.DAT. The system automatically enlarges the file to this size, but the space must be available on the disk. The amount of virtual memory available to the system is the amount of RAM plus the amount of free disk space.

In Chapter 10, on memory, we'll look into this further, and show an example where available RAM is exceeded and the system must create the swap file.

Configuration Files

The configuration file for OS/2 is called CONFIG.SYS, just as in MS-DOS. It executes when OS/2 is first booted, just as when MS-DOS is first booted. The CONFIG.SYS file is applicable whether you're going to switch to the compatibility box or continue to use protected mode in OS/2. If you have the dual-boot feature, then the MS-DOS configuration will be called CONFIG.SYS, while the OS/2 file will be CONFIG.OS2.

The CONFIG.OS2 file sets a number of different parameters. In OS/2 many of these parameters relate to processes unique to a multitasking environment. In this section we'll look at some of the key configuration commands used in a typical development environment. There are more commands than we cover here; for a description of other commands, and more details on those we mention, see the setup guide.

Buffers is a configuration command that specifies how many open disk file buffers there can be. (Its purpose is the same in MS-DOS.) More buffers are generally needed in OS/2 than in MS-DOS. Too many buffers waste memory, since each takes 512 bytes; on the other hand, you don't want to run out in the middle of a program. The more programs running at the same time, using files, the more buffers you'll want to use. The format is:

```
buffers=35
```

Specifying a value of 50 should avoid problems with running out of buffers, even in a multitasking situation.

Libpath must be used to specify the location of the dynamic link library. The command

```
libpath=c:\
```

specifies that the dynamic link (.DLL) files are in the root directory of drive C. Several pathnames can be used if they are separated by semicolons.

Memman selects two memory management options. The first, swap or noswap, specifies whether the system can swap segments in and out of memory. Since being able to swap segments is an important feature of OS/2—and in many cases is necessary when running several large programs at the same time, or running a program that is too big by itself for memory—this option should normally be set to swap. The second option is move or nomove, which specifies whether OS/2 is permitted to move data segments in memory. Normally this should be set to move. Thus, for the examples in this book, this command should look like this:

```
memman=swap,move
```

In certain non-typical situations, such as a real-time system where timing considerations are critical, it might be necessary to prevent the operating system from moving things around in memory, by using the noswap and nomove options.

Swappath specifies where the swap file is located when segments from a running program are swapped out to the disk. It has the format

```
swappath=c:\swapdir
```

where swapdir is the directory to which the swap file (which is called swapper.dat) will go. This command has an effect only if swapping is enabled by the memman command. The swap file is usually placed in the root directory.

Protectonly can be used to disable the real mode compatibility box, making the memory below 640K, normally used for real mode applications, available for protected mode applications. The format is:

```
protectonly=yes
```

If you want more protected mode memory, or are sure you will never want to run a real mode application, the option for this command should be set to yes. Otherwise, it should be set to no (the default) to allow the use of both protected mode and compatibility box programs.

Rmsize can be used to specify how much of the memory below 640K is to be reserved for real mode applications. Assuming you've selected protectonly=no, you can still save memory by restricting real mode programs to a number smaller than 640; for instance:

```
rmsize=300
```

Remember that the low part of the operating system takes up some room.

Shell loads the real-mode command processor, command.com, by specifying the pathname used to find this processor. The command.com program itself can take several switches (command-line arguments), so, for example, the command

```
shell=c:\os2sys\command.com /e:512
```

not only gives the pathname of command.com, but specifies an environmental size of 512 bytes.

Protshell is used to load and run the program selector and to specify the protected mode command interpreter. An example is

```
protshell=c:\shell.exe c:\cmd.exe c:\os2init.cmd
```

where shell.exe is the program selector and cmd.exe is the protected mode command interpreter. Files to be executed when cmd.exe is executed can be appended; in this example the batch file os2init.cmd will be executed by cmd.exe.

Device, as it did in MS-DOS, tells the system a special device driver is installed and where to find it. For example, the command

```
device=c:\os2\mousea04.sys
```

specifies the pathname for the device driver MOUSEA04.SYS.

Two commands can be used to control the operation of the scheduler. These are set to appropriate default values and do not normally need to be changed, but examining them may cast some light on the operation of the scheduler.

Timeslice sets the minimum and maximum timeslice values the scheduler allots to a process. The default value of the timeslice is a few hundred milliseconds, but this command can change it. The command has the format

```
timeslice=50,100
```

where the first number is the minimum value for the timeslice, the second the maximum. The minimum can't be any less than 31 milliseconds, and the maximum must be greater than the minimum. The maximum can be omitted, in which case the system assumes the maximum and minimum are the same.

Maxwait specifies a maximum for how long a process must wait. If many processes are running in the system it may take several seconds before a particular process is serviced. This maximum waiting time can be set to a particular value to minimize this time. The command has the format

```
maxwait=2
```

where the value is expressed in seconds. When this command has been given, the priority of any process that has not been serviced in the specified time is temporarily raised, guaranteeing that it receives service.

Batch Files

Batch files execute a series of DOS commands, automating what would otherwise be a tedious job for the computer operator. Certain batch files are executed automatically when the system is first booted; it's those we'll look at here. In MS-DOS the batch file that is automatically executed at boot time is AUTOEXEC.BAT.

In OS/2 two different auto-execute batch files are used. The file STARTUP.CMD executes automatically when the system is first booted into protected mode, and the file AUTOEXEC.BAT executes when the compatibility box is first used.

In general, the extension .CMD identifies batch files that run in protected mode, and .BAT identifies batch files that run in real mode, just as it does in MS-DOS. In protected mode, files with the extension .BAT are not recognized as batch files, and are not executable; in real mode files with the extension .CMD are not executable.

STARTUP.CMD: As noted, this file is executed when OS/2 is first booted. It plays the same role in protected mode that AUTOEXEC.BAT plays in MS-DOS. Note however, that STARTUP.CMD is executed only when the *first* screen group is started. When you switch to another screen group, the environmental information set in STARTUP.CMD will not exist.

STARTUP.CMD actually has few responsibilities in the present system. By executing the command os2init this file turns control over to another batch file, OS2INIT.CMD.

OS2INIT.CMD: In a C language development system OS2INIT.CMD sets the environmental variables to configure the system for using the C compiler and other development tools. Equivalencies can be set for the LIB, INCLUDE, and other variables used by the compiler. The PATH command can be set so the various development tools can be invoked from any directory.

OS2INIT.CMD is usually executed automatically at the beginning of each session you invoke.

If you're using dual-boot mode, AUTOEXEC.BAT works in MS-DOS, while another file, AUTOEXEC.OS2, is executed when the compatibility box is first invoked in OS/2.

Compiler Options

Since we're going to be developing programs in C, we need to know how to use the compiler. (As we noted earlier, we'll assume that you're using the Microsoft C compiler; with other compilers the settings may be different).

Almost all the example programs in this book were compiled with the following command line for the Microsoft compiler:

```
cl -Lp -G2 -Zp %1.c
```

Let's look at the various options used in this line. First, the program cl.exe invokes both the compiler and linker together (you can call the compiler and linker separately if you prefer).

The -Lp option, which exists only on the OS/2 compiler, produces an executable file which runs in the OS/2 protected mode. To produce executable files for the compatibility box, you would use the -Lc option. (Options can be preceded either by a dash or a slash, so /Lp is the same as -Lp.)

The -G2 option enables the instruction set for the 80286 microprocessor. Without this option the compiler restricts itself to the 8086 instruction set. This works, but you lose the advantages of the additional instructions in the 80286, resulting in applications that run, in some cases, less quickly.

The -Zp option may be important when your programs use structures. Used without an argument, as shown here, it causes structure members to be packed on one-byte boundaries. This is what OS/2 expects, so using this option ensures accurate communication between your application and the OS/2 API.

Some OS/2 programmers routinely use the -AL option, which specifies use of the large memory model. This permits programs to be written that are so large they need multiple segments for both code and data. It also means that all references to code and data are made by **far** (32-bit) pointers. In certain situations where you want to call C library routines with arguments that are pointers, you may need the **far** versions of these routines; these are included automatically if you're using the large memory model.

On the other hand, if you use the large memory model, normal references to code and data will also use **far** pointers. This is more cumbersome than necessary and slows down program execution. For the examples in this book we feel it is better to explicitly label pointers as **far** when necessary, rather than using the -AL option and assuming all pointers are **far**. This makes it clearer what pointers must be **far** and what pointers can be **near**.

You can use the MAKE utility to compile your programs. For the simple examples in this book, however, a simple batch (.CMD) file incorporating the compiler command-line argument shown above is sufficient.

Editors

Since you'll be compiling and running programs from this book in protected mode, it's most convenient to have an editor which will work in protected mode. However, as of this writing few such editors are available. Microsoft makes two editors which run in protected mode. The MEP editor is appropriate for creating programs. We won't go into detail on using this editor here; you can read about it in the user's guide. The disadvantage is that you need to learn how to use a new editor, although MEP can be configured to resemble other editors.

Another option is to use an old-style MS-DOS editor or word processor in the compatibility box. You can edit the program in real mode, then toggle into protected mode to compile and run it. This way you can use an editor you're already familiar with. This approach works well unless you don't have enough memory to run the compatibility box, or you don't want to use the box at all.

At this point we assume that you've set up your OS/2 system and are ready to develop OS/2 programs.

Simple OS/2 Programs

We start out in this section with some short examples. One of the points we want to demonstrate with this approach is just how simple OS/2 programming can be. However, we'll also be getting a first glimpse of some more complicated concepts.

The sleep.c Program

This is just about the simplest program you can write using an OS/2 API function.

```
/* sleep.c */
/* causes program to pause for fixed period */
#define INCL_DOS
#include <os2.h>
main()
{
   printf("Pause is beginning\n");
   DosSleep(3000L);
   printf("Pause is over\n");
   exit(0);
}
```

This program uses the API function DosSleep(), which, as its name implies, causes the application to pause—or puts it to sleep—for a specified time. The time period is specified by the function's single argument, in this case 3000L. This is the time, in milliseconds, that the application sleeps.

Type in this program, compile and link it, and try it out. You should see the two messages

```
Pause is beginning
Pause is ending
```

appear on your screen, the second message three seconds after the first.

API Functions

The programmer's reference manual, which is included in both the IBM and Microsoft OS/2 development systems, contains complete descriptions of the API functions. This manual should be consulted whenever a question arises about the correct way to use a function. However, the wealth of information and the format used in these manuals can be confusing to newcomers to OS/2. In this book we present simpler descriptions of the API functions. We describe what each function does, and summarize the function and its arguments in a box. Here's the box for the DosSleep() function:

DosSleep() — Delays execution of current thread

```
DosSleep(interval);
unsigned long interval;    /* delay time in milliseconds */
```

There are several points to notice about this function and the format used for it.

First, the function name contains both upper and lower case letters. Prerelease versions of the Microsoft Programmer's toolkit specified all upper case API function names, but the newer format is more readable. (The current IBM development system still uses all uppercase.)

The type of the DosSleep() function is **extern unsigned far pascal**. Almost every OS/2 API function is of this type. Let's examine its components.

The **pascal** keyword determines how the function's parameters are placed on the stack. This keyword specifies that the *first* argument supplied to the function (reading from left to right) goes on the stack first. In normal C functions the *last* argument (the one on the right) goes on the stack first. (The normal C order permits certain functions, like printf(), to use a variable number of arguments.) The **pascal** convention further implies that the *called function* removes the arguments from the stack before returning control to the calling program; in normal C functions the *calling program* must remove the arguments. The **pascal** convention also changes the function name into all upper case.

C programmers won't ordinarily need to worry about this convention or the contents of the stack. In some cases, however—as we'll see when we learn how to pass arguments to threads—knowing how the stack is organized is important.

All API functions use the storage class **external**, and all are referenced by **far** pointers. Most API functions are of type **unsigned**, since they return an error code of this type. A few, however, do not return an error code, and are of type **void**.

Argument Data Types

The programmer's reference included in the Microsoft programmer's toolkit specifies the data types of functions, and their arguments, using identifiers derived using **typedef** and **#define** definitions. For example, the DosSleep() function is shown like this:

```
USHORT DosSleep(ulTime)
ULONG ulTime;
```

USHORT is **typedef**ed to be of type **unsigned int**, while **ULONG** is **unsigned long**. Dozens of these derived types are used in the function descriptions, and some can be rather obscure. For example, **HSYSSEM** is **void far ***, and **PHDIR** is **unsigned short far ***. These derived types shorten the functions descriptions, and may be easier for experienced OS/2 programmers to read. However, we feel that beginners to the subject will prefer function descriptions that use the normal C types. With such descriptions it isn't necessary to search for the meaning of a derived type when learning about the function. Accordingly the boxes used to summarize the functions in this book will use the normal C data types.

The IBM development system currently does not use the Microsoft derived types. The correspondence between the Microsoft data types and the real thing are summarized in Appendix A.

Header Files

It is necessary to use a prototype (definition) for every API function in your application. Prototypes are always desirable to avoid unflagged errors due to type mismatches in the arguments. In OS/2 the prototypes are essential to define the types of the functions themselves, which would otherwise be type **int** instead of **extern unsigned far pascal**.

You can write your own prototypes and insert them at the beginning of your program, but it is usually more convenient to use those provided in the header files supplied with the development system. Microsoft provides a rather sophisticated way to manage these files, in an attempt to shorten the amount of header material included in each source file. Here's how it works.

Selective Inclusion with #define: The function prototypes are contained in two files, BSESUB.H and BSEDOS.H. The BSESUB.H file contains the prototypes for the functions that manage the video display, the keyboard, and the mouse. (These function names all start with the letters "Vio", "Kbd", or "Mou", as in VioScrollDn.) The BSEDOS.H file handles all the remaining functions (which start with the letters "Dos"). The BSEDOS.H file, which is considerably larger than BSESUB.H, is divided into sections. Each section contains the prototypes for a particular group of functions, such as file management, memory management, semaphore support, and so on. Each section is surrounded by an **#ifdef #endif** pair. By using an appropriate definition in your program source file, only the necessary part of the header file will be included.

For example, the prototype for the DosSleep() function is in the section of BSEDOS.H devoted to process and thread support. This section starts with the directive:

```
#ifdef INCL_DOSPROCESS
```

and ends with an **#endif**. If the program source file contains the directive:

```
#define INCL_DOSPROCESS
```

then this part of the BSEDOS.H header file will be included in the program. There are more than a dozen such **#define** constants, such as **INCL_DOSFILEMGR** for file-related functions, **INCL_DOSMEMMGR** for memory management, **INCL_DOSDATETIME** for date and time support, and so forth.

Including the Header Files: The header files are arranged in hierarchical fashion. At the top of the organization chart is OS2.H. To cause the various header files to be included, a program should contain the directive:

```
#include <os2.h>
```

In OS/2 version 1.0 the OS2.H file consists of only two directives:

```
#include "os2def.h"
#include "bse.h"
```

A third **#include** is added in OS/2 version 1.1 to include a file containing definitions for the Presentation Manager.

The OS2DEF.H file contains definitions used in the other header files, including the derived data types mentioned earlier. It also contains macros and some structure definitions.

The BSE.H file contains the following directives:

```
#include <bsedos.h>
#include <bsesub.h>
#include <bseerr.h>
```

The first two files contain prototypes, as mentioned earlier. The last one, BSEERR.H, contains error message definitions, such as:

```
#define ERROR_FILE_NOT_FOUND 2
```

This file is very long, but it is only needed if such error identifiers are used but not defined in the program.

Which Approach to Header Files? There are a variety of ways to make use of the hierarchical arrangement of the Microsoft header files.

The simplest approach is to include all the header files in your program. To do this, use the directives:

```
#define INCL_BASE
#include <os2.h>
```

The INCL_BASE definition will pull in all three files: BSESUB.H, BSEDOS.H, and BSEERR.H. The disadvantage of this approach is that it takes several additional seconds for the preprocessor to handle all this material (some 60K of files) when you compile your program.

To minimize compile time, you can use only those files that are necessary, and only those sections of the BSEDOS.H file that are necessary. For example, if the only API function in a program is DosSleep(), use:

```
#define INCL_NOCOMMON
#define DOS_PROCESS
#include <os2.h>
```

The INCL_NOCOMMON is necessary to exclude those sections of BSEDOS.H not specifically requested. DOS_PROCESS will include the section of BSEDOS.H containing the process and thread management prototypes, which includes DosSleep().

This approach excludes BSESUB.H and BSEERR.H, and includes only one section of BSEDOS.H, thus creating the smallest source file for this situation. The disadvantage is that you must remember which **#define** to use with each function. Also, the time saving realized by selective exclusion of parts of BSEDOS.H is not as significant as that gained by excluding an entire file.

In this book we use a middle-of-the-road approach. If a program uses a function prototyped in BSESUB.H, we include this file:

```
#define INCL_SUB
#include <os2.h>
```

If the program uses a function from BSEDOS.H, we include this file in its entirety:

```
#define INCL_DOS
#include <os2.h>
```

If the program uses functions from both files, we include them both:

```
#define INCL_DOS
#define INCL_SUB
#include <os2.h>
```

We don't use the BSEERR.H file. When it is occasionally necessary to use error definitions in a program, they are defined explicitly in the source file.

The IBM header files do not currently use such an elaborate system. Two files, DOSCALLS.H, and SUBCALLS.H, correspond to the files BSEDOS.H and BSESUB.H used in the Microsoft system. One or both of these files is **#included** in the program as necessary; **#define** statements are not used.

Eliminating Header Files

There is another way to provide function prototypes. You can write them yourself, inserting them into your program as needed. For example, here's how the sleep.c program would look, rewritten with a prototype for DosSleep():

```
/* sleep2.c */
/* causes program to pause for fixed period */
/* uses prototype in program, rather than header file */

extern unsigned far pascal DosSleep( unsigned long );

main()
{
    printf("Pause is beginning\n");
    DosSleep(3000L);
    printf("Pause is over\n");
    exit(0);
}
```

Notice that the header files and their **#defines** have been eliminated. If the program used other functions, their prototypes would be included as well. Structures could also be defined in the program rather than in the header files.

This approach is less convenient than using header files, but it does have some advantages. First, it makes it easy to see the data types of arguments used in the function: they're set forth overtly in the program. Second, the program is potentially more portable. If structures from header files are used, then the structure member names in the program must correspond with those in the header files. Different systems (IBM and Microsoft, for example) may use different structure names, so, if header files are used, a program that compiles in one system may not compile in another. Inserting your own prototypes and structure definitions avoids this problem. Finally, if you don't have access to header files, writing your own prototypes and structure definitions provides an alternative.

The exit() C Library Function

You'll notice we've terminated the sleep.c program with the exit() C library function. It is considered bad form to end an OS/2 program by simply letting control fall through the final brace. Using the exit() function ensures that things are cleaned up properly. In most situations, including the example shown above (if it is running by itself in the system), the program works fine without the exit(). However, troubles can arise with certain library functions (printf() for example) if exit() is not used.

When we investigate threads we'll see that an API function, DosExit(), is used instead of exit() in specific circumstances.

A Dreamless Sleep

The DosSleep() function actually shuts down the sleep.c program and returns control to the operating system. The program does not sit in a loop or perform any other activity waiting for its interval to be over; it is not using any CPU cycles while it is asleep. The DosSleep() function causes the operating system to set a timer so it reminds itself when it's time to wake up the calling program. The calling program then becomes inactive.

This is important, because one of the elements of good program design in a multitasking environment is to avoid stealing CPU cycles. If you use a wait-loop or similar timekilling device in your program, you unnecessarily slow down the entire system, using cycles that could be put to better use by other applications.

Another point of interest about DosSleep() is that, even if you call it with a value of 0 for its argument, it still returns control to the operating system. The calling program then loses the remainder of its time slice, but gets the next scheduled time slice. You can usefully employ DosSleep() with a 0 value whenever your program wants the operating system to pass control to another process. We'll learn more about this in the chapters on processes and threads.

Return Codes: the beep.c Program

Here's another simple program, one that beeps the speaker for a fixed duration and frequency:

```
/* beep.c */
/* beeps speaker */
#define INCL_DOS
#include <os2.h>
```

(continued)

```
main()
{
    unsigned frequency = 500;   /* frequency in Hertz */
    unsigned duration = 1000;   /* duration in milliseconds */
    unsigned rc;                /* return code */

    if( rc=DosBeep( frequency, duration ) )
        { printf("DosBeep error=%u\n", rc); exit(1); }
    exit(0);
}
```

This program uses the function DosBeep() to beep the speaker. The two arguments to the function are the frequency (in Hertz) and the duration of the beep (in milliseconds); both are unsigned integers.

When you run the program nothing appears on the screen, but the speaker beeps for one second.

DosBeep() — Beeps the speaker

```
DosBeep(Frequnecy, Duration);
unsigned Frequency;     /*frequency in Hertz (37 to 32767) */
unsigned Duration;      /* time in milliseconds */
```

The major difference between this program and sleep.c (besides what they do) is that we have added statements in beep.c to examine the code number returned by the API function. As we noted earlier, the return code for API functions is 0 if everything went all right, or an error number if the function could not complete its task properly. The program reads the return code into variable **rc**, and, if it is any value other than 0, prints an error message and exits.

Checking the return code is an important detail when most API functions are called. The code is easy to check, as the example indicates. To save space we've telescoped the two statements executed as the result of the **if** statement together on one line. This is standard format in other programs in this book.

When should the return code be checked? Almost always. Especially when you're learning about the system, checking the return code helps you track down errors in input parameters as well as other problems. Some API functions, like DosSleep() and DosBeep(), do not return errors very often, so you can probably get by with leaving them off. But if you have any doubt a function will work right 100 percent of the time, you should have your program check the return code. Of course, in a serious application you would want to use a more friendly technique to let the user know that something had gone wrong.

If an error is returned, you can look up its meaning in the description of the function in Appendix B of this book, or in the OS/2 programmers reference. For example, the function DosBeep() must be given a frequency in the range 37 to 32767 (decimal). If we modified the program to give DosBeep() a frequency value of 20, here's what would appear on the screen when we ran the program:

`DosBeep error=395`

Looking up 395 in the error codes list we see it corresponds to the message ERROR_INVALID_FREQUENCY. This particular error code applies, as you can see, explicitly to the DosBeep() function. Other error codes, however, such as number 13 (ERROR_INVALID_DATA), may be applicable to many functions.

Investigating Errors: the beep2.c Program

While we're on the subject of errors, we might mention an API function that helps a program figure out how to handle errors internally without automatically terminating the program. Here's a modification of the beep.c program that incorporates the new function, DosErrorClass(). This example also shows how an API function returns values to the calling program.

```
/* beep2.c */
/* beeps speaker; returns error information */
#define INCL_DOS
#include <os2.h>
#include <stdlib.h>          /* for atoi() */
main(argc,argv)
int argc;
char *argv[];
{
    unsigned frequency;      /* frequency in Hertz */
    unsigned duration;       /* duration in milliseconds */
    unsigned rc;             /* return code */
    unsigned Class;          /* error classification */
    unsigned Action;         /* recommended action */
    unsigned Locus;          /* error locus */
```

(continued)

```
    if( argc != 3)
       {printf("Syntax: beep freq duration\n",rc); exit(1);}
    frequency = atoi( argv[1] );
    duration = atoi( argv[2] );
    if( rc=DosBeep(frequency, duration) )  {
       printf("DosBeep error=%u\n", rc);
       DosErrClass(rc, &Class, &Action, &Locus);
       printf("Class=%u, Action=%u, Locus=%u\n",
                                    Class, Action, Locus);
       exit(1);
    }
    exit(0);
}
```

For ease of experimentation this program accepts commandline arguments for the frequency and duration of the beep. If we run the program with acceptable values for the parameters, it beeps the speaker appropriately. However, if we call it with an out-of-bounds frequency value, here's what happens:

```
C>beep2 20 500
DosBeep error=395
Class=7, Action=4, Locus=1
```

For a given return code the function DosErrorClass() returns three different numbers, specifying the class of the error, the probable action that should be taken, and the origin of the error.

DosErrClass() — Classifies error code

```
DosErrClass(Code, AClass, AAction, ALocus);
unsigned Code              /* return code */
unsigned far *AClass;      /* address for error
                              classification */
unsigned far *AAction;     /* address for recommeded action */
unsigned far *ALocus;      /* address for error location */
```

The values for the variable **Class** range from 1 to 15. The meanings for each value, and for the values of the **Action** and **Locus** variables, are found in the description of DosErrClass() in the programmer's reference. Class 7 is listed as "Probable application error," an accurate assessment of the source of the error: a smart application wouldn't have accepted an out-of-bounds value from the user. Action 4 is "Terminate in an orderly manner", which is a reasonable action to take. A locus (the source of the error) of 1 is "unknown"—the function knows only about random access devices, networks, serial devices, and memory, so the speaker is unknown.

DOS Errors: Besides the API return code errors, caused by the improper use of an API function, OS/2 may also print DOS errors, which arise in the operating system itself. These have the form:

```
SYS0021: The drive is not ready
```

A more complete explanation of the error, and suggestions for correcting the problem, can be obtained using OS/2's HELP utility. Enter the command **help** followed by the error number. In the case above, you would enter:

```
C>help SYS0021
```

Returned Arguments and Far Pointers

The DosErrClass() function returns three values to the calling program. Since C passes values by reference, rather than by value, the addresses of the three arguments must be used in the function, rather than the arguments themselves. And, since the API functions are in a different segment than the program, **far** pointers must be used. In fact, the prototype for this function in BSEDOS.H specifies the type of all three parameters to be:

```
unsigned far *
```

As you can see in the listing, the addresses in DosErrClass() are not typecast to be **far** pointers. Why is there no warning of this from the compiler? Because the prototype in the header file causes the compiler to assume that all addresses used in a **far** function are **far** (32-bit) addresses. This saves us from having to typecast all the local addresses used as parameters in API functions, or from having to use the -AL compiler option. (This is at least true of the Microsoft OS/2 compiler; other compilers may not be so accommodating.)

As you can see in the DosErrClass() box, address parameters are preceded by the letter "A" as a reminder that the address operator or a pointer should be used for this parameter. (This convention is not followed in the case of ASCIIZ strings.)

Using Structure Declarations

In addition to function prototypes, the BSEDOS.H and BSESUB.H files contain declarations for certain structures used by the API. As an example, here's a program that obtains the date and time from the system and displays it:

```
/* getdate.c */
/* prints system date and time information */
#define INCL_DOS
#include <os2.h>
main()
{
    struct _DATETIME datetime;    /* defined in bsedos.h */
    unsigned rc;                  /* return code */

    if( rc=DosGetDateTime( &datetime ) )
       { printf("DosGetDateTime error=%u",rc); exit(1); }
    printf("Hour=      %u\n", datetime.hours);
    printf("Minutes=   %u\n", datetime.minutes);
    printf("Seconds=   %u\n", datetime.seconds);
    printf("Hundredths=%u\n", datetime.hundredths);
    printf("Day=       %u\n", datetime.day);
    printf("Month=     %u\n", datetime.month);
    printf("Year=      %u\n", datetime.year);
    printf("Timezone=  %d\n", datetime.timezone);
    printf("Day/week=  %u\n", datetime.weekday);
    exit(0);
}
```

This program uses the function DosGetDateTime() to return the time
and date information, which is placed in a structure defined in the
BSEDOS.H file. Here's some sample output from the program:

```
Hour=       12
Minutes=    17
Seconds=    39
Hundredths=59
Day=        21
Month=      9
Year=       1988
Timezone=   -1
Day/week=   1
```

On our particular machine the time zone can't be set by the DOS
TIME and DATE commands, so the system sets it arbitrarily to -1.
The other values are those set with the time and date commands, and
maintained by the system clock.

DosGetDateTime() — Gets date and time information

```
DosGetDateTime(Adatetime)
struct _DATETIME far *Adatetime;   /* address of structure
```

This function takes as its only argument the address of a structure of type **struct _DATETIME**. The definition of this structure in the Microsoft header file BSEDOS.H and in the programmer's reference looks like this:

```
typedef struct _DATETIME  {
   UCHAR  hours;
   UCHAR  minutes;
   UCHAR  seconds;
   UCHAR  hundredths;
   UCHAR  day;
   UCHAR  month;
   USHORT year;
   SHORT  timezone;
   UCHAR  weekday;
} DATETIME;
```

UCHAR means **unsigned char**, **USHORT** means **unsigned int**, and **SHORT** means **int**. We can use the original name of the structure rather than the name derived from the **typedef**; this clarifies that we're defining a structure in our program listing, since we can say

```
struct _DATETIME datetime
```

instead of the more obscure

```
DATETIME datetime.
```

With these changes the structure looks like this:

```
struct _DATETIME  {
   unsigned char  hours;
   unsigned char  minutes;
   unsigned char  seconds;
   unsigned char  hundredths;
   unsigned char  day;
   unsigned char  month;
   unsigned int   year;
   int            timezone;
   unsigned char  weekday;
};
```

We'll use this format for showing structures in this book.

Writing Your Own Structure Definitions

Another approach is to ignore the structure definitions in the header files altogether, and use your own. For example, here's the getdate.c program rewritten to incorporate its own definition of the _DATETIME structure. We've changed the name of the structure to DateTime, but kept the same names for the structure members. We've also added the prototype for the function, which is necessary if header files are not used.

```
/* getdate2.c */
/* prints system date and time information */
/* uses structure definition in program, no header files */

                                    /* function prototype */
extern unsigned far pascal DosGetDateTime(struct DateTime
                                                    far *);

struct DateTime  {                  /* structure definition */
    unsigned char hours;
    unsigned char minutes;
    unsigned char seconds;
    unsigned char hundredths;
    unsigned char day;
    unsigned char month;
    unsigned int  year;
    int           timezone;
    unsigned char weekday;
};

main()
{
    struct DateTime datetime;    /* defined above */
    unsigned rc;                 /* return code */

    if( rc=DosGetDateTime( &datetime ) )
        { printf("DosGetDateTime error=%u",rc); exit(1); }
    printf("Hour=       %u\n", datetime.hours);
    printf("Minutes=    %u\n", datetime.minutes);
    printf("Seconds=    %u\n", datetime.seconds);
    printf("Hundredths=%u\n", datetime.hundredths);
    printf("Day=        %u\n", datetime.day);
    printf("Month=      %u\n", datetime.month);
    printf("Year=       %u\n", datetime.year);
    printf("Timezone=  %d\n", datetime.timezone);
    printf("Day/week=  %u\n", datetime.weekday);
    exit(0);
}
```

As we noted earlier, this approach has the advantage of making your program independent of changes in the header files. You can also name the structure and its members anything you like. The disadvantage is that you must write the structure definition into any program that needs it. (Or you could create your own header files, incorporating the structures you commonly use.)

The programs in this book use the Microsoft header files for structure definitions. However, it's easy to convert them to be independent of external header files, as shown in getdate2.c.

Here hours can have values from 0 to 23, minutes and seconds from 0 to 59, hundredths of seconds from 0 to 99, the day from 1 to 31, the month from 1 to 12, and the year from 1980 to 2079. The timezone gives the time in minutes between the current time zone and Greenwich, England. The day of the week ranges from 1 to 7.

The function DosGetDateTime() places the current values of this information in the structure **_DATETIME**, where our program can access them.

Note that the DosGetDateTime() function expects a **far** pointer to a variable of type **struct _DATETIME**. That's what it gets, since the compiler realizes it's dealing with a function of type **far**. Again, we don't need to do any typecasting (although, as we'll see soon, this is not always the case in API functions).

Setting Date and Time

If you want to change any of the date or time information, a function called DosSetDateTime(), which uses the same _DATETIME structure, will do the job. Here's a program that sets the time zone value, which can't be set with the ordinary DOS time and date commands.

```
/* setzone.c */
/* sets time zone */
#define INCL_DOS
#include <os2.h>
main(argc,argv)
int argc;
char *argv[];
{
    struct _DATETIME datetime;   /* defined in doscalls.h */
    unsigned rc;                 /* return code */
```

(continued)

```
    if(argc != 2)
       { printf("Syntax: setzone zone\n"); exit(1); }
    if( rc=DosGetDateTime( &datetime ) )
       { printf("DosGetDateTime error=%u",rc); exit(1); }
    datetime.timezone = atoi( argv[1] );
    if( rc=DosSetDateTime( &datetime ) )
       { printf("DosSetDateTime error=%u",rc); exit(1); }
    exit(0);
}
```

The timezone value is expressed in minutes from Greenwich Mean Time, with positive values west of Greenwich and negative values east. So the value for Pacific Standard Time, for instance, would be 8 hours multiplied by 60 minutes. You'd set it like this:

C>setzone 480

The program first uses DosGetDateTime() to read values into the **datetime** structure, then changes the timezone member of the structure, and finally sends all the information back to the system with DosSetDateTime().

DosSetDateTime() — Sets date and time information

```
DosSetDateTime(Adatetime);
struct _DATETIME far *Adatetime; /* address of structure */
```

This function is similar to DosGetDateTime(), and takes the same single parameter: the address of a structure of type **struct _DATETIME**.

If you're curious, subsequent use of getdate.c will confirm that setzone.c has in fact changed the value of the time zone in the system.

Typecasting Function Arguments

In the next example we can't escape typecasting one of the arguments to an API function. This program displays information on the physical aspects of a particular disk drive or other file system device. The drive number (0=default, 1=A, 2=B, etc.) is furnished by the user to the program on the command line.

```
/* filesys.c */
/* returns info on file system of specified drive */
#define INCL_DOS
#include <os2.h>
#include <stdlib.h>
#define LEVEL 1                      /* 1=file, 2=volume */
main(argc,argv)
int argc;
char *argv[];
{
    unsigned drive;                  /* drive number */
                                     /* 0=default, 1=A, 2=B, etc */
    struct _FSALLOCATE buffer;  /* defined in bsedos.h */
    unsigned size;                   /* size of buffer */
    unsigned rc;                     /* return code */

    if(argc != 2 )
        { printf("Syntax: fileinfo drive#\n"); exit(1); }
    drive = atoi( argv[1] );
    size = sizeof(struct _FSALLOCATE);
    if( rc=DosQFSInfo(drive, LEVEL,
                        (unsigned char far *)&buffer, size) )
        { printf("DosQFSInfo error=%u",rc); exit(1); }
    printf("File system ID =    %lu\n", buffer.idFileSystem);
    printf("Number of sectors = %lu\n", buffer.cSectorUnit);
    printf("Allocation units =  %lu\n", buffer.cUnit);
    printf("Available units  =  %lu\n", buffer.cUnitAvail);
    printf("Bytes per sector =  %u\n",  buffer.cbSector);
    exit(0);
}
```

The program creates the following output when given a 30 mega-byte hard disk, installed as drive C: as a parameter:

```
C>filesys 3
File system ID =    0
Number of sectors = 4
Allocation units =  15512
Available units  =  7405
Bytes per sector =  512
```

With this information, a program could figure out, before writing to it, whether a device has enough room for a particular file. (We'll have more to say about the disk file system in Chapter 8).

```
┌─────────────────────────────────────────────────────────┐
│         DosQFSInfo — Query file system information        │
│ DosQFSInfo(Drive, Level, ABuffer, Buffsize);              │
│ unsigned Drive;         /* drive number 0=default, 1=A, etc */ │
│ unsigned Level;         /* 1=file into, 2=volume info */   │
│ unsigned char far *ABuffer; /* address of buffer for info */ │
│ unsigned Buffsize;      /* buffer size */                 │
└─────────────────────────────────────────────────────────┘
```

The structure _FSALLOCATE, altered from its definition in BSEDOS.H, looks like this:

```
struct _FSALLOCATE  {
   unsigned long idFileSystem;
   unsigned long cSectorUnit;
   unsigned long cUnit;
   unsigned long cUnitAvail;
   unsigned int cbSector;
};
```

We should note a naming convention used in many (but not all) structure definitions in the Microsoft header files. The initial lower case letters of the name are intended to convey information about the purpose and data type of the variable. These letters are divided into two groups: prefixes, which designate the purpose of the variable, and bases, which designate the data type. For instance, **id** is a prefix designating an identifier, and **c** is a prefix meaning a count. The designator **b** is a base referring to a byte of data, so **cb** implies a variable which holds a variable used for counting, which occupies one byte. Other bases are **f** for a flag or boolean variable, **ch** for a character, and **us** for **unsigned short**. A complete list can be found in the programmer's reference manual.

We don't employ this naming convention in this book, except where Microsoft has used it for structure members.

Notice that the Abuffer parameter in filesys.c has to be typecast to avoid a warning error from the compiler. This is because the prototype of DosQFSInfo() specifies the address of the buffer to be a pointer to type **unsigned char**, while really it is a pointer to type **struct _FSALLOCATE**.

We will encounter this situation fairly often, in which a prototype considers a buffer to be composed of bytes, when the logic of the situation implies that the buffer is a structure.

Summary

In this chapter we discussed how to set up your system to compile C programs in OS/2, and we looked at programs which employ a few simple API functions. We saw how a program can delay itself with DosSleep(), sound the speaker with DosBeep(), get information on errors with DosErrClass(), get and set the time and date with Dos-GetDateTime() and DosSetDateTime(), and obtain information about a disk drive from DosQFSInfo(). We explained how arguments are sent to and returned from these functions, and how errors are handled.

You have, as it were, completed your first day's trek into the OS/2 programming wilderness. You can now relax around the camp-fire, and congratulate yourself, not only for your survival, but for not even finding things too difficult.

In the next chapter we employ a more systematic approach and examine some API functions pertaining specifically to the keyboard and the video screen. In the following chapter we then move on to the real heart of OS/2: multitasking.

KEYBOARD AND SCREEN

Chapter 3

Chapter 3

The most essential I/O devices on a personal computer are the video screen and the keyboard. In this chapter we focus on the API functions OS/2 makes available for using these two devices. These functions are fairly straightforward: they perform tasks, such as writing a string to the screen or reading a keyboard character, that we're all familiar with. For this reason these functions make a good starting point for our exploration of OS/2. They will also be used from time to time in later programs.

Since our goal in this chapter is to provide a relatively easy introduction to these functions, we won't cover all there is to know about the keyboard and screen. (We will examine some more advanced aspects of the display in Chapter 13.)

We'll talk first about writing to the screen, moving the cursor, and scrolling a window on the screen. Then we'll shift our attention to the keyboard, and see how to read characters and various other data from this device. We'll finish up by finding out how to set the keyboard status, how to read data directly from the screen, and how to get and set the video mode and find out what video display equipment is attached to the computer.

If a program is running under the Presentation Manager, the API calls described in this chapter will continue to work as described. Output appears in a window on the screen, rather than on the entire screen, but otherwise there is little change. The routines that carry out the API function calls will be replaced with ones designed to work in a windowing environment, but this will not affect the way programs that call these functions are written.

Writing to the Screen

OS/2 makes available a half-dozen or so functions for writing in various ways to the screen. In this section we'll look at several of these functions.

When should API functions be used, rather than C library functions such as printf()? API functions are lower-level functions, well suited to some situations, but lacking the ability to format complex output as printf() can. Their main advantage is that they are designed to be as fast as possible, and are typically faster than the equivalent C library functions. API functions are also guaranteed to work in a multitasking situation, where two threads are attempting to write to the screen at the same time. Assembly language programmers can use them as primary I/O routines, but, depending on the circumstances, C programmers have a choice.

Of course using an API function makes your program less portable, since API functions aren't used on non-OS/2 systems. However, programs that make full use of OS/2's multitasking and other advanced features will not be portable to single-tasking systems anyway.

There is another difference between C library routines and the OS/2 API functions described in this chapter: API functions cannot be redirected. If you want to send the normal screen output to a file or perform other sorts of redirection, you should stick to the C library routines. (You can redirect the output from DosWrite(), a file-oriented API function we'll learn about in the chapter on files.)

Writing at a Fixed Location

An important API function for placing characters on the screen is VioWrtCharStrAttr(). This function takes a character string from a buffer supplied by the program and writes it on the screen at a location specified by arguments given to the function. You can also specify the attribute of the string, and use this function to write in bold, underline, reverse video, or colors, as desired.

Here's a program that reads a string from the user with the normal C library function gets(), stores it in a buffer, and then uses VioWrtCharStrAtt() to display it in the middle of the screen. The phrase is displayed in reverse video for clarity.

```
/* viowrt.c */
/* demonstrates use of VioWrtCharStrAtt() function */
#define INCL_SUB
#include <os2.h>
#include <stdio.h>                  /* for gets() */
#include <string.h>                 /* for strlen() */
#define LENGTH 81                   /* length of string buffer */
#define HANDLE 0                    /* vio handle always 0 */
main()
{
    char buffer[LENGTH];            /* buffer for string */
    unsigned length;               /* length of string */
    unsigned char attr = 0x70;     /* reverse video attribute */
    unsigned row = 12;             /* set to middle row */
    unsigned column = 0;           /* set to left-most column */

    gets(buffer);                  /* get string from user */
    length = strlen(buffer);       /* find its length */
                                   /* display it */
    VioWrtCharStrAtt(buffer, length, row, column, &attr,
                                            HANDLE);
    exit(0);
}
```

Clear the screen before running the program. As soon as the program starts you can type any message of up to 80 characters. Terminate with [Enter]. No matter where you typed the message on the screen, it will be printed starting in the middle of the screen, at row 12.

VioWrtCharStrAtt — Writes character string with attribute

```
VioWrtCharStrAtt(String, Length, Row, Column, AAttr,
                                               Handle);
unsigned char far *String;   /* address of string to be
                                written */
unsigned Length;             /* length of string */
unsigned Row;                /* row to start writing */
unsigned Column;             /* column to start writing */
char far *AAttr;             /* address of attribute byte */
unsigned short Handle;       /* handle is always 0 */
```

The VioWrtCharStrAtt() function is useful when you want to write on the screen at a fixed location: you could use it when creating a form, for example.

The **String** variable is the address of the buffer holding the string. **Length** is the length of the string, and **Row** and **Column** specify the starting position on the screen. Note that this function assumes (as do other VIO functions) that the top-most row and left-most column are numbered 0 (not 1, as in some systems).

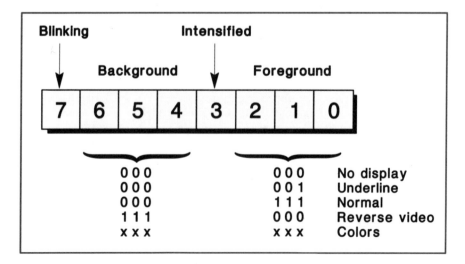

Figure 3-1
The Attribute Byte

The attribute byte (variable **Attr**) specifies the attribute the entire string is given on the screen. The structure of the attribute byte (common to all IBM-compatible systems) is shown in Figure 3-1. The color values for background and foreground are:

Value	Color
0	black
1	blue
2	green
3	cyan
4	red
5	magenta
6	brown
7	white

In the viowrt.c program we used reverse video, so the attribute byte is 70 hex. (Normal white-on-black is 07 hex.) Later in this chapter we'll show an example of a program that permits you to experiment with attributes in both color and monochrome.

Notice the **Handle** variable. This parameter, common to most video and keyboard API functions, always has a value of 0 in this release of OS/2. It's provided for increasing the functionality of OS/2 in the future, without having to change the format of the API calls.

There are other API functions similar to VioWrtCharStrAtt(). One function, VioWrtCharStr() writes a string without changing the attribute; we'll look at an example of its usage later. Another function, VioWrtCellStr(), writes a string of character/attribute combinations, allowing use of more than one attribute in the same string.

·VioWrtCharStrAtt() and similar functions will all wrap at the end of a line, continuing to the next line if necessary. However, once the function reaches the end of the screen, it terminates, whether it has more characters to print or not. It won't scroll the screen upward to write additional characters.

In some situations, there are drawbacks to using the VioWrt-CharStrAtt() function. For one thing, it does not recognize special characters such as the tab and newline. When you try to print these characters you get the corresponding graphics character instead of the action. Another possible problem is that this function doesn't move the cursor along with it, as printf() and similar C functions do. Thus if you use it for interactive I/O, where the program prints a prompt and the user replies, you need to move the cursor in a separate step (we'll see how shortly).

Another API function, however, solves both these problems at the expense of some generality. We'll examine it next.

Writing at the Cursor Position

The VioWrtTTy() function emulates teletype printing action. It starts writing to the screen wherever the cursor happens to be, and when it's done it leaves the cursor at the end of the string just printed.

Here's a program that makes use of this function to perform a short interaction with the user:

```c
/* tty.c */
/* writes on screen in teletype mode */
#define INCL_SUB
#include <os2.h>
#include <stdio.h>                      /* for gets() */
#include <string.h>                     /* for strlen() */
#define LENGTH 80                       /* length of buffer */
#define HANDLE 0                        /* vio handle always
                                           0 */
char s1[] = "Name: ";                   /* prompts */
char s2[] = "Rank: ";
char s3[] = "Serial number: ";

main()
{
    char name[LENGTH];                  /* buffers for */
    char rank[LENGTH];                  /*    user input */
    char serial[LENGTH];

    VioWrtTTy(s1, strlen(s1), HANDLE);  /* print first
                                           prompt */
    gets(name);                         /* get the user's
                                           name */
    VioWrtTTy(s2, strlen(s2), HANDLE);  /* print second
                                           prompt */
    gets(rank);                         /* get user's rank */
    VioWrtTTy(s3, strlen(s3), HANDLE);  /* print third
                                           prompt */
    gets(serial);                       /* get user's
                                           serial # */

    exit(0);
}
```

This program prints a prompt, waits for the user to reply, prints another prompt, and so on. A sample interaction looks like this:

```
Name:   George Melby
Rank:   Colonel
Serial number:   102947289
```

Notice that we don't give VioWrtTTy() any row or column information; it uses the cursor as its starting point, and it carries the cursor along with it, so the cursor is correctly positioned for the user's next input.

VioWrtTTy — Writes string in teletype mode

```
VioWrtTTy(String, Length, Handle);
char far *String;        /* address of string to be written */
unsigned Length;         /* length of string */
unsigned short Handle;   /* handle is always 0 */
```

As you'll see if you want to modify the prompts in the program, the VioWrtTTy() function performs translations of the common control characters. It tabs over for tabs, rings the bell when it sees the bell character, and performs carriage returns, linefeeds, and backspaces in response to the appropriate characters. Other VIO functions, by contrast, print the graphics symbol for these characters. VioWrtTTy() will also, unlike functions like VioWrtCharStrAtt(), scroll the screen upward if hasn't finished printing its buffer when the end of the screen is reached. VioWrtTTy() can also use ANSI escape sequences.

Because it performs these added functions, VioWrtTTy() is considered a "high-level" VIO function, as opposed to the other VIO functions, which are low level.

Writing One Character Many Times

There are situations where it is desirable to write multiple instances of the same characters. OS/2 includes several functions for this purpose. We'll look at one, VioWrtNCell(), which permits any number of screen locations to be filled with the same *cell*. A cell is a two-byte quantity that contains both the character and the attribute.

Our example program writes a string of 2000 cells, which fills the entire screen with the same character. The program then permits you to change the character used to fill the screen, and also the attribute. You can turn blinking and intensified on and off, switch to reverse video, go back to normal, and—if you are using a color display—change the foreground and background color of the characters. The program's prompts tell you how to make these selections. Exit with the [Esc] key.

```
/* attr.c */
/* writes various attributes to screen */
#define INCL_SUB
#include <os2.h>
#define TRUE 1
#define HANDLE 0                /* vio handle, always 0 */
#define FOREGROUND 0x07         /* mask for foreground bits */
#define BACKGROUND 0x70         /* mask for background bits */
#define INTENSITY 0x08          /* mask for intensity bit */
#define BLINKING 0x80           /* mask for blinking bit */
#define UNDERLINE 0x01          /* value for underline */
main()
{
    char command_letter;        /* typed by user */
    unsigned char cell[2];      /* character-attribute cell */
    unsigned color;             /* color number */

    printf("Type 'n' for normal, 'u' for underline,\n");
    printf("     'i' for intensified, 'b' for blinking,\n");
    printf("     'r' for reverse video.");
    printf("Type +n to change foreground color,\n");
    printf("     -n to change background color,\n");
    printf("     where 'n' is digit from 0 to 7");

    cell[0] = 'x';              /* character byte */
    cell[1] = 0x07;             /* normal attribute */
                                /* read command letter, */
                                /*    quit on [Esc] key */
    while( (command_letter=getche()) != 27)  {
      switch(command_letter)  {
      case 'n':                         /* normal */
        cell[1] |= FOREGROUND;          /* foreground on */
        cell[1] &= ~BACKGROUND;         /* background off */
        break;
      case 'u':                         /* underline */
        cell[1] &= ~FOREGROUND;         /* foreground = 1 */
        cell[1] |= UNDERLINE;
        break;
      case 'i':                         /* intensity */
        cell[1] ^= INTENSITY;           /* toggle intensity bit */
        break;
      case 'b':                         /* intensity */
        cell[1] ^= BLINKING;            /* toggle blinking bit */
        break;
      case 'r':                         /* reverse video */
        cell[1] &= ~FOREGROUND;         /* foreground off */
        cell[1] |= BACKGROUND;          /* background off */
        break;
```

(continued)

```
        case '+':                         /* foreground color */
            cell[1] &= ~FOREGROUND;       /* put in foreground */
            cell[1] |= getche() - 0x30;
            break;
        case '-':                         /* background color */
            cell[1] &= ~BACKGROUND;       /* put in background */
            cell[1] |= (getche() - 0x30) << 4;
            break;
        default:                          /* if not command,*/
            cell[0] = command_letter; /* change character */
        }                                 /* write entire screen */
        VioWrtNCell( (char far *)cell, 2000, 0, 0, HANDLE);
    }
    exit(0);
}
```

Like VioWrtCharStrAtt(), the function VioWrtNCell() must be given a starting row and column (which in this case are both 0), and a length. For a 25 row by 80 column screen this is 2000. It must then be given the address of a cell to hold the character attribute cell to be written. We use a character array to represent the cell, with the first byte being the character and the second byte the attribute.

VioWrtNCell — Write N character/attribute cells

```
VioWrtNCell(ACell, Times, Row, Column, Handle);
char far *ACell;          /* address of cell to be written */
unsigned Times;           /* number of cells to write */
unsigned Row;             /* row to start writing */
unsigned Column;          /* column to start writing */
unsigned short Handle;    /* handle is always 0 */
```

Note, while running this program, how quickly the entire screen changes from one character to another or one attribute to another. With API routines this fast it's not necessary to write your own routines for direct screen access (as it often is in MS-DOS).

Similar API functions write N characters without changing the existing attribute, and write N attributes without changing the existing characters (so you can underline existing text, for example). See the programmer's reference for more information.

The Logical Video Buffer

What happens when you use one of the VIO calls to write to the screen when your program is in the background? Perhaps you've started a program using the START command, so it is running in a different session; or you've started a program in the normal way and switched to a different screen group. Where does the background program's output go?

Each session (screen group) has its own *logical video buffer*, or LVB. If a process is running in a session in the background, any "writes" to the screen are made not to the physical display, but to the LVB for that session. They are invisible there, but are saved in case they will be needed. Then, if the session is moved to the foreground (the user switches to that session from the session manager), the contents of the LVB are written to the physical display buffer and appear on the screen.

Of course, material that scrolls off the top of the LVB is lost forever, just as material that scrolls off the top of the physical screen is lost.

The Cursor

The OS/2 API provides functions for manipulating the cursor. Its position can be set to any point on the screen, its type can be changed, and its position and type can be read by the program. In this section we'll explore some of these functions.

Setting the Cursor Position

The VioSetCurPos() function needs to know only the row and column where you want the cursor. It does the rest.

```
            VioSetCurPos — Set cursor position
VioSetCurPos(Row, Column, Handle);
unsigned Row;              /* row to place cursor */
unsigned Column;           /* column to place cursor */
unsigned short Handle;     /* handle is always 0 */
```

The arguments **Row** and **Column** are the coordinates the cursor moves to. As with the video writing functions discussed earlier, the top-most row and the left-most column are defined as 0.

One situation where it may be necessary to set the cursor position is when you want to place a prompt at an arbitrary location on the screen, and then await a user's input. The VioWrtTTy() function won't start itself at an arbitrary screen location (it always starts at the existing cursor position), and the VioWrtCharStrAtt() group of functions write to the screen but don't move the cursor in the process.

Here's a program that places prompts in four different locations on the screen, then asks for user input at each location. The locations are arranged in two vertical columns in the middle of the screen. Clear the screen before running the program.

```
/* curpos.c */
/* demonstrates setting cursor position */
#define INCL_SUB
#include <os2.h>
#include <stdio.h>                  /* for gets() */
#include <string.h>                 /* for strlen() */
#define LENGTH 80                   /* length of buffers */
#define HANDLE 0                    /* vio handle always 0 */

char s1[] = "Name: ";              /* prompts */
char s2[] = "Age: ";
char s3[] = "Height: ";
char s4[] = "Weight: ";

main()
{
    char name[LENGTH];              /* buffers for */
    char age[LENGTH];               /*     user input */
    char height[LENGTH];
    char weight[LENGTH];
    VioSetCurPos(12, 0, HANDLE;   /* cursor to left column */
    VioWrtTTy(s1, strlen(s1), HANDLE);
    gets(name);
    VioSetCurPos(12, 40, HANDLE); /* cursor to right column */
    VioWrtTTy(s2, strlen(s2), HANDLE);
    gets(age);
    VioSetCurPos(13, 0, HANDLE); /* cursor to left column */
    VioWrtTTy(s3, strlen(s3), HANDLE);
    gets(height);
    VioSetCurPos(13, 40, HANDLE); /* cursor to right column */
    VioWrtTTy(s3, strlen(s4), HANDLE);
    gets(weight);
    exit(0);
}
```

A sample interaction with the program would appear in the middle of the screen (rows 12 and 13) and might look like this:

```
Name: Johann Kepler              Age: 30
Height: 5'-7"                    Weight: 150
```

Changing the Cursor Type

The cursor is composed of a number of horizontal lines, each one character wide. The lines are numbered, starting with 0 on the top line. On the monochrome and EGA displays the bottom line is 13, while on the CGA display it is 7.

The number of lines used can be changed by specifying the starting and ending lines. The normal cursor consists of two lines in the bottom of the character box, so (for the monochrome cursor) the starting line is 12 and the ending line is 13. If you want a block cursor that occupies the entire character rectangle, you can specify a starting line of 0 and an ending line of 13.

You can also choose to hide the cursor entirely. This is useful if there will be no user input, and the cursor would only distract from the display.

Here's a program that allows you to change the cursor type interactively. If you're using a CGA text mode you'll want to change the user prompts shown in the listing to refer to 0 to 7, rather than 0 to 13.

```
/* curtype.c */
/* sets type of cursor */
#define INCL_SUB
#include <os2.h>
#include <stdlib.h>              /* for atoi() */
#include <stdio.h>               /* for gets() */
#define LENGTH 80                /* length of input buffer */
#define HANDLE 0                 /* Vio Handle always 0 */
main()
{
    struct _VIOCURSORINFO cursor;  /* defined in bsesub.h */
    char string[LENGTH];         /* buffer for user input */
                                 /* get cursor type */
    VioGetCurType( &cursor, HANDLE );
                                 /* starting line number */
    printf("Start line is %d.  ", cursor.yStart);
    printf("Enter new start line (0 to 13): ");
    cursor.yStart = atoi( gets(string) );
                                 /* ending line number */
```

(continued)

```
    printf("End line is %d.  ", cursor.cEnd);
    printf("Enter end line (0 to 13): ");
    cursor.cEnd = atoi( gets(string) );
                            /* hidden attribute */
    printf("Width is %d\n", cursor.cx);
    printf("Attribute is %d.  ", cursor.attr);
    printf("Hide cursor (y/n)?  ");
    cursor.attr = (getche()=='y')  ?  -1  :  0;
                            /* set cursor */
    VioSetCurType( &cursor, HANDLE );
}
```

The structure members **yStart** and **cEnd** are the start and stop lines. In text mode **cx** is always 1, while in graphics mode it's the number of horizontal pels (pixels) occupied by one character. If **attr** is set to -1, then the cursor will be hidden. If it's set to any other value, the cursor will be visible.

Here's how the interaction with the program looks when you want a split cursor: with one line on the top, and one on the bottom, assuming a monochrome or EGA screen:

```
C>curtype
Start line is 12.  Enter new start line (0 to 13): 13
End line is 13.  Enter new end line (0 to 13): 0
Width is 0
Attribute is 0.  Hide cursor (y/n)? n
C>
```

You can also hide the cursor if you want, but you'll find it makes interacting with your computer surprisingly difficult.

VioGetCurType — Get cursor type

```
VioGetCurType(ACurdata, Handle);
struct _VIOCURSORINFO far *ACurdata;   /* address of
                                          structure */
unsigned short Handle;                 /* handle is always 0 */
```

VioSetCurType — Set cursor type

```
VioSetCurType(ACurdata, Handle);
struct _VIOCURSORINFO far *ACurdata;   /* address of
                                          structure */
unsigned short Handle;                 /* handle is always 0 */
```

The program uses VioGetCurType() to read the cursor data into the **_VIOCURSORINFO** structure, where it can be changed if necessary. It then writes the data back out from the structure to the system with VioSetCurType().

Using ANSI Cursor Control

Besides providing its own cursor control, OS/2 permits you to activate ANSI support for cursor control (and ANSI's other capabilities). The following table shows some of the commonly-used ANSI codes for cursor control.

Code	Cursor action
Esc[2J	Erase screen and home cursor
Esc[K	Erase to end of line
Esc[A	Move cursor up one row
Esc[B	Move cursor down one row
Esc[C	Move cursor right one column
Esc[D	Move cursor left one column
Esc[r;cf	Move cursor to row r, column c

Each ANSI code starts with the escape character, shown as "Esc" in the table. In C the escape character can be represented by the character '\x1B' (a hex value equal to 27 decimal). For a complete list of ANSI codes, see the OS/2 setup guide. In the table the letters r and c stand for integer numbers; all other characters are sent as shown.

One API function, VioGetAnsi(), determines if ANSI support is active or not; and another, VioSetAnsi(), lets you activate or deactivate it. Here's a program that uses both functions to let you change the ANSI state of the display:

```
/* setansi.c */
/* enables or disables ansi support */
#define INCL_SUB
#include <os2.h>
#define HANDLE 0            /* always 0 */
main()
{
    unsigned indicator;     /* 0=not active, 1=active */
    unsigned rc;            /* return code */
                            /* get current ansi state */
    if( rc=VioGetAnsi( &indicator, HANDLE ) )
        { printf("VioGetAnsi error=%u\n",rc); exit(1); }
    printf("Ansi is %s.\n", indicator ? "active" : "not
                                                active");
                            /* set ansi state */
```

```
printf("Activate or deactivate ansi (a/d)? ");
indicator = (getche()=='a') ? 1 : 0;
if( rc=VioSetAnsi( indicator, HANDLE ) )
   { printf("VioSetAnsi error=%u\n",rc); exit(1); }
                            /* check if ansi really active */
printf("\nIf ansi active, row and col will be accurate");
printf("\x1B[12;40f");
printf("Row=12, Col=40");
exit(0);
}
```

This program first tells you the current ANSI status: active or not active. Then it asks if you want to activate or deactivate ANSI support. To check that the ANSI cursor controls actually work, it uses the ANSI code to set the cursor to the middle of the screen, where it prints the message "Row=12, Col=40". If there is no ANSI support, this message is not printed in the middle of the screen, but wherever the cursor happens to be, and the ANSI code itself is printed as a normal string, rather than causing the desired action.

VioGetAnsi — Get ANSI state

```
VioGetAnsi(AIndicator, Handle);
unsigned far *AIndicator;   /* address for indicator */
unsigned short Handle;      /* handle is always 0 */
```

VioSetAnsi — Set ANSI state: active or inactive

```
VioSetAnsi(Indicator, Handle);
unsigned Indicator;         /* indicator: 0=inactive,
                               1=active */
unsigned short Handle;      /* handle is always 0 */
```

VioGetAnsi() takes as an argument the address **AIndicator**, where the system returns the indicator. VioSetAnsi() uses the **Indicator** variable itself. Its possible values are 0, indicating ANSI support is not active, and 1, indicating it is active.

The ANSI escape codes can be imbedded in character strings to be printed by VioWrtTTY() and by C library functions such as printf(). In C, using the ANSI escape codes for cursor control will sometimes be more convenient than using the API functions.

Reading from the Screen

OS/2 includes a function which makes it possible to read a character string directly from the screen. Here's an example program that reads all the characters from the top half of the screen and writes them onto the bottom half.

```
/* readscr.c */
/* reads text directly from screen */
#define INCL_SUB
#include <os2.h>
#define LENGTH 1000          /* length of buffer */
#define HALF 12              /* half the screen height */
#define TOP 0                /* top-most row */
#define LEFT 0               /* left-most column */
#define HANDLE 0             /* vio handle always 0 */
main()
{
    char buffer[LENGTH];
    unsigned length = LENGTH;
    unsigned rc;
                             /* read top half of screen */
    if( rc=VioReadCharStr(buffer, &length, TOP, LEFT,
                                              HANDLE) )
       { printf("VioReadCharStr error=%u\n",rc); exit(1); }
                             /* reposition cursor */
    VioSetCurPos(HALF, LEFT, HANDLE);
    puts(buffer);           /* write to bottom half */
    exit(0);
}
```

The program uses the VioSetCurPos() function to reposition the cursor to the bottom half of the screen after the read, and the C library function puts() to do the writing.

VioReadCharStr — Reads character string from screen

```
VioReadCharStr(String, ALength, Row, Column, Handle);
char far *String;       /* address of string to be written */
unsigned far *ALength;  /* address of length of string */
unsigned Row;           /* row to start reading */
unsigned Column;        /* column to start reading */
unsigned short Handle;  /* handle is always 0 */
```

The API function VioReadCharStr() reads the screen. It requires the address of the string to be read, **String**; the address of the length of the string, **ALength**; and the **Row** and **Column** where reading should begin.

The read, as this example shows, continues past the end of the line on the screen, wrapping around to the next line. However, it cannot read past the end of the screen. If VioReadCharStr() is told to read too far it terminates at the end of the screen, and sets the **length** variable equal to the number of characters actually read (this is why the address of the length is passed, rather than the length itself).

Scrolling

There are many reasons for scrolling the screen. You may be using an API function like VioWrtCharStrAtt() which does not scroll the screen when it reaches the end. Or, you might want multiple text windows on the screen. If you then add data to a window, you want to scroll only the part of the screen devoted to the window. Even on a full screen, the text lines to be displayed are sometimes wider than the screen width; in this case it's convenient for the user to scroll the screen left and right to see all the data.

The OS/2 API contains four similar scrolling functions, one each for scrolling up, down, left, and right. Here's a program which uses VioScrollUp() to scroll a small window (10 by 25 characters) upward in the middle of the screen.

```
/* scroll.c */
/* scrolls a portion of the screen */
#define INCL_DOS              /* for dossleep() */
#define INCL_SUB              /* for vio calls */
#include <os2.h>
#define LINES 25              /* height of screen */
#define LINE_LENGTH 80        /* width of screen */
#define SCR_LENGTH (LINES * LINE_LENGTH)
#define HANDLE 0              /* vio handle, always 0 */
#define HEIGHT 10             /* height of small window */
                             /* strings to put in window */
char *string[] = { "One", "Two", "Three", "Four", "Five",
           "Six", "Seven", "Eight", "Nine", "Ten" };
main()
{
   unsigned Top = 0;          /* top left corner of screen */
   unsigned Left = 0;
   unsigned Xcell = 0x0758;   /* normal attr, 'X' char */
   unsigned blank = 0x7020;   /* reverse video, blank char */
   unsigned TopRow = 10;      /* outline of window */
   unsigned LeftCol = 24;
   unsigned BotRow = 20;
```

(continued)

```
      unsigned RightCol = 50;
      unsigned lines = 1;        /* number of lines to scroll */
      unsigned char attr = 0x70;   /* string attr: reverse
                                      video */
      unsigned rc;               /* return code */
      int j;                     /* loop counter */

                                 /* fill entire screen with 'X' */
      if( rc=VioWrtNCell( (char far *)&Xcell,
                          SCR_LENGTH, Top, Left, HANDLE ) )
         { printf("VioWrtNCell error=%u",rc); exit(1); }

      for(j=0; j<HEIGHT; j++)  {
                                 /* scroll central window up */
         if( rc=VioScrollUp(TopRow, LeftCol, BotRow, RightCol,
                         lines, (char far *)&blank, HANDLE ) )
            { printf("VioScrollUp error=%u",rc); exit(1); }
                                 /* write string on window bottom */
         if( rc=VioWrtCharStr( string[j],  strlen(string[j]),
                             BotRow, LeftCol+1, HANDLE ) )
            { printf("VioWrtCharStr error=%u",rc); exit(1); }
         DosSleep(500L);         /* pause */
      }
      exit(0);
}
```

The entire screen area is first filled with the character X, using the VioWrtNCell() function. Then, in the **for** loop, one line at a time is added to the bottom line of the window, and the lines above are scrolled up using VioScrollUp(). On the new bottom line a message is printed, consisting of the word "one" the first time through the loop, "two" the second, and so on. A delay, using DosSleep(), is inserted between each scroll to make the scrolling action easy to see.

Figure 3-2 shows what the program looks like when the window has scrolled up halfway.

The VioScrollUp() function takes as arguments the top and bottom rows **Top** and **Bottom**, and the left and right columns **Left** and **Right**, of the window to be scrolled. It also needs to know **Lines**, i.e., how many lines to scroll upward (this is often 1, as in the scroll.c program); and **ACell**, the address of the cell holding the character/attribute combination. This character and attribute are used in the line added to the window by the scroll.

In the program we use an unsigned integer to hold both the character and the attribute; this is simpler, although perhaps not quite so clear, than using a two-element character array as we did in the attr.c program earlier. (It could also cause trouble in a system that did not use a two-byte integer.)

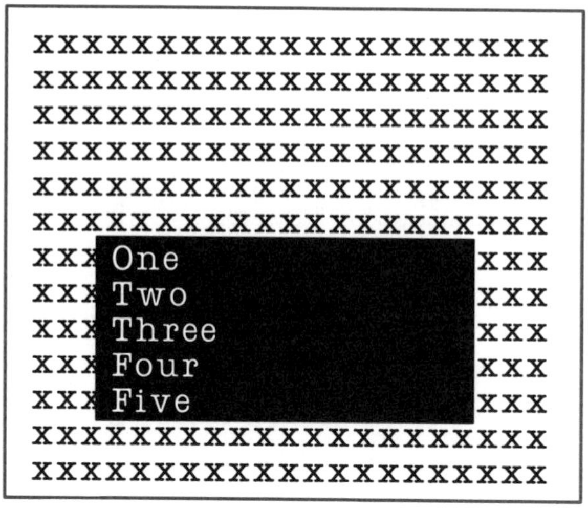

```
XXXXXXXXXXXXXXXXXXXXX
XXXXXXXXXXXXXXXXXXXXX
XXXXXXXXXXXXXXXXXXXXX
XXXXXXXXXXXXXXXXXXXXX
XXXXXXXXXXXXXXXXXXXXX
XXXXXXXXXXXXXXXXXXXXX
XXX One              XXX
XXX Two              XXX
XXX Three            XXX
XXX Four             XXX
XXX Five             XXX
XXXXXXXXXXXXXXXXXXXXX
XXXXXXXXXXXXXXXXXXXXX
```

Figure 3-2

Output of the
scroll.c program

VioScrollUp — Scrolls the screen up

```
VioScrollUp(Top, Left, Bottom, Right, Lines, ACell,
                                             HANDLE);
unsigned Top;          /* top row of scrolled area */
unsigned Left;         /* left column of scrolled area */
unsigned Bottom;       /* bottom row of scrolled area */
unsigned Right;        /* right column of scrolled area */
unsigned Lines;        /* number of blank lines to insert */
unsigned char far *ACell;   /* address of char/attr cell */
unsigned short Handle;      /* handle is always 0 */
```

We've used another new function in this program, VioWrtChrStr().
This is similar to VioWrtCharStrAtt(), discussed earlier, except that it
doesn't change the attribute of the characters being written.

VioWrtCharStr — Writes character string

```
VioWrtCharStr(String, Length, Row, Column, Handle);
char far *String;      /* address of string to be written */
unsigned Length;       /* length of string */
unsigned Row;          /* row to start writing */
unsigned Column;       /* column to start writing */
unsigned short Handle; /* handle is always 0 */
```

We don't need to change the attribute of the characters in this case,
even though we want to use reverse video, because the VioScrollUp()
function has already set the attribute of the line to be scrolled.

Clearing the Screen

The scrolling functions, such as VioScrollUp(), also provide the preferred method for clearing the screen. If the **Top** and **Left** arguments in the function are set to 0, and the **Bottom**, **Right**, and **Lines** arguments are set to -1, then the entire screen will be filled with the character/attribute combination specified for **Cell**. If **Cell** is defined as shown, then this use of VioScrollUp() will clear the screen:

```
unsigned Cell = 0x0720;

VioScrollUp( 0, 0, -1, -1, -1, (char far *)&Cell, 0);
```

We'll see an example of this usage later in the chapter.

The Keyboard

In this section we'll look at some of the API functions for interacting with the keyboard.

Reading a Keyboard Character

OS/2 provides a new, powerful function for reading characters from the keyboard: KbdCharIn(). Not only does this function read the ASCII code of the character, it tells you the scan code of the key and the status of the shift keys as well.

The data read from the keyboard is placed in a structure, which is defined in BSESUB.H Here's what the structure looks like:

```
struct _KBDKEYINFO {
    unsigned char chChar;        /* ASCII character code */
    unsigned char chScan;        /* scan code */
    unsigned char fbStatus;      /* language support status */
    unsigned char bNlsShift;     /* language support shift */
    unsigned fsState;            /* shift state */
    unsigned long time;          /* time */
};
```

The **chChar** variable is the ASCII code of the character. The system gets it from the scan code.

The **chScan** will be familiar to MS-DOS programmers: each key including the function keys, cursor keys, and so forth, has its own scan code, which is related to its position on the keyboard. The scan code can be useful for purposes such as distinguishing between standard digits and digits on the numeric keypad. It gives an unambiguous indication of which key has been pressed. It does not, however, report the state of the shift keys.

The **fbStatus** and **bNlsShift** are concerned with national language support. We'll ignore them in this example.

The **fsState** tells the state of the various shift keys, as summarized in Figure 3-3.

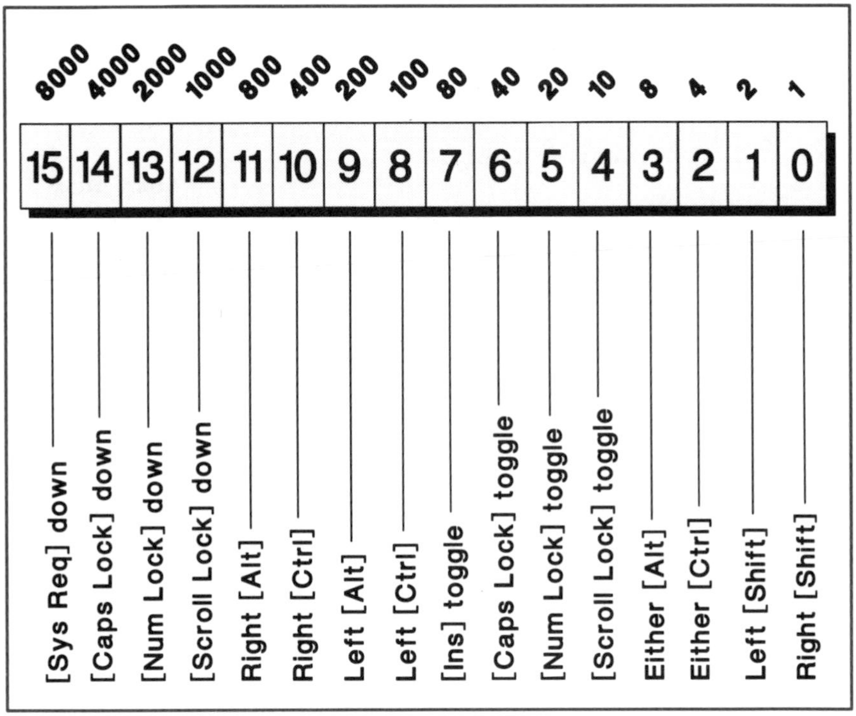

8000	4000	2000	1000	800	400	200	100	80	40	20	10	8	4	2	1
15	14	13	12	11	10	9	8	7	6	5	4	3	2	1	0
[Sys Req] down	[Caps Lock] down	[Num Lock] down	[Scroll Lock] down	Right [Alt]	Right [Ctrl]	Left [Alt]	Left [Ctrl]	[Ins] toggle	[Caps Lock] toggle	[Num Lock] toggle	[Scroll Lock] toggle	Either [Alt]	Either [Ctrl]	Left [Shift]	Right [Shift]

Figure 3-3
Shift State Values

The [Alt] and [Ctrl] keys turn on two bits at a time. The lock keys and the [Ins] key all use toggle bits: press them once to set the bit, press again to clear it.

The **time** variable gives the system time in milliseconds. This value can be used to see how closely together two characters were typed.

Here's a program that reads and displays the shift state each time any keyboard key (except a shift key) is pressed:

```
/* chardata.c */
/* reads character data for each keystroke */
#define INCL_SUB
#include <os2.h>
#define WAIT 0                       /* wait = 0, no wait = 1 */
#define HANDLE 0                     /* kbd handle always 0 */
#define ESC 27                       /* ASCII for [Esc] key */
main()
{
    struct _KBDKEYINFO keydata; /* defined in subcalls.h */
    unsigned rc;                    /* return code */

    while(TRUE) {
                                     /* read char into buffer */
        if( rc=KbdCharIn( &keydata, WAIT, HANDLE) )
            { printf("KbdCharIn error=%u\n",rc); exit(1); }
                                     /* print out char data */
        printf("Ascii=%u\nScan=%u\nStatus=%x\n",
            keydata.chChar,
            keydata.chScan,
            keydata.fbStatus);
        printf("Dshift=%x\nShift=%x\n",
            keydata.bNlsShift,
            keydata.fsState);
        printf("Time (milliseconds) = %ld\n\n", keydata.time);
                                     /* check for [Esc] key */
        if( keydata.chChar == ESC )
            exit(0);
    }
}
```

The program reads and reports the data for each key you press. It terminates when you press the [Esc] key. Here are some examples of the program at work. When you press the [a] key you get:

```
Ascii=97
Scan=30
Status=40
Dshift=0
Shift=0
Time (milliseconds) = 9491156
```

If you hold down the [Ctrl] key and press [a] you get:

```
Ascii=1
Scan=30
Status=40
Dshift=0
Shift=104
Time (milliseconds) = 95665662
```

The function key [F1] gives you:

```
Ascii=0
Scan=59
Status=40
Dshift=0
Shift=0
Time (milliseconds) = 9588718
```

Any key can be deciphered with this information, whether it's a function key, shift key, ASCII key, or a combination.

KbdCharIn — Read keyboard character data

```
KbdCharIn(Akeydata, Wait, Handle);
struct _KBDKEYINFO far *Akeydata;   /* address of
                                        structure */
unsigned Wait;                      /* 0=wait for char, 1=no wait */
unsigned short Handle;              /* handle is always 0 */
```

The API function KbdCharIn() reads the data for a particular keystroke into the structure **_KBDKEYINFO**, where the program displays it on the screen. The function must be given the address of such a structure as the first argument: **Akeydata**. The function can be set to either wait until a key is pressed, or return immediately even if no key has been pressed. This program uses a value for **Wait** of 0, so the function waits. Not waiting would permit the program to determine the status of the shift keys even when no other key had been pressed.

Like DosSleep(), this function does not waste any CPU cycles if it is set to **wait** and there is no character available. The operating system takes control away from the program, and doesn't give it back until a character is typed: the program itself does not need to continuously check the status of the keyboard.

Notice that we don't need to **#define** TRUE to be 1 in the chardata.c program. This definition already exists in the OS2DEF.H header file. FALSE is also defined in this file.

Reading a String from the Keyboard

The API function KbdStringIn() reads a complete string from the keyboard. Here's a program that uses this function to read a string typed by the user, and then prints out the string on the screen using VioWrtCharStrAtt():

```
/* keystr.c */
/* demonstrates use of KbdStringIn() function */
#define INCL_SUB
#include <os2.h>
#define LENGTH 80              /* length of string buffer */
#define WAIT 0                 /* 0=wait, 1=no wait */
#define HANDLE 0               /* always 0 */
main()
{
    char buffer[LENGTH];       /* buffer for string */
    struct _STRINGINBUF length; /* from bsesub.h */
    unsigned char attr = 0x07;  /* normal attribute */
    unsigned space = 0x0720;    /* space, normal attribute */
    unsigned row = 12;          /* set row */
    unsigned column = 0;        /* set column */
    unsigned rc;                /* return code */
                                /* clear screen */
    VioScrollUp( 0, 0, -1, -1, -1, (char far *)&space, 0);
    length.cb = LENGTH;         /* set max length */
                                /* get string from kbd */
    if( rc=KbdStringIn( buffer, &length, WAIT, HANDLE) )
        { printf("KbdStringIn error=%u",rc); exit(1); }
                                /* display string */
    VioWrtCharStrAtt( buffer, length.cchIn, row,
                                column, &attr, HANDLE);
    exit(0);
}
```

The program first uses VioScrollUp() to clear the screen. The user then types the input string which appears at the top of the screen. As soon as the user presses [Enter] the phrase is echoed in the middle of the screen.

The KbdStringIn() function uses a small structure, defined in BSESUB.H, to hold two length values: the length of the buffer available for reading the string, and the number of characters actually read in by the function. Here's what the structure looks like:

```
struct _STRINGINBUF {
    unsigned cb;      /* length of buffer (255 bytes max) */
    unsigned cchIn;   /* number of chars actually read */
    };
```

The KbdStringIn() function takes three arguments, besides the usual **Handle**.

KbdStringIn — Read character string from keyboard

```
KbdStringIn(Buffer, ALength, Wait, Handle);
char far *Buffer;              /* address where string will be
                                  placed */
struct _STRINGINBUF far *ALength;  /* address of struct */
unsigned Wait;                 /* 0=wait, 1=no wait */
unsigned short Handle;         /* handle is always 0 */
```

The arguments are **Buffer**, the address of the buffer where the string will be placed; **ALength**, the address of the buffer where the length information will be stored; and **Wait**, which indicates whether or not we want the function to wait if no characters are available: 0 indicates wait, 1 is no wait.

Before using the KbdStringIn() function we place the size of our buffer in the first member of the **_STRINGINBUF** structure. This value must be less than 256 characters. When the function returns, the number of characters actually read is in the second member of the structure. This value is then used in the VioWrtCharStrAtt() function to print the string.

In our example we use the **wait** option in the function. When the system is in *cooked* mode this is the only option. (We'll see soon what "cooked" means.)

KbdStringIn() is sometimes called a "high-level" keyboard function, since it deals with an entire string at one time, instead of a single character.

Keyboard Status

The keyboard can be in various states. The states reflect which shift keys are pressed and how other parameters are set. The keyboard state can be determined by the function KbdGetStatus(), and it can be altered by the function KbdSetStatus(). Some of this data, like the position of various shift keys, duplicates what you obtain with KbdCharIn(). However, KbdGetStatus() reveals more information than KbdCharIn().

Here's a program that uses KbdGetStatus() to read the status of the keyboard and display it on the screen:

```
/* kbdstat.c */
/* gets keyboard status using KbdGetStatus */
#define INCL_SUB
#include <os2.h>
#define HANDLE 0               /* always 0 */
main()
{
    struct _KBDINFO keystat;   /* struct in BSESUB.H*/
    unsigned rc;               /* return code */
    unsigned blank = 0x0720;   /* normal attr, blank char */

                               /* set length of structure */
    keystat.cb = sizeof(struct _KBDINFO);
                               /* clear screen */
    VioScrollUp( 0, 0, -1, -1, -1, (char far *)&blank, 0);

    while(TRUE)  {             /* get keyboard status */
       if( rc=KbdGetStatus( &keystat, HANDLE ) )
          { printf("KbdGetStatus error=%u\n",rc); exit(1); }
       VioSetCurPos( 10, 0, 0 );   /* cursor at row 10 */
       printf("Mask = %x\n",         keystat.fsMask);
       printf("Turnaround = %x\n",   keystat.chTurnAround);
       printf("Flags = %x\n",        keystat.fsInterim);
       printf("Shift state = %4x\n", keystat.fsState);
    }
}
```

This function uses a structure defined in BSESUB.H to hold the data returned from the system. The structure looks like this:

```
struct _KBDINFO  {
    unsigned cb;                /* length of this structure */
    unsigned fsMask;            /* echo, cooked, etc. */
    unsigned chTurnAround;      /* char to end KbdStringIn() */
    unsigned fsInterim;         /* for language support */
    unsigned fsState;           /* state of shift keys */
    };
```

The **cb** variable is the length of the structure itself, in bytes; it's 10. The **fsMask** variable is divided into individual bit fields, whose meaning is shown in Figure 3-4.

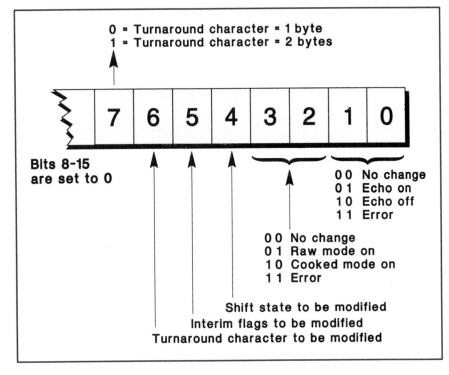

Figure 3-4
Keyboard Status Mask

Echo information in the status mask indicates whether a character typed will be echoed to the screen, and we'll discuss the raw/cooked status soon. We needn't be concerned with the other bits in the mask. In KbdGetStatus() the bits in **fsMask** simply report the status of the keyboard. When it is used with the function KbdSetStatus() the status can be changed, and then these bits are used to specify what will be changed.

The **chTurnAround** in the **_KBDINFO** structure is normally the [Enter] key, but it can be modified. This is the character used to signal the end of a string in the KbdStringIn() function. We won't be concerned with the **fsInterim** variable. The **fsState** variable reports the state of all the shift keys. This is similar to the information returned by the KbdCharIn() function.

KbdGetStatus — Gets keyboard status information

```
KbdGetStatus(AStatus, Handle);
struct _KBDINFO far *AStatus;     /* address of structure */
unsigned short Handle;            /* always 0 */
```

Besides the handle, the only argument to KbdGetStatus() is **AStatus**, the address for the **_KBDINFO** structure.

The program continuously displays the status information on the screen. With no keys pressed the display looks like this:

```
Mask = 9
Turnaround = d
Flags = 0
Shift state =     0
```

The mask number indicates that cooked mode and echo are on, and the turnaround character is set to the carriage return (0D hex). If you press any of the shift keys, you'll see the shift state change. Terminate the program with [Ctrl] [c].

Raw and Cooked Modes

What is the difference between *raw* and *cooked* modes? The distinction has to do with how much translation the system does of characters typed at the keyboard. In cooked mode, which is the default, the system interprets certain standard key-combinations. For instance, if you type [Ctrl] [c], a signal will be generated which will (usually) cause your program to terminate. The [Ctrl] [s] key combination will cause screen output to halt, and the next character typed will not be interpreted as a character, but will cause screen output to resume.

In raw mode these interpretations are no longer made. The [Ctrl] [c] key combination, for instance, is sent right on to the program. This is useful if your program needs these key combinations for its own purposes.

Here's a program that demonstrates the difference between raw and cooked mode by using KbdSetStatus() to set the keyboard status to raw or cooked, as the user chooses.

```
/* raw.c */
/* sets raw/cooked status using KbdSetStatus() */
#define INCL_SUB
#include <os2.h>
#define HANDLE 0                        /* always 0 */
```

(continued)

```
main()
{
   struct _KBDINFO keystat;     /* struct in bsesub.h */
   int j;                       /* loop counter */
   unsigned rc;                 /* return code */
                                /* set length of structure */
   keystat.cb = sizeof(struct _KBDINFO);
                                /* get keyboard status */
   if( rc=KbdGetStatus( &keystat, HANDLE ) )
      { printf("KbdGetStatus error=%u\n",rc); exit(1); }
   if( keystat.fsMask & 0x0004 )
      printf("Bit 2 set: raw mode on\n");
   if( keystat.fsMask & 0x0008 )
      printf("Bit 3 set: cooked mode on\n");
   printf("\nCooked mode on (y/n)? ");
   if( getche() == 'y' ) {
      keystat.fsMask &= 0xFFFB;   /* set bit 2 = 0 */
      keystat.fsMask |= 0x0008;   /* set bit 3 = 1 */
   } else {
      keystat.fsMask |= 0x0004;   /* set bit 2 = 1 */
      keystat.fsMask &= 0xFFF7;   /* set bit 3 = 0 */
      }
                                /* set new status */
   if( rc=KbdSetStatus( &keystat, HANDLE ) )
      { printf("KbdSetStatus error=%u\n",rc); exit(1); }
   for(j=0; j<500; j++)         /* test for cooked */
      printf("%d -- Testing...testing...\n", j);
   exit(0);
}
```

This program first reads in the keyboard status. It then examines the **raw** and **cooked** bits and reports their status. It asks the user whether raw or cooked mode is desired, and uses KbdSet-Status() to set the raw/cooked bits accordingly. Finally, it enters a loop which prints a phrase over and over; this gives the user the chance to experiment with the [Ctrl] [c] and [Ctrl] [s] key combinations. In cooked mode these will have their usual effects: scrolling can be stopped with [Ctrl] [s], and the program can be terminated with [Ctrl] [c]. In raw mode, however, these keys will not work, and the program will continue to print the "testing...testing" message.

KbdSetStatus — Sets keyboard status

```
KbdSetStatus(AStatus, Handle);
struct _KBDINFO far *AStatus;   /* address of structure */
unsigned short Handle;          /* always 0 */
```

Like KbdGetStatus(), the KbdSetStatus() function takes only one argument (besides the handle), **AStatus**, the address of a structure of type **_KBDINFO**.

Don't panic if you can't stop the program in raw mode; after 500 lines have been printed it stops by itself. Switch to a different screen group and do something else until it finishes.

Video Modes

OS/2 can operate in many different video modes: monochrome text, CGA with 40 columns text, CGA graphics, and so on. When the system is first started it queries the attached equipment—the adaptor card (or cards)—to see what video mode is appropriate, and then sets this mode.

In this section we'll show how a program determines what video mode is in use, and how to change to a different mode.

Reading the Video Mode

In MS-DOS modes are numbered, and each number has a certain set of characteristics: number of colors, number of rows and columns in text mode, horizontal and vertical graphics resolution, and so on. The OS/2 functions which deal with the video modes don't operate in terms of mode numbers, but in terms of the video characteristics themselves. Thus the function to read the video mode, VioGetMode(), returns a whole structure full of characteristics. Here's what it looks like:

```
struct _VIOMODEINFO {
    unsigned length;cb      /* length of _VIOMODEINFO
                               structure */
    unsigned char fbType;   /* bitmask of mode
                               characteristics */
    unsigned char color;    /* number of color bits */
    unsigned col;           /* number of character columns */
    unsigned row;           /* number of character rows */
    unsigned hres;          /* horizontal graphics
                               resolution */
    unsigned vres;          /* vertical graphics resolution */
    unsigned char fmt_ID;   /* reserved, must be 0 */
    unsigned char attrib;   /* reserved, must be 0 */
};
```

The **cb** variable is the length of the structure itself, which is 14 bytes. You can specify fewer bytes if you don't want all the information.

The **fbType** variable is divided into bit fields, as shown in Figure 3-5.

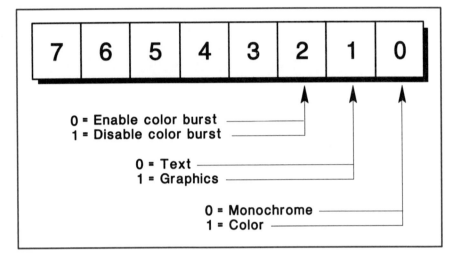

Figure 3-5
The Type Field in the __VIOMODEINFO Structure

The **color** field is the number of bits necessary to represent the number of colors.

Colors	Bits
2	1
4	2
16	4

Columns and **rows** apply to characters; typical values are 80 and 25, 40 and 25, or 80 and 43. **hres** and **vres** are the horizontal and vertical resolution—in pixels—in graphics mode.

The last two variables in this structure are currently reserved and must be set to 0.

Here's the program that displays this information:

```
/* getvio.c */
/* gets and displays the video mode parameters */
#define INCL_SUB
#include <os2.h>
```

(continued)

```
#define COLOR      0x01          /* bit 0 in type parameter */
#define GRAPHICS   0x02          /* bit 1 in type parameter */
#define NO_BURST   0x04          /* bit 2 in type parameter */
#define HANDLE 0                 /* vio handle always 0 */
main()
{
    struct _VIOMODEINFO modedata;        /* from bsesub.h */

    modedata.cb = sizeof(modedata);      /* length of buffer */
    VioGetMode( &modedata, HANDLE );     /* get mode data */
    if( modedata.fbType & COLOR )        /* adaptor type */
       printf("Color adaptor\n");
    else
       printf("Monochrome adaptor\n");
    if( modedata.fbType & GRAPHICS )     /* text or graphics */
       printf("Graphics adaptor\n");
    else
       printf("Text mode\n");
    if( modedata.fbType & NO_BURST )     /* color burst */
       printf("Color burst disabled\n");
    else
       printf("Color burst enabled\n");
                                         /* number of colors */
    printf("Number of color bits: %d\n", modedata.color );
                                         /* resolutions */
    printf("Alpha columns:    %u\n", modedata.col);
    printf("Alpha rows:       %u\n", modedata.row);
    printf("Horiz resolution: %u\n", modedata.hres);
    printf("Vert resolution:  %u\n", modedata.vres);
    exit(0);
}
```

And here's the output when the program is run on a system with an EGA graphics monitor:

```
Graphics adaptor
Text mode
Color burst enabled
Number of color bits: 4
Alpha columns:      80
Alpha rows:         25
Horiz resolution: 640
Vert resolution:  350
Format ID:          25
Attribute:           0
```

If you are using a different graphics mode, your system will report different information. The monochrome adaptor, for example, reports a resolution of 720 by 350, among other changes.

VioGetMode — Gets video mode information

```
VioGetMode(AData, Handle);
struct _VIOMODEINFO far *AData;    /* address of structure */
unsigned short Handle;             /* always 0 */
```

The function that gets the video mode information, VioGetMode(), needs to know only the location of the structure to hold the data, **AData**, and the handle.

The following table shows the video modes currently available in OS/2:

Mode (dec)	Colors	Resolution Horiz	Vert	Text Cols	Rows	VGA	EGA	CGA	Mono
0 text	16 gray	320	200	40	25	X	X	X	
0 text	16 gray	320	350	40	43	X	X		
0 text	16 gray	360	400	40	50	X			
1 text	16	320	200	40	25	X	X	X	
1 text	16	320	350	40	43	X	X		
1 text	16	360	400	40	50	X			
2 text	16 gray	640	200	80	25	X	X	X	
2 text	16 gray	640	350	80	43	X	X		
2 text	16 gray	720	400	80	50	X			
3 text	16	640	200	80	25	X	X	X	
3 text	16	640	350	80	43	X	X		
3 text	16	720	400	80	50	X			
4 graph	4	320	200	40	25	X	X	X	
5 graph	2 B&W	320	200	40	25	X	X	X	
6 graph	2 B&W	640	200	80	25	X	X	X	
7 text	2 B&W	720	350	80	25				X
7 text	2 B&W	720	400	80	25	X			
13 graph	16	320	200	80	25	X	X		
14 graph	4	640	200	80	25	X	X		
15 graph	2 B&W	640	350	80	25	X	X		
16 graph	16	640	350	80	25	X	X		
17 graph	2 B&W	640	480	80	30	X			
18 graph	16	640	480	80	30	X			
19 graph	256	320	200	40	25	X			

Now we know how to read the existing video mode; is it also possible to change from one mode to another?

Setting the Video Mode

To change the video mode, a program first fills a _VIOMODEINFO structure with the appropriate information, and then calls VioSetMode() to send this information on to the system. The information to put in the buffer can come either from the user, a previous use of Vio-GetMode(), or a combination. In the following program it comes entirely from the user:

```c
/* setvio.c */
/* sets the video mode */
#define INCL_SUB
#include <os2.h>
#include <stdio.h>                    /* for printf() */
#define COLOR    0x01                 /* bit 0 in type parameter */
#define GRAPHICS 0x02                 /* bit 1 in type parameter */
#define NO_BURST 0x04                 /* bit 2 in type parameter */
#define STRLEN 12                     /* amount of data to set */
#define HANDLE 0                      /* vio handle always 0 */
main()
{
    struct _VIOMODEINFO modedata;  /* defined in bsesub.h */
    char string[80];               /* buffer for input */
    unsigned rc;                   /* return code */

    modedata.cb = STRLEN;          /* length of struct */
    modedata.fbType &= ~COLOR;     /* AND off color bit */
    printf("\nMonochrome/color (m/c)? ");
    if( getche()=='c' )            /* if color, */
       modedata.fbType |= COLOR;   /* OR on the bit */

    modedata.fbType &= ~GRAPHICS; /* graphics */
    printf("\nGraphics or text (g/t)? ");
    if( getche()=='g' )
       modedata.fbType |= GRAPHICS;

    modedata.fbType &= ~NO_BURST; /* color burst */
    printf("\nColor burst (y/n) ");
    if( getche()=='n' )
        modedata.fbType  |= NO_BURST;
    printf("\nType parameter = %02x\n", modedata.fbType );
                                   /* color bits */
    printf("\nNumber of color bits: ");
       modedata.color = (char)atoi( gets(string) );
                                   /* resolutions */
    printf("Number of text columns: ");
       modedata.col = atoi( gets(string) );
```

(continued)

```
   printf("Number of text rows: ");
      modedata.row = atoi( gets(string) );
   printf("Number of horizontal pixels: ");
      modedata.hres = atoi( gets(string) );
   printf("Number of vertical pixels: ");
      modedata.vres = atoi( gets(string) );

                                    /* set the mode */
   if( rc=VioSetMode( &modedata, HANDLE ) )
      { printf("VioSetMode error=%u\n",rc); exit(1); }
   exit(0);
}
```

The program takes the user's answers to the questions about color, text/graphics, and color burst, and puts them together into the **fbType** variable, which is then printed out for the user's information. The other parameters are entered similarly, and the function VioSetMode() then causes the mode to change. This does not clear the screen, but it does initialize the cursor position and type.

Here's a sample session where the program is used to change to CGA text mode, with 80 by 25 characters:

```
Monochrome/color (m/c)? c
Graphics or text (g/t)? t
Color burst (y/n) y
Type parameter = 01
Number of color bits: 4
Number of text columns: 80
Number of text rows: 25
Number of horizontal pixels: 640
Number of vertical pixels: 200
```

Or, if you have an EGA or VGA monitor, you can change to a 43 line mode:

```
Monochrome/color (m/c)? c
Graphics or text (g/t)? t
Color burst (y/n) y
Type parameter = 01
Number of color bits: 4
Number of text columns: 80
Number of text rows: 43
Number of horizontal pixels: 640
Number of vertical pixels: 350
```

The VioSetMode() function, like VioGetMode(), takes only two parameters: the address of the structure where the mode characteristics are stored, and the handle.

VioSetMode — Alters the video mode information

```
VioSetMode(AData, Handle);
struct _VIOMODEINFO far *AData;   /* address of structure */
unsigned short Handle;            /* always 0 */
```

The _VIOMODEINFO structure is the same as that used in VioGetMode(). In this program we specify a length of 12 as the first element of the structure. This avoids having to deal with the last two elements of ModeData.

If you attempt to use this program with arguments which don't constitute a possible mode for your equipment, you'll get the message:

```
VioSetMode error=355
```

This means "unsupported screen mode." The program could check for this specific return code, and offer a more specific message to the user. Or, better yet, the program could contain parameters for known modes, such as this program that changes to CGA text mode:

```
/* setcga.c */
/* sets video mode to CGA color text, 80x25 */
#define INCL_SUB
#include <os2.h>
#define HANDLE 0                  /* vio handle always 0 */
#define STRLEN 12                 /* amount of data to set */
main()
{
    struct _VIOMODEINFO modedata; /* defined in bsesub.h */
    unsigned rc;                  /* return code */

    modedata.cb=STRLEN;           /* length of structure */
    modedata.fbType = 0x01;       /* color, text, burst */
    modedata.color = 4;           /* color bits */
    modedata.col = 80;            /* columns */
    modedata.row = 25;            /* rows */
    modedata.hres = 640;          /* horiz pixels */
    modedata.vres = 200;          /* vertical pixels */
                                  /* set the mode */
    if( rc=VioSetMode( &modedata, HANDLE ) )
       { printf("VioSetMode error=%u\n",rc); exit(1); }
    exit(0);
}
```

In this same way any graphics mode can be quickly set.

Discovering the Adaptor and Display Type

Your program can find out not only a machine's graphics mode, it can also determine the type of video adaptor card being used, and the type of display attached to the card (or at least the type of display the adaptor *thinks* is attached to it).

Here's a program that tells you whether the adaptor is running in monochrome, CGA, EGA, or VGA, and which of these types the monitor is. It also tells you how much graphics memory your adaptor has.

```
/* gconfig.c */
/* gets the video configuration (adaptor and display) */
#define INCL_SUB
#include <os2.h>
#define HANDLE 0                    /* always 0 */
main()
{
    struct _VIOCONFIGINFO config;  /* defined in bsesub.h */
    unsigned rc;                   /* return code */

    config.cb = sizeof(config);
    if( rc=VioGetConfig( 0, &config, HANDLE ) )
        { printf("VioGetConfig error=%u\n",rc); exit(1); }
    switch(config.adapter)  {
        case 0: printf("Monochrome adaptor\n"); break;
        case 1: printf("CGA adaptor\n"); break;
        case 2: printf("EGA adaptor\n"); break;
        default: printf("Unknown adaptor\n");
        }
    switch(config.display)  {
        case 0: printf("Monochrome display\n"); break;
        case 1: printf("CGA display\n"); break;
        case 2: printf("EGA display\n"); break;
        default: printf("Unknown display\n");
        }
    printf("Display memory size is %lu\n", config.cbMemory);
    exit(0);
}
```

The system returns this information in a structure, defined in BSESUB.H, that looks like this:

```
struct _VIOCONFIGINFO {
    unsigned cb;
    unsigned adapter;
    unsigned display;
    unsigned long cbMemory;
    };
```

For the **adaptor_type** and **display_type** the possible values are:

Value	Adaptor type
0	Monochrome
1	CGA
2	EGA
3	VGA

Value	Display type
0	Monochrome
1	Color
2	Enhanced color

The **cbMemory** variable is the amount of memory, in bytes. Thus a typical readout, for an EGA system with fully loaded memory, would be:

```
EGA adaptor
EGA display
Display memory is 262144 bytes
```

With the information about display and adaptor type, as well as the various characteristics of the video mode being used, your program should have no trouble getting what it needs to know about the display.

The function used to write the configuration information into the _VIOCONFIGINFO structure is VioGetConfig().

VioGetConfig — Get video display information

```
VioGetConfig(Reserved, AInfo, Handle);
unsigned Reserved;                /* reserved, must be 0 */
struct _VIOCONFIGINFO far *AInfo;   /* address of
                                         structure */
unsigned short Handle;            /* kbd handle, always 0 */
```

The first argument is reserved and must be 0. The second argument is the address of the _VIOCONFIGINFO structure. The third is the keyboard handle, which must be 0.

Subsystems and the Presentation Manager

The VIO calls, collectively, are contained in a special OS/2 entity called a *subsystem*. The KBD calls and the mouse (MOU) calls also form subsystems. A subsystem is an easily-replaceable module. Thus, if your system uses the Presentation Manager (PM), the VIO, KBD and MOU subsystems are different than if you are using OS/2 version 1. However, this change is invisible to the programmer. It is also possible to install custom subsystems.

These subsystems are designed to be very fast. They avoid the standard file system, and the complexities, such as redirection, that slow it down. In most cases it should not be necessary to resort to the stratagems that are common in MS-DOS, such as directly writing characters to the physical screen buffer.

If redirection is more important than speed, then you can use the DosRead() and DosWrite() functions from the file system, which we'll examine in Chapter 8. In fact, DosRead() and DosWrite() make use of the low-level functions VioWrtTTy() and KbdStringIn() to do their reading and writing, after they have dealt with the redirection issue. The normal C library routines, such as printf(), are also redirectable.

Character Mode

The routines described in this chapter read and write characters, not graphics. For this reason they are called *character mode* functions. The graphics calls built into the old MS-DOS BIOS to read and write dots are not supported in OS/2.

If your system is running the Presentation Manager, it is possible to read the keyboard and write to the screen in two ways. You can use either the character mode functions described here, or you can use a different set of functions built into the Presentation Manager. When should you use the VIO routines, and when the PM?

The PM is much more difficult to program than the VIO API described in this chapter. If you are writing, say, a commercial-level word processor, you will probably want to make the time investment necessary to learn how to program the PM.

However, for less ambitious applications, this is not necessary. Some programs won't profit very much from the visual interface of the PM: a sorting routine, for example, or a linker. Also, many custom applications will not have the high sales volume to justify a full-scale windows interface, and will perform admirably in character mode. These character mode applications will run perfectly well under the PM; they are only restricted from using the graphics and visual interface routines built into the PM.

Summary

In this chapter we've looked at a number of API functions which perform simple operations involving the screen and keyboard.

We've seen how to write to a specific location on the screen with a new attribute using VioWrtCharStrAttr(), how to write with the existing attribute with VioWrtCharStr(), how to write at the cursor position with VioWrtTTy(), and how to write the same character many times with VioWrtNCell().

The cursor's position can be changed with VioSetCurPos(), and the type of the cursor can be queried and changed with VioGetCurType() and VioSetCurType(). We can also find out if the ANSI keyboard driver is in use with VioGetAnsi(), and turn ANSI on or off with VioSetAnsi(). A character string can be read from a screen location with VioReadCharStr(), and the screen can be scrolled with a family of four API functions, of which VioScrollUp() is one.

A character, and detailed information about it, can be read from the keyboard with KbdCharIn(), and a string can be read with KbdStringIn(). The status of the shift keys and other information about the keyboard can be queried with KbdGetStatus() and set with KbdSetStatus().

Finally, we saw how to get information about the video mode with VioGetMode(), and change the mode with VioSetMode().

This chapter should have reinforced your familiarity with the style used in the API functions. We're now ready to investigate the heart of OS/2: multitasking.

PROCESSES

Chapter 4

Chapter 4

In Chapter 1 we discussed the three kinds of OS/2 multitasking: screen groups, processes, and threads. A screen group is a virtual computer: it has its own logical screen and keyboard. To the user, a screen group looks almost like a complete computer system. The user can create new screen groups using the session manager, and can switch back and forth from one screen group to another.

A process, on the other hand, is more like our intuitive idea of a program. A user can start a foreground process merely by typing its name at the DOS prompt, and—as we saw in Chapter 1—can also start background processes by using DETACH.

If a user can start a process, is it also possible for one process to start another? Not surprisingly, it is. In this chapter we focus on how to write programs that create child processes and how to manage these processes once they're running. After looking at examples of processes and some of their capabilities, we'll discuss in a more general way how they fit into the programming picture and why you might want to use them.

One Parent, One Child

A parent process can start many child processes, and each child can start children of its own, as shown in Figure 4-1.

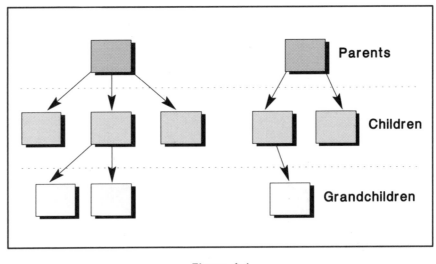

Figure 4-1
Parents Starting Children

Of course, unlike the biological world, each child process has only one parent.

Our first example consists of the simplest possible arrangement: one parent and one child. The parent first starts the child, then sits in a loop printing X's on the screen. The child, once started, prints dashes. Since each program reveals the fact that it's running by printing a distinctive character, we have a visual display of how the scheduler allots time slices to the two processes.

When a key is pressed, the parent first kills the child, then exits (yes, it sounds like a Greek tragedy).

Here's the parent program:

```c
/* parent.c */
/* starts a child process */
/* continuously writes 'X' to screen */
#define INCL_DOS
#define INCL_SUB
#include <os2.h>
#define LENGTH 40       /* length of object name buffer */
#define FLAGS 1         /* asynchronously, no trace */
#define ARGS 0L         /* no command-line arguments */
#define ENVS 0L         /* no environment variables */
#define KILLALL 0       /* kill process and children */
main()
{
   char fbuf[LENGTH];            /* buffer for fail-object */
   struct _RESULTCODES childID;  /* defined in doscalls.h */
   unsigned rc;                  /* return code */
                                 /* start child */
   if( rc=DosExecPgm( fbuf, LENGTH, FLAGS, ARGS, ENVS,
                      &childID, "CHILD.EXE" ) )
      { printf("DosExecPgm error=%u\n",rc); exit(1); }
   while( !kbhit() )             /* print until key struck */
      VioWrtTTy("X", 1, 0 );
                                 /* kill child */
   if( rc=DosKillProcess( KILLALL, childID.codeTerminate ) )
      { printf("DosKillProcess error=%u\n",rc); exit(1); }
   exit(0);
}
```

And here's the child, which will be started by the parent:

```c
/* child.c */
/* runs as child process under parent.exe */
/* continuously prints dash on screen */
#define INCL_SUB
#include <os2.h>
```

(continued)

```
main()
{
   while(TRUE)
      VioWrtTTy( "-", 1, 0 );
}
```

Here's what the screen looks like after the parent has been started, it has started the child, and they are running together:

```
-----------------------------------------------------XXXXXXXXXX
X--------------------------------------------------------------
--------------------------------------------------------------
---------------XXXXXXXXXXXXXXXXXXXXXXXXXXXXXXXXXXXXXXXXXXXXXXXXX
XXXXXXXXXX----------------------------------------------------
------------------------------------------XXXXXXXX-------------
------XXXXXXXXXXXXXXXXXXXXXXXXXXXXXXXXXXXXXXXXXXXXXXXXXXXXXXXXXX
XX------------------------------------------------------------
-------------XXXXXXXX-----------------------------------------
----------XXXXXXXXXXXXXXXXXXXXXXXXXXXXXXXXXXXXXXXXXXXXXXXXXXXXXX
XXXXXX-------------------------------------------------------
--------------------------------------------------------------
----------------XXXXXXXX--------------------------------------
```

(So it will fit on the page, we've rearranged this output by making the lines shorter than they are on an 80-column screen. The effect is the same.)

Since both processes are running in the foreground in the same screen group, they both have access to the screen. The screen shows both outputs intermixed.

In this particular case the child seems to get more time than the parent. This is dependent on many factors, such as what other programs may be running, which version of the system is being used, and how priorities and time slice parameters have been set in the config.os2 file. The speed of the processor and display also determine how many characters are printed before one process's time slice is over and another process takes over.

The DosExecPgm() Function

The child simply uses the VioWrtTTy() function to write a dash to the screen over and over. (We could also have used the printf() function.) The child is simple, but the parent process uses some new functions. The function which starts the child process is DosExecPgm().

DosExecPgm — Executes child process

```
DosExecPgm(ABuffer, Length, Flags, AArgs, AEnvs, ACodes,
                                               Name);
char far *ABuffer; /* address of buffer for object name */
unsigned Length;   /* length of buffer */
unsigned Flags;    /* synch or asynch, trace or no trace */
char far *AArgs;   /* address of command-line arguments */
char far *AEnvs;   /* address of environmental variables */
struct _RESULTCODES far *ACodes;  /* process ID, or exit
                                     code */
char far *Name;    /* drive and pathname of child */
```

When this function is executed the operating system finds the intended child program, in this case CHILD.EXE, on the disk, and loads it into memory. Then it executes it. This is similar to a user invoking a program by typing its name at the keyboard. However, there is a closer relationship between the parent and the child than there is between independently running programs.

The first parameter of DosExecPgm() is a buffer in which the name of an object that contributed to the failure of the function is placed. In complex situations starting a program may involve loading a variety of dynalink library routines along with a program; a problem with any one of these could cause a failure. This field helps pinpoint which routine is responsible. In the situation such as that shown here, this field returns relatively simple information. For instance, if the parent tries to start a program that doesn't exist, the name of the nonexistent file is placed in this buffer.

The second parameter is simply the length of this buffer; this is provided so the system won't overrun the space available. The third parameter, **Flags**, specifies one of six possible situations:

Value	Meaning
0	Child executes synchronously to parent
1	Child executes asynchronously to parent, result code discarded
2	Child executes asynchronously to parent, result code saved for DosCWait()
3	Tracing enabled, parent will debug child
4	Asynchronous child runs outside parent's screen group
5	Child does not run until "thawed" by call from session manager

Executing *synchronously*, option 0, means the parent waits until the child has terminated, before continuing past the DosExecPgm() call. This is more like an overlay than multitasking, and is provided for upward compatibility of MS-DOS programs. Otherwise, it should be avoided. We are interested in **asynchronous** operation: options 1 and 2. In these modes the parent starts the child, and both continue to run simultaneously. Figure 4-2 shows the difference between synchronous and asynchronous operation of two processes.

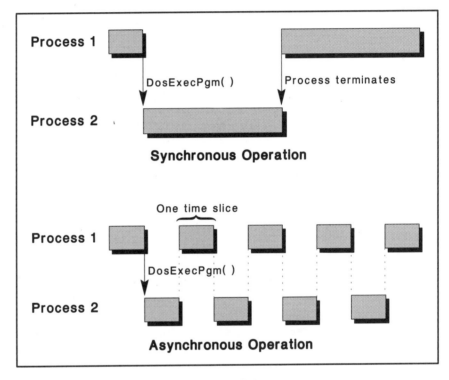

Figure 4-2
Synchronous and Asynchronous Operation

Options 1 and 2 are similar, except that in option 1 the parent does not remember the termination code of the child and can't use DosCWait() to find out when the child terminated. This is a "start it and forget it" approach. Use this option if you don't intend to use DosCWait() and want to find out what happened to the child. In option 2 the termination code is retained, and the parent can be notified of the child's termination using DosCWait() (which we'll examine soon).

Option 3 is used when the parent is debugging the child; we won't examine this option here, although writers of debugging programs will find it interesting. It's used, for example, by CodeView. Option 4 is for processes that execute entirely in the background, with no access to screen or keyboard. This is similar to using the DETACH command from the keyboard. Such processes are considered to be parentless, and are called **daemon** processes. Option 5 leaves a program ready to run, but not yet executed. The user can then start it from the session manager screen.

The **AArgs** and **AEnvs** variables are used to transmit the address of command-line arguments and environmental strings to the child. Null pointers, which we have used in this example, indicate that no command-line arguments or environmental strings will be passed. We'll see later how to use these parameters.

The **ACodes** variable is the address of a structure. The structure is defined in BSEDOS.H, and looks like this:

```
struct _RESULTCODES  {
    unsigned codeTerminate;   /* process ID or termination
                                 code */
    unsigned codeResult;      /* exit code */
    };
```

If we requested *synchronous* operation, the first member of this structure would be filled in by the termination code of the child when it terminates and returns control to the parent. Also, the second member of the structure would be used to pass the result code from an exit() or DosExit() statement. However, we requested *asynchronous operation*, so the first member of the structure, **codeTerminate**, will be filled in by the process ID of the child. As we noted earlier, the ID of a process is a number assigned to it by the operating system, with each succeeding process getting the next number in line. If option 2 is selected for FLAGS, the result code of the child is saved in **codeResult**, the second variable in the structure. In our program, since we selected option 1, the process ID of the child will be stored in **childID.codeTerminate**, a fact which we'll make use of when we kill the child.

The last parameter we need to give DosExecPgm() is the address of a string which is the drive and pathname of the child program we want to start. In our case, this is the string "CHILD.EXE", which is assumed to be in the same directory as the parent. The current directory is searched first for the filename. If the file isn't found there, then the operating system looks in the parent's environment for additional paths to the file.

Instead of a filename, a complete pathname can be used for this parameter. If it is "fully qualified," meaning it appears to contain all the information to find the file (it starts with '\' or a drive letter and colon), then the pathname is used to find the file.

We might note that, even when you start a program by typing its name at the DOS prompt, the command processor CMD.EXE uses DosExecPgm() to start the program; it's the universal OS/2 program starter.

Killing the Child

The parent uses the API function DosKillProcess() to terminate the child. Why is this necessary? The fact that the parent has terminated itself with exit() has no effect on the child. Unless something is done, the child continues to run, printing dashes all over the screen long after the parent is gone. Worse yet, the normal way to terminate a runaway program, [Ctrl] [C], has no effect on the child (although it will terminate the parent). If a child process is written so it terminates itself after it has performed its task, all is well. If not, we must rely on the parent to kill it off, lest it run forever as an "orphan" process (or at least until we reboot).

```
                 DosKillProcess — Terminate process
DosKillProcess(Code, ProcessID);
unsigned Code;        /* 0=kill children too; 1=only process */
unsigned ProcessID;    /* ID of process to kill */
```

This function needs only the process ID of the child (so it knows what process to kill) and a parameter specifying whether to kill only the process, or the process and all its children.

It is possible to notify a process about to be killed by DosKill-Process(). This allows it to perform any necessary house-cleaning tasks, such as closing files. (Granting one last request to the condemned man.) We'll find out more about this when we discuss signals in Chapter 12.

One Parent, Several Children

A parent can start as many children as it likes, all of which can run concurrently. Here's an example that uses this fact to explore the time slices apportioned to different processes. It uses one parent and two children, which all sit in loops printing the time. Here's the parent:

```
/* p3time.c */
/* three time-printer processes run simultaneously */
/* uses child processes */
#define INCL_DOS
#include <os2.h>
#define LENGTH 40       /* length of object name buffer */
#define FLAGS 1         /* asynchronously, no trace */
#define ARGS 0L         /* no command-line arguments */
#define ENVS 0L         /* no environment variables */
#define KILLALL 0       /* kill process and children */

main()
{
   struct _DATETIME now;            /* for DosGetDateTime() */
   char fbuf[LENGTH];               /* buffer for fail-object */
   struct _RESULTCODES childID1;    /* for first child */
   struct _RESULTCODES childID2;    /* for second child */
   unsigned rc;                     /* return code */
                                    /* start first child */
   if( rc=DosExecPgm( fbuf, LENGTH, FLAGS, ARGS, ENVS,
                      &childID1, "CH3TIME1.EXE" ) )
      { printf("DosExecPgm error=%u\n",rc); exit(1); }
                                    /* start second child */
   if( rc=DosExecPgm( fbuf, LENGTH, FLAGS, ARGS, ENVS,
                      &childID2, "CH3TIME2.EXE" ) )
      { printf("DosExecPgm error=%u\n",rc); exit(1); }
                                    /* print time continuously */
   while( !kbhit() )  {
      DosGetDateTime( (struct _DATETIME far *) &now);
      printf("[%d:%d]", now.seconds, now.hundredths);
   }                                /* kill children */
   if( rc=DosKillProcess( KILLALL, childID1.codeTerminate) )
      { printf("DosKillProcess error=%u", rc); exit(1); }
   if( rc=DosKillProcess( KILLALL, childID2.codeTerminate) )
      { printf("DosKillProcess error=%u", rc); exit(1); }
   exit(0);
}
```

And here is one of the children. The other child is identical except that it is called ch3time2.c, and prints an asterisk before and after the time, instead of a dash.

```
/* ch3time1.c */
/* continuously prints the time */
/* to be used as child process(s) of p3time.exe */
#define INCL_DOS
#include <os2.h>
```

(continued)

```
main()
{
    struct _DATETIME now;

    while(TRUE) {
       DosGetDateTime( (struct _DATETIME far *)&now);
       printf("-%d:%d-", now.seconds, now.hundredths );
    }
}
```

We discussed the DosGetDateTime() function in Chapter 1: it returns the time from the system clock. Here both parent and children use this function to display the time in seconds and hundredths. For simplicity we've used the C library function printf() to do the printing.

Here's an example of this application's output:

```
-47:18--47:18--47:21--47:21--47:25--47:25--47:25--47:25--47:25-
-47:28--47:28--47:28--47:28--47:28--47:28--47:37--47:37--47:37-
-47:37--47:37--47:40--47:40--47:40--47:40--47:40--47:40--47:40-
-47:43--47:43--47:43--47:43--47:43--47:43--47:46--47:46--47:46-
-47:46--47:46--47:46-*47:50**47:50**47:50**47:50**47:50**47:53*
*47:53**47:53**47:53**47:53**47:53**47:56**47:56**47:56**47:56*
*47:56**47:56**47:56**47:59**47:59**47:59**47:59**47:59**47:59*
*47:62**47:62**47:62**47:62**47:62**47:62**47:65**47:65**47:65*
*47:65**47:65**47:65**47:65**47:68**47:68**47:68**47:68**47:68*
*47:68**47:71**47:71**47:71**47:71**47:71**47:71*[47:75][47:75]
[47:75][47:75][47:75][47:78][47:78][47:78][47:78][47:78][47:81]
[47:81][47:81][47:81][47:84][47:84][47:84][47:84][47:84][47:87]
[47:87][47:87][47:87][47:90][47:90][47:90][47:90][47:90][47:93]
[47:93][47:93][47:93][47:96][47:96][47:96][47:96][47:96]-47:49-
-47:99--48:0--48:0--48:0--48:0--48:0--48:3--48:3--48:3--48:3-
```

The output reveals that each process gets the CPU for about a quarter of a second. (The times displayed do not change every hundredth of a second because the system clock doesn't count intervals that small.)

Notice that we can use printf() in a multitasking situation. The three routines all use printf(). This works, if the messages they are sending to the screen are short. If the messages are longer there can be trouble. For instance, if one process is trying to write *Hamlet* to the screen, using a series of printf() statements, while another is trying to write *Macbeth*, an incomprehensible mixture of the two plays is likely to result. In this situation it is necessary to coordinate access to the screen by the different processes. Semaphores, which we'll examine in Chapter 6, provide one way to do this.

Knowing When Your Child Has Died

Suppose a parent launches a child, then goes about some processing of its own, and when it has finished needs to know if the child has also finished. As an example, suppose in a spreadsheet program that the main process calls a child process (perhaps called HELP.EXE) whenever the user asks to see a "help" screen. The child process loads the help files and interacts with the user, while the main process goes on recalculating the spreadsheet. But the main process must wait for the child to finish before it prints a prompt to the user, lest it interfere with the output from HELP.

One way the parent can handle this problem is to use the function DosCWait() to wait for the child. When it executes this function, the parent is put in a wait state (it doesn't get any more time slices) until the child terminates. At this point the system wakes up the parent. The situation is shown in Figure 4-3.

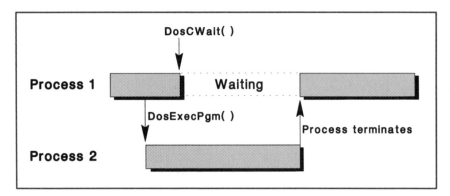

Figure 4-3
Operation of DosCWait( )

When the process that DosCWait() has been waiting on terminates, the function returns considerable information about the process. It can also be set up to wait in several different ways. Let's look at its arguments.

DosCWait — Wait for another process to terminate

```
DosCWait(Scope, Wait, ACodes, APid, ProcessID);
unsigned Scope;      /* 0=wait for process, 1=children too */
unsigned Wait;       /* 0=wait if not ended, 1=no wait */
struct _RESULTCODES far *ACodes;    /* address for result
                                       codes */
unsigned far *APid;  /* address for ID of ending process */
unsigned ProcessID;  /* 0=any child, or ID of process */
```

The first argument to DosCWait() is **Scope**; it is set to 0 if the function should wait only for the specified process to end. It is set to 1 if the function should wait not only for the process, but for all its descendants to end as well. The second argument, **Wait**, is set to 0 if the function should not return until the appropriate process (or processes) has ended, and to 1 if the function should return immediately whether the process has ended or not.

Acodes is the address of a structure of type **_RETURNCODES**. This is the same structure as that used in DosExecPgm(), but used somewhat differently. The structure is filled in with a termination code and a result code. The termination code can have the following values:

Code	Meaning
0	Normal exit
1	Hard error abort
2	Trap operation
3	Unintercepted DosKillProcess()

Normally the termination code will be 0.

The result code is that supplied in the DosExit() function by the terminating thread. We'll learn more about this function in the next chapter.

The fourth argument, **APid**, is filled in by the function with the ID of the process that activated DosCWait(). This could be different than the process requested, since it might be a child. The last argument is the ID of the process to be waited for. If this argument is set to 0, then DosCWait() will return after any of its child processes have ended.

The following pair of programs demonstrates DosCWait(). The parent program starts a child and then executes DosCWait() to wait for it to end. The child prints 100 lines on the screen and then exits. When it exits, DosCWait() releases the parent, which prints out what it has learned about the death of the child (the obituary, as it were).

Here's the listing for the parent:

```
/* pwait.c */
/* starts child, waits for it to finish, using DosCWait() */
#define INCL_DOS
#include <os2.h>
#define LENGTH 40      /* length of object name buffer */
#define FLAGS 2        /* must be 2 for DosCWait() */
#define ARGS 0L        /* no command-line arguments */
#define ENVS 0L        /* no environment variables */
#define ACTION 1       /* 0=process only, 1=children too */
#define WAIT 0         /* 0=wait, 1=no wait */
main()
{
    char fbuf[LENGTH];           /* buffer for fail-object */
    struct _RESULTCODES ExResult;  /* results from
                                        DosExecPgm() */
    unsigned childID;            /* child ID from DosExecPgm */
    struct _RESULTCODES CwResult;  /* results from
                                        DosCWait() */
    unsigned procID;             /* ID of terminated process */
    unsigned rc;                 /* return code */

                                 /* start child */
    if( rc=DosExecPgm( fbuf, LENGTH, FLAGS, ARGS, ENVS,
                            &ExResult, "CHWAIT.EXE" ) )
        { printf("DosExecPgm error=%u\n",rc); exit(1); }
    childID = ExResult.codeTerminate;
    printf("Started child\n");
    printf("Proc ID = %u\n", childID);
                                 /* wait for child to exit */
    if( rc=DosCWait(ACTION, WAIT, &CwResult, &procID,
                                                childID) )
        { printf("DosCWait error=%u\n",rc); exit(1); }
                                 /* display exit info */
    printf("Child terminated.  Process ID = %u\n", procID );
    switch( CwResult.codeTerminate )  {
        case 0: printf("Normal exit\n"); break;
        case 1: printf("Hard error abort\n"); break;
        case 2: printf("Trap operation\n"); break;
        case 3: printf("DosKillProcess()\n"); break;
    }
}
```

Note that for DosCWait() to work, the **FLAGS** variable in Dos-ExecPgm() must have the value 2. Otherwise, the termination of the child won't be recognized, and its result code won't be saved.

Here's the listing of the child process:

```
/* chwait.c */
/* prints lines, then exits */
/* to be used as child process of pwait.exe */
#define LINES 100
main()
{
   int j;
   for(j=1; j<=LINES; j++)
      printf("Child is printing line %d of %d\n", j, LINES);
   printf("Child is exiting\n");
   exit(99);
}
```

And here's what's printed on the screen when you run the program:

```
Started child
Proc ID = 84
Child is printing line 1 of 100
Child is printing line 2 of 100
Child is printing line 3 of 100
- - - - - - - - - - - - - - - -
- - - - - - - - - - - - - - - -
Child is printing line 98 of 100
Child is printing line 99 of 100
Child is printing line 100 of 100
Child is exiting
Child terminated.   Process ID = 84
Normal exit
Result code = 99
```

In some cases the two lines printed by the parent just after starting the child may be mixed in with those printed by the child, since the two processes run concurrently.

Passing Arguments to the Child

When, as a user, you start a program by typing its name at the DOS prompt, you can specify command-line arguments, which the program can then make use of. For instance, typing

C>prog one two

causes the arguments **one** and **two** to be sent to the program prog.exe.

A program can also make use of "environmental" information which was set up earlier using the PATH and SET commands. For instance, the command

`PATH=c:\bin`

causes this string to be placed in the environment, where it is available to all programs in a given screen group.

A C language program can access both command-line arguments and environmental information using parameters in the main() function

`main( argc, argv, envp )`

where **argc** is the number of command-line arguments, **argv** is the address of an array of pointers to the arguments, and **envp** is the address of an array of pointers to environmental variables. For a program invoked from the DOS command line, all this information is provided by the user in the form of command-line arguments or as a previously-written batch file. It would be nice if there were a way to pass command-line arguments and environmental information to a child process directly from a parent.

Happily, the creators of OS/2 have provided just such a capability. The **Args** and **Envs** parameters in the DosExecPgm() function are strings which contain command-line arguments or environmental variables.

Here's a parent process which creates a child and at the same time sends it command-line and environmental arguments:

```
/* pargenv.c */
/* starts child, sends it arguments */
#define INCL_DOS
#include <os2.h>
#include <stdio.h>               /* for NULL definition */
#define LENGTH sizeof(fbuf)
#define FLAG 2                    /* asynch, store child ID */

char ArgStr[] = "PARGENV.EXE\0arg1 arg2 arg3\0";

char EnvStr[] = "TEMP=c:\\work\\temp\0LIB=c:\\lib\0";
```

(continued)

```
main()
{
   unsigned rc;                        /* return code */
   char fbuf[32];                      /* failed object buffer */
   struct _RESULTCODES childID;        /* result codes buffer */
                                       /* start child */
   if( rc=DosExecPgm(fbuf, LENGTH, FLAG, ArgStr, EnvStr,
                        &childID, "CHARGENV.EXE" ) )
      { printf("DosExecPgm error=%u\n", rc); exit(1); }
   exit(0);
}
```

The parent sets up pointers to the command-line arguments and to several environmental statements.

Here's a child process that reads these arguments and displays them:

```
/* chargenv.c */
/* prints out arguments provided by parent */
/* to be used with pargenv.c (or alone) */
main(argc, argv, envp)
int argc;
char *argv[];                       /* command-line ptr */
char *envp[];                       /* environment ptr */
{
   char **ptr;

   for( ptr=argv; argc; argc-- )    /* use argc for count */
      printf("Arg = %s\n", *ptr++); /* print com-line arg */

   for( ptr=envp; *ptr; ptr++ )     /* until NULL pointer */
      printf("Env = %s\n", *ptr);   /* print env string */
   exit(0);
}
```

Here's the output from the child when the parent is executed:

```
Arg = PARGENV.EXE
Arg = arg1
Arg = arg2
Arg = arg3
Env = TEMP=c:\work\temp
Env = LIB=c:\lib
```

The argument string **ArgStr** starts with the program name, followed by a '\0' (null) character. Following this are the command-line arguments separated by spaces. A double null terminates the string (one null occurs normally at the end of the string, the second is inserted explicitly).

The environmental variables occupy the string **EnvStr**. They are separated by nulls, with a double null at the end of the string.

You can use this same program, chargenv.c, to display arguments typed at the command line from DOS, and the existing environment. In this case the program name, typed by the user, is the first command-line argument, and the environmental variables are supplied by previous uses of the PATH and SET commands.

Command-line arguments provide a convenient way for a parent to pass information to a child without resorting to more complex kinds of interprocess communication, such as pipes and queues. We'll see an example in the next section. The parent can also create a particular environment for the child, different from that of the parent, customized for the child's needs.

One Parent and Twins

It is possible for a parent program to start several versions of the same program. For instance, the parent program could use DosExecPgm() to start a process called CHILD.EXE. Then, in another call to DosExecPgm(), it could start the same CHILD.EXE again. There would then be two CHILD.EXE files in memory, and two instances of the program running at the same time.

Although they use identical code, each process might behave differently, depending on the information each received from the parent at its creation or from the outside world later in life.

Here's an example in which a parent starts the same child twice. The file used for the children is CHTWINS.EXE. This application is much like our earlier p3time.c example, except that here the three programs print only single letters, instead of the time; and, although there are two child processes, they are not different files but instances of the same .EXE file.

Here's the parent program:

```
/* ptwins.c */
/* starts two instances of one child process */
/* continuously writes 'X' to screen */
#define INCL_DOS
#include <os2.h>
```

(continued)

```
#define LENGTH 40      /* length of object name buffer */
#define FLAGS 1        /* asynchronously, no trace */
#define ENVS 0L        /* no environment variables */
#define KILLALL 0      /* kill process and children */

main()
{
    char fbuf[LENGTH];              /* buffer for fail-object */
    struct _RESULTCODES childID1; /* defined in doscalls.h */
    struct _RESULTCODES childID2; /* defined in doscalls.h */
    unsigned rc;                   /* return code */
                                   /* start first child */
    if( rc=DosExecPgm( fbuf, LENGTH, FLAGS, "-", ENVS,
                   &childID1, "CHTWINS.EXE" ) )
        { printf("DosExecPgm error1=%u\n",rc); exit(1); }
                                   /* start second child */
    if( rc=DosExecPgm( fbuf, LENGTH, FLAGS, "*", ENVS,
                   &childID2, "CHTWINS.EXE" ) )
        { printf("DosExecPgm error2=%u\n",rc); exit(1); }
    while( !kbhit() )              /* print until key struck */
        printf("X");
                                   /* kill first child */
    if( rc=DosKillProcess( KILLALL,
                             childID1.codeTerminate ) )
        { printf("DosKillProcess error1=%u\n",rc); exit(1); }
                                   /* kill second child */
    if( rc=DosKillProcess( KILLALL,
                             childID2.codeTerminate ) )
        { printf("DosKillProcess error2=%u\n",rc); exit(1); }
    exit(0);
}
```

Notice in this program how the same filename is used in both invocations of DosExecPgm(). Although the same filename is used, two different process IDs are returned, since two processes will be running.

The parent sends a string consisting of a single character as a command-line argument to the children. This is how we can tell which child is which.

The child process is very simple. It takes the first letter of the command-line argument and uses it as a character to be printed continuously on the screen. Here's the listing for both children:

```
/* chtwins.c */
/* runs as child process under ptwins.exe */
/* prints character, passed in command-line, on screen */
#define TRUE 1

main(argc,argv)
int argc;
char *argv[];
{
    while(TRUE)
        printf("%c", *argv[0] );
}
```

The output, when ptwins.exe is executed, looks like this:

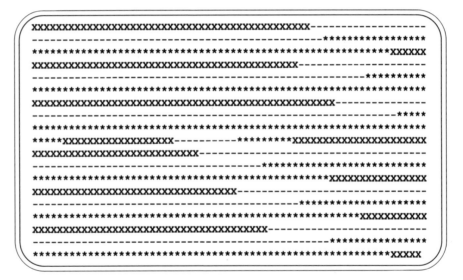

Again, the display shows how all three processes use the screen, and how the scheduler divides CPU time among them.

We mentioned earlier the difference between a program and a process. The example above points out the difference. We have only one program, the file CHTWINS.EXE. However, there are two processes using this file. One prints out dashes and the other prints out asterisks.

Flashing Signs

Here's a variation on the preceding program. It shares the screen in a different way: each of three processes uses one row of the screen to flash its own name. The parent flashes "PARENT" on the top of the screen, the first child flashes "CHILD1" in the middle of the screen, and the second child flashes "CHILD2" on the bottom of the screen. Each process flashes at a different rate.

```c
/* pflash.c */
/* starts two instances of one child process */
/* flashes program name on the screen */
#define INCL_DOS
#define INCL_SUB
#include <os2.h>
#define LENGTH 40  /* length of object name buffer */
#define FLAGS 1    /* asynchronously, no trace */
#define ENVS 0L    /* no environment variables */
#define COUNT 10   /* number of times to flash on and off */
#define ROW 5      /* row to place flashing message */
#define COL 35     /* same column for all processes */
#define HANDLE 0   /* vio handle always 0 */

main()
{
    char fbuf[LENGTH];          /* buffer for fail-object */
    struct _RESULTCODES childID; /* defined in doscalls.h */
    unsigned cell = 0x0720;     /* blank, normal attr */
    int j;                      /* loop variable */
    unsigned rc;                /* return code */

                                /* clear screen */
    VioScrollUp( 0, 0, -1, -1, -1, (char far *)&cell,
HANDLE);
                                /* start first child */
    if( rc=DosExecPgm( fbuf, LENGTH, FLAGS, "1", ENVS,
                      &childID, "CHFLASH.EXE" ) )
      { printf("DosExecPgm error1=%u\n",rc); exit(1); }
                                /* start second child */
    if( rc=DosExecPgm( fbuf, LENGTH, FLAGS, "2", ENVS,
                      &childID, "CHFLASH.EXE" ) )
      { printf("DosExecPgm error2=%u\n",rc); exit(1); }
                                /* flash name on screen */
    for(j=0; j<COUNT; j++)  {
      VioWrtCharStr( "PARENT", 6, ROW, COL, HANDLE );
      DosSleep( 500L );
      VioWrtNChar( " ", 6, ROW, COL, HANDLE );
      DosSleep( 500L );
    }
    exit(0);
}
```

In this situation it is not necessary to kill the children, since they terminate themselves after they have counted through their loops. The same code is used for both children:

```c
/* chflash.c */
/* child process of pflash.c */
/* flashes program name on the screen */
#define INCL_DOS
#define INCL_SUB
#include <os2.h>
#define COUNT 10    /* number of times to flash on and off */
#define COL 35      /* same column for all processes */
#define HANDLE 0    /* vio handle always 0 */

main(argc,argv)
int argc;
char *argv[];
{
    unsigned cell = 0x0720;     /* blank, normal attr */
    int row;                    /* row to place message */
    unsigned long delay;        /* delay for flashing */
    int j;                      /* loop variable */

                                /* values for this process */
    if( *argv[0] == '1' )  {
       row = 10;
       delay = 600L;
    }  else  {
       row = 15;
       delay = 700L;
    }
                                /* flash name on screen */
    for(j=0; j<COUNT; j++)  {
       VioWrtCharStr( "CHILD", 5, row, COL, HANDLE );
       VioWrtCharStr( argv[0], 1, row, COL+5, HANDLE );
       DosSleep( delay );
       VioWrtNChar( " ", 6, row, COL, HANDLE );
       DosSleep( delay );
    }
    exit(0);
}
```

The children discover who they are by reading the first character of the command-line argument, which is either 1 or 2. They then set their row position and time delay accordingly.

The children continue flashing somewhat longer than the parent, and the user does not regain control of the screen until the last child has finished (unless the program is executed with the START command). The three names flashing at different rates provide graphic evidence that the three processes are operating independently, and suggest ways in which different processes could share the screen in more interesting ways: each placing data in a separate window, for example.

Priority

The priority of a process determines how often the scheduler lets it run. The priority consists of two parts: the *class* and the *level*. There are three classes: *idle-time*, *regular*, and *time-critical*. The operating system thinks of these in terms of numbers:

Value	Class
1	Idle-time
2	Regular
3	Time-critical

Most programs are regular class; that is the default. However, if it is essential that a program, or part of a program, not be interrupted, then it can be given the time-critical class. Time-critical class might be appropriate for a program which controls a chemical reaction, or one which saves the computer's files in the event of a power failure.

On the other hand, if there is little urgency about when a particular program finishes its work, it can run in the idle-time class. This means it will get CPU cycles only when no program in regular (or time-critical) class needs them. A candidate for idle-time priority might be a sorting routine working on a long, and not urgent, file.

Within each priority class there are 32 levels, numbered from 0 to 31. A process starts out at level 0. If the configuration command **priority=dynamic** is set in the config.OS2 file, the CPU monitors the priority. If the process needs faster access to resources (the keyboard, screen, disk files, etc.) it can increase its priority. If config.sys has the priority set to **absolute**, the operating system cannot change the priority level of a process. Normally the priority is set to **dynamic**.

Reading the Priority

Here's a program that reports its own priority, or the priority of any other running process whose ID you know. It's invoked with one command-line parameter: the process ID. If this is 0, then the priority of the process itself is reported.

```
/* getprior.c */
/* returns priority of indicated process */
#define INCL_DOS
#include <os2.h>
#define SCOPE 0            /* first thread in process */
main(argc, argv)
int argc;
char *argv[];
{
    unsigned rc;           /* return code */
    unsigned priority;     /* high byte=class, low byte=level */
    unsigned processID;    /* 0 indicates current process */

    if( argc != 2 )
        { printf("Syntax: getprior processID\n"); exit(1); }
    processID = atoi( argv[1] );
    if( rc=DosGetPrty( SCOPE, &priority, processID ) )
        { printf("DosGetPrty error=%u\n",rc); exit(1); }
    printf("Class = %u\n", priority>>8 & 0x00FF );
    printf("Level = %u\n", priority & 0x00FF );
}
```

Used to report the priority of a process with an ID of 61, the interaction with the program looks like this:

```
C>getprior 61
Class = 2
Level = 0
```

As you can see, the normal values of class and level are reported. If you try to use the program on a process not currently running, or if you use the wrong ID number, you'll get back error number 303: invalid process ID.

DosGetPrty — Get priority of process or thread

```
DosGetPrty(Scope, APriority, ID);
unsigned Scope;            /* 0=process, 2=specified thread */
unsigned far *APriority;   /* address of class and level
                                  bytes */
unsigned ID;               /* process or thread ID (0=current) */
```

The program uses the DosGetPrty() function. This function requires a parameter called **Scope**. A zero value for this parameter indicates that the priority of the first thread in the process is returned. In this case the **ID** parameter is set to the ID of the process. (This is the situation in the example program). A value of 2 for **Scope** indicates the priority of a particular thread in the current process is to be returned; in this case **ID** specifies a thread ID. The only valid values for **Scope** are 0 and 2. The **APriority** word receives the class in the upper byte and the level in the lower byte.

Setting the Priority

It is also possible for a process to change its priority, or that of other processes, using the DosSetPrty() function. This function takes four variables. The first is **Scope**, which can take one of three values, and determines exactly what entity the priority change will effect:

Value	Scope
0	The specified process and all its threads
1	The specified process and all its descendants
2	A single thread within the current process

The second parameter is **Class**—its values were defined earlier for idle-time, regular, and time-critical. In addition, if **Class** is set to 0, no change will be made to the current value.

DosSetPrty — Set priority of process or thread

```
DosSetPrty(Scope, Class, Delta, ID);
unsigned Scope;       /* entities affected */
unsigned Class;       /* class value to be set (0 to 4) */
unsigned Delta;       /* change in level (-31 to +31) */
unsigned ID;          /* process or thread ID (0=current) */
```

The third parameter, **Delta**, is how much the current level should be changed. Since the level can range from 0 to 31, **Delta** can range from -31 to +31; this permits the level to be changed to any possible value. The final parameter is the **ID**. This indicates the ID of a process if **Scope** is 0 or 1, or the ID of a thread in the current process if **Scope** is 2.

In most situations it is not necessary for an application to change its priority. However, the time-critical class may be appropriate to a program performing process control, or data acquisition from special equipment. Or, an application performing a time-consuming but low-priority job might be nice enough to assign itself the idle-time class.

Background Processes

In Chapter 1 we showed how a DOS command such as DIR or SORT can run in background mode using the DETACH command. These utilities can run in background even though they are not designed specifically with that possibility in mind. It is also possible to design processes specifically for background operation.

Any activity requiring little or no interaction with the user is a candidate for background status. A sorting routine working on a large file, a program that searches through many files for a particular phrase, or a communications program receiving a long transmission, might all run in the background.

Notice that running in the background does not necessarily imply a program has lower priority. A background process is given the regular class and level, as are foreground processes.

Even a process running in the background, however, may need to communicate with the user. The examples above may all need, at a minimum, to signal when their task is complete. An application not designed for background operation cannot do this. But if we know in advance the application will run in the background, we can build in the necessary capability.

For this purpose OS/2 makes available a function called Vio-PopUp(), which permits a background process to temporarily take over the screen and keyboard. When the background process invokes this function the screen is blanked out, and the background process can write whatever it wants and receive user input from the keyboard. When the interaction is complete the application restores the former screen by executing a VioEndPopUp() call. Figure 4-4 shows how this process looks.

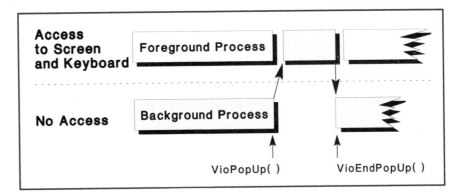

Figure 4-4
Popup Window Operation

Here's a short example program which demonstrates the difference between foreground and background operation. Once started, it delays for a ten-second interval, and then announces its existence with a popup screen.

```c
/* popup.c */
/* waits ten seconds, then pops up window */
#define INCL_DOS
#define INCL_SUB
#include <os2.h>
#define DELAY 10        /* number of seconds to delay */
#define HANDLE 0        /* vio handle always 0 */
main()
{
   unsigned WaitFlags = 0;

   printf("popup.c will wait %d sec until popup.\n", DELAY);
   DosSleep( DELAY*1000L );
   VioPopUp( &WaitFlags, HANDLE );
   printf("The popup.c program has waited %d seconds.\n",
                                                    DELAY);
   printf("Press any key to continue.\n");
   while( !kbhit() )
      ;
   VioEndPopUp( HANDLE );
   exit(0);
}
```

When the popup window appears, the program tells the user to press any key. When this is done the program closes the popup window and terminates.

You can run this program in several ways. You can invoke it from the command line in the usual way:

```
C>popup
```

This causes the popup window to appear on the screen. Until it appears the screen is frozen as the program waits for DosSleep() to time out.

You can also run the program in the background using the DETACH command:

```
C>detach popup
```

Now the operating system will tell you the program's process ID, and return control of the keyboard to you, while popup.exe continues to run in the background. After the delay the popup window blots out whatever you're doing, and remains until you strike a key.

The third way to run the program is in a separate screen group. Start it running (you don't need to use DETACH), then use the session manager to change to another screen group. When it times out it will interrupt the screen group you're in.

The VioPopUp() function takes only two arguments.

VioPopUp — Creates a popup window

```
VioPopUp(AWaitFlags, Handle);
unsigned far *AWaitFlags;      /* address of flag word */
unsigned short Handle;         /* vio handle is always 0 */
```

The **AWaitFlags** variable has only one possible value in the current version of OS/2: it's set to 0 to indicate that, if a popup window is not immediately available, the function will wait for it. The **Handle** argument, as in other VIO functions, is always 0. There are really no choices to be made in using VioPopUp(). The VioEnd-PopUp() function is even simpler, with only one invariant parameter.

VioEndPopUp — Removes a popup window

```
VioEndPopUp(Handle);
unsigned short Handle;         /* vio handle is always 0 */
```

Reminder Program

Here's a program you can use as a daily timer. At the time you specify, it interrupts whatever you're doing on the screen, and prints a message which you previously inserted in the program. The message might be "Call stock broker," for instance; or "Executive meeting in five minutes!"

```
/* remind.c */
/* pops reminder message into window at specified time */
#define INCL_DOS
#define INCL_SUB
#include <os2.h>
#define FREQUENCY 100      /* for DosBeep() */
#define DURATION 3000L     /* for DosBeep() */
#define HANDLE 0           /* vio handle always 0 */
#define BUFFLEN 80         /* length of string buffer */
#define MSECS 60000L       /* milliseconds in a minute */
#define WAIT 0             /* 0=wait, 1=no wait */
```

(continued)

```
char s1[] = "\n\rYou will be reminded at time you
                                             specify.\n\r";
char s2[] = "\n\rEnter hour (24 hour time): ";
char s3[] = "\n\rEnter minute: ";
char s4[] = "\n\rEnter message (less than one line)\n\r";
char s5[] = "\n\rREMINDER!!!\n\r";
char s6[] = "\n\n\rPress any key to continue\n\r";
main()
{
    struct _STRINGINBUF length; /* from bsesub.h */
    struct _KBDKEYINFO keydata; /* from bsesub.h */
    struct _DATETIME datetime;  /* from bsedos.h */
    int hour, minute;           /* hours and minutes from
                                            user */
    unsigned long now, then;    /* times in milliseconds */
    char string[BUFFLEN];       /* buffer for user input */
    unsigned WaitFlags = 0;     /* for viopopup() */

                                /* pop up, print prompt */
    VioPopUp( &WaitFlags, HANDLE );
    VioWrtTTy( s1, strlen(s1), HANDLE );

                                /* get hour */
    VioWrtTTy( s2, strlen(s2), HANDLE );
    length.cb = BUFFLEN;
    KbdStringIn( string, &length, WAIT, HANDLE);
    string[length.cchIn] = '\0';
    hour = atoi( string );
    if( hour>23 || hour<0 )
       { printf("Hours from 0 to 23 only\n"); exit(1); }

                                /* get minute */
    VioWrtTTy( s3, strlen(s3), HANDLE );
    KbdStringIn( string, &length, WAIT, HANDLE);
    string[length.cchIn] = '\0';
    minute = atoi( string );
    if( minute>59 || minute<0 )
       { printf("Minute from 0 to 60 only\n"); exit(1); }

                                /* get message */
    VioWrtTTy( s4, strlen(s4), HANDLE );
    KbdStringIn( string, &length, WAIT, HANDLE);
    string[length.cchIn] = '\0';
                                /* end this popup */
    VioEndPopUp( HANDLE );
                                /* sleep until time */
    then = (hour*60 + minute) * MSECS;
    DosGetDateTime( &datetime );
    now = (datetime.hours*60 + datetime.minutes) * MSECS;
```

(continued)

```
    DosSleep( then - now );
                                        /* pop up message */
    VioPopUp( &WaitFlags, HANDLE );
    VioWrtTTy( s5, strlen(s5), HANDLE );
    VioWrtTTy( string, strlen(string), HANDLE );
    VioWrtTTy( s6, strlen(s6), HANDLE );
    DosBeep( FREQUENCY, DURATION );

                                        /* wait for keypress */
    KbdCharIn( &keydata, WAIT, HANDLE );
    VioEndPopUp( HANDLE );
    exit(0);
}
```

This program avoids potential conflicts with C library routines by using API calls exclusively. Note that the API calls do not check for error returns. We have deleted this code to make the listing (which is already long enough) easier to read. If you plan to experiment with the program you should put error statements back in for all but the most foolproof API functions.

A sample session with this program, for an appointment at 1:30 pm, might be:

```
C>detach remind
Enter hour (24 hour time): 13
Enter minute: 30
Enter message (less than one line):
Meet Gloria in the cafeteria
```

At 1:30 p.m. whatever is on your screen is wiped out and the message about Gloria appears. A beep also sounds. When you push any key the foreground program resumes where it left off.

This program should be run in detached mode, or as a separate screen group. You can detach as many instances of the program as you need; they will all run happily at the same time, alerting you with different messages at different times.

Further Thoughts on Processes

Now that you've seen some examples of processes in use, let's review some of the things we've learned and talk more about processes in general.

Inheriting Resources

Any process, including programs in older single-tasking systems like MS-DOS, can be said to "own" resources. In fact, this is one of the defining aspects of a process: its ability to own resources. What are resources? They are files the program has opened, memory it is accessing, and devices (like the printer or display) it is using. Some resources can be inherited by a child process when a parent passes control to it. In particular, if the parent process has opened files or pipes, these can be inherited by the child (provided the file or pipe was opened with the proper parameters set). We'll have more to say about files and pipes in later chapters.

Processes Slow to Create

Creating a process using DosExecPgm() is not a particularly quick activity, as you've probably noticed in executing the examples in this chapter. The executable file must be read in from the disk, and considerable bookkeeping must be done to set up the necessary tables and segments. Starting a child process is not something a program should do all the time.

We haven't discussed threads yet, but we should point out that each process starts off with a single thread of execution. It can then create additional threads as it goes along. In contrast to creating a new process, which is slow, creating a new thread is very fast. We'll see what this means in the next chapter.

A process is isolated from other processes. Ordinarily it doesn't know anything about other processes which may be running in the same computer (except for child processes it has started). However, if the decision is made beforehand, a process can use interprocess communication to communicate with other processes.

Interprocess Communication

We've already seen how processes can pass command-line arguments and environmental variables to their children. There are also more sophisticated techniques which one process can use to communicate with another. The important methods are shared memory, pipes, and queues. Processes can also coordinate their activities using system semaphores and signals. We'll look into all these methods in later chapters.

Why Use Processes?

Why would you want to start a separate process? One reason is to make more efficient use of memory. If a particular part of your program is not needed in memory, system performance will be improved if it can be swapped out to the disk. In fact, your complete application may be too large to fit in memory at one time. Even if your program is a single process, OS/2 will automatically swap parts of it to disk, but dividing it up can give you more control over when the swapping process takes place. System swaps are arbitrary decisions based on which parts of your system haven't been used recently. You can control the this action yourself, creating processes as necessary and killing them off when they are no longer needed.

Processes are also useful in isolating functionally different parts of a program. An accounting program with separate modules for accounts receivable and inventory might want to use separate processes, for example. A control program could then swap in the appropriate module, as requested by the user. Or, your program might be an "integrated" application incorporating a spreadsheet, database, word processor, and telecommunications program. It would probably be a good idea to make each of these entities a separate process, invoked only as needed.

Due to the overhead involved in creating them, processes should be used only for major sections of a program that are invoked infrequently. A section of a program the size of a function, on the other hand, should be represented by a thread, not a process.

Doing It from C

The Microsoft and IBM versions of C for OS/2 provide, as library functions, equivalents to several of the API functions we have discussed in this chapter. In particular, it is possible to create child processes using one of a family of C library functions called spawn(), spawnle(), spawnlp(), and so on. Each function in this group handles the arguments to be passed to the child slightly differently. These functions are a multitasking version of the exec() family of library functions, which perform a similar role for children that run synchronously (not at the same time) to their parents.

Other C library functions duplicate to varying degrees the action of API functions. For instance, the C functions wait() and cwait() perform a role similar to DosCWait().

Summary

This chapter focused on the process, which can be called a program in action. We've seen examples of a parent starting one or more child processes using DosExecPgm(). Other examples showed how a parent can find out if a child is still alive, using DosCWait(), and kill it if necessary using DosKillProcess(). We looked at passing command-line arguments and environmental variables from parents to children, and at querying and changing the priority of a process with DosGetPrty() and DosSetPtry(). Finally we saw how a background process, using VioPopUp() and VioEndPopUp(), can employ popup windows to communicate when necessary with the outside world.

In the next chapter we change our focus from processes, which are comparatively large-scale, to threads, a smaller-scale unit of multitasking. Threads are handier and more commonly used than processes.

THREADS

Chapter 5

In the last chapter we talked about processes, which are program-sized multitasking units. In this chapter we shift our focus to threads, which are multitasking units with the size and flavor of C language functions. If you want two major program units to run at the same time, you use processes; but if you want two functions within a process to run at the same time, you use threads. Threads are easier to employ and used more often than processes. If anything can be said to lie at the heart of multitasking in OS/2, it is threads.

We start with a simple example of threads at work. Then we show how to exit from one thread without stopping the others in the same process, and how local and global variables are used in threads. We then examine how several threads can share the same code and how, with a little effort, it's possible to pass arguments to a thread. We explore critical sections, which permit one thread to turn off all the other threads in a process; this is useful when one thread is engaged in activities where timing is important. We also look at how a thread can suspend the operation of another thread. We finish up with some examples of threads used in real-world situations.

Creating Threads

A computer program, when it is running, executes a sequence of instructions which are stored in the computer's memory. This activity—executing a sequence of stored instructions—is called a *thread*, or sometimes a *thread of execution*. Think of an instruction pointer that points to the next instruction to be executed. Generally the instruction pointer moves forward through memory, pointing to each instruction in sequence, but sometimes it jumps to a different part of memory (to accommodate loops, function calls, and other non-sequential activities). This instruction pointer tracks the activity of a particular thread.

When a process is started it begins executing a single thread. So far in this book, the examples have used only a single thread in each process. However, just as one process can create a new process using an API function, so a thread can create a new thread. Both threads can then run at the same time. What does this mean? Again, imagine that each thread has its own instruction pointer, showing where it is in the instruction sequence in memory. The scheduler lets one instruction pointer move through memory for a while, then the other. These time slices are very short, making the two threads appear to run simultaneously.

Here's a very simple example in which one thread starts another. The first thread then prints a series of Xs, while the second prints a series of dashes.

This is similar to examples in the last chapter in which different processes placed characters on the screen. However, in the case of threads, the entities placing characters on the screen are part of the same process and are stored in the same file. This works like a normal C program, where a main() function occupies the same file as the other user-written functions which it calls.

```
/* simpleth.c */
/* one thread starts another */
#define INCL_DOS
#include <os2.h>
#include <malloc.h>          /* for malloc() */
#define STACK_SIZE 1024       /* size of new thread's stack */

main()
{
    char far *stkptr;          /* stack pointer for new thread */
    void far NewThread();      /* prototype for new thread */
    unsigned threadID;         /* thread ID number */
    unsigned rc;               /* return code */

                               /* get stack space */
    stkptr = (char far *)malloc(STACK_SIZE) + STACK_SIZE;
                               /* start new thread */
    if( rc=DosCreateThread( NewThread, &threadID, stkptr) )
       { printf("DosCreateThread error=%u\n",rc); exit(1); }

    while( !kbhit() )          /* loop until key struck */
       printf("X");
    exit(0);                   /* exit all threads */
}

/* NewThread() */
/* second thread in this process */
void far NewThread()
{
    while(TRUE)
       printf("-");
}
```

The thread called NewThread looks very much like a function. It is declared or prototyped at the beginning of main(), and it is written like a function, with its definition at the beginning and its body surrounded by braces.

However, control is not transferred to the thread in the same way it is to a function, nor is it invoked in the same way from main(). Instead of executing a statement containing the function name, as in

```
NewThread();    /* not how threads are started *
```

the thread is started by the API function DosCreateThread(). When a program calls a function, control is transferred from the calling program to the function; the calling program then stops running until the function returns control to it. Starting a thread, on the other hand, creates another, different thread of control: both the calling program and the thread it creates continue to run.

You can see this by examining the output of the simpleth.c program:

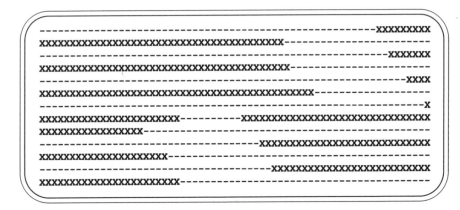

The Xs and dashes are interspersed much as they were when two processes were putting characters on the screen. Both threads are running at the same time.

The DosCreateThread() Function

The programmer must furnish two parameters to the DosCreateThread() function. It returns one. The programmer must specify the address of the section of code where the new thread begins. Since the code for the new thread is written in the form of a function, we can use the C convention of representing the address of a function by its name. In our program, that is simply the variable **NewThread**.

> ### DosCreateThread — Creates a new thread of execution
>
> ```
> DosCreateThread(Address, AThreadID, StackPtr);
> void (far *)(void)Address;      /* address of thread */
> unsigned far *AThreadID;        /* address for thread ID */
> unsigned char far *StackPtr;    /* address of stack area */
> ```

Like processes, each thread is given a unique ID number when it is created by the system. DosCreateThread() returns the new thread's ID in the variable whose address is provided in the second argument of the function. The program can then use this ID number whenever it wants to access the thread. Reasons to do this include temporarily stopping the thread (as we'll see soon) or changing its priority.

Allocating Stack Space

The third parameter in DosCreateThread() is the address of an area in memory which will hold the new thread's stack. Like ordinary C functions, each thread uses its own separate stack space, distinct from that of the calling program. The stack space holds **automatic** variables: local variables created when the function or thread is created and destroyed when it ends.

However, while the stack space for C functions is created automatically, the stack space for threads must be created explicitly by the programmer. This may not be very user-friendly, but it gives the programmer control over the stack size. Memory for the stack is allocated using the C library function malloc(). This program line allocates the stack space:

```
stkptr = (char far *)malloc(STACK_SIZE) + STACK_SIZE;
```

The malloc() function returns a far pointer to the *lowest* address in the newly allocated memory space. However, since stacks grow downward in memory, what must be furnished to DosCreateThread() is the *highest* address of the memory space, which is the starting point of the stack. For this reason we add the size of the originally-requested memory to the pointer, as shown in Figure 5-1.

Actually, as you can see in the figure, the resulting pointer points to the space one word higher in memory than the top of the stack. We'll see in a later section how this affects our coding when we want to pass arguments to the thread.

For brevity, we have omitted from the example any code to check for a NULL return from malloc(). Such a return indicates that the requested memory could not be found, perhaps because memory was full. A serious program would check for this possibility when allocating space for a new thread, and alert the user or take other appropriate action if the operation was unsuccessful.

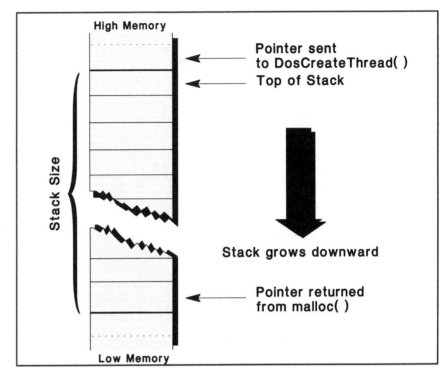

Figure 5-1
Thread Stack Pointer

Unit of Dispatchability

Threads are referred to as the "unit of dispatchability." This means the scheduler allots CPU time to threads, not processes. Each thread gets its share of time before control is passed to the next thread. Thus a process with more threads will get more CPU time, as shown in Figure 5-2.

We might also say that processes themselves do not run—threads in a process run. As we noted in the last chapter, the process owns resources. But without at least one thread, a process cannot run.

Speed of Thread Creation

In the last chapter we saw that it takes a comparatively long time to create a new process, since a file must typically be read from disk and installed in memory. Creating a thread, on the other hand, is very fast. The overhead is comparable to calling a C function, where the function is in the same file as the calling program. The thread, like a

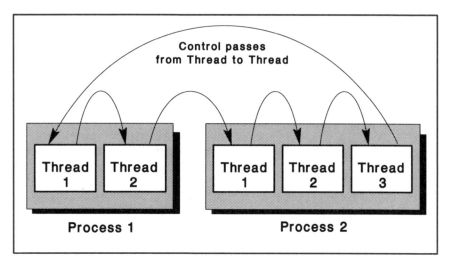

Figure 5-2
Units of Dispatchability

function, is loaded into memory along with the calling program, so no disk access is necessary when it is invoked by another thread.

It is also easier to share data between threads than it is between processes, as we'll see shortly.

Threads Inherit Resources

As C functions do, threads inherit resources from the calling thread. If the calling thread (or parent thread) has open files, for instance, they are accessible to the child thread. If the child threads open files, they are also accessible to the parent thread and any other threads it created. This is another way of saying that it is the *process* that owns resources. All the threads in a process have access to the same resources, no matter which thread has opened or created them.

Only two things (besides ID numbers) distinguish one thread from another. Each thread has its own stack space, and each thread has its own set of virtual CPU registers, including the program counter (which points to the address of the instruction currently being executed). When a thread is executing, the contents of its virtual registers are loaded into the real CPU registers. When the thread is not executing, the contents of the registers are saved, to be restored the next time the thread is run.

Threads and Processes

Let's summarize the difference between threads and processes:

Processes	Threads
Program-sized	Function-sized
Creation is time-consuming	Creation is fast
Complex and slow to share data	Easy and fast to share data
Owns resources (files, memory)	Owns stack space and registers
	Unit of dispatchability

Exiting from a Single Thread

When a normal C function completes its task, it can return to the calling program by "falling through" the last brace, or by executing a **return** statement. A thread, however, cannot use either of these stratagems (and trying to use them will lead to erratic results). When a thread finishes its task it does not return control to the caller, since the caller is usually doing something else. Instead the thread simply stops executing. It does this with the API function DosExit().

```
              DosExit — Exit from thread or process
DosExit(Action, Result);
unsigned Action;        /* 0=current thread, 1=all threads */
unsigned Result;        /* code to be returned to parent */
```

This function takes two parameters. The first, the action code, indicates whether the thread that issues the DosExit() will be the only one terminated (Action=0), or whether all the threads in the process, and thus the process itself, will terminate (Action=1). The second option should not be used, because in C programs, the C library function exit() is used to terminate an entire process.

The result code is an arbitrary number supplied by the thread which is terminating, just as a code can be supplied in the C library function exit(). If the thread is part of a child process, the result code can be read by the parent process using DosCWait(), as described in the last chapter. Ordinarily, if a thread exits normally, the result code is set to 0. A result code of 1 is commonly used to indicate an error return. In more sophisticated programs a range of non-zero values can indicate the reasons for the termination.

We might note that there is no way for one thread to kill another, as DosKillProcess() does with processes. One thread can suspend another's operation temporarily, but it can't remove it from its place in the program.

Exiting from Two Threads Separately

Here's an example in which two threads use DosExit() to terminate themselves separately, while the main program continues to run until stopped by a keypress from the operator. This program also shows how the parent thread can create two children, rather than one as in the previous example.

```c
/* threxit.c */
/* demonstrates dosexit() */
#define INCL_DOS
#include <os2.h>
#include <malloc.h>          /* for malloc() */
#define STACK_SIZE 1024      /* size of new thread's stack */
#define ACTION 0             /* 0=this thread, 1=all threads */
#define RESULT 0             /* code returned to caller */
main()
{
    char far *stkptr;        /* stack pointer for threads */
    void far thread1();      /* prototype for thread 1 */
    void far thread2();      /* prototype for thread 2 */
    unsigned thread1ID;      /* thread ID number 1 */
    unsigned thread2ID;      /* thread ID number 2 */
    unsigned rc;             /* return code */

                             /* get stack space */
    stkptr = (char far *)malloc(STACK_SIZE) + STACK_SIZE;
                             /* start first thread */
    if( rc=DosCreateThread( thread1, &thread1ID, stkptr) )
       { printf("DosCreateThread error=%u\n",rc); exit(1); }
                             /* get stack space */
    stkptr = (char far *)malloc(STACK_SIZE) + STACK_SIZE;
                             /* start second thread */
    if( rc=DosCreateThread( thread2, &thread2ID, stkptr) )
       { printf("DosCreateThread error=%u\n",rc); exit(1); }
    while( !kbhit() )        /* loop until key struck */
       printf("X");
    printf("\nThread 0 ending\n");
    exit(0);                 /* exit all threads */
}
```

(continued)

```
/* thread1() */
/* second thread in this process */
void far thread1()
{
   int j;
   for(j=0; j<200; j++)
      printf("-");
   printf("\nThread 1 ending\n");
   DosExit(ACTION,RESULT);
}

/* thread2() */
/* third thread in this process */
void far thread2()
{
   int j;
   for(j=0; j<300; j++)
      printf("*");
   printf("\nThread 2 ending\n");
   DosExit(ACTION,RESULT);
}
```

Two threads are created, each with its own address and separate stack space. Two thread ID's are also returned (although this program does not make use of them).

The first child thread prints 200 dashes and terminates itself; the second prints 300 asterisks. The operator can then terminate the main thread, which prints as many Xs as seem desirable.

Here's a sample of the program's output:

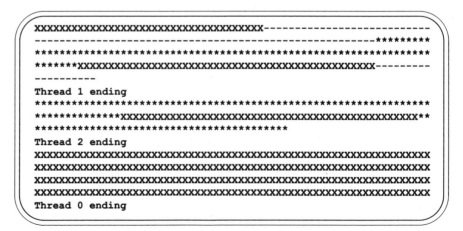

After thread 1 terminates no more dashes are printed, and after thread 2 ends there are no more asterisks. Both these threads terminated with DosExit(), with the **Action** argument set to 0 to indicate that only the current thread was to be terminated. Finally, the user presses a key to exit from the entire process, killing any remaining threads; this is done with the C library function exit().

Local and Global Variables

Threads use variables in much the same way C functions do. As in functions, automatic variables used in a thread have a lifetime and visibility limited to the thread in which they are defined. The loop counter **j** in the above threads is an example.

Global variables can also be used as they are in normal C programs. Any thread in a process can access a global variable declared at the beginning of the file. The following program demonstrates the situation. It contains a main thread and a child thread. There is one global variable, **alpha**, a local variable **beta** in the main thread, and a local variable **gamma** in the child thread.

```c
/* thrvars.c */
/* shows threads use of variables */
#define INCL_DOS
#include <os2.h>
#include <malloc.h>          /* for malloc() */
#define STACK_SIZE 1024       /* size of new thread's stack */

int alpha = 33;              /* global variable */

main()
{
    int beta = 44;           /* local variable */
    char far *stkptr;        /* stack pointer for new thread */
    void far NewThread();    /* prototype for new thread */
    unsigned threadID;       /* thread ID number */
    unsigned rc;             /* return code */
                             /* get stack space */
    stkptr = (char far *)malloc(STACK_SIZE) + STACK_SIZE;
                             /* start new thread */
    if( rc=DosCreateThread( NewThread, &threadID, stkptr) )
        { printf("DosCreateThread error=%u\n",rc); exit(1); }
    DosSleep( 1000L );       /* wait for child to finish */
    printf("\nParent knows alpha=%d, beta=%u\n", alpha,
beta);
    exit(0);                 /* exit all threads */
}
```

(continued)

```
/* NewThread() */
/* second thread in this process */
void far NewThread()
{
    int gamma = 55;                /* local variable */
    printf("\nChild knows alpha=%d, gamma=%d", alpha,
                                                    gamma );

    DosExit(0,0);                  /* exit this thread */
}
```

When we run the program, the output, not surprisingly, is:

```
Child knows alpha=33, gamma=55
Parent knows alpha=33, beta=44
```

This is just what we'd see if NewThread were a function rather than a thread. If we try to reference **beta** from NewThread(), or **gamma** from the main() thread, we get a compiler error, just as we would using functions.

Being able to access global variables gives threads a convenient way of sharing data with other threads in a process. Contrast this with the complexity of passing command-line arguments (or using pipes, queues, or shared memory segments, which we'll learn about later), which is necessary for interprocess communication.

There are potential pitfalls when sharing global variables between threads. Several threads, running simultaneously, can reference a global variable at roughly the same time. To avoid confusion, it may be necessary to coordinate access to the variable using semaphores; this is a topic we'll explore in the next chapter.

Accessing a Routine from Multiple Threads

In many situations it would be convenient for several threads in a process to access the same user-written C function. For instance, an application might have two threads running, each of which needs to perform a certain calculation. Can they both call the same function for this purpose, without worrying about interfering with each other? Yes, if the function is written correctly. In particular, the function must not use any global variables.

A function in C creates its own stack space and local variables each time it is called. Thus if two threads each call a function, a new set of local variables are created for each instance of the call. OS/2 requires that executable code not be modifiable, so there is no reason why two threads cannot be executing at different places in the code of the same function.

However, if the function uses global variables, there is only one copy of a particular variable for all the threads that access the function. Thread 2, for example, may then alter the value of the variable before thread 1 has finished with it. The moral: avoid global variables in functions that may be accessed simultaneously by different threads.

Here's an example in which three threads access a single function. We've contrived the program in such a way that we can guarantee that one thread will be interrupted by another before it has exited from the function. This tests our assertion that a correctly written function can be accessed by more than one thread at the same time.

A main thread creates two child threads. Each of the resulting three threads then continuously fills an array with a constant, and calls on the function **sum()** to sum the contents of an array. Since **sum()** requires many steps to sum the array for a particular thread, it is certain to be interrupted by other threads from time to time.

```
/* xaccess.c */
/* demonstrates several threads accessing the same
   routine */
#define INCL_DOS
#include <os2.h>
#include <malloc.h>          /* for malloc() */
#define STACK_SIZE 1024       /* size of new stacks */
#define ARRAY_SIZE 10         /* size of test array */

main()
{
    int far sum(int far *, int); /* prototype for function */
    char far *stkptr;        /* stack pointer for new thread */
    void far thread1();      /* prototype for thread 1 */
    void far thread2();      /* prototype for thread 2 */
    unsigned threadID;       /* thread ID number */
    int j;                   /* loop counter */
    int list[ARRAY_SIZE];    /* array for main routine */

                            /* start first thread */
    stkptr = (char far *)malloc(STACK_SIZE) + STACK_SIZE;
    DosCreateThread(thread1, &threadID, stkptr);
                            /* start second thread */
    stkptr = (char far *)malloc(STACK_SIZE) + STACK_SIZE;
    DosCreateThread(thread2, &threadID, stkptr);
```

(continued)

```
    while( !kbhit() )  {    /* fill array, sum it, check total */
        for(j=0; j<ARRAY_SIZE; j++)
            list[j] = 3;
        printf("\nThread 0 calling sum(%d)\n", ARRAY_SIZE);
        if( sum(list, ARRAY_SIZE ) != ARRAY_SIZE * 3 )
            { printf("Wrong sum\n"); exit(1); }
        printf("\nThread 0 returned\n");
    }
    exit(0);                /* exit all threads */
}

/* thread1() */
/* calls the sum() function */
#define ARRAY_SIZE 20
void far thread1()
{
    int list[ARRAY_SIZE];
    int j;
    while(TRUE)  {        /* fill array, sum it, check total */
        for(j=0; j<ARRAY_SIZE; j++)
            list[j] = 5;
        printf("\nThread 1 calling sum(%d)\n", ARRAY_SIZE);
        if( sum(list, ARRAY_SIZE) != ARRAY_SIZE * 5 )
            { printf("Wrong sum\n"); DosExit(1,1); }
        printf("\nThread 1 returned\n");
    }
}

/* thread2() */
/* calls the sum() function */
#define ARRAY_SIZE 30
void far thread2()
{
    int list[ARRAY_SIZE];
    int j;

    while(TRUE)  {        /* fill array, sum it, check total */

        for(j=0; j<ARRAY_SIZE; j++)
            list[j] = 7;
        printf("\nThread 2 calling sum(%d)\n", ARRAY_SIZE);
        if( sum(list, ARRAY_SIZE) != ARRAY_SIZE * 7 )
            { printf("Wrong sum\n"); DosExit(1,1); }
        printf("\nThread 2 returned\n");
    }
}
```

(continued)

```
/* sum() */
/* function to sum contents of an array */
int far sum(ptr, n)
int far *ptr;                   /* pointer to array */
int n;                          /* number of elements in array */
{
    int j;
    int total = 0;
    for(j=0; j<n; j++)  {  /* sum the elements */
        total += *ptr++;
        printf("%d/%d ", j, n ); /* display progress */
    }
    return(total);              /* return the total */
}
```

The **sum()** function is frequently in the midst of summing one thread's array when a second thread interrupts. However, for the reasons mentioned, it has no trouble keeping track of its progress with each thread.

Here's some typical output. In each pair of numbers the first shows which element of an array is being summed. The second shows the size of the array, and (since each thread operates with a different sized array) the thread calling **sum()**.

```
Thread 0 calling sum(10)
0/10 1/10 2/10 3/10
Thread 1 calling sum(20)
0/20 1/20 2/20 3/20 4/20 5/20 6/20 7/20 8/20 9/20 10/20 11/20

12/20 13/20 14/20 15/20 16/20 17/20 18/20 19/20
Thread 1 returned
Thread 1 calling sum(20)
0/20 1/20 2/20 3/20 4/20 5/20
Thread 2 calling sum(30)
0/30 1/30 2/30 3/30 4/30 5/30 6/30 7/30 8/30 9/30 10/30 11/30

12/30 13/30 14/30 15/30 16/30 17/30 18/30 4/10 5/10 6/10
7/10 8/10 9/10
Thread 0 returned
```

Here thread 0 has time to sum only four elements of a 10-element array before it is interrupted by thread 1, which gets a big time slice and sums all 20 elements of its first array and six more of its next array before being interrupted by thread 2, which sums 19 elements before being interrupted by the continuation of thread 0, and...but you get the idea.

The program runs as long as you like without making errors. This demonstrates that it's all right for any number of threads to call a C function at the same time, provided the function is written with this possibility in mind.

Passing Parameters to a Thread

We've seen that threads can communicate easily using global variables. However, global variables are not ideal in some circumstances. They are vulnerable to inadvertent modification by functions which should not address them, and, since their lifetime is the same as the entire process, they make inefficient use of memory. It is possible to pass arguments to C functions, using statements like

```
funct(arg1, arg2, arg3);
```

thus avoiding the use of global variables. Can we do the same with threads?

While it is possible to pass parameters to threads, it is not as convenient as passing them to functions. Since we need to manage the creation of a thread's stack ourselves, we must also place into the stack, "by hand," any arguments we want sent to the thread.

Here's an example which shows three arguments—two integers and a character—being passed to a thread on the stack.

```c
/* thparam.c */
/* demonstrates passing parameters to threads */
#define INCL_DOS
#include <os2.h>
#include <malloc.h>        /* for malloc() */
#define STACK_SIZE 1024    /* stack size for threads */

main()
{
    int far *stkptr;        /* stack pointer for new thread */
    void far thread();      /* define thread */
    unsigned threadID;      /* thread ID number */
    unsigned rc;            /* return code */

                            /* get stack space */
    stkptr = (int far *)malloc(STACK_SIZE) + STACK_SIZE;
```

(continued)

```
   *(stkptr-3) = 1234;        /* insert first arg */
   *(stkptr-2) = 'b';         /* insert second arg */
   *(stkptr-1) = 3456;        /* insert last arg */
   stkptr -= 3;               /* set pointer to top of stack */
                              /* start new thread */
   if(rc=DosCreateThread(thread, &threadID, (char far
                                                 *)stkptr) )
      { printf("DosCreateThread error=%u", rc); exit(1); }
   DosExit(0,0);              /* exit only this thread */
}

/* thread() */
/* prints out parameters passed to it */
void far thread(intvar1, charvar, intvar2)
int intvar1;
char charvar;
int intvar2;
{
   printf("Intvar1=%d\n", intvar1);
   printf("Charvar=%c\n", charvar);
   printf("Intvar2=%d\n", intvar2);
   exit(0);                   /* exit all threads */
}
```

In this program the first thread places the three parameters in the stack space it has obtained for the child thread. Then it starts the child. The child removes the values from the stack just as a C function would, and prints out the results. The output generated by the child thread looks like this:

```
Intvar1=1234
Charvar=b
Intvar2=3456
```

The convention in C programs is to place the last argument (reading from left to right) on the stack first (at the highest memory location). The other arguments follow as the stack grows downward, so the first argument is at the top of the stack (at the lowest memory location). Also, the pointer given to the function should point to the top of the stack and the first argument. Figure 5-3 shows how this looks.

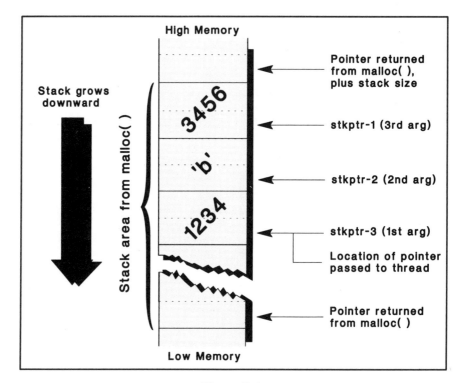

Figure 5-3
Stack Used for Passing Parameters

The heart of the program is the group of statements that place the arguments on the stack:

```
*(stkptr-3) = 1234;        /* insert first arg */
*(stkptr-2) = 'b';         /* insert second arg */
*(stkptr-1) = 3456;        /* insert last arg */
stkptr -= 3;               /* set pointer to top of stack */
```

The first three statements put the arguments in the appropriate addresses. The last statement resets the stack pointer to the top of the stack.

This same effect can be accomplished by the statements:

```
*--stkptr = 3456;
*--stkptr = 'b';
*--stkptr = 1234;
```

This is shorter but perhaps slightly less clear.

The machine language instructions that put items on the stack and remove them operate on words, not bytes. Thus the stack must be thought of as an array of integers, not characters. Notice that in the example program the pointer to the stack is a pointer to type **int**. However, the **stkpr** argument in the DosCreateThread() function must be typecast back to a pointer of type **char**, which is what this function expects. If we had made this pointer of type **char** as in previous examples, our pointer arithmetic would not have worked: decrementing the pointer would have moved the pointer to the next byte in the stack, rather than the next word.

For the same reason, the character argument passed to the function must occupy an integer-sized area of the stack, even though the high byte of the word is not used.

There is no way to return a value from a thread as **return()** does from functions, since it's unclear where in the calling program such a value would be returned. However, a thread can send any number of arguments back to the calling thread using addresses passed on the stack, as described above.

Sharing Code

Threads can not only access the same routine, as shown in the xaccess.c example, they can consist entirely of code that is shared by several different threads. This is useful when several "objects" in a program all act in the same way. Such objects can be elements in a game, such as race cars or spacecraft, or they might be mathematical formulas waiting for data so they can calculate their own solution.

Here's an example in which five race horses race across the screen. Each horse is represented by a different thread, but all the threads share the same code, at address **horse**. The only way each thread knows its own identity is by a number passed to the thread on the stack (as described in the last section). The variable **j**, used in the loop that creates the horses, is also the thread or horse ID number.

Each horse is represented on the screen by a string of four graphics characters. This horse shape is represented by a global variable, which can be accessed by all the threads.

```
/* horsrace.c */
/* multiple threads program -- each horse is a thread */
#define INCL_DOS
#define INCL_SUB
#include <os2.h>
#include <malloc.h>          /* for malloc() */
```

(continued)

```
#define STACK_SIZE 400      /* size of stack for threads */
#define NUM_HORSES 5         /* number of horses */
#define FINISH_LINE 75       /* length of track */

char shape[] = "\xDD\xDF\xDD\xDF";            /* horse shape */

main()
{
   int far *stkptr;        /* stack pointer for new thread */
   void far horse();       /* prototype for new thread */
   unsigned threadID;      /* thread ID number */
   int j;                  /* loop var and thread ID */
   int blank = 0x0720;     /* blank, normal attribute */
   struct _DATETIME TimeBuff;  /* date time buffer */
   unsigned rc;            /* return code */

                           /* clear screen */
   VioScrollUp( 0, 0, -1, -1, -1, (char far *)&blank, 0 );
   VioSetCurPos( 0, 0, 0);  /* set cursor to upper left */

                           /* use time to seed randoms */
   DosGetDateTime( &TimeBuff);
   srand( (unsigned)TimeBuff.hundredths );

   /* loop starts each horse separately */
   for(j=0; j<NUM_HORSES; j++)  {
                           /* get stack space */
      stkptr = (int far *)malloc(STACK_SIZE) + STACK_SIZE;
      *--stkptr = j;        /* j is arg to thread, on stack */
                           /* start new thread */
      if(rc=DosCreateThread(horse,&threadID,(char far
*)stkptr))
          { printf("DosCreateThread error=%u",rc); exit(1); }
   }
   DosExit(0,0);           /* exit this thread */
}

/* horse() */
/* each instance of this thread represents one horse */
void far horse(horseID)
int horseID;               /* ID of this horse */
{
   int blank = 0x0720;     /* blank, normal attribute */
   int dist = 0;           /* distance horse has gone */
```

(continued)

```
while(TRUE)  {              /* move horse */
    dist += rand() % 4; /* can go 0, 1, 2 or 3 */
                            /* clear row and draw horse */
    VioWrtNCell( (char far *)&blank, 80, horseID*2, 0, 0);
    VioWrtCharStr( (char far *)shape, 4, horseID*2, dist, 0);
    if( dist >= FINISH_LINE)  {
        VioSetCurPos( 20, 0, 0); /* cursor to lower left */
        printf("HORSE %d IS THE WINNER!!!\n", horseID);
        exit(0);              /* kill all threads */
        }
    DosSleep(200L);       /* slow down the horses */
    }
}
```

We use the C function srand() to seed the random number generator, and rand() to generate the actual random number. The seed is the time, in hundredths of a second, obtained from DosGetDateTime().

Figure 5-4 shows the horses at the end of a close race.

Figure 5-4
Horses at End of Race

When, in any one of the threads, the distance a horse has gone (the variable **dist**) exceeds the distance to the finish line, that horse is the winner. That thread announces the winner and terminates all the threads. In this example there are five threads sharing the same code.

The single-tasking approach to this situation would be a loop which calls a function over and over, using different parameters each time to represent the different horses, and moving each horse a short distance each time it is called. In effect such a program would need to be its own scheduler, allotting time to each horse function in round-robin fashion. The multitasking approach eliminates the need for this overhead, and makes the situation conceptually simpler, since once each thread is started it becomes an independent entity, which need not be accessed again by the main program. Such independent threads provide a greater degree of isolation from the main program, so they are less likely to suffer inadvertent interference.

A minor problem with this program is that the horses don't get an even start. Those threads that are created first get a few extra time-slices while the other threads are being created. We'll see a solution to this in the next chapter.

Critical Sections

It sometimes happens that one thread in a process is doing something in which timing is important. In this case it is essential that the thread not be interrupted by the other threads: it must be the only thread running.

For instance, one thread in a process control application might be controlling a robot arm that pours molten glass into a mold. If this thread is interrupted, by another thread accessing a disk file for example, hot glass might be spilled all over the floor. Or, a thread might be drawing an animation effect on the screen that needs to proceed at a constant pace; interruptions by other threads might create a jerky appearance.

For these situations OS/2 defines what is called a *critical section*. When a thread enters a critical section it calls the API function DosEnterCritSec(). This stops all the other threads. The thread issuing this call is guaranteed to be the only one running in its process. (It's up to the user to ensure other processes, which might disrupt the critical thread, are not running.) When the critical processing has been completed the thread calls DosExitCritSec(), which causes the other threads to resume their operation.

Our example program starts two threads which continuously print dashes and asterisks, respectively, on the screen. The main thread then uses a critical section to stop the other threads while it

beeps the speaker. When the main thread exits from the critical
section the other threads resume their operation.

```c
/* critsec.c */
/* demonstrates critical sections */
#define INCL_DOS
#define INCL_SUB
#include <os2.h>
#include <malloc.h>          /* for malloc() */
#define STACK_SIZE 1024       /* for each thread */

main()
{
    char far *stkptr;         /* stack pointer for threads */
    void far thread1();       /* prototype for thread 1 */
    void far thread2();       /* prototype for thread 2 */
    unsigned threadID;        /* thread ID number */
    int j;                    /* loop counter */

                              /* get stack space */
    stkptr = (char far *)malloc(STACK_SIZE) + STACK_SIZE;
                              /* start first thread */
    DosCreateThread( thread1, &threadID, stkptr );
                              /* get stack space */
    stkptr = (char far *)malloc(STACK_SIZE) + STACK_SIZE;
                              /* start second thread */
    DosCreateThread( thread2, &threadID, stkptr );

    DosSleep( 1000L );        /* let other threads run */

    DosEnterCritSec();        /* stop other threads */

    for(j=0; j<10; j++) {     /* do critical processing */
      DosBeep( 200, 300 );        /* beep speaker */
      DosSleep( 300L );           /* ten times */
    }
    DosExitCritSec();         /* start other threads again */

    DosSleep(1000L);          /* let other threads continue */
    exit(0);                  /* exit all threads */
}

/* thread1() */
void far thread1()
{
    while(TRUE)               /* continuously print dash */
      VioWrtTTy("-", 1, 0);
}
```

(continued)

```
/* thread2() */
void far thread2()
{
    while(TRUE)                    /* continuously print
                                       asterisk */

        VioWrtTTy("*", 1, 0);
}
```

Here's what the output looks like. The main thread sleeps for one second while the other threads print dashes and asterisks. The main thread enters its critical section and when it is done sleeps for another second while the other threads continue.

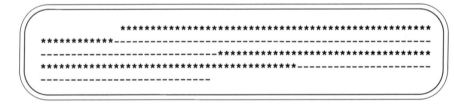

(Here printing stops and the speaker beeps ten times)

The functions DosEnterCritSec() and DosExitCritSec() are among the simplest in the API; they take no arguments. They are so simple they don't even return an error code, so they are of type **void**.

DosEnterCritSec — Stop other threads

```
DosEnterCritSec(void);
```

DosExitCritSec — Restart other threads

```
DosExitCritSec(void);
```

Critical sections are also useful in debugging. If you can't use CodeView for some reason, and you are debugging a multi-threaded application where some threads may be interfering with others, you can insert DosEnterCritSec() functions at appropriate places in the code so that only a single thread is running. If it goes wrong you know it is not because of the actions of other threads.

Critical sections can also be used in some situations to avoid *race conditions*, which we'll examine later in this chapter.

Critical sections should not be used in every situation. For instance, if several threads both need to access a resource, such as the screen, they should not enter a critical section in order to keep others away from the resource. The situation is better handled by semaphores. Critical sections defeat the advantages of multitasking, because multiple threads can no longer run at the same time, so this expedient should be used only when necessary.

Suspending Threads

A thread can use a critical section to stop *all* other threads in a process from executing. It is also possible for one thread to stop *one* other thread from executing. This is a less extreme action. Only the thread that absolutely must be stopped is stopped; the others can continue. The DosSuspendThread() function stops the thread and DosResumeThread() restarts it.

This example is similar to that for critical sections, except only one of the two child threads is suspended. Also, performed by the main thread the critical task is printing Xs to the screen, rather than beeping the speaker.

```
/* suspend.c */
/* demonstrates suspending a thread */
#define INCL_DOS
#define INCL_SUB
#include <os2.h>
#include <malloc.h>          /* for malloc() */
#define STACK_SIZE 1024      /* for each thread */

main()
{
    char far *stkptr;        /* stack pointer for threads */
    void far thread1();      /* prototype for thread 1*/
    unsigned thread1ID;      /* thread 1 ID number */
    void far thread2();      /* prototype for thread 2 */
    unsigned thread2ID;      /* thread 2 ID number */
    int j;                   /* loop variable */
```

(continued)

```
                                 /* get stack space */
        stkptr = (char far *)malloc(STACK_SIZE) + STACK_SIZE;
                                 /* start thread 1 */
        DosCreateThread(thread1, &thread1ID, stkptr);
                                 /* get stack space */
        stkptr = (char far *)malloc(STACK_SIZE) + STACK_SIZE;
                                 /* start thread 2 */
        DosCreateThread(thread2, &thread2ID, stkptr);

        DosSleep(1000L);         /* let all threads run */
        DosSuspendThread( thread1ID ); /* stop thread 1 */
        printf("\nSuspending thread 1\n");
        for(j=0; j<160; j++)     /* print series of Xs */
            printf("X");
        printf("\nResuming thread 1\n");
        DosResumeThread( thread1ID );  /* resume thread 1 */
        DosSleep(1000L);         /* let all threads continue */
        exit(0);                 /* exit all threads */
}

/* thread1() */
void far thread1()
{
    while(TRUE)                 /* continuously print dash */
        printf("-");
}

/* thread2() */
void far thread2()
{
    while(TRUE)                 /* continuously print asterisk */
        printf("*");
}
```

The main thread allows both child threads to run while it sleeps for one second. Then it wakes up, suspends the first child (the one that prints dashes), prints its series of Xs, resumes (restarts) thread 1 and finally goes back to sleep for another second.

As the printout shows, there are no dashes printed while thread 1 is suspended, although thread 2 does continue to intrude with asterisks while the main thread is busy displaying its series of Xs.

```
-----------------------------------------------------------------
----------------*************************************************
****************************--------------------------------------
----------------------------------------------------*************
*****************************************************************
***-----------
Suspending thread 1
XXXXXXXXX****************************************
****************************************XXXXXXXXXXXXXXXXXXXXXXXX
XXXXXXXXXXXXXXXXXXXXXXXXXXXXXXXXXXXXXXXXXXXXXXXXXXX********
*****************************************************************
******XXXXXXXXXXXXXXXXXXXXXXXXXXXXXXXXXXXXXXXXXXXXXXXXXXXXXXXXXX
XXXXXXXXXXXX
Resuming thread 1
***************************************************
***************************-------------------------------------
-----------------------------------------********************
****************************************************************------
-----------------------------------------------------------------
----------*******************************************************
```

DosSuspendThread — Suspends another thread's execution

```
DosSuspendThread(threadID);
unsigned threadID;        /* ID of thread to be suspended */
```

DosResumeThread — Resume another thread's execution

```
DosResumeThread(threadID);
unsigned threadID;        /* ID of thread to be resumed */
```

DosSuspendThread() and DosResumeThread() take only one argument: the ID of the thread to be suspended or resumed. This is the ID returned by DosCreateThread().

It is possible for a thread to suspend itself. However, if all the threads in a process are suspended, the process falls into deadlock, a sort of spell from which it can not be reawakened.

Exit Lists

It often happens, even in single-tasking operating systems like MS-DOS, that a program is terminated prematurely, leaving unfinished business. For example, the user of a word processing program may have made changes to a document. If the user forgets this and exits the program with a [Ctrl] [C], the changes will be lost before they can be saved to the disk.

In multitasking systems the problem of premature program termination is more severe, because programs can be terminated not only by the user with [Ctrl] [C], but by other processes and by the session manager. Also, there are more resources to clean up. A process may need to release semaphores, memory segments, pipes, queues, and similar resources which it is sharing with other processes.

It is desirable to make a program aware of its imminent termination so it can perform these types of last minute housekeeping tasks. OS/2 includes this capability in the *exit list*. This is a list of addresses of routines that are to receive control when a particular process is terminated.

The exit list is implemented with an API function called DosExitList(). This function is actually used in three different ways. First, it can place the address of a routine on the list. This is done by the main program, probably during initialization. The effect is to tell the operating system, "Listen, if anything happens to me, I want you to execute this routine." Second, DosExitList() can remove an address from the list. This might happen in response to changing conditions in the program, when it is determined that a particular clean-up action will no longer be needed if the program is terminated. And third, the exit routine itself invokes DosExitList() to tell the operating system it has finished; it is used instead of exit() or DosExit().

Here's a short example that demonstrates this function's usage:

```
/* exitlist.c */
/* creates list of routines to execute on exit */
#define INCL_DOS
#include <os2.h>
#include <malloc.h>             /* for malloc() */
#define ADD_ADDR 1              /* add address to exit list */
#define DONE 3                  /* exit routine complete */
main()
{
    void far exit1();           /* prototype for exit routine */
    void far exit2();           /* prototype for exit routine */
    unsigned rc;                /* return code */
                                /* set up first exit routine */
    if( rc=DosExitList( ADD_ADDR, exit1 ) )
        {printf("DosExitList error=%u\n",rc); exit(1); }
                                /* set up second exit routine */
    if( rc=DosExitList( ADD_ADDR, exit2 ) )
        {printf("DosExitList error=%u\n",rc); exit(1); }
```

(continued)

```
   while( !kbhit() )              /* loop until key struck */
      printf("X");
   exit(0);                       /* exit all threads */
}
/* exit1() */
/* first routine to execute at exit */
void far exit1()
{
   unsigned rc;
   printf("\nClearing flags and semaphores");
   if( rc=DosExitList( DONE, 0L ) )
      printf("DosExitList error=%u\n",rc);
}

/* exit2() */
/* second routine to execute at exit */
void far exit2()
{
   unsigned rc;
   printf("\nFreeing resources");
   if( rc=DosExitList( DONE, 0L ) )
      printf("DosExitList error=%u\n",rc);
}
```

This program sets up two exit routines, called exit1() and exit2(). They're written in the form of C language functions, but they operate differently. The operating system rather than a calling program transfers control to them; they do not return in the way functions do, but through the DosExitList() function. Since the process that contains them is no longer among the living, they return to the operating system.

The DosExitList() function takes two parameters. The first is a function code with the following possible values:

Value	Function
1	Add the address, given as the second parameter, to the exit list.
2	Delete the address, given as the second parameter, from the exit list.
3	Used to terminate exit routine.

For the first two of these options the second parameter is the address of the routine to be placed on (or deleted from) the exit list. If the third option is used, the second parameter is not applicable and can be the NULL pointer or 0L.

DosExitList — Manage list of exit routines

```
DosExitList(FnCode, Address);
unsigned FnCode;        /* 1=add to list, 2=delete, 3=exit */
void (far *)(void);     /* address of exit routine */
```

The exit routines in our example don't actually free any resources or perform other such tasks, but they do print messages *saying* that's what they're doing (not unlike many politicians).

When the main program is started it prints the usual series of Xs to the screen. The user can stop it by pressing any key. This causes the main program to execute the exit() function. At this point the routines on the exit list are executed. Here's a sample run:

```
XXXXXXXXXXXXXXXXXXXXXXXXXXXXXXXXXXXXXXXXXXXXXXXXXXXXXXXXXXXXXXX
XXXXXXXXXXXXXXXXXXXXXXXXXXXXXXXXXXXXXXXXX
Clearing flags and semaphores
Freeing resources
C>
```

Once the exit routines are complete, control returns to the operating system.

The exit routines are also triggered if the program is terminated by [Ctrl] [C], as shown in this sample run:

```
XXXXXXXXXXXXXXXXXXXXXXXXXXXXXXXXXXXXXXXXXXXXXXXXXXXXXXXXXXXXXXXX
XXXXXXXXXXXXXXXXXXXXXXXXXXXXXXXXXXXXXXX
Clearing flags and semaphores
Freeing resources
The process has stopped.
The process was cancelled either by itself,
another process, or by pressing Ctrl+Break.
^C
C>
```

Execution of the DosKillProcess() function by another process has the same effect.

Of course in a real application the exit routines would be expanded to perform more serious tasks. As we learn more about memory and interprocess communication we'll see more situations where exit lists would be useful.

Examples Using Threads

We'll close this chapter with a pair of somewhat more complex example programs. These examples give a hint of how threads may be used in real programming situations, and they also point out potential problems that can be solved by semaphores, the subject of the next chapter.

Reading and Writing to a Buffer

Data from the outside world often arrives at the computer faster than a program can process it. In such a situation it is desirable for the incoming data to be stored temporarily in a buffer, so none of it is lost before it can be used.

A simple example of this situation is displaying typed characters. If the user types faster than the display routine can put the characters on the screen, characters are lost, and the user finds the performance of the program unsatisfactory. In a multitasking situation this problem can arise because another process interrupts the read/display process between the time a character is typed and when it is displayed.

The solution is the type-ahead buffer, in which typed characters are stored while they await their turn to be displayed. Since the routine that reads characters from the keyboard, and the routine that displays characters on the screen, operate asynchronously, they can be implemented by different threads. The reader thread waits for a character to be typed and places it in the buffer. The writer waits for a character to appear in the buffer, and when it finds one, displays it on the screen. Thus if there is an interruption between reading and display, no harm is done.

The writer and the reader each maintain a pointer to the buffer. The reader increments its pointer when it places a character in the buffer, and the writer increments its pointer after displaying a character. Both pointers move along through the buffer, the distance between them indicating how far the display lags the keyboard. Figure 5-5 shows the arrangement.

What should be done if the buffer fills up? One solution is the ring buffer, in which the end of the buffer is conceived of as being connected to the beginning. Our program uses a simpler approach: if the buffer is full, the program sounds a beep. Whenever the writer catches up with the reader, the reader's and the writer's pointers are both set back to the beginning of the buffer. So, if the user receives a beep when pressing a key, it is only necessary to wait until the display catches up, then typing can be continued.

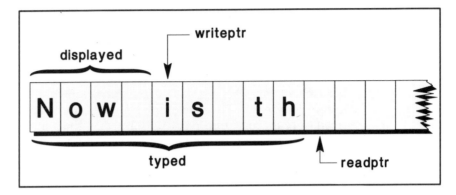

Figure 5-5
Type-ahead Buffer

Here's the listing:

```
/* readwrit.c */
/* 1st thread reads keyboard, 2nd writes to screen */
#define INCL_DOS
#define INCL_SUB
#include <os2.h>
#include <malloc.h>          /* for malloc() */
#define STACKSIZE 1024       /* stack size for new thread */
#define ARRAY_SIZE 50        /* size of character buffer */
#define HANDLE 0             /* kbd handle always 0 */
#define WAIT 0               /* 0=wait, 1=no wait */
#define FREQ 1000            /* frequency for DosBeep */
#define DURATION 100         /* DosBeep duration */
char charbuff[ARRAY_SIZE];   /* character buffer */
char *writeptr;              /* pointer to charbuff */
char *readptr;               /* pointer to charbuff */

main()
{
   struct _KBDKEYINFO keydata;  /* struct in bsesub.h */
   char far *stkptr;            /* pointer to stack space */
   unsigned writerID;          /* thread ID */
   void far writer();          /* declare writer() */

   readptr = charbuff;         /* set pointers to */
   writeptr = charbuff;        /* start of buffer */
                               /* start writer thread */
   stkptr = (char far *)malloc(STACKSIZE) + STACKSIZE;
   DosCreateThread( writer, &writerID, stkptr );
```

(continued)

```
    while(TRUE)   {
        KbdCharIn( &keydata, WAIT, HANDLE );   /* read char */
        if( readptr < charbuff + ARRAY_SIZE ) /* if room, */
            *readptr++ = keydata.chChar;      /* put in buffer */
        else                                  /* otherwise, */
            DosBeep( FREQ, DURATION );         /* beep instead */
    }
}

/* writer() */
/* writes characters from buffer to display */
void far writer()
{
    while(TRUE)   {
        if( writeptr < readptr )   {           /* if char, */
            VioWrtTTy( writeptr++, 1, HANDLE ); /* display
                                                    it */
            if( writeptr==readptr )           /* if caught up, */
                writeptr = readptr = charbuff;  /* reset ptrs */
        }
    DosSleep(200L);              /* delay for slow typists */
    }
}
```

We've included a 200 millisecond delay in the writer thread. This is a long delay for most typists, but it makes the program's operation clearer. Run the program, and try typing a phrase on the screen. You will easily outstrip the display. If you stop typing, the display will catch up. If you reach the end of the buffer before the writer thread can catch up and reset the pointers (type 50 characters rapidly), you'll hear the beep. To exit from the program, type [Ctrl] [C].

The heart of the program is the buffer **charbuff[]** and the two pointers to it, **readptr** and **writeptr**. Both pointers are initialized to the beginning of the buffer. The reader thread reads a character with KbdCharIn(), then copies it from the **_KBDKEYINFO** structure to **charbuff** and increments **readptr**. It also checks to see if **readptr** has reached the end of the buffer. If so, it beeps instead of putting the character in the buffer.

The writer thread asks if **writeptr** is less than **readptr**. If so, it knows there are undisplayed characters in the buffer and displays the next one just before incrementing **writeptr**. It also checks to see if **writeptr** is equal to **readptr**; if so it sets them both back to the beginning of **charbuff**.

The Interprocess Synchronization Problem

There is a potential problem with this program that illustrates one of the pitfalls of programming in a multitasking situation. Suppose the writer thread has just checked to see if the two pointers are equal and has found they are. We'll say both are pointing to position 5 in the buffer. That is, the writer thread has executed the first of the following two lines of code:

```
if( writeptr==readptr )              /* if caught up, */
   writeptr = readptr = charbuff;    /* reset ptrs */
```

The writer is about to reset both pointers to the start of **charbuff** using the second of these two lines. However, before it can do so, its time slice is over and the reader thread takes over. The reader finds that a character has been typed, and places it at position 5 in the buffer. Now control happens to return to the writer, which continues where it left off and resets both pointers to the beginning of **charbuff**. But the character is lost: it is left, undisplayed, in position 5, while both threads start out again at the beginning of the buffer, oblivious to its fate.

Such a lost character incident will probably not occur very often. It only happens when the writer catches up to the reader and when the scheduler interrupts the writer between reading and resetting the pointers. To see more consistently how this problem affects the operation of the program, we can modify the code to provide a delay between the two critical lines. Here's the modified writer thread:

```
/* writer() */
/* writes characters from buffer to display */
/* causes trouble with delay */
void far writer()
{
   while(TRUE)   {
      if( writeptr < readptr )  {           /* if char, */
         VioWrtTTy(writeptr++, 1, HANDLE);  /* display it */
         if( writeptr==readptr )  {         /* if caught up, */

            DosSleep(200L);                 /* cause trouble */
```

(continued)

```
            writeptr = readptr = charbuff; /* reset ptrs */
        }
    }
  DOSSLEEP(200L);              /* delay for slow typists */
    }
}
```

With this modification the program still works all right if you type very slowly, or if your typing is consistently faster than the display. But whenever the display catches up with your typing, characters are lost. Without the addition of DosSleep(), characters are also lost, but much less often, because it is less likely that the writer thread will be interrupted between these two instructions.

The trouble is that the two lines of code in which the pointers are tested and then reset should not be permitted to be interrupted by other threads. This situation, in which the operation of the program is dependent on the exact timing of two different threads, is called a *race condition*. In a program with a race condition a problem may occur only once in a hundred or once in a thousand times. Such a bug is particularly frustrating to track down: you can run CodeView on the program over and over without seeing the error occur, and even in the real world it occurs only rarely. However, rarely may be often enough to make a program's operation unacceptable.

The moral: be on the lookout for possible race conditions, and either program in such a way that they don't occur, or eliminate the problem with semaphores, critical sections, or by suspending a thread. Semaphores provide the most general and flexible solution. In the next chapter we'll see how semaphores can eliminate the race condition in readwrit.c.

Using Threads to Improve Performance

The next example gives a hint of how threads can be used to make programs run faster. This program accepts numbers typed by the user and determines if they are prime. This is not something everyone wants to do, rather we use it to symbolize any computation-intensive task, in which the computer requires substantial time to process data and the user requires substantial time to enter it.

In a traditional single-tasking operating environment this program would be written in a simple loop, as shown in Figure 5-6.

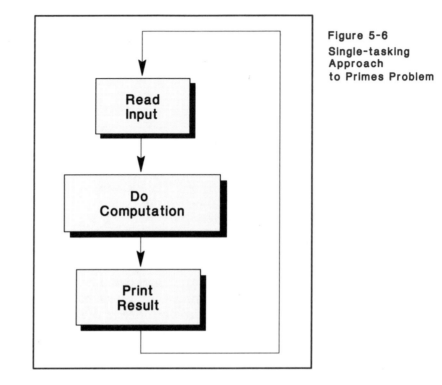

Figure 5-6
Single-tasking
Approach
to Primes Problem

The user types in a number and then waits for the program to determine if it is prime. If the number is in fact prime this can take a little time—perhaps several seconds—depending on the speed of the processor and the number typed in. The delay may be enough to make the user wish he had purchased a different program.

Here's a program showing the single-tasking approach:

```
/* prime1.c */
/* tells whether a number is a prime */
#define TRUE 1
main()
{
    unsigned long div, number;
    unsigned long isprime(unsigned long);

    while(TRUE)  {
        printf("\nEnter an integer: ");
        scanf("%U", &number);
        if( div=isprime(number) )
            printf("%lu is divisible by %lu\n", number, div);
```

(continued)

```
        else
            printf("%lu is prime\n", number);
    }
}

/* isprime() */
/* returns 0 if argument is prime, divisor if not */
unsigned long isprime(unsigned long number)
{
    unsigned long j;
    for( j=2; j<number; j++ )
        if( (number % j)==0 )
            return(j);              /* number is divisible by j */
    return(0);                      /* number is prime */
}
```

Our method for calculating the prime is not the fastest, but it is simple. It divides the original number by all the integers less than the number. If the remainder of any such division is 0, then the number is not prime; otherwise it is. The isprime() function returns 0 if the number is prime, and the divisor if it is not.

The most obvious improvement that could be made to this scheme is to stop the loop when the divisor has grown to the square root of the number, rather than the number itself. (There's no point, for example, in checking 100 for divisors greater than 10.) We could also divide by only odd numbers, since only an even number can be divided exactly by an even number. But an even number is not prime. However, our purpose is not to make the most efficient prime-finder, but to investigate multitasking.

Experiment to find numbers that take a second or so to calculate. Try 33331, 77773, or 99991, which are prime. They cause a small but perceptible delay on our 80286-based machine. (Of course faster computers will process the numbers more quickly, so you may need to use larger primes, like 333331.) Notice that every such number takes about two seconds to process: one second to type in, and another second to do the analysis. It would save time if these two activities could be carried out at the same time.

Here's the prime1.c program rewritten to use multitasking. It uses two threads and a two-dimensional array with two columns.

The first thread initializes the second thread, and then enters a loop where it reads the numbers typed by the user and stores them in the first column of the array. The user signals that the last number has been entered by entering 0. At this point the first thread starts to print out the results. If there are results in the buffer already, they are printed. If the results are not yet calculated, the thread waits for them.

The second thread continuously checks the array to see if there are any numbers that need to be analyzed. If there are, it analyzes the number and leaves the result—the divisor if the number is not prime and 0 if it is—in the second column of the array. If there are no unanalyzed numbers in the array, it waits for them. Figure 5-7 shows what the different threads do.

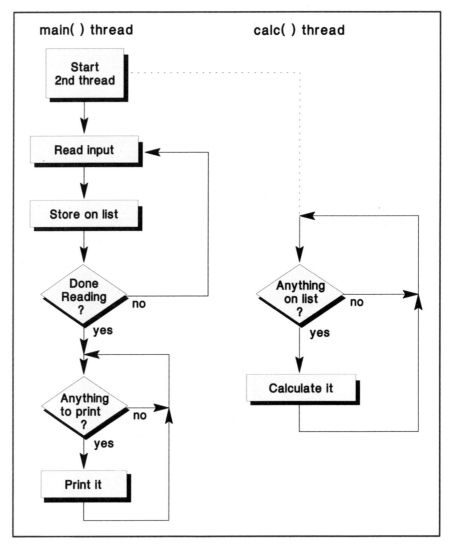

Figure 5-7
Multitasking Approach to Primes Problem

While the user is inputting new numbers, the program is analyzing ones previously input. While the results are being printed out, the program is calculating numbers entered but not yet printed. (We could have three threads, one for input, one for calculation, and one for printing, but it's disconcerting for the user if we intersperse input and output on the screen, so we wait for the input to be completed before starting to print the results.)

This program is related to the readwrit.c program, in that different threads manipulate a single data buffer. However, in the prime2.c program there are three activities involved—reading, analysis, and writing—rather than only reading and writing as in readwrit.c.

```c
/* prime2.c */
/* tells whether numbers typed in are primes */
#define INCL_DOS
#include <os2.h>
#include <malloc.h>          /* for malloc() */
#define STACKSIZE 1024        /* stack size for threads */
#define ARRAYSIZE 50          /* size of array */
                             /* array for primes and divisors */
unsigned long number[ARRAYSIZE][2];
int index=0;                  /* index to input */
int calcdex=0;                /* index to calculation */
main()
{
    int outdex;               /* index to output */
    char far *stkptr;         /* pointer to stack space */
    unsigned rc;              /* return code */
    unsigned threadID;        /* thread ID */
    void far calc();          /* prototype for 2nd thread */
                             /* start calculation thread */
    stkptr = (char far *)malloc(STACKSIZE) + STACKSIZE;
    if( rc=DosCreateThread(calc, &threadID, stkptr) )
        { printf("DosCreateThread error=%d",rc); exit(1); }
                             /* get numbers, put in array */
    printf("Enter possible primes, terminate list with 0.\n");
    for(index=0; index<ARRAYSIZE; index++)   {
        printf("Enter an integer: ");
        scanf("%U", &number[index][0]);
        if( number[index][0] == 0L )
            break;
    }
```

(continued)

```
    while(TRUE)  {                          /* print results */
       if(outdex==calcdex && calcdex==index)   /* if all
                                                      calced */
          exit(0);                          /* and printed, quit */
       if( outdex < calcdex )  {            /* if unprinted items */
          if( number[outdex][1] )           /* print them */
             printf("%lu is divisible by %lu\n",
                 number[outdex][0], number[outdex][1] );
          else
             printf("%lu is prime\n", number[outdex][0]);
          outdex++;
          }
       else
          DosSleep(0L);     /* no data; let calc work */
    }
}

/* calc() */
/* puts 0 in array if argument is prime, divisor if not */
void far calc()
{
   unsigned long isprime(unsigned long);
   while(TRUE)  {
      while( index <= calcdex )    /* wait for input */
         DosSleep(0L);
      number[calcdex++][1] = isprime(number[calcdex][0]);
   }
}

/* isprime() */
/* returns 0 if argument is prime, divisor if not */
unsigned long isprime(unsigned long number)
{
   unsigned long j;
   for( j=2; j<number; j++ )
      if( (number % j)==0 )
         return(j);
   return(0);
}
```

In this program the pointers **index** and **calcdex**, which are global variables, mark the position of the next incoming data item and the next item to be calculated. The local variable **outdex** indicates the next item to be printed. Figure 5-8 shows the data buffer and pointers, first during data input, and then, after the user has signaled that input is complete, during output.

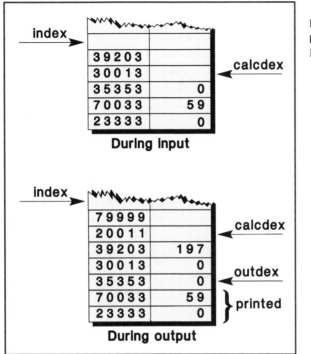

Figure 5-8
Pointers in the
prime.c program

If you have a list of potential primes that take a second or so to calculate, you'll find this program completes the task more quickly than the single-tasking version. While you're typing, it's thinking.

The Stolen Time Slice Problem

There is one problem with this example. It violates one of the golden rules of programming in a multitasking environment: don't wait in a loop. Waiting in a loop steals machine cycles, which could be used by other threads or processes. In this example, the first thread, while it prints the results, cycles in a **while** loop if it is waiting for results to be calculated. The thread used for calculating waits in another **while** loop if there are no new values to calculate.

True, both these loops turn over control to the system with a DosSleep() when they find they can't do anything. However, this only releases control for one time slice. The scheduler must keep allotting time slices to these processes whether they can use them or not. What is needed is a way for a routine, while waiting for a particular condition, to release control completely *until that condition is met.*

The answer to this problem, and to the synchronization problem in the previous example, is the semaphore, which we'll investigate in the next chapter.

Other Uses for Threads

In what circumstances should threads be used? The horsrace.c program showed how threads can be used to simplify the organization of a program, and the primes2.c example demonstrated the use of threads to improve performance by permitting I/O to take place at the same time as processing. Threads can also be used to perform housekeeping tasks unrelated to user input. For instance, a word processing program might save the contents of a file to disk at fixed intervals, so data would not be lost in the event of a power failure. A separate thread would keep track of the time, and perform the save, without interfering with the user.

In general, a thread is useful whenever a program must wait for something. One thread can do the waiting, while other threads go about more useful business. If a telecommunications program is waiting for data to arrive from another terminal, another thread can be rewriting the screen display, while a third waits for user input. Or, one process might be waiting for a message to arrive from another process via some form of interprocess communication. The process could use one thread to wait for the message, while other threads communicate with the user.

Summary

In this chapter, we discussed the use of threads, a function-like unit of multitasking in OS/2. We've learned how one thread can create another with DosCreateThread(), how a thread can terminate using DosExit() without affecting other threads, and how threads can share global variables. We examined how more than one thread can access the same C function at the same time, how multiple threads can share the same section of code, and how arguments can be passed to a thread using the stack.

We covered several other API functions which deal with threads. Critical sections, in which all threads but one are stopped, can be entered with DosEnterCritSec() and exited with DosExitCritSec(). One thread can be halted with DosSuspendThread() and restarted with DosResumeThread(). A list of routines to be executed when a program is terminated can be created and managed with DosExitList().

Finally we looked at examples of threads in use in a type-ahead buffer and a program that checks whether numbers are primes. These examples reveal the need for an additional mechanism to synchronize threads. This brings us to semaphores and our next chapter.

SEMAPHORES

Chapter 6

Chapter   6

Semaphores are the principle means OS/2 uses to coordinate the activities of different tasks. (We'll use the term "task" in this discussion to mean either a process or a thread.) Semaphores are used in two kinds of situations: to provide mutually exclusive access to a shared resource, and to enable one process or thread to signal another.

There are two kinds of semaphores: *RAM semaphores*, which are used between threads, and *system semaphores*, which are used mostly between processes.

In this chapter we first discuss the idea of semaphores in general. Then we'll cover RAM semaphores and their use for mutual exclusion and signaling and finally look at system semaphores.

Problems with Interprocess Coordination

What are semaphores and why do we need them? Timing and coordination problems arise when several tasks are running at the same time. Semaphores provide a solution to these problems.

The most common use of semaphores is to provide a way for several tasks to coordinate access to a shared resource. The resource can be any entity which would become confused if two tasks tried to access it simultaneously. The resource might be the screen (where two processes should not try to write a paragraph of text to the screen at the same time) or a printer or a disk drive. In some cases, a data buffer in memory should not be accessed by more than one process at a time. This type of resource is sometimes called a "serially reusable resource," or SRR.

As an example of the need for coordination between tasks, consider the following program, in which two threads simultaneously write a three-line paragraph to the screen:

```
/* xdisp.c */
/* two threads write to the screen */
#define INCL_DOS
#define INCL_SUB
#include <os2.h>
#include <malloc.h>          /* for malloc() */
#define STACK_SIZE 1024       /* stack for thread */
#define WAIT -1L              /* 1=wait, 0=return, >0=msecs */
#define HANDLE 0              /* vio handle always 0 */

char a1[] = "Semaphores provide\n\r";
char a2[] = "exclusion and signalling\n\r";
char a3[] = "between processes and threads.\n\r\n\r";
```

(continued)

```
char b1[] = "Life's but a walking shadow, a poor
                                        player\n\r";
char b2[] = "That struts and frets his hour upon the
                                        stage\n\r";
char b3[] = "And then is heard no more.\n\r\n\r";

main()
{
   char far *stkptr;        /* stack pointer for new thread */
   void far thread();       /* prototypes for new thread */
   unsigned threadID;       /* thread ID number */
                            /* get stack, start thread */
   stkptr = (char far *)malloc(STACK_SIZE) + STACK_SIZE;
   DosCreateThread( thread, &threadID, stkptr );
                            /* write data to screen */
   while( !kbhit() )  {     /* until keypress */
      VioWrtTTy( a1, sizeof(a1), HANDLE );
      VioWrtTTy( a2, sizeof(a2), HANDLE );
      VioWrtTTy( a3, sizeof(a3), HANDLE );
   }
   exit(1);                 /* exit all threads */
}

/* thread() */
/* writes data to screen */
void far thread()
{
   while(TRUE) {
      VioWrtTTy( b1, sizeof(b1), HANDLE );
      VioWrtTTy( b2, sizeof(b2), HANDLE );
      VioWrtTTy( b3, sizeof(b3), HANDLE );
   }
}
```

One thread displays a statement about semaphores, while the other displays a paragraph from Shakespeare's *Macbeth*. Unfortunately, when the program is run, the output of the two threads are mixed, with results like this:

```
Semaphores provide
exclusion and signaling
That struts and frets his hour upon the stage
between processes and threads.
And then is heard no more.
```

It is important to keep technology and drama more firmly separated than this, so we look for a way to coordinate the activities of the two threads. What is needed is a simple system whereby one thread can say to the other, "Sorry, I'm using the screen now, you'll have to wait," or, "I'm done with the screen now, it's your turn." Figure 6-1 shows how such mutual exclusion looks schematically.

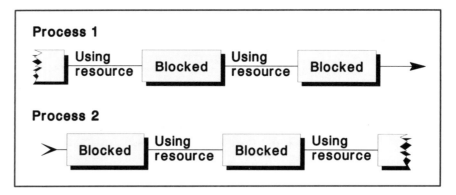

Figure 6-1
Mutually Exclusive Use of a Resource

Using a Variable for Coordination

In the case of threads, one might imagine using a single global variable to provide this capability. Setting the variable to 0 would mean the resource was free and could be used, while setting it to 1 would mean the resource was occupied. When a thread was ready to use the resource, it would check the variable. If it was 0, the thread would set it to 1 and start using the resource. If it was 1 the thread would realize the resource was in use and perhaps sleep for a while before checking again. When a thread finished with the resource, it would set the variable to 0.

This scheme seems reasonable, but it suffers from several flaws.

Atomic Versus Non-atomic

The most serious problem with the use of a variable for interprocess coordination, as outlined above, is its susceptibility to occasional failure.

Suppose thread 1 and thread 2 both decide to write a paragraph to the screen (or access some other resource) at roughly the same time. Let's say thread 1 is running, so it reads the variable that we've set up to control access to the screen. It's 0, so thread 1 says to itself, great, I can start displaying my paragraph. Thread 1 is about to set the variable equal to 1 to indicate that the resource is busy. But, at this exact moment, the scheduler snatches control away from thread 1 and gives it to thread 2. Thread 2 reads the variable and also finds it to be 0. It sets it to 1 and starts writing to the screen. Now when thread 1 regains control, it also sets the variable to 1 and starts writing to the screen. The result is total confusion.

The problem is that the two operations—checking the variable to see if the resource is free, and changing the variable to indicate the resource is busy—are two separate actions, performed by separate CPU instructions. They are not *atomic*, or indivisible. The scheduler can interrupt one process and schedule another between any two instructions; and so, according to the dictates of Murphy's law, a thread will eventually be interrupted between these two critical instructions. This is another example of a race condition, mentioned in the last chapter. As with all race conditions, the problem, because it *doesn't* happen very often, is very difficult to track down.

What is needed is an atomic mechanism: one that checks the variable and sets it at the same time. In this context "at the same time" means that no other process can start running in between these two actions.

Avoiding Busy-waiting

There is another problem with using a simple variable for interprocess coordination. A thread that finds a resource being used by another thread must keep checking the variable to know when the resource becomes available. Here it finds itself in a dilemma. If it sits in a loop, continuously checking the variable, it wastes many time slices which could be put to better use by other tasks. On the other hand, if it goes to sleep with DosSleep() for a short time after checking the variable each time through the loop, it may waste time because it is not immediately awake when the resource becomes available. What is needed here is a way to put a process to sleep and awaken it *as soon as* the resource is available.

Can't Use Variables Between Processes

Even if global variables were the solution for coordination between *threads*, there would remain the problem of synchronizing different *processes*. This might be done with a variable in a shared memory segment (which we'll learn about in Chapter 10), but this is a somewhat cumbersome approach, and in any case is subject to the same problems noted above.

Semaphores to the Rescue

The semaphore is the device used in OS/2 to solve all these problems. A RAM semaphore is essentially still a variable in memory. However, the operating system, and not the application, controls the semaphore through system calls by the application. Since it is the operating system that checks and sets the semaphore variable, and since the operating system can ensure that it itself is not interrupted by another task, the check-and-set operation cannot be interrupted. Also, when a resource becomes available, the operating system is informed immediately of this fact (either by another task or by an interrupt from a hardware device) and can immediately wake up a process which is waiting for the resource.

Thus, using system calls, OS/2 provides a simple and effective approach to interprocess coordination. It solves problems inherent in using non-atomic test-and-check instructions, and avoids busy-waiting.

RAM Semaphores

In this section we'll look at RAM semaphores, which are used for coordination between threads. As the name implies, RAM semaphores use a global variable in memory: a variable which is accessible to all the threads wishing to use the semaphore.

The problem we posed in the xdisp.c program is an example of resource sharing. We'll look at this situation first, and then examine the second use for semaphores: where one task needs to signal one or more other tasks. Later we'll look at system semaphores.

Mutually Exclusive Access to a Shared Resource

How can we solve the problem presented in the xdisp.c program? Here's a modification to that program, which shows how to use a RAM semaphore to coordinate access to the screen by two threads.

```
/* xdisp2.c */
/* uses semaphore to coordinate access to screen */
#define INCL_DOS
#define INCL_SUB
#include <os2.h>
#include <malloc.h>        /* for malloc() */
#define STACK_SIZE 1024     /* stack for thread */
#define WAIT -1L            /* -1=wait, 0=return, >0=msecs */
#define HANDLE 0            /* vio handle always 0 */

unsigned long semaphore=0; /* RAM semaphore */

char a1[] = "Semaphores provide\n\r";
char a2[] = "exclusion and signalling\n\r";
char a3[] = "between processes and threads.\n\r\n\r";
```

(continued)

```c
char b1[] = "Life's but a walking shadow, a poor
                                          player\n\r";
char b2[] = "That struts and frets his hour upon the
                                          stage\n\r";
char b3[] = "And then is heard no more.\n\r\n\r";

main()
{
    char far *stkptr;        /* stack pointer for new thread */
    void far thread();       /* prototypes for new thread */
    unsigned threadID;       /* thread ID number */
                             /* get stack, start thread */
    stkptr = (char far *)malloc(STACK_SIZE) + STACK_SIZE;
    DosCreateThread( thread, &threadID, stkptr );
                             /* write data to screen */
    while( !kbhit() )  {      /* until keypress */
       DosSemRequest( &semaphore, WAIT );
       VioWrtTTy( a1, sizeof(a1), HANDLE );
       VioWrtTTy( a2, sizeof(a2), HANDLE );
       VioWrtTTy( a3, sizeof(a3), HANDLE );
       DosSemClear( &semaphore );
    }
    exit(1);                 /* exit all threads */
}

/* thread() */
/* writes data to screen */
void far thread()
{
    while(TRUE) {
       DosSemRequest( &semaphore, WAIT );
       VioWrtTTy( b1, sizeof(b1), HANDLE );
       VioWrtTTy( b2, sizeof(b2), HANDLE );
       VioWrtTTy( b3, sizeof(b3), HANDLE );
       DosSemClear( &semaphore );
    }
}
```

Only a few changes have been made to the program to install the semaphore. The semaphore itself is a global variable, declared at the beginning of the listing. It must be of type **unsigned long**. When this variable is 0, the resource it protects is assumed to be available. When it is non-zero then the resource is considered to be in use. Semaphore variables should be initialized to 0 before being used, as shown in the example. Thereafter, however, their value should be changed only by API semaphore functions. Avoid the temptation to interfere with semaphores using assignment statements like:

```
semaphore = 1;        /* don't set it this way */
```

As you can see in the listing, each section of code containing the VioWrtTTy() functions is preceded by the DosSemRequest() function, and followed by the DosSemClear() function. Each thread, before it attempts to write to the screen, calls DosSemRequest(). If the semaphore is set to 0 (or "cleared"), this indicates the resource is available. DosSemRequest() then sets the semaphore to 1 ("owned") and returns control to the thread. The thread can then execute the three VioWrtTTy() functions. When it's done, the thread calls DosSemClear() which sets the semaphore back to 0 (or clears the semaphore to "unowned").

But suppose that when a thread executes the DosSemRequest() function, the semaphore is owned (set to 1). In this case the function simply waits—that is, control is not given back to the thread. Control is returned to the thread as soon as the semaphore does become 0, so there is no delay in the thread's access to the screen.

In this way the two sections of prose will not become intermixed. The output from xdisp2.c looks like this:

```
Semaphores provide
exclusion and signaling
between processes and threads.

Life's but a walking shadow, a poor player
That struts and frets his hour upon the stage
And then is heard no more.
```

The DosSemRequest() function takes two arguments. The first is the address of the RAM semaphore. This has the type **void far ***. Why is this? The semaphore itself is **unsigned long**, so one would think its address would be **unsigned long far ***. This would work perfectly well in the case of RAM semaphores. However, DosSem-Request() and other semaphore functions are also used for *system* semaphores. In this case the semaphore is a different type. Using a pointer to a **void** type allows DosSemRequest() and the other semaphore functions to be used with both RAM and system semaphores, without the need to typecast the semaphore handle. (We discuss this further in the section on system semaphores.)

DosSemRequest — Waits for semaphore to clear, resets it

```
DosSemRequest(SemHandle, Timeout);
void far *SemHandle;      /* semaphore handle or address */
long Timeout;            /* -1=wait, 0=return, >0=msecs */
```

The second parameter in DosSemRequest(), which is a long integer, indicates what happens if the semaphore is owned (set to non-zero). There are three possibilities:

Value	Action
-1	The thread will sleep until the semaphore is cleared
0	The function will immediately return control to the thread
>1	The value is the number of milliseconds the function will wait before returning control to the thread

The most common choice is for the thread to wait until the semaphore is cleared, but we'll see an example later where it's useful to return immediately.

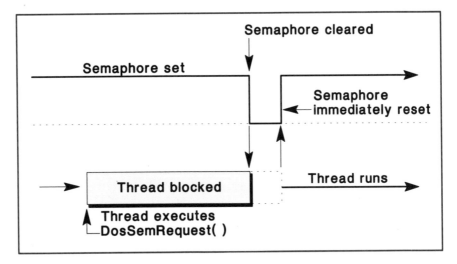

Figure 6-2
Operation of DosSemRequest( )

Figure 6-2 shows the situation when the semaphore is initially set and a thread is waiting for it with DosSemRequest(). When the semaphore is cleared by another thread the DosSemRequest() function sets it immediately to owned and then returns control to the calling thread.

DosSemClear — Clears a semaphore

```
DosSemClear(SemHandle);
void far *SemHandle;      /* semaphore handle or address */
```

The DosSemClear() function takes a single variable, the address of the semaphore. DosSemClear() clears the semaphore no matter what state it was in before. There is no effect on the thread that issued the call, although clearing the semaphore may cause another thread, which was waiting on the semaphore, to be released from a DosSemRequest() and start up.

Coordinating Access to Shared Memory

Here's another situation in which semaphores can be usefully employed for mutually exclusive access to a resource. In this case, the resource is a buffer in memory.

Suppose the buffer contains data about a particular individual, as in a personnel file. Perhaps several tasks need to write to this buffer and several others need to read from it. (Imagine a database being accessed by separate terminals in the personnel department.)

If one task is permitted to read from the buffer at the same time another is writing a record to it, the reader task may come away with a garbled record. That is, it may read part of the record, be interrupted long enough for a writer task to change the record, and read a second part of the record about a different individual. Thus we need to make sure that only one task at a time has access to the buffer. (Actually no harm is done if more than one *reader* accesses it at the same time, but we'll ignore this situation for simplicity.)

The next example models this situation with a main thread that repeatedly reads the buffer, and two other threads that each continuously place data in it. The buffer consists of a structure containing information about novelists: their name, date of birth, and a brief description.

```
/* dbsem.c */
/* accesses common structure */
/* uses semaphore to coordinate access */
#define INCL_DOS
```

```c
#include <os2.h>
#include <malloc.h>          /* for malloc() */
#include <string.h>          /* for strcpy() */
#define STACK_SIZE 1024      /* stack for each thread */
#define WAIT -1L             /* -1=wait, 0=return, >0=msecs */

struct personnel  {          /* structure for novelist info */
   char name[30];            /* name */
   int birth;                /* birthdate */
   char descr[40];           /* description */
} novelist;                  /* shared structure */

unsigned long semaphore=0; /* RAM semaphore */

main()
{
   char far *stkptr;         /* stack pointer for new threads */
   void far thread1();       /* prototypes for new threads */
   void far thread2();
   unsigned threadID;        /* thread ID number */

   stkptr = (char far *)malloc(STACK_SIZE) + STACK_SIZE;
   DosCreateThread( thread1, &threadID, stkptr );

   stkptr = (char far *)malloc(STACK_SIZE) + STACK_SIZE;
   DosCreateThread( thread2, &threadID, stkptr );

   while( !kbhit() )  {  /* loop until key struck */
      DosSleep( 200L );  /* avoid lockstep */
      DosSemRequest( &semaphore, WAIT );
      printf("\nName   %s\n", novelist.name);
      printf("DOB:   %4d\n", novelist.birth);
      printf("Descr: %s\n", novelist.descr);
      DosSemClear( &semaphore );
   }
   exit(1);                  /* exit all threads */
}

/* thread1() */
/* fills structure with data */
void far thread1()
{
   while(TRUE) {
      DosSemRequest( &semaphore, WAIT );
      strcpy( novelist.name, "Herman Melville" );
      novelist.birth = 1819;
      strcpy( novelist.descr, "Seafarer and mystic" );
      DosSemClear( &semaphore );
   }
}
```

(continued)

```
/* thread2() */
/* fills structure with data */
void far thread2()
{
   while(TRUE) {
      DosSemRequest( &semaphore, WAIT );
      strcpy( novelist.name, "Scott Fitzgerald" );
      novelist.birth = 1896;
      strcpy( novelist.descr, "Disillusioned socialite" );
      DosSemClear( &semaphore );
   }
}
```

The semaphore prevents any thread, whether it wants to read or write to the buffer, from doing so until no other thread is using it. Without the semaphore the output from the program is jumbled, as you can see by removing the semaphore functions and running the program. With no semaphores you'll get readouts like this:

```
Name    Scott Fitzgerald
DOB:    1896
Descr: Seafarer and mystic
```

Fitzgerald was never a seafarer or a mystic, so this isn't very satisfactory. You might even see something like

```
Name    Scott Fitzgelle
DOB:    1819
Descr: Seafarer and mystic
```

where the novelist's name becomes a hybrid.

With the semaphore functions installed and working, the integrity of the output is guaranteed:

```
Name    Herman Melville
DOB:    1819
Descr: Seafarer and mystic

Name    Scott Fitzgerald
DOB:    1896
Descr: Disillusioned socialite
```

As we go along we'll see other examples of semaphores used to provide mutually exclusive access to a shared resource.

Lockstep

The DosSleep() function is inserted in the main() function of dbsem.c to prevent a lockstep situation from developing. In lockstep, running threads always receive their time slices in the same order: thread 1, thread 2, thread 3; thread 1, thread 2, thread 3; and so on. In the present example we want both thread1() and thread2() to have a chance at filling the buffer just before the main() thread gets its time slice and displays it. The use of DosSleep() causes main() to awaken at a time that is out of synch with the other threads.

The NO WAIT Option

The **Timeout** argument in DosSemRequest() gives the programmer the option of returning immediately from the function even if the semaphore is owned. This is useful if you want the thread to do something while it's waiting for the resource.

If you specify the NO WAIT option, and the semaphore is owned, the function returns immediately with a return code of 121, or ERR_SEM_TIMEOUT.

Here's the dbsem.c program rewritten so nothing is printed without a specific request from the user. If the user decides to display the contents of the data buffer, pressing [Enter] makes this request to the program. If no other thread is using the buffer its contents are printed out. However, if another thread is using it, the program returns the message "Data not ready. Try again."

```
/* nowait.c */
/* accesses common structure */
/* one thread does not wait on owned semaphore */
#define INCL_DOS
#include <os2.h>
#include <malloc.h>        /* for malloc() */
#include <string.h>        /* for strcpy() */
#define STACK_SIZE 256      /* stack for each thread */
#define WAIT -1L            /* -1=wait, 0=return, >0=msecs */
#define NOWAIT 0L           /* return if sem not available */
#define ERR_SEM_TIMEOUT 121 /* return code if sem owned */

struct personnel  {         /* structure for novelist info */
    char name[30];          /* name */
    int birth;              /* birthdate */
    char descr[40];         /* description */
} novelist;                 /* shared structure */
```

(continued)

```
unsigned long semaphore=0;   /* RAM semaphore */

main()
{
   char far *stkptr;       /* stack pointer for new threads */
   void far thread1();     /* prototypes for new threads */
   void far thread2();
   unsigned threadID;      /* thread ID number */
   unsigned rc;            /* return code */

   stkptr = (char far *)malloc(STACK_SIZE) + STACK_SIZE;
   DosCreateThread( thread1, &threadID, stkptr );

   stkptr = (char far *)malloc(STACK_SIZE) + STACK_SIZE;
   DosCreateThread( thread2, &threadID, stkptr );

   while( TRUE )  {
      printf("\nPress [Enter] to read data: ");
      if( getche() != '\r' )   /* exit on non-[Enter] */
         exit(0);
      if( rc=DosSemRequest(&semaphore, NOWAIT) )
         if ( rc == ERR_SEM_TIMEOUT )
            printf("\nData not ready.  Try again.\n");
         else  {
            printf("\nDosSemRequest error=%u\n",rc);
            exit(1);
         }
      else  {
         printf("\nName   %s\n", novelist.name);
         printf("DOB:   %4d\n", novelist.birth);
         printf("Descr: %s\n", novelist.descr);
      }
      DosSemClear( &semaphore );
   }
}

/* thread1() */
/* fills structure with data */
void far thread1()
{
   while(TRUE) {
      DosSemRequest( &semaphore, WAIT );
      strcpy( novelist.name, "Joseph Conrad" );
      novelist.birth = 1857;
      strcpy( novelist.descr, "Polish sea captain" );
      DosSemClear( &semaphore );
   }
}
```

(continued)

```
/* thread2() */
/* fills structure with data */
void far thread2()
{
   while(TRUE) {
      DosSemRequest( &semaphore, WAIT );
      strcpy( novelist.name, "Ernest Hemingway" );
      novelist.birth = 1899;
      strcpy( novelist.descr, "Boxer, fisherman, hunter" );
      DosSemClear( &semaphore );
   }
}
```

Here's an example of output from the program:

```
Press [Enter] to read data:
Data not ready.  Try again.

Press [Enter] to read data:
Data not ready.  Try again.

Press [Enter] to read data:
Name   Joseph Conrad
DOB:   1857
Descr: Polish sea captain
```

In this session the buffer was being used the first two times the user tried to access it, but was free on the third occasion, having just been filled by thread1().

Press [Ctrl] [C] to exit from the program.

Cleaning Up the Keyboard Buffer Problem

In the last chapter we examined a program, readwrit.c, in which one thread placed keystrokes in a buffer and another thread took them from the buffer and displayed them on the screen. We saw that a problem could occur because the steps to check whether the writer had caught up with the reader, and to reset their pointers to the start of the buffer, were not atomic. If the reader thread interrupted the writer between these two steps, trouble would result.

In the following example this problem is fixed by using semaphores to prevent simultaneous access to the buffer by the two threads.

```
/* rwsem.c */
/* 1st thread reads keyboard, 2nd writes to screen */
/* uses semaphores to avoid race condition */
#define INCL_DOS
#define INCL_SUB
#include <os2.h>
#include <malloc.h>         /* for malloc() */
#define STACKSIZE 1024      /* stack size for new thread */
#define ARRAY_SIZE 50       /* size of character buffer */
#define HANDLE 0            /* kbd handle always 0 */
#define KBDWAIT 0           /* 0=wait, 1=no wait */
#define FREQ 1000           /* frequency for DosBeep */
#define DURATION 100        /* DosBeep duration */
#define SEMWAIT -1L         /* -1=wait, 0=no wait,
                                  >0=msecs */

char charbuff[ARRAY_SIZE]; /* character buffer */
char *writeptr;            /* pointer to charbuff */
char *readptr;             /* pointer to charbuff */
unsigned long sem;         /* semaphore */
main()
{
    struct _KBDKEYINFO keydata;  /* struct in bsesub.h */
    char far *stkptr;       /* pointer to stack space */
    unsigned writerID;      /* thread ID */
    void far writer();      /* declare writer() */

    readptr = charbuff;     /* set pointers to */
    writeptr = charbuff;    /* start of buffer */
                            /* start writer thread */
    stkptr = (char far *)malloc(STACKSIZE) + STACKSIZE;
    DosCreateThread( writer, &writerID, stkptr );
    while(TRUE)  {
        KbdCharIn( &keydata, KBDWAIT, HANDLE ); /* read char
                                                      */
        DosSemRequest( &sem, SEMWAIT );
        if( readptr < charbuff + ARRAY_SIZE )   /* if room, */
            *readptr++ = keydata.chChar;    /* put in buffer */
        else                                /* otherwise, */
        DosBeep( FREQ, DURATION );          /* beep instead */
        DosSemClear( &sem );
    }
}
```

(continued)

```
/* writer() */
/* writes characters from buffer to display */
void far writer()
{
   while(TRUE)  {
      if( writeptr < readptr )  {            /* if char, */
         VioWrtTTy( writeptr++, 1, HANDLE ); /* display it
                                                         */
         DosSemRequest( &sem, SEMWAIT );
         if( writeptr==readptr )  {       /* if caught up, */
            DosSleep(200L);               /* cause trouble */
            writeptr = readptr = charbuff;   /* reset ptrs */
         }
         DosSemClear( &sem );
      }
   DosSleep(200L);     /* delay for slow typists */
   }
}
```

This version of the program incorporates the delay, in the write thread, that we used in the last chapter to make certain the program would fail. In this case, however, the program works fine because the test and reset operations in the write thread cannot be interrupted by the read thread. Try it. You'll find the dropped-out characters you encountered before are no longer a problem.

Signaling Between Threads

The second major use of semaphores, after coordinating access to a shared resource, is signaling. Signaling is simply a way for one task to get the attention of another. (Don't confuse this use of the term "signal" with the concept of *signals*, such as [Ctrl] [C], which we cover in Chapter 12.) There are many reasons why one task might want to alert another. We look at several possibilities in this section.

When semaphores are used for mutually exclusive access to shared resources, the API function DosSemRequest() is appropriate because, as soon as the semaphore is cleared by another process, DosSemRequest() immediately sets it again so only one process at a time is given access to the shared resource. On the other hand, when semaphores are used for signaling, it may be that several different threads must all be signaled and start to run at the clearing of a single semaphore. For this reason different API functions are used in signaling: DosSemWait() or DosSemSetWait(), rather than DosSem-Request().

Let's look at an example. In this program one thread reads the keyboard, while another prints messages on the screen. This division of labor into separate threads is not really necessary in such a small program, but in a more sophisticated application it might be advantageous. One thread could concentrate on reading keystrokes without fear of losing any, while another could spend all the time it needed to modify the display, perhaps in a complex and fancy way.

In our example the display thread prints a series of prompts to the user, and the keyboard thread captures the user's replies from the keyboard. In action there should be one prompt, followed by a response, followed by another prompt, and so on. This is the coordination the semaphore is designed to provide.

```c
/* alert.c */
/* one thread alerts another using semaphore */
#define INCL_DOS
#define INCL_SUB
#include <os2.h>
#include <malloc.h>          /* for malloc() */
#define STACK_SIZE 1024       /* stack for each thread */
#define SEMWAIT -1L           /* -1=wait, 0=return, >0=msecs */
#define KBDWAIT 0             /* 0=wait, -1=no wait */
#define BUFFLEN 80            /* length of input buffer */
#define HANDLE 0              /* vio handle always 0 */

char name[BUFFLEN];          /* buffer for name */
char position[BUFFLEN];      /* buffer for position */
char age[BUFFLEN];           /* buffer for age */

unsigned long semaphore=0; /* RAM semaphore */

main()
{
    char far *stkptr;        /* stack pointer for new thread */
    void far keyboard();     /* prototype for new thread */
    unsigned threadID;       /* thread ID number */
                             /* start keyboard thread */
    stkptr = (char far *)malloc(STACK_SIZE) + STACK_SIZE;
    DosCreateThread( keyboard, &threadID, stkptr );
                             /* start dialogue */
    printf("Enter your name: ");
    DosSemSetWait( &semaphore, SEMWAIT );
    printf("Enter your position: ");
    DosSemSetWait( &semaphore, SEMWAIT );
    printf("Enter your age: ");
    DosSemSetWait( &semaphore, SEMWAIT );
    printf("At %s, aren't you too old\n", age );
    printf("to be a %s, %s?", position, name );
    exit(0);
}
```

(continued)

```
/* keyboard() */
/* gets data from keyboard */
void far keyboard()
{
    gets(name);
    DosSemClear( &semaphore );
    gets(position);
    DosSemClear( &semaphore );
    gets(age);
    DosSemClear( &semaphore );
    DosExit(0,0);
}
```

The first thread prints a prompt, then waits for a semaphore to be cleared. The second thread gets the user's response from the keyboard and then clears the semaphore, permitting the first thread to go on to the next prompt. This interchange is repeated three times before the first thread goes on to print a message making use of the information provided by the user. Here's a sample of interaction with the program:

```
Enter your name: Ebenezer Brown
Enter your position: programmer
Enter your age: 23
At 23, aren't you too old
to be a programmer, Ebenezer Brown?
```

In this program we use the function DosSemSetWait() in the main thread. This function sets the semaphore, and at the same time starts the thread waiting for the semaphore to be cleared. We could also have used the DosSemWait() function, which works the same but does not set the semaphore, and preceded it with DosSemSet(). However, the portmanteaux version is more convenient here.

DosSemSetWait — Sets semaphore and waits for it to clear

```
DosSemSetWait(SemHandle, Timeout);
void far *SemHandle;        /* semaphore handle or address */
long Timeout;               /* -1=wait, 0=return, >0=msecs */
```

The format of this call is identical to that of DosSemRequest(), and the operation is also quite similar. The only difference, as we noted, is that DosSemSetWait() does not reset the semaphore when it becomes clear. Figure 6-3 shows the operation of this function.

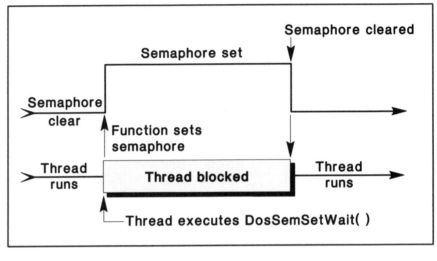

Figure 6-3
Operation of DosSemSetWait( )

When the user has typed the response to a prompt, the second thread clears the semaphore with DosSemClear. This permits the first thread to go on to the next prompt.

One Semaphore Signaling Multiple Threads

In the example above a single thread waited for the semaphore to be cleared. It is also possible for more than one thread to be triggered by the clearing of a semaphore. In the next program five different threads will start to run when a semaphore is cleared. This program is a slight revision of horsrace.c from the last chapter; the only modification is the addition of a semaphore. This semaphore is used to guarantee a fair start to the race. In the original version of the program, each horse started running as soon as its thread was created. This gave an unfair advantage (although not a large one) to those horses created first.

In horstart.c all the horse threads are created as before, but they all wait on a semaphore before beginning to advance the horses. The main program finishes creating all the threads and then clears the semaphore, permitting all the horses to start running at once. The horses appear at half-second intervals on the left edge of the screen, then are released from the "starting gate." Here's the listing:

```
/* horstart.c */
/* semaphore used to start horses */
#define INCL_DOS
#define INCL_SUB
#include <os2.h>
#include <malloc.h>
#define STACK_SIZE 400     /* stack size for threads */
#define NUM_HORSES 5       /* number of horses */
#define FINISH_LINE 75     /* length of track */

unsigned long StartSem=0; /* semaphore to start race */
int dist[NUM_HORSES];      /* table of current distances */
char shape[] = "\xDD\xDF\xDD\xDF";          /* horse shape */

main()
{
    int far *stkptr;        /* stack pointer for new thread */
    void far horse();       /* prototype for new thread */
    unsigned threadID;      /* thread ID number */
    unsigned rc;            /* return code */
    int j;                  /* loop var and thread ID */
    int blank = 0x0720;     /* blank, normal attribute */
    struct _DATETIME TimeBuff;  /* date time buffer */
                            /* clear screen */
    VioScrollUp( 0, 0, -1, -1, -1, (char far *)&blank, 0 );
    VioSetCurPos( 0, 0, 0); /* set cursor to upper left */
                            /* use time to seed randoms */
    DosGetDateTime( &TimeBuff);
    srand( (unsigned)TimeBuff.hundredths );
                            /* set sem until threads going */
    DosSemSet( &StartSem );
    /* loop creates each horse separately */
    for(j=0; j<NUM_HORSES; j++)  {
                            /* get stack space */
        stkptr = (int far *)malloc(STACK_SIZE) + STACK_SIZE;
        *--stkptr = j;      /* j is arg to thread, on stack */
                            /* start new thread */
        if(rc=DosCreateThread(horse,&threadID,(char far
*)stkptr))
            { printf("DosCreateThread error=%u",rc); exit(1); }
        DosSleep( 500L );   /* create horses slowly */
    }                       /* clear semaphore to start race */
    DosSemClear( &StartSem );
    DosExit(0,0);           /* exit this thread */
}
```

(continued)

```
/* horse() */
/* each instance of this thread represents one horse */
void far horse(horseID)
int horseID;                  /* ID of this horse */
{
    int blank = 0x0720;       /* blank, normal attribute */

    while(TRUE)   {

                               /* clear row and draw horse */
        VioWrtNCell( (char far *)&blank, 80, horseID*2, 0, 0);
        VioWrtCharStr( (char far *)shape, 4, horseID*2,
                                        dist[horseID], 0);
                               /* wait for start of race */
        DosSemWait( &StartSem, -1L );
                               /* move horse */
        dist[horseID] += rand() % 4; /* can go 0, 1, 2 or 3 */
                               /* check if race is won */
        if( dist[horseID] >= FINISH_LINE)   {
            VioSetCurPos( 20, 0, 0); /* cursor to lower left */
            printf("HORSE %d IS THE WINNER!!!\n", horseID);
            exit(0);          /* kill all threads */
            }
        DosSleep( 200L );     /* slow down the horses */
    }
}
```

This program operates the same as horsrace.c, but with the improved version a fair start is guaranteed. When several threads are waiting on the same semaphore, it is difficult to predict which one will awaken when it is released, since this depends on which thread happens to be scheduled next.

In this program the threads waiting on the semaphore do not set it. The main thread sets the semaphore as part of its initialization process, then creates the other threads, and finally clears the semaphore to start the race. Since the other threads don't need to set the semaphore when they start waiting on it, they use DosSemWait() rather than DosSemSetWait().

DosSemWait — Waits for semaphore to clear

```
DosSemWait(SemHandle, Timeout);
void far *SemHandle;          /* semaphore handle or address */
long Timeout;                 /* -1=wait, 0=return, >0=msecs */
```

Again, this function looks very much like DosSemRequest() and DosSemSetWait(). The only difference between it and DosSemSet-Wait() is that it does not set the semaphore when it is first invoked. Figure 6-4 shows its operation.

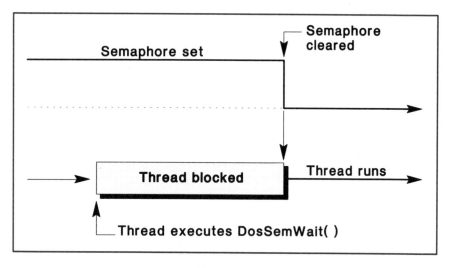

Figure 6-4
Operation of DosSemWait( )

One Thread Waiting on Multiple Semaphores

We've seen how clearing one semaphore can start more than one thread. The inverse situation is also possible: a single thread can wait for one of several different semaphores to be cleared. This might occur, for example, if a thread needed to process the data returned when either one of two disk drives completed a file access, and each drive was associated with a different semaphore.

The API function used for this purpose is DosMuxSemWait(). The function performs a role similar to DosSemWait(), except instead of waiting on only one semaphore, it waits on many and returns when any one of them clears.

The following example demonstrates this function. The main thread creates two semaphores and starts two child threads. Then it uses DosMuxSemWait() to wait until one or the other of the child threads is cleared. Each child thread waits a fixed time and then clears one semaphore. When either semaphore is cleared the main thread awakens and displays a message. Here's the listing:

```
/* mux.c */
/* demonstrates DosMuxSemWait() function */
#define INCL_DOS
#include <os2.h>
#include <malloc.h>
#define STACK_SIZE 1024 /* stack for thread */
#define WAIT -1L         /* -1=wait, 0=no wait, >0=msecs */

unsigned long s1 = 0;   /* first RAM semaphore */
unsigned long s2 = 0;   /* second RAM semaphore */

struct {                /* DosMuxSemWait() list */
   unsigned SemCount;   /*    # of semaphores */
   unsigned res1;       /*    sem1 - reserved; must be 0 */
   unsigned far *ps1;   /*    sem1 - pointer to semaphore */
   unsigned res2;       /*    sem2 - reserved; must be 0 */
   unsigned far *ps2;   /*    sem2 - pointer to semaphore */
} list;

main()
{
   char far *stkptr;       /* stack pointer for new thread */
   void far thread1();     /* prototype for new thread */
   void far thread2();     /* prototype for new thread */
   unsigned threadID;      /* thread ID number */
   unsigned rc;            /* return code */
   unsigned index;         /* semaphore number returned */

   list.SemCount = 2;   /* initialize list */
   list.res1 = 0;
   list.ps1 = (unsigned far *)&s1;
   list.res2 = 0;
   list.ps2 = (unsigned far *)&s2;

   DosSemSet( &s1 );    /* set semaphores */
   DosSemSet( &s2 );

   stkptr = (char far *)malloc(STACK_SIZE) + STACK_SIZE;
   DosCreateThread( thread1, &threadID, stkptr );

   stkptr = (char far *)malloc(STACK_SIZE) + STACK_SIZE;
   DosCreateThread(thread2, &threadID, stkptr );

   if( rc=DosMuxSemWait(&index, (unsigned far *)&list,
                                                WAIT) )
      { printf("DosMuxSemWait error=%u\n", rc); exit(1); }

   printf("The semaphore that caused the event is %d\n",
                                                index);
```

(continued)

```
    DosSleep(4000L);           /* wait for threads to exit */
    exit(0);                   /* exit all threads */
}

/* thread1() */
/* delays before clearing semaphore s1 */
void far thread1()
{
    DosSleep(3000L);           /* pause, then clear semaphore */
    DosSemClear( &s1 );
    DosExit(0,0);              /* exit this thread */
}

/* thread2() */
/* delays before clearing semaphore s2 */
void far thread2()
{
    DosSleep(2000L);           /* pause, then clear semaphore */
    DosSemClear( &s2 );
    DosExit(0,0);              /* exit this thread */
}
```

In this particular program thread 2, which has a shorter delay, is the first to clear the semaphore. When it is cleared the main thread prints the line:

The semaphore that caused the event is 1.

An index value of 1 goes with thread2(). If we had given the shorter delay to the other thread the message would have changed to reflect it. How does the program know which semaphore triggered the DosMuxSemWait() function? Let's look at the arguments to the function.

DosMuxSemWait — Wait for one of several semaphores to clear

```
DosMuxSemWait(Aindex, Alist, Timeout);
unsigned far *Aindex;      /* address to place index number */
void far *Alist;           /* address of semaphore list */
long Timeout;              /* -1=wait, 0=no wait, >0=msecs */
```

The first argument is the address of an index number returned by the function. It tells which of the semaphores on the semaphore list (which we'll look at next), caused the function to return. The numbering starts with 0 for the first semaphore on the list. In our example there are only two possibilities: 0 and 1.

The second argument is the address of a list of semaphores. These are the semaphores the function waits on. The list starts with an initial word which holds the number of semaphores on the list. Each semaphore then requires a word, which is reserved and always 0, followed by a double word which holds a far pointer to the semaphore. The word plus double-word combination is repeated as often as necessary.

In the mux.c example we placed the structure that holds the semaphore list directly into the program. The structure variable is named **list**. If we needed to expand the structure to hold more semaphores, we could add two additional lines per semaphore to the structure.

There is another approach to setting up the semaphore list. The Microsoft header file bsedos.h defines two structures: MUXSEM, which holds the information for one semaphore, and MUXSEMLIST, which holds a count and space for 16 MUXSEM structures. This arrangement can be used instead of placing a structure directly into the program as we've shown. There is even a macro, DEFINEMUXSEM-LIST, in bsedos.h that can be used to create the MUXSEMLIST structure arrangement.

The third argument to DosMuxSemWait() is the ubiquitous timeout. As in other semaphore functions, it specifies whether the function should wait for a semaphore to be cleared, return immediately, or wait a fixed amount of time, which is given in milliseconds.

A peculiarity of DosMuxSemWait() is that it is *edge-triggered*, rather than *level-triggered* as the other semaphore functions are. What does this mean? When any of the other semaphore functions such as DosSemWait(), DosSemSetWait() or DosSemRequest() are waiting on a semaphore, it must become clear *and remain clear* until the function queries it; otherwise they will not return. If a semaphore became clear, and was subsequently set again before a function like DosSemWait() queried it, the function would see only that it was set, and would not return. This is shown in parts b) and c) of Figure 6-5.

With DosMuxSemWait(), on the other hand, the semaphore need be cleared only momentarily for the function to recognize it as cleared. Even if the semaphore is reset before DosMuxSemWait() has a chance to query it, the function still returns as if the semaphore were clear. This is shown in part a) of Figure 6-5.

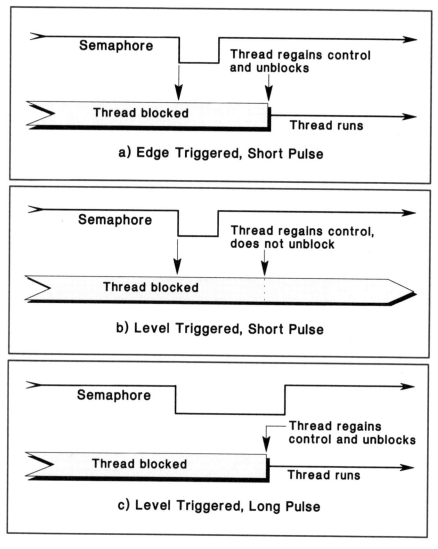

Figure 6-5
Edge and Level Triggering

More Complex Inter-Process Signaling

The next example shows how different processes or threads can be isolated from one another, but still coordinate their activities, using semaphores.

This program is a submarine game. A ship, represented by five graphics characters, moves back and forth randomly along one line of the screen. A submarine, under control of the cursor keys, moves back and forth on another line. Torpedoes can be fired from the submarine by pressing the up-arrow key. If the sub is directly under the ship when the torpedo is fired, the ship's image is replaced by waves, a tone sounds, and a message appears on the screen. Figure 6-6 shows the ship and the submarine stalking it.

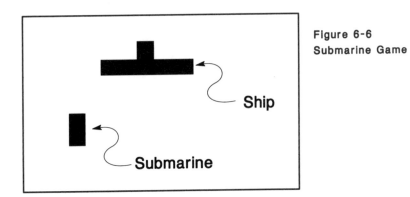

Figure 6-6
Submarine Game

In the program the submarine and the ship are represented by separate threads. The main part of the program, which is responsible for sounding the beep and placing the success message on the screen, is also a separate thread. These threads communicate by means of semaphores. When the submarine fires a torpedo, it uses a semaphore to signal this fact to the ship. The ship then compares its location and that of the torpedo to see if it has been hit. If it has, it uses a semaphore to signal the main() thread, which announces the fact to the user.

```
/* sub.c */
/* submarine game -- demonstrates DosSemWait(), etc. */
#define INCL_DOS
#define INCL_SUB
#include <os2.h>
#include <malloc.h>            /* for malloc() */
```

(continued)

```
#define STACK_SIZE 1024      /* stack for each thread */
#define SEM_WAIT -1L          /* wait for semaphore */
#define SEM_NO_WAIT 0L        /* return immediately */
#define SHIPLINE 10           /* ship will be on this line */
#define SUBLINE 13            /* sub will be on this line */
#define HANDLE 0              /* vio handle always 0 */
#define MIDDLE 40             /* center column of screen */
#define FREQ 256              /* pitch for DosBeep() */
#define DURATION 1000         /* duration for DosBeep() */

unsigned long FireSem = 0;   /* cleared when torpedo fired */
unsigned long SunkSem = 0;   /* cleared when ship sunk */
int torpedopos;              /* pos of torpedo when fired */

main()
{
   char far *stkptr;       /* stack pointer for new threads */
   void far ship();        /* prototype for ship thread */
   void far sub();         /* prototype for sub thread */
   unsigned threadID;      /* thread ID number */
   int blank = 0x7020;     /* blank, reverse video */

                           /* start ship thread */
   stkptr = (char far *)malloc(STACK_SIZE) + STACK_SIZE;
   DosCreateThread( ship, &threadID, stkptr );
                           /* start sub thread */
   stkptr = (char far *)malloc(STACK_SIZE) + STACK_SIZE;
   DosCreateThread( sub, &threadID, stkptr );
   while( TRUE )  {
                           /* clear screen, set cursor */
      VioScrollUp(0, 0, -1, -1, -1, (char far *)&blank, 0);
      VioSetCurPos( 0, 0, 0); /* set cursor to upper left */
                           /* initialize torpedo sem */
      DosSemSet( &FireSem );
                           /* wait for sinking */
      DosSemSetWait( &SunkSem, SEM_WAIT );
      VioWrtTTy("IT'S A HIT!", 11, HANDLE );
      DosBeep( FREQ, DURATION );    /* sound trumpet */
      DosSleep( (long)DURATION*3 ); /* savor victory */
   }
}


/* ship() */
/* calculates ship position and displays it */
/* position determined by random number generator */

char far Xship[] = "\xDC\xDC\xDB\xDC\xDC";  /* ship shape */
char far Xwave[] = "\xF7\xF7\xF7\xF7\xF7";  /* wave shape */
```

(continued)

```
void far ship()
{
    int shippos = MIDDLE;           /* column number of ship */
    int blank = 0x0720;             /* blank, normal attr */
    unsigned rc;                    /* return code */

    while(TRUE)  {                   /* move ship randomly */
       shippos = (rand() & 0x01) ? shippos + rand() % 4 :
                                    shippos - rand() % 4;
                                    /* clear line, draw ship */
       VioWrtNCell( (char far *)&blank, 80, SHIPLINE, 0, 0);
       VioWrtCharStr( Xship, 5, SHIPLINE, shippos, 0);
       rc=DosSemWait( &FireSem, SEM_NO_WAIT );
       if( rc == 0 )  {             /* if torpedo fired, */
          if( torpedopos == shippos+2 )  {  /* and it's a
                                                      hit, */
                                    /* tell main */
             DosSemClear( &SunkSem );
                                    /* draw waves */
             VioWrtCharStr( Xwave, 5, SHIPLINE, shippos, 0);
             DosSleep( (long)DURATION*3 );
             shippos = MIDDLE;      /* start ship in middle */
          }                         /* if sem clear, reset it */
          DosSemSet( &FireSem );
       }
       DosSleep(200L);             /* slow down motion */
    }
}

/* sub() */
/* calculates sub position and displays it */
/* position determined by left-right arrow keys */
#define LEFT_ARROW 75               /* cursor key scan codes */
#define RIGHT_ARROW 77
#define UP_ARROW 72
#define ESCAPE 27                   /* [Esc] key */
#define KBD_WAIT 0                  /* wait for keystroke */
char Xsub[] = "\xDB";               /* sub shape */

void far sub()
{
    int blank = 0x0720;             /* blank, normal attribute */
    int subpos = MIDDLE;            /* column number of sub */
    struct _KBDKEYINFO keydata; /* defined in bsesub.h */
```

(continued)

```
    while(TRUE)  {                    /* clear line, draw sub */
       VioWrtNCell( (char far *)&blank, 80, SUBLINE, 0, 0);
       VioWrtCharStr( (char far *)Xsub, 1, SUBLINE,
                                                    subpos, 0);
                                  /* read keystroke */
       KbdCharIn( &keydata, KBD_WAIT, HANDLE );
       if( keydata.chScan == RIGHT_ARROW )      /* go right */
          subpos++;
       else if( keydata.chScan == LEFT_ARROW ) /* go left */
          subpos--;
       else if( keydata.chScan == UP_ARROW ) { /* shoot */
          torpedopos = subpos;                  /* (tell */
          DosSemClear( &FireSem );              /* ship) */
       }
       else if( keydata.chChar == ESCAPE )      /* exit */
          exit(0);
    }
}
```

The main program sets **SunkSem**, the semaphore indicating that the ship has been sunk, and waits for it to be cleared by the ship. It doesn't need to do anything except wait for the ship to be sunk, so it uses DosSemSetWait() with the WAIT option. On the other hand, while the ship thread is waiting (nervously) for **FireSem**—the semaphore indicating a torpedo has been fired—it also must continuously move the ship. So it uses DosSemWait() with the NO_WAIT option. The sub thread clears this semaphore when the user presses the up-arrow to fire a torpedo. Figure 6-7 shows the relationship of the threads and semaphores.

Notice in this program that the only communication between the different threads is via semaphores (except for the location of the torpedo). This provides a way to isolate the various parts of the program and at the same time simplify the relationships between them. Semaphores can aid structured, modular programming.

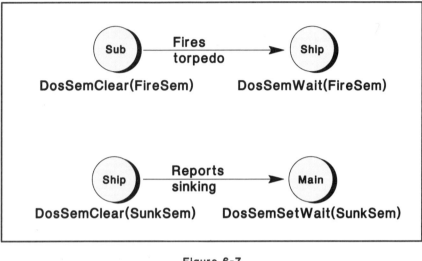

Figure 6-7
Threads and Semaphores in sub.c

System Semaphores

So far we've seen semaphores used to coordinate only between threads. Semaphores can also be used for coordination between different processes. However, different processes can't use global variables for their semaphores, since the memory space of one process is not (ordinarily) known to other processes. For this reason semaphores used between processes must rely on a semaphore variable which is set up and maintained by the system. The semaphore is still in memory, but it is in the operating system's memory space, and is under the system's control. This kind of semaphore is called, not surprisingly, a *system semaphore*.

A program asks the system to create a system semaphore using the DosCreateSem() function. This establishes the semaphore and returns a handle to it, which the program can use thereafter to refer to it. A handle is simply a number (of type **unsigned long**) assigned by the system to a particular semaphore. It is similar to the file handles used to identify files.

When the semaphore is created it is given a name which looks very much like a file name. The name is preceded by the "pathname" **\SEM**, and just as with files, consists of up to eight letters followed by an optional three-letter extension.

Processes other than the one that created it can access a system semaphore using the DosOpenSem() function, specifying the same name as that used in DosCreateSem(). DosOpenSem() will return the handle so the semaphore can be accessed by the new process.

Here's an example of two processes using a system semaphore for mutual exclusion: coordinating access to the screen. The effect is similar to that in the xdisp2.c program in the section on RAM semaphores. As in that example, if no semaphores are used, the output of the two processes is scrambled on the screen. Coordination is necessary to ensure that the message from one process has a chance to finish before the message from the other process begins. The messages are lower- and upper-case versions of an old Turkish proverb.

Here's the parent process:

```
/* psysem.c */
/* shares screen with chsysem.c, using system semaphore */
#define INCL_DOS
#include <os2.h>
#define LENGTH 40              /* length of object buffer */
#define FLAGS 1                /* asynchronously, no trace */
#define COMS 0L                /* no command-line args */
#define ENVS 0L                /* no environment variables */
#define WAIT -1L               /* semaphore waits for clear */
#define NO_EX 1                /* sem not exclusively owned */
#define KILLALL 0              /* kill process and children */
main()
{
    void far *SemHandle;        /* handle of system sem */
    struct _RESULTCODES childID;  /* new process ID */
    char fbuf[LENGTH];          /* buffer for fail-object */
    unsigned rc;                /* return code */
                                /* create system semaphore */
    if( rc=DosCreateSem( NO_EX, &SemHandle,
                                    "\\SEM\\DISP.EXC" ) )
        { printf("DosCreateSem error=%u\n",rc); exit(1); }
                                /* start child process */
    if( rc=DosExecPgm( fbuf, LENGTH, FLAGS, COMS, ENVS,
                            &childID, "CHSYSEM.EXE" ) )
        { printf("DosExecPgm error=%u\n",rc); exit(1); }
                                /* continuously print text */
    while( !kbhit() )  {        /* until key is pressed */
        DosSemRequest( SemHandle, WAIT );
        printf("He that would ");
        printf("speak truth ");
        printf("must have one foot ");
        printf("in the stirrup.\n");
        DosSemClear( SemHandle );
    }                           /* close semaphore */
    if( rc=DosCloseSem( SemHandle ) )
        { printf("DosCloseSem error=%u\n",rc); exit(1); }
    exit(0);                    /* return to dos */
}
```

This process creates the semaphore with DosCreateSem(), and then starts a child process. It then uses DosSemRequest() and DosSemClear() to implement mutual exclusion on a group of printf() statements. The statements are printed over and over until the user presses any key, at which point the process closes the semaphore with DosCloseSem() and terminates itself.

DosCreateSem — Create system semaphore

```
DosCreateSem(Ownership, Ahandle, Name);
unsigned Ownership;        /* 0=exclusive, 1=not exclusive */
void far * far *Ahandle;   /* address for handle */
char far *Name;            /* semaphore name */
```

The DosCreateSem() function takes three parameters. The first is a flag with two possible settings. A value of 0 indicates the semaphore will be unknown to other processes; the caller maintains exclusive ownership. A value of 1 indicates that other processes will be able to access the semaphore; this is the more usual setting. The second parameter is the address where the function can return the file handle, and the third is the name of the semaphore. The creator of the semaphore can use any name, so long as it begins with the pathname **\SEM** and follows the conventions for naming files.

Notice that the backslashes in the semaphore's pathname are doubled. This is because the backslash is an escape character in C; to be interpreted literally this character must be preceded by another backslash.

DosCloseSem — Close system semaphore

```
DosCloseSem(Handle);
void far *Handle;          /* semaphore handle */
```

The DosCloseSem() function takes only one argument: the semaphore handle. We'll talk more about this function in a moment.

Here's the child process executed by psysem.c:

```
/* chsysem.c */
/* child process of psysem.c */
/* prints text on screen */
#define INCL_DOS
#include <os2.h>
#define TIMES 40               /* number of times to loop */
#define WAIT -1L               /* wait for semaphore to clear */
```
(continued)

```
main()
{
    void far *SemHandle;   /* handle for system semaphore */
    int count;             /* loop variable */
    unsigned rc;           /* return code */

                           /* open existing system semaphore */
    if( rc = DosOpenSem( &SemHandle, "\\SEM\\DISP.EXC" ) )
        { printf("DosOpenSem error=%u\n",rc); exit(1); }
    for( count=0; count<TIMES; count++)  {
        if( rc = DosSemRequest( SemHandle, WAIT ) )
            { printf("DosSemRequest error=%u\n",rc); exit(1); }
        printf("%d ", count);
        printf("HE THAT WOULD ");
        printf("SPEAK TRUTH ");
        printf("MUST HAVE ONE FOOT ");
        printf("IN THE STIRRUP\n");
        if( rc=DosSemClear( SemHandle ) )
            { printf("DosSemClear error=%u\n",rc); exit(1); }
    }
    exit(0);                /* exit this process */
}
```

The child process establishes contact with the semaphore using DosOpenSem(). Having done this, it then uses a **for** loop to execute all the **printf()** statements a fixed number of times. As in the parent, DosSemRequest() and DosSemWait() provide mutually exclusive access to the screen, using the semaphore handle obtained in DosOpenSem(). When the loop has terminated, the child exits.

DosOpenSem — Opens an existing system semaphore

```
DosCreateSem(Ahandle, Name);
void far *far *Ahandle;         /* address to put handle */
char far *Name;                 /* semaphore name */
```

The DosOpenSem() function uses the name of the semaphore as its second argument. This must be the same name as that used in DosCreateSem(). The two processes know they are talking about the same semaphore because they use the same name when creating and opening it. The first argument of this function is the address where the semaphore's handle will be placed. This is the same handle as that returned by other processes for this semaphore.

The DosOpenSem() function cannot be used on a semaphore that does not exist. An attempt to open a semaphore that has not yet been created with DosCreateSem() results in an error return.

Once a semaphore has been created, it remains in existence until all the processes that have created it or opened it have either closed it with DosCloseSem() or exited.

Closing a System Semaphore

A semaphore cannot be closed with DosCloseSem() unless it is already cleared, (that is, unowned). An attempt to close a set semaphore results in return code 102, ERROR_SEM_IS_SET. This makes sense: there's no point in leaving a semaphore set—and claiming you own its associated resource—if you no longer exist. Other processes waiting on the semaphore would wait forever for the non-existent process to clear it.

Semaphore Data Types

The data types used for system semaphores, as defined in Microsoft header files, deserve a word of explanation.

The reality of the situation, independent of C language data types, is that semaphores are variables occupying four bytes of memory. This is what an assembly language programmer works with.

In the case of RAM semaphores, this four-byte variable occupies memory in the application's data space. The API semaphore functions, such as DosSemRequest(), work with the address of this semaphore variable.

System semaphores are different. When DosCreateSem() or DosOpenSem() is invoked, the system returns a four-byte quantity which is the *handle* of the semaphore. This is not an address, it is only a number identifying the semaphore. DosSemRequest() and the other API semaphore functions work with this number directly, not with its address.

Since the semaphore API functions work with both RAM and system semaphores, their semaphore argument is sometimes the address of a four-byte variable and sometimes simply the four-byte variable itself. Given this situation, what C data types should be used for the semaphore in the prototype of the API functions?

One solution is to make the type of the argument in the functions **unsigned long**, and make both RAM semaphores and system semaphore handles **unsigned long.** Using this scheme, no typecasting is necessary for system semaphores, but RAM semaphores must be cast from **unsigned long far *** to **unsigned long**. This is the solution used in the first release of Microsoft's software development kit, and still used in the IBM development kit.

The scheme currently used in the Microsoft header files avoids the need to typecast the argument. The prototypes for the API semaphore functions define the semaphore argument as type **void far ***. RAM semaphores are defined as type **unsigned long**, so their addresses match this type. System semaphore handles are placed in a variable of type **void far ***, so they match the type as well, even though they are not really pointers to anything.

The Untimely Death of the Semaphore Owner

What happens if the process that owns a system semaphore at a particular moment dies, leaving the semaphore set? All the other processes that are waiting for the resource protected by the semaphore will wait forever for the semaphore to be freed. The resource will be lost to the system, and if it is an important resource, the system may be paralyzed.

In the psysem.c program we do our duty on termination: the semaphore is cleared at the end of the loop, before the program closes it and exits. This permits the child program, chsysem.c, to continue running correctly even if the parent is terminated first. You can experiment with this by hitting any key before the child has printed all forty lines. The parent stops printing, but the child continues. In the sample output shown below, the user hits a key following line 26. At this point the parent exits, leaving the child to continue with no difficulty until all 39 lines were printed.

```
- - - - - - - - - - - - - - - - - - - - - - - - - - - - - - -
He that would speak truth must have one foot in the stirrup.
He that would speak truth must have one foot in the stirrup.
25 HE THAT WOULD SPEAK TRUTH MUST HAVE ONE FOOT IN THE STIRRUP
He that would speak truth must have one foot in the stirrup.
He that would speak truth must have one foot in the stirrup.
26 HE THAT WOULD SPEAK TRUTH MUST HAVE ONE FOOT IN THE STIRRUP
He that would speak truth must have one foot in the stirrup.
27 HE THAT WOULD SPEAK TRUTH MUST HAVE ONE FOOT IN THE STIRRUP
28 HE THAT WOULD SPEAK TRUTH MUST HAVE ONE FOOT IN THE STIRRUP
29 HE THAT WOULD SPEAK TRUTH MUST HAVE ONE FOOT IN THE STIRRUP
30 HE THAT WOULD SPEAK TRUTH MUST HAVE ONE FOOT IN THE STIRRUP
- - - - - - - - - - - - - - - - - - - - - - - - - - - - - - -
```

But what happens if a program is irresponsible and leaves a semaphore in the set position when it exits? Or if it is killed by another process, or experiences a fatal system error, and must be terminated? It turns out that it is possible for other processes, if they are prepared, to avoid catastrophe. Here's how it works.

If the owner of a set semaphore dies, the next process to ask for the semaphore will return with code 105, ERROR_SEM_OWNER_DIED. At the same time, this process inherits ownership of the semaphore, like a soldier taking the flag from a falling comrade. Now the new process, and other processes using the resource, can go on using the semaphore, doing their jobs as before.

Here are revised versions of the psysem.c and chsysem.c that demonstrate how this works. The parent has been modified to exit, with the semaphore set, when the user presses a key:

```c
/* psysem2.c */
/* shares screen with chsysem.c, using system semaphore */
/* semaphore remains set on exit */
#define INCL_DOS
#include <os2.h>
#define LENGTH 40            /* length of object buffer */
#define FLAGS 1              /* asynchronously, no trace */
#define COMS 0L              /* no command-line args */
#define ENVS 0L              /* no environment variables */
#define WAIT -1L             /* semaphore waits for clear */
#define NO_EX 1              /* sem not exclusively owned */
#define KILLALL 0            /* kill process and children */
main()
{
    void far *SemHandle;     /* handle of system sem */
    struct _RESULTCODES childID;  /* new process ID */
    char fbuf[LENGTH];       /* buffer for fail-object */
    unsigned rc;             /* return code */
                             /* create system semaphore */
    if( rc=DosCreateSem( NO_EX, &SemHandle,
                                  "\\SEM\\DISP.EXC" ) )
       { printf("DosCreateSem error=%u\n",rc); exit(1); }
                             /* start child process */
    if( rc=DosExecPgm( fbuf, LENGTH, FLAGS, COMS, ENVS,
                             &childID,"CHSYSEM2.EXE" ) )
       { printf("DosExecPgm error=%u\n",rc); exit(1); }
    while(TRUE)  {           /* continuously print text */
      DosSemRequest( SemHandle, WAIT );
      printf("He that would ");
      printf("speak truth ");
      if( kbhit() )          /* if keypress, exit with */
         exit(0);            /* semaphore set to owned */
      printf("must have one foot ");
      printf("in the stirrup.\n");
      DosSemClear( SemHandle );
    }
}
```

The exit takes place in the loop, while the parent owns the semaphore and is writing to the screen.

Here's a revised child process, modified to deal with the untimely death of the parent:

```c
/* chsysem2.c */
/* child process of psysem2.c */
/* prints text on screen, recovers semaphore */
#define INCL_DOS
#include <os2.h>
#define TIMES 40         /* number of times to loop */
#define WAIT -1L          /* wait for semaphore to clear */
main()
{
    void far *SemHandle; /* handle for system semaphore */
    int count;           /* loop variable */
    unsigned rc;         /* return code */

                         /* open existing system semaphore */
    if( rc = DosOpenSem( &SemHandle, "\\SEM\\DISP.EXC" ) )
       { printf("DosOpenSem error=%u\n",rc); exit(1); }
    for( count=0; count<TIMES; count++)  {
                         /* try to obtain semaphore */
       rc = DosSemRequest( SemHandle, WAIT );
       if( rc == 105 )
          printf("\n*** Owner has died ***\n");
       else if( rc != 0 )
          { printf("DosSemRequest error=%u\n",rc); exit(1); }
       printf("%d ", count);
       printf("HE THAT WOULD ");
       printf("SPEAK TRUTH ");
       printf("MUST HAVE ONE FOOT ");
       printf("IN THE STIRRUP\n");
       if( rc=DosSemClear( SemHandle ) )
          { printf("DosSemClear error=%u\n",rc); exit(1); }
    }
    exit(0);              /* exit this process */
}
```

If the child finds an error code returned from DosSemRequest(), it checks to see if it is error 105. If so, it knows it has acquired ownership of the semaphore, and that it (and other processes) can go on using the semaphore as before.

Here's a sample of output when the user terminates the irresponsible program in the middle of its output:

```
- - - - - - - - - - - - - - - - - - - - - - - - - - - - - - - - - -
He that would speak truth must have one foot in the stirrup.
7 HE THAT WOULD SPEAK TRUTH MUST HAVE ONE FOOT IN THE STIRRUP
8 HE THAT WOULD SPEAK TRUTH MUST HAVE ONE FOOT IN THE STIRRUP
He that would speak truth must have one foot in the stirrup.
He that would speak truth
*** Owner has died ***
9 HE THAT WOULD SPEAK TRUTH MUST HAVE ONE FOOT IN THE STIRRUP
10 HE THAT WOULD SPEAK TRUTH MUST HAVE ONE FOOT IN THE STIRRUP
11 HE THAT WOULD SPEAK TRUTH MUST HAVE ONE FOOT IN THE STIRRUP
- - - - - - - - - - - - - - - - - - - - - - - - - - - - - - - - - -
```

The new owner prints a message indicating its discovery that the previous owner has died, and then goes on operating the semaphore and printing its numbered lines as before. (Although not shown in the example, the new owner should also close the semaphore when it terminates.)

Recursive Semaphore Use

System semaphores, if they are created with the exclusive option set, can be set recursively. What does this mean, and why would it be necessary?

Imagine a situation where a thread in a word processing program writes text, supplied by the user, to the screen. This function uses a semaphore to control screen access, so other processes will not interfere with it. Another function in the same thread is occasionally used to write certain predefined phrases to the screen, perhaps in response to the user pressing special keys. This function also uses the semaphore. Now, suppose the first function is in the middle of writing something and needs to call the second function to insert a phrase in the text.

The first function has set the semaphore, indicating ownership of the screen. It can't release it because it isn't done writing. So when it calls the second function, the second function will find the screen semaphore set, and will be denied access. Or will it?

It turns out that if the second function is in the same thread as the first, it will be allowed access to the semaphore (and presumably to the associated resource). This is a convenience to the programmer: the assumption is that it is all right for *the same thread* to access the resource a second time, since a thread would not attempt to interfere with its own operation.

But if two functions have successfully claimed ownership of the semaphore, how does the system know when to release it? If it's released when the second function does a DosSemClear(), other processes might then interfere with the first function, which is not yet done with it. To solve this problem, the semaphore maintains a count. Each time it is successfully requested, the count is incremented; and each time it is cleared, the count is decremented. In the case of the two functions described, the count will be incremented from 0 to 1 by the first function, and again from 1 to 2 by the second function. When the second function releases the semaphore, the count will be decremented from 2 to 1, and when the first function releases it, the count will return to 0, so other processes can use the resource.

Other Uses of System Semaphores

The examples we showed earlier for RAM semaphores could all be modified to work between processes as system semaphores. One process creates the system semaphore with DosCreateSem(), and other processes can access it with DosOpenSem(). From then on, the other semaphore functions can be used just as they were between threads. These include DosSemSet(), DosSemClear(), DosSemWait(), DosSemSetWait(), and DosMuxSemWait().

Timer Functions and System Semaphores

Sometimes a program needs to be reminded when a certain time interval has passed. Perhaps the program is waiting for something that may never happen (such as a dial tone or carrier in a telecommunications program). While it is waiting, we want the program to continue processing (perhaps it needs to continue reading keyboard characters, for example). After a time we want the program to realize it has been waiting for a long time, and say to itself, "Well, I guess the event is never going to happen, so I better do something else." The "something else," for example, might be notifying the user that there is no dial tone.

Or, a program may need to be reminded to do something at fixed intervals. Perhaps it is desirable to sample the temperature of the cooling water in a nuclear reactor every ten seconds.

OS/2 makes available several functions which provide asynchronous delay and interval timing. ("Asynchronous" means that the timers run independently of the program.) These functions make use of system semaphores. A delay function causes a semaphore to be cleared after a fixed delay, and a timer function causes a semaphore to be cleared repeatedly at fixed intervals.

The following example shows the delay function, called Dos-TimerAsync(), at work. When started, the program begins to print a series of numbers. When the delay, which has been set to one second (1000 milliseconds) is over, the program stops. In a more realistic situation, instead of printing numbers on the screen, the program would presumably accomplish useful work while waiting for the delay to time out.

```c
/* delay.c */
/* waits fixed time before stopping */
/* uses asynchronous time delay */
#define INCL_DOS
#include <os2.h>
#define NO_EX 1              /* no exclusive ownership */
#define NO_WAIT 0L           /* -1=wait, 0=nowait, >0=msecs */
#define FREQ 1000            /* hertz for DosBeep() */
#define DURATION 300         /* msecs for DosBeep() */
#define MSECS 1000L          /* msecs for DosTimerAsync() */
#define ERR_SEM_TIMEOUT 121 /* return code if sem owned */
main()
{
    void far *SemHandle;     /* from DosCreateSem() */
    unsigned short TimerHandle;  /* from DosTimerAsync() */
    char far *SemName = "\\SEM\\DELAY.SEM";
    int count;               /* loop counter */
    unsigned rc;             /* return code */

                             /* create semaphore */
    if( rc=DosCreateSem( NO_EX, &SemHandle, SemName ) )
        { printf("DosCreateSem error=%u\n",rc); exit(1); }
    DosSemSet( SemHandle ); /* set semaphore */
                             /* start timer */
    if ( rc=DosTimerAsync( MSECS, SemHandle, &TimerHandle) )
         { printf("DosTimerAsync error=%u\n",rc); exit(1); }
    do {                     /* wait for semaphore */
       printf("%d ", count++);              /* busy work */
       rc = DosSemWait( SemHandle, NO_WAIT );/* sem clear? */
    } while ( rc==ERR_SEM_TIMEOUT );        /* not yet */
    if( rc != 0 )                           /* check error */
        { printf("DosSemWait error=%u\n",rc); exit(1); }
                             /* wait is over */
    printf("\nThe delay has timed out.\n");
    DosBeep( FREQ, DURATION );
}
```

The output from the program looks something like this (the dotted line is substituted for the intermediate numbers to save space):

```
0 1 2 3 4 5 6 7 8 9 10 11 12 13 14 15 16 17 18 19 20 21 22 23 24
- - - - - - - - - - -- -- -- -- -- -- -- -- -- -- -- -- -- -- --
221 222 223 224 225 226 227 228 229 230 231 232 233 234 235 236
237 238 239
The delay has timed out.
```

The actual number of digits printed varies, depending on how much time the scheduler gives to the program before the delay is over. The actual time interval should always be the same.

The timer needs a semaphore to communicate with the program. Thus the program must first create a system semaphore, and set it. It is important that the **no exclusive** option is used when creating the semaphore. The program then passes the handle of the semaphore, obtained from DosCreateSem(), along to DosTimerAsync().

DosTimerAsync — Starts asynchronous time delay

```
DosTimerAsync(Interval, SemHandle, ATimerHandle);
unsigned long Interval;            /* delay time in msecs */
void far *SemHandle;               /* semaphore handle */
unsigned short far *ATimerHandle;  /* address for timer
                                      handle */
```

DosTimerAsync() takes three arguments. The first is the delay time in milliseconds. The timer starts running as soon as the function is issued, even if the semaphore is set later. The second argument is the semaphore handle. The third is the address of a word to hold the timer handle. The timer handle is a number returned by the system to identify a particular timer. This number can be used by the DosTimerStop() function, which we'll encounter in the next example.

Once the timer is started, the program can wait for it to clear the semaphore with DosSemWait() function, just as the program might wait for any other semaphore to be cleared. In delay.c we use the NO_WAIT option with DosSemWait() so the program can continue with its task of printing numbers.

An Interval Timer

A function similar to DosTimerAsync() is used to clear a semaphore repeatedly at fixed intervals, rather than only once. This is DosTimerStart(). In the following example this function is used to provide a beep from the speaker every second, while at the same time the program prints numbers on the screen. When the user presses a key, the timer is turned off by another function, DosTimerStop(). The numbers continue to be printed, but the beeping ceases. Use [Ctrl] [C] to exit the program.

```
/* timer.c */
/* beeps every second */
/* uses asynchronous time interval */
#define INCL_DOS
#include <os2.h>
#define NO_EX 1              /* no exclusive ownership */
#define NO_WAIT 0L           /* -1=wait, 0=nowait, >0=msecs */
#define FREQ 1000            /* hertz for DosBeep() */
#define DURATION 300         /* msecs for DosBeep() */
#define MSECS 1000L          /* msecs for DosTimerAsync() */
#define ERR_SEM_TIMEOUT 121 /* return code if sem owned */
main()
{
   void far *SemHandle;      /* from DosCreateSem() */
   unsigned short TimerHandle;  /* from DosTimerStart() */
   char far *SemName = "\\SEM\\INTERVAL";
   int count;                /* loop counter */
   unsigned rc;             /* return code */
                            /* create semaphore */
   if( rc=DosCreateSem( NO_EX, &SemHandle, SemName ) )
      { printf("DosCreateSem error=%u\n",rc); exit(1); }
   DosSemSet( SemHandle ); /* set semaphore */
                            /* start timer */
   if ( rc=DosTimerStart( MSECS, SemHandle, &TimerHandle) )
       { printf("DosTimerStart error=%u\n",rc); exit(1); }

   while (TRUE)   {
      printf("%d ", count++);                 /* busy work */
      rc = DosSemWait( SemHandle, NO_WAIT );/* sem clear? */
      if( rc==0 )  {                          /* if so, */
         DosBeep(FREQ, DURATION );            /* beep, */
         DosSemSet( SemHandle );              /* reset sem */
      }
      else                                    /* check for */
         if( rc != ERR_SEM_TIMEOUT )          /* error */
            { printf("DosSemWait error=%u\n",rc); exit(1); }
      if( kbhit() )  {                         /* if keypress */
         DosTimerStop( TimerHandle );         /* stop timer */
         getch();                             /* clear char */
      }
   }
}
```

Once the semaphore has been created and set, and the timer started, the program enters a loop. In the loop it prints its number and executes DosSemWait(). If the result code from this function indicates the semaphore has been cleared, the program sounds a beep and resets the semaphore. The system will clear it again in one second.

DosTimerStart — Starts interval timer

```
DosTimerStart(Interval, SemHandle, ATimerHandle);
unsigned long Interval;            /* delay time in msecs */
void far *SemHandle;               /* semaphore handle */
unsigned short far *ATimerHandle;  /* address for timer
                                      handle */
```

The DosTimerStart() function takes the same arguments as DosTimerAsync().

The function DosTimerStop() stops the timer. Stopping the timer has no effect on the associated semaphore; it remains in whatever state it was set to when DosTimerStop() was issued.

DosTimerStop — Stops delay or interval timer

```
DosTimerStop(TimerHandle);
unsigned short TimerHandle;        /* timer handle */
```

DosTimerStop() takes only one argument: the timer handle returned by DosTimerAsync() or DosTimerStart(), whichever started the timer.

Deadlocks

We should not leave a chapter devoted to questions of interprocess synchronization without mentioning the problem of deadlocks. A deadlock arises when two or more processes acquire ownership of resources in such a way that each process is waiting for another to release a resource. None can continue because all are waiting, so the application comes to a halt.

For example, consider two processes, 1 and 2, each of which simultaneously requires two resources, A and B, to carry out a task. Suppose process 1 wants to use resource A, and sets a semaphore with DosSemRequest() to indicate that it has acquired ownership of the resource. It is about to acquire resource B, but at that moment it is interrupted by process 2, which acquires resource B. Now process 1 can't continue because it can't acquire resource B, and process 2 can't continue because it can't acquire resource A. The result is shown in Figure 6-8. Here the fact that the arrows form a loop indicates deadlock: each process is waiting for a resource owned by another process that is waiting for another resource. The application is halted and cannot start again without outside intervention.

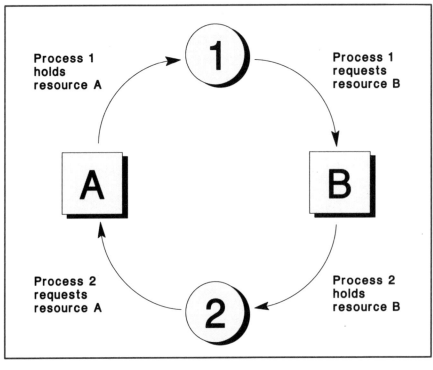

Figure 6-8
Deadlock

Here's a program example which shows a deadlock in action. Two threads each try to write a buffer of data to the screen. The memory buffer is considered to be a resource, and is protected by the semaphore **BuffSem** so that only one thread can access it at a time. The screen is another resource, protected by the semaphore **DispSem**.

The main thread fills the buffer with data and starts thread 1 and thread 2. These threads occupy themselves in writing the contents of the buffer to the screen. However, each one is careful to do no writing until it has established—using the two semaphores—that it has exclusive access to both the buffer and the screen.

```
/* deadlock.c */
/* demonstrates deadlock */
/* two threads require access to two resources */
#define INCL_DOS
#include <os2.h>
#include <malloc.h>        /* for malloc() */
#include <string.h>        /* for strcpy() */
#define STACK_SIZE 1024     /* stack for each thread */
#define WAIT -1L            /* -1=wait, 0=return, >0=msecs */

struct  {                   /* mathematician info */
    char name[30];          /* name */
    int birth;              /* birthdate */
    char accomp[40];        /* accomplishment */
} math;                     /* shared structure */

unsigned long DispSem = 0; /* screen semaphore */
unsigned long BuffSem = 0; /* data semaphore */

main()
{
    char far *stkptr;       /* stack pointer for new threads */
    void far thread1();     /* prototypes for new threads */
    void far thread2();
    unsigned threadID;      /* thread ID number */

                            /* fill data structure */
    strcpy( math.name, "Pierre de Fermat" );
    math.birth = 1601;
    strcpy( math.accomp, "Fermat's last theorem" );

                            /* start threads */
    stkptr = (char far *)malloc(STACK_SIZE) + STACK_SIZE;
    DosCreateThread( thread1, &threadID, stkptr );

    stkptr = (char far *)malloc(STACK_SIZE) + STACK_SIZE;
    DosCreateThread( thread2, &threadID, stkptr );
    DosExit(0,0);           /* exit this thread */
}

/* thread1() */
/* reads and displays data */
void far thread1()
{
    int j;
    while(TRUE)  {
        DosSemRequest( &DispSem, WAIT );
        for(j=0; j<100; j++)
            j = j + (j-j);
        DosSemRequest( &BuffSem, WAIT );
```

(continued)

```
        printf("\nThread 1 displaying data\n");
        printf("Mathematician:    %s\n", math.name);
        printf("Date of birth:    %4d\n", math.birth);
        printf("Accomplishment:   %s\n", math.accomp);
        DosSemClear( &DispSem );
        DosSemClear( &BuffSem );
    }
}

/* thread2() */
/* reads and displays data */
void far thread2()
{
    while(TRUE)   {
        DosSemRequest( &BuffSem, WAIT );
        DosSemRequest( &DispSem, WAIT );
        printf("\nThread 2 displaying data\n");
        printf("Mathematician:    %s\n", math.name);
        printf("Date of birth:    %4d\n", math.birth);
        printf("Accomplishment:   %s\n", math.accomp);
        DosSemClear( &DispSem );
        DosSemClear( &BuffSem );
    }
}
```

To make sure the deadlock occurs fairly often we inserted a delay loop in thread 1, between the DosSemRequest() functions for the display and the buffer. If we'd used a DosSleep() here deadlock would have occurred immediately; and if we'd omitted it, deadlock would occur only rarely. As it is, deadlock occurs after the program has been running for half a minute or so. The effect is disconcerting: the program displays a large number of copies of the data file with no problem, and then suddenly freezes. (You may need to adjust the delay loop to achieve comparable results on your computer.)

The Dining Philosophers Problem

Deadlocks are the subject of much research in computer science. There is even a famous problem, called the "Dining Philosophers," which demonstrates deadlocks. In this problem five philosophers (representing processes) are imagined to be sitting around a circular table, eating spaghetti. Each spends part of his time thinking (presumably about weighty philosophical issues) and part of his time eating. To eat the spaghetti each philosopher must use two forks (representing resources) at once. However, only five forks have been provided, one between each plate, as shown in Figure 6-9.

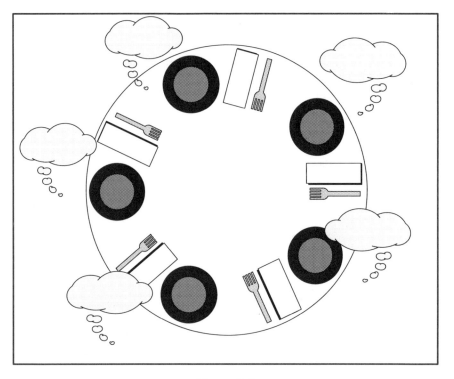

Figure 6-9
The Dining Philosophers

Each philosopher from time to time tries to pick up the fork on his left. If successful, he tries to pick up the fork on his right. If he obtains both forks he eats for a while before putting them both down to resume thinking. This system might work for a while, assuming the philosophers have impulses to eat at random times. However, imagine what happens if, say, each philosopher takes the fork on his right and then waits for the fork on his left to become available. Deadlock ensues and they all starve.

It is difficult to find a strategy that is guaranteed to prevent deadlock in all situations. Fortunately deadlock can usually be avoided in simple programming situations with few shared resources. In the deadlock.c program, for example, deadlock can be avoided by having the two threads request the resources in the same order, rather than in opposite orders as in the listing. However, when programs become complex, with many processes using many resources, deadlock can become a problem.

Summary

In this chapter we've learned how semaphores are used to coordinate the activities of different processes and threads. There are two main kinds of semaphores: RAM semaphores and system semaphores. Their characteristics are summarized in the tables below.

RAM Semaphores

Usage:	between threads
Consist of:	external *unsigned long* variable
Created by:	declaring variable
Initialized:	by setting variable to 0 (unowned)
Known to:	other threads with access to external variable
Altered by:	any thread with access to variable
Removed:	exists for life of file containing variable

System Semaphores

Usage:	between processes
Consist of:	variable controlled by system
Created by:	DosCreateSem()
Initialized:	set to unowned when created
Known to:	other process using DosSemOpen()
Altered by:	process that created it, other processes if *NoExclusive* flag set
Removed:	when all processes that opened or created it issue DosCloseSem() or exit

The following table summarizes the semaphore API functions. Listed are the function, the effect the function has on the semaphore, and the effect it has on the thread that issued it.

API function	Effect on semaphore	Effect on thread
DosSemClear()	clear to unowned	none
DosSemSet()	set to owned	none
DosSemRequest()		
if sem clear	set to owned	return to caller
if sem owned	none	wait until cleared
when sem clears	set to owned	return to caller
DosSemWait()		
if sem clear	none	return to caller
if sem owned	none	wait until cleared
when sem clears	none	return to caller
DosSemSetWait()		
if sem clear	set to owned	wait until cleared
if sem owned	none	wait until cleared
when sem clears	none	return to caller
DosMuxSemWait()		
if any sem clear	none	return to caller
if all sems owned	none	wait until cleared
(even momentary clearing unblocks thread)		

The phrase "wait until cleared" in the chart above actually offers three options: wait indefinitely for the semaphore to clear, wait a fixed length of time, or return immediately. The last two return with the ERROR_SEM_TIMEOUT return code (number 121 decimal) if the semaphore is set. Note that "set" and "owned" are synonyms, and are the opposite of "cleared" and "unowned".

In this chapter we learned that mutually exclusive access to a shared resource can be arranged using the functions DosSem-Request() and DosSemClear(). Signals can be sent between threads, or between processes, using DosSemSet() and DosSemClear() to directly manipulate the semaphore, while waiting for it to clear with DosSemWait(), DosSemSetWait(), and DosMuxSemWait() as appropriate.

We also learned about the timer functions, DosTimerAsync(), DosTimerStart(), and DosTimerStop(), which provide time delays and intervals through the medium of semaphores.

Finally we learned that it is possible for a system to come to a halt in a state of deadlock, if several processes make the wrong decisions about when to access resources.

DIRECTORIES

Chapter 7

A large number of API functions are provided to handle various aspects of the file system. We divide these functions into two groups. Functions in the first group treat files as unopened units: they are concerned with directory and file management. Functions in the second group read, write, and make other changes to the contents of opened files. In this chapter we examine functions in the first group. Chapter 8 covers the second group, and Chapter 9 discusses the use of files in a multitasking environment.

The structure of files in OS/2 is essentially the same as in MS-DOS. Many OS/2 directory and file API functions have counterparts in MS-DOS, as INT-21 calls, so the purpose of some functions we discuss may be familiar. However, there are differences between OS/2 and MS-DOS file functions. API functions must operate in a multitasking environment, so they are, in some cases, more complex than their MS-DOS equivalents. Also, some API functions are designed specifically to take advantage of a multitasking environment.

The first part of this chapter examines directories, and the functions that manipulate them. In the second part we see how to manipulate files as units: how to search for them, move them, and delete them.

Manipulating Directories

There are many reasons why it might be desirable to manipulate directories from within a program. For example, an installation routine in an application might want to create a new directory to contain the application's files. Or, to facilitate file access, an application might want to change the current directory to one containing certain files. Or a utility program might copy a directory tree from one place on a disk to another, or from one disk to another.

In this section we'll examine the API functions dealing with such operations.

Making and Removing Directories

Let's look first at a pair of programs, one which creates directories, and one which removes them. These programs work very much like the DOS commands MKDIR and RMDIR.

Here's the first program:

```
/* mkdir2.c */
/* creates a sub-directory */
/* at end of current directory or specified path */
#define INCL_DOS
#include <os2.h>
```

(continued)

```
main(argc, argv)
int argc;
char *argv[];
{
    unsigned rc;

    if( argc != 2 )
        { printf("Syntax mkdir2 dirname"); exit(1); }
    if( rc=DosMkdir( argv[1], 0L ) )  {
        if( rc==3 )
            printf("Path not found");
        else if ( rc==5 )
            printf("Can't make directory");
        else
            printf("DosMkdir error=%u",rc);
        exit(1);
    }
    exit(0);
}
```

This program uses a command-line argument to obtain the pathname, and the API function DosMkdir() to create the new directory.

DosMkdir — Make new directory

```
DosMkdir(Pathname, Reserved);
char far *Pathname;   /* ASCIIZ pathname of new directory */
unsigned long Reserved;   /* reserved; must be 0 */
```

This function needs only one piece of data: the pathname of the new directory. The second parameter, a long word, is reserved for future expansion of OS/2, and must be initialized to zero. This reserved double word is common to many API file functions.

To create a sub-directory in the current directory, type only its name on the command-line:

`C>mkdir2 newdir`

To create a sub-directory in a directory other than the current one, type a complete pathname:

`C>mkdir2 \letters\xyzcorp\newdir`

The pathname can include a drive letter (A to Z or a to z, followed by a colon) to create directories on different drives.

The program prints explicit messages for the most common errors encountered with this function. Attempts to create directories on non-existent disk drives (such as G), or at the end of non-existent paths, elicit the "Path not found" message. "Can't make directory" results if a directory of the specified name and path already exists.

The next program removes directories. Here's the listing:

```
/* rmdir2.c */
/* removes a sub-directory */
#define INCL_DOS
#include <os2.h>

main(argc, argv)
int argc;
char *argv[];
{
   unsigned rc;

   if( argc != 2 )
      { printf("Syntax: rmdir2 dirname"); exit(1); }
   if( rc=DosRmdir( argv[1], 0L ) )  {
      if( rc==3 )
         printf("Directory not found");
      else if ( rc==5 )
         printf("Can't remove directory");
      else
         printf("DosRmDir error=%u",rc);
      exit(1);
   }
   exit(0);
}
```

This program is similar to mkdir2.c. It uses the function DosRmdir() to remove the directory specified by the command-line argument.

DosRmdir — Directory

```
DosRmdir(Pathname, Reserved);
char far *Pathname;        /* ASCIIZ pathname of directory */
unsigned long Reserved;    /* reserved; must be 0 */
```

This function requires only the pathname of the directory to be removed. As with the DOS command RMDIR, the directory must be empty before it can be removed. If it is not empty, the error message "Can't remove directory" appears. If the drive or the pathname specified is not valid, the program prints "Directory not found".

The Current Drive and Directory

The concepts of the "current drive" and "current directory" are somewhat different in OS/2 protected mode than they are in MS-DOS. In MS-DOS, the current drive and directory are system-wide states. If one application changes the current drive or directory, then all applications, including the operating system, find themselves in the new drive or directory when the application terminates.

In OS/2, on the other hand, the current drive and directory are local to a particular process, and (while the process is running) to a particular session. Changing the drive or directory in a running program in one session has no effect on the current drive or directory in other sessions. Also, if a process changes the current drive or directory, they will be restored to their former values when the process terminates. In other words, the instance of CMD.EXE in your session will continue to operate with the same drive and directory, even if your application changes to a new drive and directory.

Changing the Current Directory

The following example demonstrates how an application can change its current directory. First it finds the current drive number and directory, and prints out that pathname. Then it changes to the drive and directory specified on the command line, and finally, for confirmation, it prints out the pathname of the new drive and directory.

```
/* chdir2.c */
/* changes current directory (for this process only) */
#define INCL_DOS
#include <os2.h>
#define BUFF_LEN 80                /* size of path buffer */

main(argc, argv)
int argc;
char *argv[];
{
    unsigned drive;              /* drive number (A=1, etc) */
    unsigned long map;           /* drive map (not used) */
    unsigned bufflen = BUFF_LEN; /* size of path buffer */
    char pathbuff[BUFF_LEN];     /* buffer for path */
    unsigned rc;                 /* return code */

    if( argc != 2 )
       { printf("Syntax: chdir2 pathname"); exit(1); }
    if( rc=DosQCurDisk( &drive, &map ) )
       { printf("DosQCurDisk error=%u",rc); exit(1); }
```

```
                                        /* find current directory */
            if( rc=DosQCurDir( drive, pathbuff, &bufflen ) )
               { printf("DosQCurDir error=%u",rc); exit(1); }
            printf("Old directory = %c:\\%s\n", drive+('A'-1),
                                                          pathbuff );

            if( argv[1][1] == ':' )  {          /* if drive spec, */
               drive = toupper( argv[1][0] );   /*    get letter */
               drive -= 'A'-1;                  /*   convert to number */
               if( rc=DosSelectDisk( drive ) )  /*   change drive */
                  if( rc==15 )
                     { printf("Invalid drive"); exit(1); }
                  else
                     { printf("DosSelectDisk error=%u",rc);
                                                          exit(1); }
            }
                                        /* change directory */
            if( rc=DosChdir( argv[1], 0L ) )
               if( rc==3 )
                  { printf("Invalid directory path"); exit(1); }
               else
                  { printf("DosChDir error=%u",rc); exit(1); }

                                        /* display new directory */
            if( rc=DosQCurDir( drive, pathbuff, &bufflen ) )
               { printf("DosQCurDir error=%u",rc); exit(1); }
            printf("New directory = %c:\\%s\n", drive+64, pathbuff );
            exit(0);
         }
```

This program uses four new API functions. To find out the current pathname we need to know the current disk drive, so the first API function in the program is DosQCurDisk(), which returns the drive number.

DosQCurDisk — Find current disk drive

```
DosQCurDisk(APath, AMap);
unsigned far *APath;       /* address for drive number */
unsigned long far *AMap;   /* address for drive map */
```

The "Q" in DosQCurDisk() stands for "query". This function is one of a family of query functions used to return various kinds of information about files and the file system. We'll encounter more of these query functions as we go along.

DosQCurDisk() returns two pieces of information: the current drive number (where the number 1 represents drive A, 2 represents

B, etc.), and a drive map. The map is a double word which shows which drives exist in the system. Bit 0 stands for drive A, bit 1 for drive B, and so on, up to bit 25 for drive Z. If a bit is set to 1, the corresponding drive is installed in the system. This map might be useful information for an application, although our example does not make use of it.

The drive number is used as an input parameter for another query function, DosQCurDir(). This function returns the pathname of the current directory.

DosQCurDir — Find current directory

```
DosQCurDir(Drive, APath, ALength);
unsigned Drive;            /* drive number */
char far *APath;           /* address for pathname */
unsigned far *ALength;     /* address of length of path
                              buffer */
```

This function also requires the address of the length of the buffer where the path name will be placed. The pathname produced by DosQCurDir() is in all upper case characters. It does not include the drive specification, nor the initial backslash, so the program adds this information when printing out the pathname.

To discover if the user wants to change to a new disk drive, the program examines the second character in the command line: **argv[1][1]**. If this character is a semicolon, the character preceding it is assumed to represent a drive letter. The user may type either an upper or lower case letter, so we convert it to upper. To convert from the character 'A' to the number 1 (or from 'B' to 2, etc.) the quantity 'A'-1 (64) is subtracted from the value of the character.

The new drive number is used as an argument in the function DosSelectDisk().

DosSelectDisk — Change current disk drive

```
DosSelectDisk(Drive);
unsigned Drive;            /* drive number (1=A, 2=B, etc.) */
```

This function causes the current drive to change to the number specified. As we noted earlier, this change applies only for the life of the process calling the function: once this process terminates, the current drive reverts to its previous value. If an invalid drive number is used, the program prints the message "Invalid drive".

The key to the program is the function DosChdir(), which changes the current directory.

DosChdir — Change current directory

```
DosChdir(Path, Reserved);
char far *Path;          /* pathname of new directory */
unsigned long Reserved;  /* reserved; must be 0 */
```

The only information required by this function is the pathname of the new directory. If an incorrect pathname is used, the function prints the message "Invalid directory path."

After the current directory has been changed, the program prints out the new pathname using DosQCurDir(). This demonstrates that the program is in fact operating in the new directory. As with the disk drive number, this change lasts only for the duration of the current process; when the process terminates, the current path reverts to whatever it was before.

Here's a sample interchange with the program. We show the full OS/2 prompt, which includes the current directory path.

```
[C:\SAMPLES\WED]chdir2 b:\notes\thurs
Old directory = C:\SAMPLES\WED
New directory = B:\NOTES\THURS
[C:\SAMPLES\WED]
```

The prompt printed by OS/2 after the program terminates shows that the drive and directory revert to their previous values.

Manipulating Files

From the major functions for manipulating directories, we move on to functions that deal with files. We'll see how to delete, move, and search for files.

Deleting Files

Here's a short program that deletes a file typed as a command-line argument. Either the file name itself (if the file is in the current directory) or the complete pathname may be typed. A drive specification may also be used.

```
/* delete.c */
/* demonstrates DosDelete() */
#define INCL_DOS
#include <os2.h>
```

(continued)

```
main(argc, argv)
int argc;
char *argv[];
{
    unsigned rc;

    if( argc != 2 )
        { printf("Syntax: delete filename"); exit(1); }
    if( rc=DosDelete( argv[1], 0L ) )   {
        if( rc==2 )
            printf("File not found");
        else if( rc==32 )
            printf("Sharing violation");
        else
            printf("DosDelete error=%u",rc);
        exit(1);
    }
    printf("%s deleted", argv[1] );
    exit(0);
}
```

This program uses the API function DosDelete(). The function needs only one piece of information: the pathname of the file to be deleted.

DosDelete — Delete file

```
DosDelete(FileName, Reserved);
char far *FileName;       /* ASCIIZ string for filename */
unsigned long Reserved;   /* reserved; must be 0 */
```

If the program is used to delete a non-existent file, the message "File not found" is printed. If an attempt is made to delete a file which is in use by another process, the message "Sharing violation" appears. This happens if, for example, you attempt to delete the system file SWAPPER.DAT.

Moving Files

The next example moves a file from one directory to another. The name of the file to be moved, and the directory it is to be moved to, are given as command-line arguments.

```
/* move.c */
/* moves file to directory */
#include <doscalls.h>
#include <string.h>
```

(continued)

```
main(argc, argv)
int argc;
char *argv[];
{
   int rc;
   char *LastSlash;        /* ptr to last backslash */
   char FileName[80];      /* file name, without path */
   char OldName[80];       /* old path for DosMove() */
   char NewName[80];       /* new path for DosMove() */

   if( argc != 3 )
      { printf("Syntax: C>move filename directory");
exit(1); }
   strcpy( OldName, argv[1] );
   strcpy( NewName, argv[2] );

                     /* extract filename from old path */
   if( LastSlash=strrchr(OldName, '\\') ) /* if slash, */
      strcpy( FileName, LastSlash+1 );    /* name follows */
   else                                   /* if no slash, */
      strcpy( FileName, OldName );        /* it's name only */
                           /* add backslash if necessary */
   if( NewName[strlen(NewName)-1] != '\\' )
strcat(NewName, "\\");
                     /* add file name to new path name */
   strcat( NewName, FileName );

                     /* move the file */
   printf("Moving %s to %s\n", OldName, NewName );
   if( rc=DOSMOVE( OldName, NewName, 0L) )
      if( rc==2 )
         { printf("No such file"); exit(1); }
      else if( rc==3 )
         { printf("No such directory"); exit(1); }
      else if( rc==5 )
         { printf("Can't move to that directory");
                                            exit(1); }
      else
         { printf("DosMove error=%d",rc); exit(1); }
   exit(0);
}
```

This program uses the function DosMove(). DosMove() requires two arguments. The first is the name of the file to be moved. This can be a complete pathname if the file is in another directory. The second parameter is the complete pathname where the new file will be installed. This includes both the directory sequence *and* the new file-name.

Most users will not want to type the new filename (unless it's to be changed) when they type the directory the file will be moved to. That is, to move the file NOTE.TXT to the directory \LETTERS\NOV you want to type:

```
C>move note.txt \letters\nov
```

not:

```
C>move note.txt \letters\nov\note.txt
```

However, since the second parameter of DosMove() requires the file-name as part of the directory pathname, the program must figure out the filename by looking at the first command-line argument, and then append it to the directory path given in the second command-line argument. A backslash may also need to be inserted if the user didn't type one at the end of the directory path. Figure 7-1 shows how this looks.

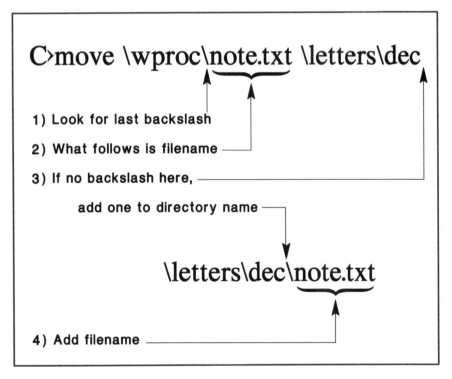

Figure 7-1
Modifying the Pathname for DosMove( )

To make its operation clearer, the program prints out the arguments being given to DosMove(). Here's the interchange if a file called SMITH.INV is moved from the current directory, \CALCS, to a different one, \INVOICES\NOV:

```
[C:\CALCS]move smith.inv \invoices\nov
Moving smith.inv \invoices\nov\smith.inv
```

And here's how it looks if the file is moved back again to the original directory:

```
[C:\CALCS]move \invoices\nov\smith.inv \calcs
Moving \invoices\nov\smith.inv \calcs\smith.inv
```

Notice how the program adds a backslash and the filename to the second command-line argument. The first command-line argument can consist of either the filename alone or a full pathname. The program decides which of these two situations it is and constructs the filename accordingly. The filename is then added to the second command-line argument to create the second parameter for Dos-Move().

DosMove — Move file
```
DosMove(OldName, NewName);
char far *OldName;   /* ASCIIZ pathname of original file  */
char far *NewName;   /* ASCIIZ pathname of new location */
unsigned long Reserved;   /* reserved; must be 0 */
```

If the user attempts to move a file which doesn't exist, the program will print the "No such file" message. Attempting to move a file to a non-existent directory elicits "No such directory". The message "Can't move to that directory" results from trying to move a file to a directory which already contains a file of the same name.

Renaming a File

For simplicity, the move.c program shown above does not permit the file to be renamed while it is being moved. However, this is possible with DosMove(). Here's a somewhat simpler program that permits files to be renamed. The user invokes the program with the old name and the new name as command-line arguments.

```
/* rename2.c */
/* renames a file */
#define INCL_DOS
#include <os2.h>

main(argc, argv)
int argc;
char *argv[];
{
   int rc;

   if( argc != 3 )
      { printf("Syntax: rename2 oldname newname");
                                                  exit(1); }

                           /* move file to new name */
   if( rc=DosMove( argv[1], argv[2], 0L) )
      if( rc==2 )
         { printf("No such file"); exit(1); }
      else if( rc==3 )
         { printf("No such pathname"); exit(1); }
      else if( rc==5 )
         { printf("New name is invalid"); exit(1); }
      else
         { printf("DosMove error=%d",rc); exit(1); }
   exit(0);
}
```

Because the user is expected to type a filename for both arguments, no manipulation of the input is necessary and it is simply passed to the DosMove() function. A file in the current directory can be renamed like this:

`C>rename2 joe.let harry.let`

Or a file can be moved to a different directory and renamed at the same time:

`C>rename2 joe.let \letters\nov\harry.let`
`C>rename2 \letters\nov\harry.let \archive\harry.let`

If the program can't find the old name, it prints, "No such file". If it can't follow the path to the new name, it prints "No such pathname," and if a file with the new name already exists "New name is invalid" appears.

It would be easy to combine move.c and rename2.c to imitate the functionality of the COPY command, or to improve upon it.

Finding Files

The OS/2 API includes a trio of powerful functions for finding files with a particular file specification. This specification can include wildcard characters, so these functions can be used to find groups of files matching the specification.

Finding a Single File

The first of these functions is DosFindFirst(), which finds the first file meeting the specification. The second function, DosFindNext(), finds all subsequent files meeting the specification. Finally, DosFind-Close() is used when the search process has been completed.

In our first example we'll use only DosFindFirst() and DosFind-Close(). This program takes a file specification as a command-line argument, and prints out the name and some information about the first file it finds meeting this specification in the current directory.

```
/* findfirs.c */
/* demonstrates DosFindFirst() */
#define INCL_DOS
#include <os2.h>
#include <string.h>            /* for strcpy() */
#define ATTR 0x0037            /* find any type file */
#define LENGTH sizeof(buff)    /* size of results buffer */
#define READ_ONLY 0x0001       /* attribute word values */
#define HIDDEN    0x0002
#define SYSTEM    0x0004
#define DIRECT    0x0010
#define ARCHIVE   0x0020
main(argc,argv)
int argc;
char *argv[];
{
    char pathname[80];          /* buffer for entry name */
    unsigned short handle = 0xFFFF;  /* allocate handle */
    struct _FILEFINDBUF buff;   /* defined in os2def.h */
    unsigned count = 1;         /* number of entries */
    unsigned rc;                /* result code */

    if( argc != 2 )
        { printf("Syntax: findfirs pathname"); exit(1); }
    strcpy( pathname, argv[1] );

    if( rc=DosFindFirst( pathname, &handle, ATTR, &buff,
                              LENGTH, &count, 0L ) )
```

(continued)

```
        if( rc==18 )
            { printf("No such file"); exit(1); }
        else
            { printf("DosFindFirst error=%u",rc); exit(1); }
    printf("Name = %s\n", buff.achName );     /* file name */
    printf("Size = %ul\n", buff.cbFile );     /* file size */
    if( buff.attrFile & READ_ONLY ) printf("Read-only\n");
    if( buff.attrFile & HIDDEN )    printf("Hidden\n");
    if( buff.attrFile & SYSTEM )    printf("System\n");
    if( buff.attrFile & DIRECT )    printf("Directory\n");
    if( buff.attrFile & ARCHIVE )   printf("Archive\n");
    DosFindClose( handle );
    exit(0);
}
```

The program prints the name of the file, its size, and any attributes (read-only, hidden, system, sub-directory, and archive) it may have.

For example, if the first file with the extension .EXE in the current directory was appl.exe, an interchange with the program might look like this:

```
C>findfirs *.exe
Name = APPL.EXE
Size = 12084
Archive
```

The archive bit is set when a file is created or modified, and cleared by such programs as BACKUP and XCOPY (with the /m option) that are presumably making "archival" copies of the file. A better name for the bit would be "not yet archived".

If we gave findfirs.c a specification that applied to directories, it might return something like this:

```
C>findfirs \os*
Name = OS2
Size = 0
Directory
```

To see a file with the other attributes, we can use a specification that applies to a system file:

```
C>findfirs \ibm*.*
Name = IBMBIO.COM
Size = 16369
Read-only
Hidden
System
```

The function that returns all this information is DosFindFirst().

DosFindFirst — Find first file matching specification

```
DosFindFirst(Name, AHandle, Attr, ABuff, Length, ACount,
                                                    Res);
char far *Name;                 /* ASCIIZ pathname */
unsigned short far *AHandle;    /* address for find handle */
unsigned Attr;                  /* attributes to search for */
struct _FILEFINDBUF far *ABuff; /* buffer for results */
unsigned Length;                /* length of results buffer */
unsigned far *ACount;           /* address for entry count */
unsigned long Res;              /* reserved; must be 0 */
```

Let's look at the arguments for this function.

First is the *pathname* to be searched for, in the form of a normal ASCIIZ string. The function returns a *handle*, which is used to refer to this particular search activity. This handle is used as an argument to the DosFindNext() and DosFindClose() functions, directing all three functions to the same search activity. This permits several such search activities to take place in the system at the same time.

The handle variable is used not only to return the handle from the function to the application, but also by the application to supply information to the function. If the application sets this variable to -1, (0xFFFF), the system knows to supply a handle value, which over-writes the -1. Using a value of 1 obtains a standard handle which is always available. In our program we want to obtain a new handle, so we supply the -1 value.

If the handle value returned by a DosFindFirst() call is used again in another DosFindFirst() call, its association with the previous search activity is broken, and a new one is established.

The *attribute* word tells the function what kinds of files we want to search for. It uses bit fields to represent the attributes, as shown in Figure 7-2.

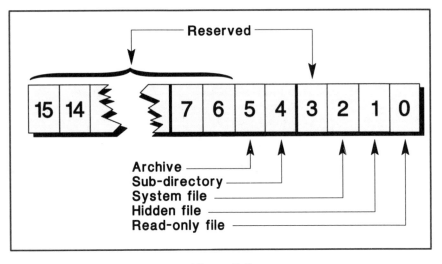

Figure 7-2
The Attribute Word

If none of these bits are set to 1, it searches only for normal files. If one or more bits are set, then it searches for corresponding types of files, as well as normal files.

The *result buffer* has the data type **struct _FILEFINDBUF**. This structure is defined in os2def.h. With normal C datatypes it looks like this:

```
struct _FILEFINDBUF  {
   struct _FDATE fdateCreation;
   struct _FTIME ftimeCreation;
   struct _FDATE fdateLastAccess;
   struct _FTIME ftimeLastAccess;
   struct _FDATE fdateLastWrite;
   struct _FTIME ftimeLastWrite;
   unsigned long cbFile;           /* size allocated */
   unsigned long cbFileAlloc;      /* actual size */
   unsigned      attrFile;         /* attributes */
   unsigned char cchName;          /* length of file name */
   char          achName[13];      /* file name */
};
```

The structures for **_FDATE** and **_TIME** use bit fields to hold the various quantities, and look like this:

```
struct _FTIME  {
   unsigned twosecs : 5;    /* seconds divided by two */
   unsigned minutes : 6;
   unsigned hours   : 5;
};
struct _FDATE  {
   unsigned day    : 5;
   unsigned month  : 4;
   unsigned year   : 7;    /* 1980 is 0 */
};
```

DosFindFirst() returns information to the caller in the structure _FILEFINDBUF. The first four members of the structure (the dates and times of last access and creation) are not yet implemented in the OS/2 file system and are always 0. The date and time of writing are used; we'll examine them later. The file size is the size of the file in bytes, and the allocation size is the number of bytes allocated to the file. The attribute word has the same format as that described above for the attributes to be searched for. The string length member is the length of the string in the last member of the structure, which is the file name returned by the function.

The *length* of the result buffer must be specified by the caller. The buffer can, if desired, hold information for more than one file. Thus this value can either be the size of the buffer, or a multiple of this size if information on more than one file will be gathered at once.

The *count* is the number of entries desired to be returned. The actual number returned overwrites this value. The actual number of files returned is either the number asked for, the number that fit in the buffer, or the number that exist, whichever is smaller. We want to look at only one file at a time, so this value is initialized to 1.

The *reserved* variable must be 0.

If DosFindFirst() cannot find any file matching the specification given to it, it returns error 18, NO_MORE_FILES.

Finding a Group of Files

The previous program permitted the user to find the first file matching a particular description. In general, however, we want to find a group of files, not just one. For example, if we invoke the DOS command DIR like this:

```
C>dir *.c
```

we want to be able to list *all* the files with the .C extension.

In this section we look at two versions of a file-finding program. The first version is as simple as possible, to show how the functions are used. The second is more useful.

Here's the short version:

```
/* findmany.c */
/* lists files meeting specification */
#define INCL_DOS
#include <os2.h>
#define LEN sizeof(buff)
#define PATH_LEN 80              /* length of path buffer */
#define ATTR 0x0000             /* normal files only */

main(argc, argv)
int argc;
char *argv[];
{
    char path[PATH_LEN];         /* space for pathname */
    struct _FILEFINDBUF buff;    /* defined in os2def.h */
    unsigned short handle=0xFFFF; /* start with this value */
    unsigned count=1;            /* get one entry at a time */
    int rc;                      /* return code */

    if( argc != 2 )
        { printf("Syntax: findmany pathname"); exit(1); }

                                 /* find first entry */
    DosFindFirst(argv[1], &handle, ATTR, &buff, LEN, &count,
                                                     0L);

    printf("%-14s\n", buff.achName );

while( TRUE ) {                  /* find other entries */
        rc = DosFindNext(handle, &buff, LEN, &count);
        if( rc==18 ) {
            DosFindClose( handle );
            exit(0);
        }
        printf("%-14s\n", buff.achName );
    }
}
```

This program gets a file specification from the command line and uses it as an argument for DosFindFirst(), the same way findfirs.c did. However, it then enters a loop which contains the function DosFind-Next().

DosFindNext — Find next file matching specification

```
DosFindNext(Handle, ABuff, Length, ACount);
unsigned short Handle;                /* find handle */
struct _FILEFINDBUF far *ABuff;  /* buffer for results */
unsigned Length;                  /* length of results buffer */
unsigned far *ACount;             /* address for entry count */
```

This function uses four parameters. The handle is the value obtained from DosFindFirst(). The remaining parameters have usages similar to those in DosFindFirst(). The structure of the buffer for the results is the same as that in DosFindFirst(), the length is the length of this buffer, and the count tells how many instances we are looking for, and returns the amount received.

Each time this function is called it returns the next entry on the list of files matching the specification. The entry is stored in the buffer, as it is for DosFindFirst().

When DosFindNext() can find no more files meeting the specification, it returns error code 18. At this point the program executes the DosFindClose() function and exits.

DosFindClose() dissolves the association between DosFindFirst() and DosFindNext() and the search activity, and releases the handle obtained by DosFindFirst(). This function should always be executed when a search is completed.

DosFindClose — Closes find handle

```
DosFindClose(Handle);
unsigned short Handle;        /* find handle */
```

This function takes as its only argument the handle, obtained from DosFindFirst(), of the search activity to be closed.

Instead of exiting on an error code from DosFindNext(), the program could check for the value of the **count** variable. When the function returns with a zero value for this variable, no more files with the specified pathname can be found.

Here's an example of the program's output when it's used to search for files with the extension .EXE:

```
C>findmany *.exe
FINDFIRS.EXE
GETCOM.EXE
SETCOM.EXE
REVERSE.EXE
FINDMANY.EXE
C>
```

The program is an adequate substitute for DIR in such simple situations, but it suffers from several defects. It must always be used with a file specification: you can't simply type the name of the program, with no command-line argument, to list all files in the current directory. It does not understand a pathname typed without a specific filename or wildcard characters, so you can't simply type a directory name and expect it to list the files in the directory. It prints out only the filename, with no other information about the file. And, last but by no means least, if there are no instances of the files specified, it goes into an endless loop.

The following program attempts to remedy these problems and imitate the action of the DOS command DIR.

```c
/* dir2.c */
/* lists files in a directory */
#define INCL_DOS
#include <os2.h>
#include <string.h>              /* for strcpy() etc */
#define BUFLEN sizeof(buff)
#define PATH_LEN 80              /* length of path buffer */
#define ATTR 0x0037              /* all attributes */
#define DIRECTORY 0x0010         /* directory attr */
#define NO_MORE_FILES 18         /* dos error code */

struct _FILEFINDBUF buff;        /* defined in doscalls.h */
unsigned short handle=0xFFFF;    /* start with this value */
main(argc, argv)
int argc;
char *argv[];
{
    char path[PATH_LEN];         /* space for pathname */
    void pinfo(unsigned);        /* function to print info */
    unsigned SearchCount=1;
    int rc;

    if( argc < 2 )               /* if no arg, */
        strcpy( path, "*.*" );   /* search all in current dir */

                                 /* if a single backslash, */
    else if( strcmp(argv[1],"\\")==0 )  {
        strcpy( path, argv[1] ); /* it's root directory */
        strcat( path, "*.*" );   /* search all files in root */
    }
                                 /* if wildcards or period, */
    else if( strcspn(argv[1],"*?.") < strlen(argv[1]) )
        strcpy( path, argv[1] ); /* use path as is */
```

(continued)

```
      else  {                           /* if any other argument, */
         strcpy( path, argv[1] ); /* it's a pathname , */
         strcat( path, "\\*.*" ); /* search all files in it */
      }
      printf("Listing pathname %s\n", path );
                                        /* find first entry */
      rc = DosFindFirst(path, &handle, ATTR, &buff,
                                  BUFLEN, &SearchCount, 0L);
      pinfo(rc);                        /* print information */

                                        /* find other entries */
      while( TRUE )  {
         rc = DosFindNext(handle, &buff, BUFLEN, &SearchCount);
         pinfo(rc);                     /* print information */
      }
   }

   /* pinfo() */
   /* print out file or directory information */
   void pinfo(rc)
   unsigned rc;
   {
      if( rc )
         if( rc == NO_MORE_FILES )
            { DosFindClose(handle); exit(0); }
         else
            { printf("DosFindxxx error=%d\n", rc); exit(1); }
      else {
         printf("%-14s", buff.achName );    /* file name */
         if( buff.attrFile & DIRECTORY )
            printf("%11s\n", "<DIR>");       /* directory, or */
         else
            printf("%6ul\n", buff.cbFile);  /* file size */
      }
   }
```

In this program the function pinfo() handles printing the output and error messages. The function is used following both DosFindFirst() and DosFindNext(). In addition to printing the filename, the size is also printed. If the entry is a directory rather than a file, the symbol <DIR> is shown instead of the size.

The program deals with several possible inputs. If there is no argument typed on the command-line, the program uses the string "*.*" as the search path. If a backslash is the only argument, it is taken to be the root directory and the program searches for "*.*". If there is already a wild-card character in the input, the string is used as is. In all other situations it assumes a directory name has been typed, and adds "*.*".

The dir2.c program searches for entries with any attribute, whether they are normal files, directories, or hidden, system, or archival files. However, only the directory attribute is displayed. Here's an example:

```
C>dir2
FLIGHT.C        4022
FLIGHT.EXE      27518
GAMES                   <DIR>
CABBAGE.EXE     33187
FINANCE                 <DIR>
RELIVE.C        1034
RELIVE.TXT      12498
```

Of course the program could be modified to print any of the other attributes as well.

Searching for Files in Sub-directories

In the dir2.c example above we treated a sub-directory much as if it were a file, ignoring the fact that sub-directories themselves are directories that can contain files. In our next, somewhat longer, example, instead of passing over sub-directories, we plunge into them to investigate the files within.

The purpose of this example is to count all the bytes in all the files in a directory, no matter how deeply buried in sub-directories they may be. To do this the program operates recursively. Most of the program consists of a function, called countdir(), whose purpose is to count the number of bytes in a directory. The main program calls countdir() using the pathname the user typed on the command line. Whenever countdir() finds a file, it adds the number of bytes to a running total. Whenever countdir() finds a sub-directory, it calls itself, using the pathname of the sub-directory. By calling itself repeatedly it can handle any depth of sub-directory.

Actually there is a practical limit to the depth of sub-directories that can be analyzed. This limit it imposed by the stack size. Since the arguments for countdir() must be kept on the stack, too many nested calls to the function cause stack overflow. If your system uses more than a half-dozen or so layers of sub-directories, you may want to change the program's stack size, using the /F option when you compile the program. The default stack size is 2,048 bytes (800 hex). To double this, for example, include the option

```
/F 1600
```

in the CL command-line. The number of bytes is given in hex.

The example must be compiled using the -AL option, since the printf() function needs to use **far** pointers. (Alternatively, you could use the **"%fs"** format specifier in the printf() function to indicate a far pointer to the string.)

Here's the program listing:

```
/* dirsize.c */
/* finds total size of all files in directory */
/* includes files in sub-directories to any level */
/* compile with -AL model for far ptrs in printf() */
#define INCL_DOS
#include <os2.h>
#include <string.h>            /* for strcat(), etc. */
#define BUFLEN sizeof(buff)    /* length of result buff */
#define PATH_LEN 80            /* length of path buffer */
#define F_ATTR 0x0037          /* all attributes */
#define DIRECTORY 0x0010       /* directory attr */
#define NO_MORE_FILES 18       /* dos error code */

unsigned long total=0;         /* running total of dir sizes */

main(argc, argv)
int argc;
char *argv[];
{
    void countdir(char far *); /* funct counts one directory
                                               */
    char path[80];             /* directory path to search */

    if( argc < 2 )             /* if no command-line arg, */
       strcpy( path, "\0" );   /* start with null string */
    else                       /* if argument, */
       strcpy( path, argv[1] );   /* use it */
    countdir( (char far *)path ); /* analyze specified dir */
    printf("Total bytes in this directory: %lu\n", total );
    exit(0);
}

/* countdir() */
/* function to add sizes of all files in directory */
/* calls itself to analyze sub-directories */
void countdir( PathPtr )
char far *PathPtr;                 /* ptr to pathname */
```

(continued)

```
{
    char localpath[80];        /* local pathname */
    void entry( char far *, unsigned,
                                    struct _FILEFINDBUF * );
    struct _FILEFINDBUF buff;    /* defined in os2def.h */
    unsigned Scnt=1;             /* search count for DosFind() */
    unsigned short handle=0xFFFF; /* start with this value */
    unsigned rc;                 /* return code */
  if( strlen(PathPtr) > 1 )      /* if not null or root, */
      strcat( PathPtr, "\\" );   /* add backslash */
    strcpy( localpath, PathPtr ); /* start with path */
    strcat( localpath, "*.*" );   /* add search-all */

                                   /* find first entry */
    if( rc=DosFindFirst( localpath, &handle, F_ATTR, &buff,
                                    BUFLEN, &Scnt, 0L) )
        if( rc == NO_MORE_FILES )         /* if at end, */
            { DosFindClose(handle); return; } /* return */
        else
            { printf("DosFindFirst error=%d\n", rc); exit(1); }
    entry( PathPtr, handle, &buff);  /* analyze this entry */

    while( TRUE )  {                    /* find other entries */
        if( rc=DosFindNext(handle, &buff, BUFLEN, &Scnt) )
            if( rc == NO_MORE_FILES )          /* if at end, */
                { DosFindClose(handle); return; }  /* return */
            else
                { printf("DosFindNext error=%d\n", rc);
                                            exit(1); }
        entry(PathPtr, handle, &buff);  /* analyze each one */
    }
}

/* entry() */
/* get size of file, or analyze sub-directory */
#define NAME buffptr->achName         /* shorter defs */
#define SIZE buffptr->cbFile
#define ATTR buffptr->attrFile

void entry(LocPathPtr, handle, buffptr)
char far *LocPathPtr;                   /* ptr to path */
unsigned short handle;                  /* search handle */
struct _FILEFINDBUF *buffptr;           /* ptr to buffer */
```

(continued)

```
{
   char locpath[80];

   if( ATTR & DIRECTORY ) {            /* if directory, */
      if( NAME[0] == '.' )             /* if (.) or (..), */
         return;                       /*    forget it */
      strcpy( locpath, LocPathPtr );   /* start with old
                                               path */
      strcat( locpath, NAME );         /* add directory name */
      countdir( locpath );             /* analyze it */
   }
   else {                              /* if file, */
      printf("%s%s=%ul\n", LocPathPtr, NAME, SIZE );
      total += SIZE;                   /* count file size */
   }
}
```

You can call dirsize.c either with a complete pathname, with no pathname (in which case it analyzes the current directory), or with a single backslash indicating the root directory. If you choose to count all the files in the root directory, and your hard disk contains many files, the program may require several minutes to count all of them.

Figure 7-3 shows the relationship of the pathnames sent to the various functions in the program when the command-line input is respectively nothing, a backslash indicating the root directory, and a full directory pathname.

On command-line	Sent to DosFindxxx( )	Sent recursively to countdir( )
nothing	*.*	CCC
\	*.*	CCC
\AAA\BBB	\AAA\BBB*.*	\AAA\BBB\CCC

Figure 7-3
Pathnames in dirsize.c

The figure supposes that, in the course of a search, the program comes across the file CCC, and shows the resulting arguments used to send to DosFindxxx() and to the next evocation of the countdir() function, respectively.

The program prints out the name and size of each file as it adds it to the total. Here are the last few lines of a typical run, in which the current directory is being analyzed:

```
ENVFIND2.EXE=7580
VERIFY2.C=704
FILEMODE.EXE=8308
XXX\XFILE.1=345
XXX\XFILE.2=456
XXX\YYY\XFILE11=453
XXX\YYY\XFILE22=1453
XXX\YYY\ZZZ\XFILE222=8734
XXX\YYY\ZZZ\XFILE333=450
XXX\DIRSIZE.EXE=6787
DIRSIZE2.C=3843
DIRSIZE.C=3722
VERIFY2.EXE=8142
DIRSIZE.EXE=9952
DIRSIZE2.EXE=8160
Total bytes in this directory: 202795
```

Notice how dirsize.c drops down into sub-directories and sub-sub-directories in its relentless pursuit of file sizes.

The part of the program that determines if a particular entry in a directory is a sub-directory or a file, and takes the appropriate action, is placed in a separate function: entry(). This avoids duplicating the code, which is evoked twice in the countdir() function, once under DosFindFirst() and once under DosFindNext().

You can modify this program to perform other tasks involving all the functions in a directory. For instance, it could delete an entire directory, including files in all its sub-directories, if the code to count files was changed to remove them, using the DosRmdir() function.

File Attributes

We've seen functions that return information about file attributes, but we haven't focused specifically on attributes. Let's remedy that situation by examining two functions designed specifically to read and modify attributes: DosQFileMode() and DosSetFileMode().

The following example program uses these functions to find and display the attributes of any file, and then lets the user change the attributes. This is a useful program for making hidden files visible, or for permitting read-only files to be modified.

Here's the listing:

```
/* filemode.c */
/* reads and changes mode of file */
#define INCL_DOS
#include <os2.h>
#include <stdio.h>               /* for getche() etc */
#define NORMAL    0x0000         /* attribute bits */
#define READONLY  0x0001
#define HIDDEN    0x0002
#define SYSTEM    0x0004
#define DIRECTORY 0x0010
#define ARCHIVE   0x0020

main(argc, argv)
int argc;
char *argv[];
{
   unsigned attr;               /* attribute word */
   int rc;                      /* return code */

   if( argc != 2 )
     { printf("Syntax: filemode filename\n"); exit(1); }

                                 /* find attributes of file */
   if( rc=DosQFileMode(argv[1], &attr, 0L) )
     {printf("DosQFileMode error=%d", rc); exit(1); }

   if(attr == NORMAL)           /* print out attributes */
     printf("Normal file\n");
   else   {
     if(attr & READONLY)  printf("Read-only  ");
     if(attr & HIDDEN)    printf("Hidden  ");
     if(attr & SYSTEM)    printf("System  ");
     if(attr & DIRECTORY) printf("Directory  ");
     if(attr & ARCHIVE)   printf("Archive  ");
   }
```

(continued)

```
      printf("\n\nChange attributes(y/n)? ");
      if( getche() != 'y')
         exit(0);
      attr = NORMAL;                      /* change attributes */
      printf("\nSet to normal (y/n)? ");
      if( getche() != 'y' )   {
         printf("\nSet to Read-only (y/n)? ");
         if( getche() == 'y' )
            attr |= READONLY;
         printf("\nSet to Hidden (y/n)? ");
         if( getche() == 'y' )
            attr |= HIDDEN;
         printf("\nSet to System (y/n)? ");
         if( getche() == 'y' )
            attr |= SYSTEM;
         printf("\nSet to Archive (y/n)? ");
         if( getche() == 'y' )
            attr |= ARCHIVE;
      }                                   /* set attributes */
      if( rc=DosSetFileMode(argv[1], attr, 0L) )
         { printf("DosSetFileMode error=%d\n"); exit(1); }
      printf("\n");
      exit(0);
}
```

In the following sample session with this program we take a normal file called testfile.txt and turn all its attributes on. Then we call it up again, and change it back to a normal file.

```
C>filemode testfile.txt
Normal file

Change attributes(y/n)?  y
Set to normal (y/n)?  n
Set to Read-only (y/n)?  y
Set to Hidden (y/n)?  y
Set to System (y/n)?  y
Set to Archive (y/n)?  y
C>
C>filemode testfile.txt
Read-only  Hidden  System  Archive

Change attributes(y/n)?  y
Set to normal (y/n)?  y
C>
```

The directory attribute cannot be modified, so it is not included in the list of options to be changed. However, this program permits you to alter directory attributes, making them hidden, for example.

The API function used to find the attribute word of a file is DosQFileMode(), another of the query functions.

DosQFileMode — Find file attributes

```
DosQFileMode(Name, AAttribute, Reserved);
char far *Name;              /* ASCIIZ name of file */
unsigned far *AAttribute;    /* address for attribute word */
unsigned long Reserved;      /* reserved; must be 0 */
```

This function needs to know the pathname of the file. It then returns the attribute word. (The format of this word was shown in Figure 7-2). The program looks at each bit of the word in turn, and prints an appropriate message if the bit is on.

The function for setting a file's attributes is DosSetFileMode().

DosSetFileMode — Set file attributes

```
DosSetFileMode(Name, Attribute, Reserved);
char far *Name;              /* ASCIIZ name of file */
unsigned Attribute;          /* attribute word */
unsigned long Reserved;      /* reserved; must be 0 */
```

This function requires both the name of the file whose attributes are to be modified, and the attribute word with the new settings. On return the new attributes have been set.

Finding the Path for a Known File

An application program often needs to find the pathname of a specific file. The file may be in one of several directories, but the application doesn't know which one. For example, an application may need to locate an initialization file, called APP.INI, that could be in the current directory, the root directory, or a directory called \APP\INIT. How can the application retrieve the actual pathname of the file?

OS/2 makes available an API function specifically for this purpose: DosSearchPath(). This function requires the name of the file to be located and the directories to be searched for the pathname. A string containing several different directories, separated by semicolons, can be used as input to the function.

Here's a program that demonstrates DosSearchPath(). It takes two command-line arguments: the filename to be searched for, and the list of directories, separated by semicolons. It locates the file, and prints out its pathname. In a real application the pathname would likely be used to reference the file, rather than being printed out.

```
/* search.c */
/* searches for pathname of file */
#define INCL_DOS
#include <os2.h>
#define LENGTH sizeof(result) /* length of result buffer */
#define CONTROL 0x0001         /* search current directory */

main(argc,argv)
int argc;
char *argv[];
{
    char result[256];          /* result path buffer */
    unsigned rc;               /* result code */

    if( argc != 3 )
       { printf("Syntax: search file path1;path2");
                                                  exit(1);  }

    if( rc=DosSearchPath( CONTROL, argv[2], argv[1],
                                       result, LENGTH ) )
       if( rc== 2)
          { printf("File not found"); exit(1); }
       else
          { printf("DosSearchPath=error %u",rc); exit(1); }
    printf("%s\n", result);
    exit(0);
}
```

To use this program to carry out the search for APP.INI described above, the following interchange might take place:

```
C>search app.ini \;\app\init
C:\APP\INIT
```

In this case the file APP.INI was in the directory \APP\INIT, but the program would find it in the current directory or the root directory, as well. The string \;\app\init tells the program to search for the file in either the root directory or \app\init. A parameter to DosSearchPath() tells the program to look in the current directory.

If the APP.INI file had been in the current directory, called \CHAP8\NOTES, the interaction with the program would have looked like this:

```
C>search app.ini \;\app\init
C:\CHAP8\NOTES
```

If the file cannot be found in any of the possible directories, the message "File not found" is printed

DosSearchPath — Search for filename

```
DosSearchPath(Control, Path, File, Buffer, Length);
unsigned Control;    /* cur dir or not, env vars or not */
char far *Path;      /* ASCIIZ list of pathnames */
char far *File;      /* ASCIIZ name of file */
char far *ABuffer;   /* address of result buffer */
unsigned Length;     /* length of result buffer */
```

The first parameter of DosSearchPath() is a control word that uses bit fields to determine two different options. This word is shown in Figure 7-4.

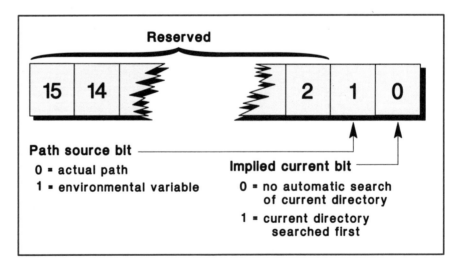

Figure 7-4
DosSearchPath( ) Control Word

Bit 0 in the control word is called the "Implied Current" bit. If this bit is set, the function searches the current directory for the file before it searches the directories named in the directory list. If the bit is not set, the current directory is not searched at all unless it is specifically named (a period may be used) in the search path. In the example it's set to 1 so the current directory is always searched.

The second bit is called the "path source" bit. We'll see what it does in the next example; in search.c it's set to 0.

The second parameter is the ASCIIZ string containing the pathnames to be searched, separated by semicolons.

The third parameter is the ASCIIZ string for the name of the file to be searched for. This filename can contain wildcards. Filenames with wildcards permit the use of this function in applications that need to return a group of pathnames instead of one. The results can be used as input for DosFindFirst() and DosFindNext().

The fourth parameter is the address of the buffer where the system will place the pathname of the file.

The last parameter is the length of the results buffer.

Finding the Path From an Environmental Variable

It is often the case that a pathname is stored in the environment so a particular directory can be referenced with an environmental variable. For example, the Microsoft C compiler uses this system to refer to the LIB directory using the variable LIB. The user can place this directory anywhere, but the environment must contain a line telling where it is, such as:

```
LIB=C:\C5\LIB
```

Using only the name LIB the compiler can figure out the pathname to use for files in that directory.

There are two ways to use API functions and environmental variables to find the pathnames of particular files. The first technique can be demonstrated simply by changing the value of the CONTROL variable in the search.c program. If the Path Source bit (position 1) is set to 1, then DosSearchPath() interprets the path argument as an environmental variable rather than a pathname. Only a single environmental variable may be used; semicolons are not appropriate when the Path Source bit is set.

The second way to use an environmental variable to search for a file is to convert the environmental variable to the corresponding pathname, using a function designed specifically for that purpose: DosScanEnv(). This function accepts the environmental variable as input, and finds the value (usually a pathname or series of pathnames) associated with it in the current environment. This technique is slightly more complicated than simply changing the CONTROL value in DosSearchPath().

DosScanEnv — Scan environment

```
DosScanEnv(VarName, BuffPtr);
char far *VarName;           /* ASCIIZ name of env variable */
char far * char far *BuffPtr;  /* address for string
                                  pointer */
```

DosScanEnv() takes as input the name of the environmental variable, and returns a pointer to the corresponding string value, as shown in Figure 7-5.

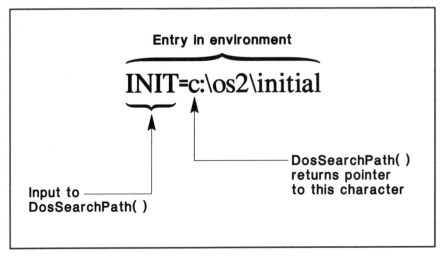

Figure 7-5
Pointer to Environmental Value

Here's a program that uses DosScanEnv() and DosSearchPath() to find a path to a file using an environmental variable.

```
/* envfind.c */
/* searches for file using environmental variable */
#define INCL_DOS
#include <os2.h>
#define LENGTH sizeof(result) /* length of result buffer */
#define CONTROL 0x0001        /* search current directory */
```

(continued)

```
main(argc,argv)
int argc;
char *argv[];
{
    char far *PathPtr;              /* pointer to env string */
    char result[256];              /* result path buffer */
    unsigned rc;                   /* result code */
    if( argc != 3 )                /* start with env variable */
        { printf("Syntax: envfind filename ENVVAR");
                                                    exit(1); }
                                   /* get actual pathname */
    if( rc=DosScanEnv( argv[2], &PathPtr ) )
        { printf("DosScanEnv error=%u",rc); exit(1); }
                                   /* search path */
    if( rc=DosSearchPath( CONTROL, PathPtr, argv[1],
                                        result, LENGTH ) )
        if( rc== 2)
            { printf("File not found"); exit(1); }
        else
            { printf("DosSearchPath error=%u",rc); exit(1); }
    printf("%s\n", result);
    exit(0);
}
```

Suppose the environment contained the line

`INIT=c:\os2\initial`

and suppose the file ED.INI was in the directory C:\OS2\INITIAL. If we invoked envfind.c to find the pathname for this file, the interaction would look like this:

`C>envfind ed.ini INIT`
`C:\OS2\INITIAL`

The environmental variable must be typed in uppercase letters, since this is how it appears in the environment. The program returns the pathname for the file.

The function DosScanEnv() takes the environmental variable INIT, and searches the environment for it, returning the corresponding pathname C:\OS2\INIT. Then, DosSearchPath() searches for the file ed.ini in this string and finds it. Since the Implied Current bit is set, it also looks in the current directory, but in this case doesn't find the file there.

Summary

In this chapter we've explored a variety of API functions that treat files as unopened units. We've seen how directories can be created and deleted with DosMkdir() and DosRmdir(), and how the current directory (for a a particular application) can be changed using DosChdir(). The current directory can be discovered using DosQCurDisk(), and the current disk drive number can be found and changed using DosQCurDisk() and DosSelectDisl().

Files can be deleted with DosDelete() and moved from one directory to another and renamed using the powerful DosMove() API function.

The trio of DosFindFirst(), DosFindNext(), and DosFindClose() can be used to return all the files matching a certain specification, which may include wildcards. We saw how these functions can be applied to several situations, including a directory search program and a directory byte count program.

The attributes of a file (whether it is read-only, hidden, system, archive, or a sub-directory) may be discovered with DosQFileMode(), and changed with DosSetFileMode().

Finally we saw how an application can use DosSearchPath() to find the path for a specific file, and DosScanEnv() to find a file whose path is specified as an environmental variable.

In the next chapter we'll show what can be done with a file when it is opened, exposing its contents for modification.

Chapter 8

Chapter 8

In the last chapter we looked at API functions that deal with files as discrete, unopened entities. In this chapter we explore functions that operate on opened files: that is, on a file's contents.

This chapter is divided into three parts. The first section shows examples of the basic API functions for opening a file and reading and writing to it. The second section discusses some API functions used to find out information about a file and change various characteristics of the file. In the last section we'll finish up with some miscellaneous file-related functions.

Many file-oriented API functions have counterparts in Microsoft C. These are new library functions created specifically to work in the multitasking environment. For example, the API function DosOpen() permits a file to be opened for sharing with other processes; the Microsoft C library function sopen() can be used in much the same way. In this chapter we use the API functions rather than similar C library functions.

As has been true in previous chapters, many of the API file functions are similar to INT 21 system calls in MS-DOS.

This chapter focuses on the use of file I/O functions in single-tasking situations. In the next chapter we'll explore the multitasking possibilities of file I/O.

Reading and Writing Files

The OS/2 API functions for opening, closing, reading, and writing files are similar in some respects to the traditional C-language system-level functions for file I/O: open(), close(), read(), and write(). The most important similarity is that both sets of functions treat data as an unformatted sequence of bytes. There is no attempt to interpret the data as integers, records, or other data types.

However, the API disk I/O functions have several additional features. Many of these features become meaningful primarily when the functions are used in a multitasking situation, but there are other differences as well.

Writing to a File

Our first example is a program that permits the user to write a simple text file. We use this program to demonstrate three API functions: DosOpen(), DosWrite(), and DosClose().

The program is invoked with a command-line argument consisting of the name of the file to be written. When the program starts, it displays a message telling whether the requested file existed already and was truncated, or whether it did not exist and was created. The program then instructs the user to enter lines of text, and signal the end of the input process by starting a line with [Enter].

Here's a sample session, in which the user inputs the first stanza of Samuel Taylor Coleridge's poem, "Kubla Khan".

```
C>wfile kubla.txt
File existed and was truncated
Enter lines of text.
To terminate, start line with [Enter].
In Xanadu did Kubla Khan
   A stately pleasure-dome decree:
Where Alph, the sacred river, ran
Through caverns measureless to man
   Down to a sunless sea.
```

You can use the DOS TYPE function to see that the keyboard data was in fact written to the disk.

Here's the program listing:

```
/* wfile.c */
/* writes a text file to disk */
/* input comes from keyboard */
#define INCL_DOS
#include <os2.h>
#include <string.h>      /* for strcat() */
#define ATTR 0           /* normal file */
#define OPENFLAG 0x12    /* truncate old or create new file */
#define OPENMODE 0x0041  /* acc=write only, share=deny
                                                    none */

main(argc, argv)
int argc;
char *argv[];
{
   char filename[81];      /* buffer for file name */
   char string[80];        /* buffer for keyboard text */
   unsigned short handle;  /* file handle from DosOpen */
   unsigned action;        /* action taken by DosOpen */
   unsigned long size=0;   /* no minimum size of file */
   unsigned length;        /* length of keyboard line */
   unsigned BytesWritten;  /* bytes written by DosWrite */
   unsigned total=0;       /* running total, bytes written */
   unsigned rc;            /* return code */

   if( argc != 2 )
      { printf("Syntex: wfile filename\n"); exit(1); }
   strcpy( filename, argv[1] );
```

(continued)

```
                              /* open file */
        if( rc=DosOpen(filename, &handle, &action, size,
                              ATTR, OPENFLAG, OPENMODE, 0L) )
            { printf("DosOpen error=%u\n", rc); exit(1); }

        switch(action)  {
           case 2: printf("File was created.\n"); break;
           case 3: printf("File existed and was truncated.\n");
        }
        printf("Enter lines of text.\n");
        printf("To terminate, start line with [Enter].\n");
        do {
           gets(string);       /* get line of text from keyboard */
           strcat(string, "\n\r");    /* add CR and LF */
           length = strlen(string);   /* DosWrite needs length */
                              /* write line to disk */
           if( rc=DosWrite( handle, string, length,
                                             &BytesWritten ) )
              { printf("DosWrite error=%d", rc); exit(1); }
           total += BytesWritten;
        }  while( length > 2 );
                              /* print bytes, close file, exit */
        printf("Total bytes written to file is %d\n", total);
        DosClose(handle);
        exit(0);
        }
```

The DosOpen() Function

The DosOpen() function is the most important, and also the most complicated, of the file-related API functions. Much of its additional complexity, compared with the traditional C system function open(), is the result of working in a multitasking environment. However, there are also improvements such as an argument returned by the system that tells whether the file existed.

DosOpen — Open file

```
DosOpen(Name, AHandle, AAction, Size, Attr, Flag, Mode,
                                                    Res);
char far *Name;            /* ASCIIZ name of file to open */
unsigned short far *AHandle;  /* address for file handle */
unsigned far *AAction;     /* address for action taken */
unsigned long Size;        /* new size of file in bytes */
unsigned Attr;             /* attribute to be used */
unsigned Flag;             /* action to be taken */
unsigned Mode;             /* open mode to be used */
unsigned long Res;         /* reserved: must be 0 */
```

Let's look at the arguments to DosOpen() one at a time. There is a great deal of information stored in these arguments, and understanding it is the key to understanding the file API functions in general.

Name is an ASCIIZ string containing the name of the file to be opened. You should avoid using filenames longer than 11 characters (eight for the name and three for the extension). Some versions of OS/2 may simply truncate longer names, but newer versions will return an error. When the OS/2 file system is revised in the future, names longer than 11 characters will be accepted. The argument used for the name can be a file in the current directory or a complete pathname.

Ahandle is the address of a word in which the system will return the handle. Three file handles are permanently assigned:

Handle	Device
0	Standard input
1	Standard output
2	Standard error

There is no "standard auxiliary" handle as there is in MS-DOS, nor is there a standard printer.

The system may use several handles for dynalink files in use for library functions, so the handle numbers returned from DosOpen() may start at 10 or so. The file handle is defined in the Microsoft C header files to have the type **unsigned short**. This is currently the same as **unsigned int** (two bytes), but is used for compatibility on new systems that might use a different integer size.

AAction is the address of a word that holds the results of the action taken by DosOpen() in response to the existence of the file to be opened. The possible values for this parameter are:

Value	Action taken
1	File existed
2	File was created
3	File existed and was truncated

Size is the size of the file in bytes. If an existing file is being opened, this value is ignored. If the file does not exist, DosOpen() allocates the number of bytes requested using as contiguous an area of the disk as possible. If the file is being created, but its size is unknown in advance, this value may be set to zero or to whatever is anticipated as the minimum file size. Then the size of the file will be determined by the data written to it.

Attr is a word specifying the attribute of the file to be opened. This is the same information dealt with by the DosQFileMode() and DosSetFileMode() functions discussed in the last chapter, except that directories cannot be accessed with DosOpen().

The **Attr** word uses the following bitfields:

Value	File attribute
0x0000	Normal
0x0001	Read-only
0x0002	Hidden
0x0004	System
0x0020	Archive

This argument permits the attribute of the file to be established when it is first opened.

Flag or **OpenFlag** is a word used by the program to specify what action it wants the system to take if the file exists or doesn't exist. The lower eight bits of the word are broken into two four-bit fields. The left-hand four bits tell the action to take if the file exists; the right-hand four bits tell what to do if the file does not exist. Figure 8-1 shows the arrangement of this argument.

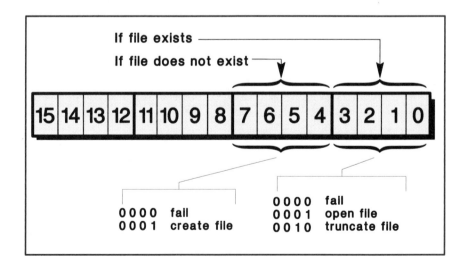

Figure 8-1
The OpenFlag Argument

In the example wfile.c, the value 0x12 is used, indicating the file should be created if it doesn't exist, or truncated (reduced to zero length) if it does exist. This setting—truncating an existing file—should be used with care, since it effectively erases the file.

Mode or **OpenMode** controls a variety of different aspects of the file, the most important having to do with how the file is accessed and shared by other files. Figure 8-2 shows how the bit fields for this argument are arranged.

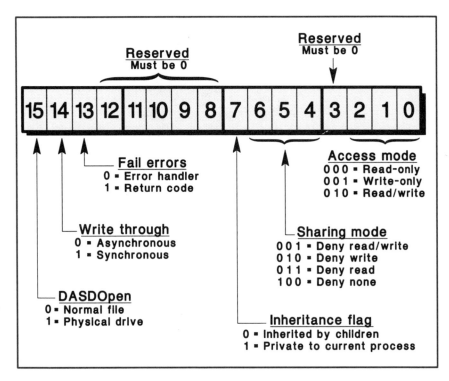

Figure 8-2
The OpenMode Argument

The **AccessMode** bit field in the **OpenMode** argument can have one of three values, as shown in the figure: read-only, write-only, and read-write. This argument tells how the current process intends to operate on the file. For instance, if the file will be written to, as in the example, it must be opened as either write-only or read/write; otherwise the DosWrite() function will return the error message ACCESS_DENIED. In the example it is opened as write-only.

The AccessMode is used in conjunction with the Sharing Mode argument to determine whether a file opened by one process can be accessed by another. We'll see later what happens when a file is opened by more than one process at a time.

The **SharingMode** bit field defines what operations other processes may perform on the file. As seen in the figure, it can have one of four values, representing deny read/write, deny write, deny read, and deny none. (A value of 000 (binary) is illegal.) It is important to set these values correctly if you expect a file to be accessed by more than one process at once. We'll look into file access by multiple processes in the next chapter.

The **InheritanceFlag** bit tells whether the file handle will be passed along to child processes. If not set, the file handle is inherited by children of the process that opened it, and may be accessed as if the child had opened it. If set, the file handle is private, and may be accessed only by the parent process.

The **FailErrors** bit specifies how physical problems, such as not having a disk in the drive or trying to read from a bad sector, are reported. If the bit is set, the function returns an error code to the application. If the bit is cleared, the "system critical error handler" reports the error directly to the user.

The **WriteThrough** bit indicates to what extent writes to the disk are buffered. If this bit is set, the information specified in the write command is physically placed on the disk before the command returns. If the bit is not set, information is sent to a buffer and not written to the disk until the buffer is full or the file is closed. In normal situations this bit may be cleared to zero.

The **DASDOpen** bit is set if the open applies to a physical drive rather than a file. This setting is provided mostly for systems programmers and is not ordinarily needed by applications programmers.

The **Reserved** bit fields in **OpenMode** must be set to zero.

Here's how the arguments to DosOpen() are used in the wfile.c example program. The **filename** is a string copied from the command-line argument **argv[1]**. The **handle** returned by the open is saved for later use by DosWrite() and DosClose(). The **action argument** is used in a **switch** statement to tell the user whether the file was created, or existed already and was truncated. The **size** is initialized to zero to indicate we don't require any minimum size for the file; the size of the file will depend on how much we write into it. The **attribute** is set to zero to indicate a normal file. The **OpenFlag** is set to create a new file (if the file does not exist) or truncate an existing file. **OpenMode** has its sharing mode set to deny none, and its access mode set to write-only.

The DosWrite() Function

Once the program opens the file, it next goes into a loop where it repeatedly obtains a line of text from the keyboard and writes it to the file.

As is usual in C programming, the decision must be made about how to store newlines. The C convention is to indicate newlines as the linefeed character: 0x0a. The DOS convention is the carriage-return linefeed combination: 0x0d 0x0a. If the contents of the file are read only by printf() or similar C statements, then the C convention is appropriate. If it is read using the OS/2 VIO functions, the DOS convention should be used, since the VIO calls do not expand a LF into a CR/LF combination. In the program we use the DOS convention, so both characters are appended to each line using strcpy().

Each line of text is written in turn to the disk using the DosWrite() API command.

```
              DosWrite — Synchronous write to file
DosWrite(Handle, Buffer, BuffLength, ABytesWritten);
unsigned short Handle;          /* handle from DosOpen() */
void far *Buffer;               /* address of data buffer */
unsigned BuffLength;            /* number of bytes to write */
unsigned far *ABytesWritten;    /* address for bytes
                                   written */
```

DosWrite() requires four parameters. The first is the file handle already obtained from DosOpen(). The second is the address of the buffer from which the data is written. The function expects this data to be of type **char**. If the data is something else, it must be cast to type **char**.

The third parameter, **length**, is the number of bytes to write. In the example this is obtained by finding the length of the string input from the keyboard. (The program assumes, somewhat dangerously, that the user will not type a string longer than the 80-column screen width.) The final parameter is the address of a word where the number of bytes actually written, **BytesWritten**, is returned by the function. This is normally the same as **length**, the number of bytes specified to be written. If it isn't the same, some error, such as the disk being full, has occurred. A conscientious write routine would check for this possibility. In the example, after each write, we add the value of **BytesWritten** to a running total, which is later printed out to tell the user the size of the file created.

The DosClose() Function

The last API function in the program is DosClose().

> ### DosClose — Close file handle
>
> ```
> DosClose(Handle);
> unsigned short Handle;      /* file handle to be closed */
> ```

This function takes only one parameter: the handle of the file to be closed.

When this function executes, the contents of any internal buffers not yet written are sent to the disk, and the directory entries for the file handle are updated. A file is normally closed when all the processes using it are terminated, so strictly speaking this function is not necessary in the example shown. However, it is good practice to specifically close every file.

Reading from a File

Reading from a file is no more complicated than writing to it. The following example program reads text files from the disk and displays them on the screen. You can use it to display files created with wfile.c, as shown here, where the same file created earlier is displayed:

```
C>rfile kubla.txt
In Xanadu did Kubla Khan
   A stately pleasure-dome decree:
Where Alph, the sacred river, ran
Through caverns measureless to man
   Down to a sunless sea.
```

You can also display files created with other programs. In operation the example program looks very much like the DOS TYPE function. The file to be displayed is entered as a command-line argument.

```
/* rfile.c */
/* reads text file from disk and displays it */
#define INCL_DOS
#include <os2.h>
```

(continued)

```
#define ATTR 0           /* normal file */
#define OPENFLAG 0x01    /* fail if no file, or open it */
#define OPENMODE 0x0040 /* acc=read-only, share=deny none */
#define BUFLEN 40         /* size of input buffer */
#define ERROR_OPEN_FAILED 110   /* explicit open failure */

main(argc, argv)
int argc;
char *argv[];
{
    char buffer[BUFLEN+1];   /* buffer for text */
    unsigned short handle;   /* file handle from DosOpen */
    unsigned action;         /* action taken by DosOpen */
    unsigned long size=0;    /* no minimum size of file */
    unsigned length;         /* length of keyboard line */
    unsigned BytesRead;      /* bytes read by DosRead */
    unsigned rc;             /* return code */

    if( argc != 2 )
       { printf("Syntex: rfile filename\n"); exit(1); }

                           /* open file */
    if( rc=DosOpen(argv[1], &handle, &action, size,
                        ATTR, OPENFLAG, OPENMODE, 0L) )
       if( rc = ERROR_OPEN_FAILED )
          { printf("Can't find that file"); exit(1); }
       else
          { printf("DosOpen error=%u\n", rc); exit(1); }

    do  {                   /* read line of text */
       if( rc=DosRead(handle, buffer, BUFLEN, &BytesRead ) )
          { printf("DosRead error=%u\n", rc); exit(1); }

                           /* display line of text */
       buffer[BytesRead] = 0;    /* put '\0' to end string */
       printf( "%s", buffer );   /* print string */
    } while( BytesRead==BUFLEN );  /* EOF when buffer not
                                      full */

    DosClose(handle);
    exit(0);
}
```

The arguments to the DosOpen() function are somewhat different than those in the wfile.c example. The **OpenFlag** parameter is set
to fail if the file doesn't exist, or open it if it does. The access bit field
in **OpenMode** is set to read-only. Also, we look for a particular return
code: 110, or ERROR_OPEN_FAILED. This is the code returned

when the conditions explicitly specified in the **OpenFlag** parameter are not met. In the example we requested a failure if the file does not exist, so when this is the case the code 110 is returned. On return of this code, the program informs the user that the file cannot be found. All other error codes are returned as numbers in the usual way.

The DosRead() Function

The DosRead() function is similar to DosWrite().

```
          DosRead — Synchronous read from file

DosRead(Handle, ABuffer, BuffLength, ABytesRead);
unsigned short Handle;       /* handle from DosOpen() */
void far *ABuffer;           /* address of data buffer */
unsigned BuffLength;         /* size of buffer in bytes */
unsigned far *ABytesRead;    /* address for bytes actually
                                read */
```

The handle and the address of the data buffer perform the same functions they do in DosWrite(). **BuffLength** is the maximum size of the data buffer. The function pours in bytes from the disk until this space is filled. **BytesRead** returns the number of bytes actually read by the function. When this is less than **BuffLength**, we can assume— for disk files—that the end of the file has been reached in mid-read. (When reading from the keyboard using KBD$ this may not be true; in that case it's important to check that **BytesRead** is actually 0, since a small value may indicate only that a short line of text was typed.) If **BytesRead** is 0, the function was trying to read from the end-of-file. The example program checks the size of **BytesRead**, and stops reading when it is smaller than **BuffLength**.

To display a line of text using the C library function printf(), the program must first insert a 0 at the end of the string to be displayed. You could use the API function VioWrtTTy() here instead; it does not require the insertion of a zero, only the length of the string to be printed.

Examining Files

Here's a program that uses the DosRead() function to display the contents of any file, whether text or binary. It uses an output format similar to that employed by DEBUG and other programs.

```
/* hexdump.c */
/* displays file in hex and ASCII characters */
#define INCL_DOS
#include <os2.h>
#define ATTR 0                  /* normal file */
#define OPENFLAG 0x01           /* fail if no file, or open it */
#define OPENMODE 0x0042         /* acc=read/write, share=deny
                                   none */
#define BUFLEN 16               /* size of input buffer */

main(argc, argv)
int argc;
char *argv[];
{
   char buffer[BUFLEN+1]; /* buffer for input */
   unsigned short handle; /* file handle from DosOpen */
   unsigned action;       /* action taken by DosOpen */
   unsigned long size=0;  /* no minimum size of file */
   unsigned length;       /* length of keyboard line */
   unsigned BytesRead;    /* bytes read by DosRead */
   int j;                 /* character counter */
   unsigned rc;           /* return code */

   if( argc != 2 )
      { printf("Syntex: rfile filename\n"); exit(1); }

                           /* open file */
   if( rc=DosOpen(argv[1], &handle, &action, size,
                     ATTR, OPENFLAG, OPENMODE, 0L) )
      { printf("DosOpen error=%u\n", rc); exit(1); }

   do {                    /* read file */
      if( rc=DosRead(handle, buffer, BUFLEN, &BytesRead ) )
         { printf("DosRead error=%u\n", rc); exit(1); }

                           /* display bytes in hex */
      for(j=0; j<BUFLEN; j++) {        /* for each char */
         if( j >= BytesRead )          /* if short line, */
            printf("   ");             /* fill in spaces */
         else {                        /* print hex value */
            printf("%2x ", buffer[j] & 0xFF );
            if( buffer[j] < 32 )       /* if not printable, */

               buffer[j] = '.';        /* substitute period */

         }
      }                    /* display ascii string */
```

(continued)

```
        buffer[BytesRead] = 0;      /* put '\0' to end string */
        printf(" %s\n", buffer );  /* print string */
    } while( BytesRead==BUFLEN );   /* EOF when buffer not
                                       full */

    DosClose(handle);
    exit(0);
}
```

The file to be displayed is entered as a command line argument.
Here's an example of the program's output, when it is used to display
its own source code. Only the last few lines of the file are shown.

```
- - - - - - - - - - - - - - - - - - - - - - - - - - - - - - - - -
20 20 70 72 69 6e 74 66 28 22 20 25 73 5c 6e 22     printf(" %s\n"
2c 20 62 75 66 66 65 72 20 29 3b 20 20 20 2f 2a     , buffer );  /*
20 70 72 69 6e 74 20 73 74 72 69 6e 67 20 2a 2f     print string */
 d  a 20 20 20 7d 20 77 68 69 6c 65 28 20 42 79     ..    } while( By
74 65 73 52 65 61 64 3d 3d 42 55 46 4c 45 4e 20     tesRead==BUFLEN
29 3b 20 20 2f 2a 20 45 4f 46 20 77 68 65 6e 20     );   /* EOF when
62 75 66 66 65 72 20 6e 6f 74 20 66 75 6c 6c 20     buffer not full
2a 2f  d  a  d  a 20 20 20 44 4f 53 43 4c 4f 53     */....   DOSCLOS
45 28 68 61 6e 64 6c 65 29 3b  d  a 20 20 20 65     E(handle);..   e
78 69 74 28 30 29 3b  d  a 7d  d  a                  xit(0);..}..
```

Dots are used to represent the ASCII version of non-printable
characters.

Standard Handles

Before leaving the subject of reading and writing, we should mention
that the three standard file handles (listed earlier) can be used without DosOpen(). This same arrangement exists in MS-DOS.

Here's a program that takes phrases typed at the keyboard and
displays them on the screen, using DosWrite() instead of printf() or
VioWrtTTy().

```
/* stdout.c */
/* writes a text file to the screen, using DosWrite() */
/* input comes from keyboard */
#define INCL_DOS
#include <os2.h>
#include <string.h>              /* for strcat() */
#define STDOUT (unsigned short)1 /* file handle for
                                    screen */
```

(continued)

```
main()
{
    char string[80];        /* buffer for keyboard text */
    unsigned length;        /* length of keyboard line */
    unsigned BytesWritten;  /* bytes written by DosWrite */
    unsigned total=0;       /* running total, bytes written */
    unsigned rc;            /* return code */

    printf("Enter lines of text.\n");
    printf("To terminate, start line with [Enter].\n");
    do {
        gets(string);       /* get line of text from keyboard */
        strcat(string, "\n\r");    /* add CR and LF */
        length = strlen(string);    /* DosWrite needs length */
                            /* write line to disk */
        if( rc=DosWrite( STDOUT, string, length,
                                        &BytesWritten ) )
            { printf("DosWrite error=%u", rc); exit(1); }
        total += BytesWritten;
    }  while( length > 2 );
                            /* display total bytes */
    printf("Total bytes written is %d\n", total);
    exit(0);
}
```

This program is considerably simpler than wfile.c, since Dos-Open() and all its arguments are not necessary.

Since we are using the screen to echo the input to the program, as well as display the output, every line (a quote from George Bernard Shaw) will appear twice:

```
C>stdout
Enter lines of text.
To terminate, start line with [Enter]
Nothing is worth doing
Nothing is worth doing
unless the consequences
unless the consequences
may be serious.
may be serious.
Total bytes written is 68
```

This approach is most commonly used in situations where the output may go either to the screen, or, if indirection is used, to a file.

We'll see another example of DosWrite() used without DosOpen() when we discuss pipes in the chapter on interprocess communication.

File Information

In the last chapter we examined some functions like DosQFileMode() and DosSetFileMode() that obtain information from, and change the characteristics of, unopened files. There is also a group of API functions which use the file handle to get and change different kinds of information in open files. In this section we look at some of these functions.

Date and Size

The date and time a file was last written to, its size, and other information about it can be obtained using an API function called DosQFileInfo().

```
         DosQFileInfo — Query file information
DosQFileInfo(Handle, InfoLevel, Buffer, BuffSize);
unsigned short Handle;      /* file handle from DosOpen() */
unsigned InfoLevel;         /* 1 is only level now in use */
struct _FILESTATUS *Buffer;    /* address of buffer for
                                  info */
unsigned BuffSize;          /* size of buffer in bytes */
```

The first argument is the file handle. The second is the information level; at present only one level is defined, so this argument must be set to 1. The third argument is the buffer where the information is stored, and the fourth is the size, in bytes, of the buffer.

The structure of the buffer for the file is defined in BSEDOS.H. Without the typedef, it looks like this:

```
struct _FILESTATUS   {
   struct _FDATE fdateCreation; /* not in current version */
   struct _FTIME ftimeCreation;
   struct _FDATE fdateLastAccess; /* not in current version
                                     */
   struct _FTIME ftimeLastAccess;
   struct _FDATE fdateLastWrite;  /* last write info */
   struct _FTIME ftimeLastWrite;
   unsigned long cbFile;          /* actual size of file */
   unsigned long cbFileAlloc;     /* size allocated */
   unsigned attrFile;             /* file attributes */
};
```

The _FDATE and _FTIME types are bitfield structures, defined in OS2DEF.H. Without the typedefs they look like this:

```
struct _FDATE   {
   unsigned day    : 5;
   unsigned month  : 4;
   unsigned year   : 7;    /* 1980 is 0 */
};

struct _FTIME   {
   unsigned twosecs : 5;   /* multiply by two for seconds */
   unsigned minutes : 6;
   unsigned seconds : 5;
};
```

The date and time of the file's creation, and the date and time of its last access, are not currently implemented. The remaining entries in the buffer report the date and time a file was last written to, the size of the file in bytes, the allocation size (currently a multiple of 2048 bytes for the hard disk, although this depends on the type of device), and the file attributes. You may obtain attributes in other ways, through such functions as DosQFileMode(), discussed in the last chapter.

The structure of the date and time information is shown in Figure 8-3.

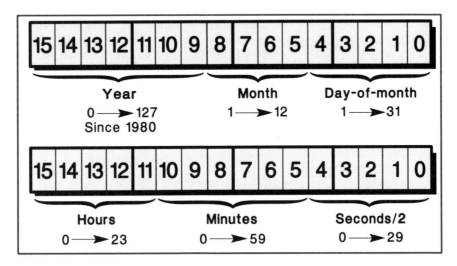

Figure 8-3
Date and Time Format

The following example program obtains and displays date, time and size information about a file whose name is typed on the command line, and displays it.

```c
/* fileinfo.c */
/* gets file information using DosQFileInfo() */
#define INCL_DOS
#include <os2.h>
#define SIZE 0L          /* no minimum size of file */
#define ATTR 0           /* normal file */
#define FLAG 0x01        /* fail if no file, or open it */
#define MODE 0x4042      /* acc=read/write, share=deny none */
#define LEVEL 1          /* only level available */
#define BUFF_SIZE sizeof(fstatus)
main(argc, argv)
int argc;
char *argv[];
{
   struct _FILESTATUS fstatus;  /* defined in bsedos.h */
   unsigned short handle;       /* file handle from DosOpen */
   unsigned action;            /* action taken by DosOpen */
   unsigned rc;                /* return code */

   if( argc != 2 )
     { printf("Syntax: fileinfo filename\n"); exit(1); }
                     /* open file */
   if( rc=DosOpen( argv[1], &handle, &action, SIZE, ATTR,
                                  FLAG, MODE, 0L ) )  {
      if( rc==32 )
        printf("Can't open file: sharing violation");
      else if( rc==5 )
        printf("Can't open file: access denied");
      else if( rc==110 )
        printf("Can't open file: doesn't exist");
      else
        printf("DosOpen error=%u", rc);
      exit(1);
   }
```

(continued)

```
                              /* query file information */
        if( rc=DosQFileInfo( handle, LEVEL, &fstatus,
                                                BUFF_SIZE ) )

          { printf("DosQFileInfo error=%u",rc); exit(1); }
                              /* print file information */
        printf("Date and time of creation: ");
                              /* print month */
        printf("%2d/", fstatus.fdateLastWrite.month );
                              /* print day of month */
        printf("%02d/", fstatus.fdateLastWrite.day );
                              /* print year */
        printf("%02d  ", fstatus.fdateLastWrite.year + 80 );
                              /* print hour */
        printf("%2d:", fstatus.ftimeLastWrite.hours );
                              /* print minute */
        printf("%02d:", fstatus.ftimeLastWrite.minutes );
                              /* print seconds */
        printf("%02d\n", fstatus.ftimeLastWrite.twosecs * 2 );
                              /* print other info */
        printf("File size = %lu\n", fstatus.cbFile );
        printf("Allocation size = %lu\n", fstatus.cbFileAlloc );
                              /* close file and exit */
        DosClose( handle );
        exit(0);
}
```

Here's a typical interaction with the program:

```
C>fileinfo wfile.exe
Date and time of creation:   6/04/88  10:44:24
File size = 8744
Allocation size = 10240
```

Notice that we look for three specific return codes when opening the file. We've already seen that 110, ERROR_OPEN_FAILED, happens when the conditions specified in the **OpenFlag** argument to DosOpen() are not met. In this case, if the file does not exist, it elicits a message to this effect. Code 5, ERROR_ACCESS_DENIED, occurs when an inappropriate access is used. An attempt to open read-only file for read/write elicits this Code 5 error. Code 32,

ERROR_SHARING_VIOLATION, occurs when a file is already in use by another process and cannot be shared. For instance, if you enter

```
C>fileinfo fileinfo.exe
```

this error will occur. We'll explore sharing violations in the next section.

Another function, DosSetFileInfo(), permits modification of the dates and times obtained by DosQFileInfo(). Since only the date and time of the last write are currently used, only these items may be modified.

DosSetFileInfo — Set file information

```
DosSetFileInfo(Handle, InfoLevel, Buffer, BuffSize);
unsigned short Handle;          /* file handle */
unsigned InfoLevel;             /* 1 is only level now used */
struct _FILESTATUS far *Buffer;  /* buffer for new file
                                    info */
unsigned BuffSize;              /* size of buffer in bytes */
```

This function takes four parameters, similar to those in DosQFileInfo(). The structure of the buffer **struct _FILESTATUS** is the same as that used in DosQFileInfo(), except that it does not use the last three members of the structure: the size, allocated size, and attributes. Only the date and time of creation, last access, and last write are available to DosSetFileInfo().

If a value of 0 is used for both the date and time parameters for any of these three events, that field is left unchanged.

Handle Type

It is sometimes important for an application to know if an open file handle applies to an actual file, to a device such as the screen or keyboard, or to a pipe. The DosQHandType() function returns this information. A program can then decide whether it is dealing with interactive screen and keyboard I/O with a user, with a normal file, or with a pipe. If it is dealing with a file, for instance, it may not want to use screen prompts that are appropriate when it is dealing with a user.

DosQHandType — Query handle type

```
DosQHandType(Handle, AType, AFlag);
unsigned short Handle; /* file handle */
unsigned far *AType;   /* address for type: 0=file, etc. */
unsigned far *AFlag; /* address for attribute, if device */
```

This function takes three parameters: the handle of the file to be investigated, the address of a word where the file type is returned, and the address where the device attribute—if the handle is a device—is returned. The handle type can have one of three values:

Value	Handle type
0	File
1	Device
2	Pipe

Here's a program that uses this function to find the file type and display it. Typically a program would use the results internally, rather than displaying them.

```c
/* handtype.c */
/* tells if handle is normal file or device */
#define INCL_DOS
#include <os2.h>
#define ATTR 0          /* normal file */
#define OPENFLAG 0x01   /* fail if no file, or open it */
#define OPENMODE 0x0040 /* acc=read-only, share=deny none */

main(argc, argv)
int argc;
char *argv[];
{
    unsigned short handle;   /* file handle from DosOpen */
    unsigned action;         /* action taken by DosOpen */
    unsigned long size=0;    /* no minimum size of file */
    unsigned HandType;       /* 0=file, 1=device, 2=pipe */
    unsigned attribute;      /* attribute if handle is file */
    unsigned rc;             /* return code */

    if( argc != 2 )
        { printf("Syntax: handtype filename"); exit(1); }
                            /* open file */
    if( rc=DosOpen(argv[1], &handle, &action, size,
                        ATTR, OPENFLAG, OPENMODE, 0L) )
        { printf("DosOpen error=%u\n", rc); exit(1); }
                            /* find handle type */
    if( rc=DosQHandType( handle, &HandType, &attribute ) )
        { printf("DosQHandType error=%u\n", rc); exit(1); }
    if( HandType==0 )        /* display handle type */
        printf("File system handle\n");
```
                        (continued)

```
    else
       printf("Device handle\n");
                            /* display attribute */
       printf("Attribute word is %x\n", attribute );

       DosClose(handle);        /* close file and exit */
       exit(0);
}
```

Here's an example of interaction when we use the name which is a normal file:

```
C>handtype wfile.exe
File system handle
Attribute word is 0
```

In this case the attribute word is 0, indicating a file.

Now here's the interaction when we use a name which is actually a device, in this case the screen:

```
C>handtype SCREEN$
Device handle
Attribute word is 8082
```

When applied to a device the attribute word contains a value other than 0. Figure 8-4 shows the layout of the device attribute word.

The appropriate bit is set in the device attribute word when the condition noted in the figure applies. The driver name for the standard output device (stdout) is SCREEN$, and the standard input device stdin is called (KBD$). The name CON (for console) applies to these two devices used together. PRN is used for the printer and CLOCK$ for the clock. A full description of the parameters in the device attribute word is beyond the scope of this book. Their explanation can be found in the Microsoft *Device Drivers Guide* or similar references.

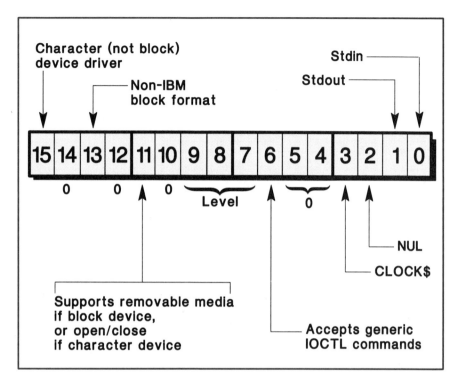

Figure 8-4
Device Attribute Word

Handle State

Once a file has been opened, a program may need to find out what values were used in the **OpenMode** argument supplied to DosOpen(). This information is called the handle state, and the API function DosQFHandState() will retrieve it. Here's a program that makes use of this function. It first prints the value of the **OpenMode** argument used in DosOpen(), and then the value of the handle state from DosQFHandState(). These should be the same.

```
/* filehand.c */
/* displays file handle state */
#define INCL_DOS
#include <os2.h>
#define SIZE 0L          /* no minimum size of file */
#define ATTR 0           /* normal file */
#define FLAG 0x01        /* fail if no file, or open it */
#define MODE 0x4040      /* acc=read-only, share=deny none */
```

(continued)

```
main(argc, argv)
int argc;
char *argv[];
{

    unsigned short handle;  /* file handle from DosOpen */
    unsigned action;    /* action taken by DosOpen */
    unsigned state;     /* handle state from DosQFHandState */
    unsigned rc;        /* return code */

    if( argc != 2 )
        { printf("Syntax: filehand filename\n"); exit(1); }
                        /* display initial open mode */
    printf("File opened with OpenMode = %x\n", MODE );
                        /* open file */
    if( rc=DosOpen( argv[1], &handle, &action, SIZE, ATTR,
                                    FLAG, MODE, 0L ) )
        { printf("DosOpen error=%u", rc); exit(1); }
                        /* query file handle state */
    if( rc=DosQFHandState( handle, &state ) )
        { printf("DosQFHandState error=%u",rc); exit(1); }
                        /* display state */
    printf("File handle state = %x\n", state );
                        /* close file and exit */
    DosClose( handle );
    exit(0);
}
```

Here's a sample interaction:

```
C>fhand wfile.exe
File opened with OpenMode = 4040
File handle state = 4040
```

The DosQFHandState() function takes only two parameters: the file handle, and the address where the handle state is returned.

DosQFHandState — Query file handle state

```
DosQFHandState(Handle, AHandleState);
unsigned short Handle;      /* file handle */
unsigned far *AHandState;   /* address for handle state */
```

The hand state word has the same format as the **OpenMode** word described under DosOpen(), and can be analyzed in the same way.

Maximum File Handles

When OS/2 is booted it sets a default maximum number of file handles which can be opened by all the processes in the system. Currently this value is 20. As we noted earlier, some of these handles are used by the system, and others may be used by DLL libraries invoked by running programs.

If an application needs to open more than a few files it may be necessary for it to increase the maximum number of file handles. This can be accomplished using the API function DosSetMaxFH(). Here's an example program that obtains the new value for the maximum number of file handles from the user as a command-line argument, and sets the value in the system with DosSetMaxFH().

```
/* maxfh.c */
/* set maximum number of file handles */
#define INCL_DOS
#include <os2.h>
main(argc, argv)
int argc;
char *argv[];
{
    unsigned maxhands;
    unsigned rc;

    if( argc != 2 )
        { printf("Syntax: maxfh maxhandles"); exit(1); }
    maxhands = (unsigned)atoi( argv[1] );
    if( rc=DosSetMaxFH( maxhands ) )
        { printf("DosSetMaxFH error=%u",rc); exit(1); }
    exit(0);
}
```

The only parameter to DosSetMaxFH() is the new value for the number of handles.

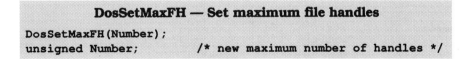

DosSetMaxFH — Set maximum file handles

```
DosSetMaxFH(Number);
unsigned Number;            /* new maximum number of handles */
```

You cannot reduce the maximum number of handles. If a value less than the initial value is used, the program returns code 87, ERROR_INVALID_PARAMETER. Values larger than 255 are also invalid.

Other File Functions

This section covers some additional file-oriented API functions that reset the file pointer, change a file's size, reset the I/O buffer, and duplicate a file handle.

File Pointers

The OS/2 API includes a function, DosChgFilePtr(), to change the file pointer within a file. This provides random access to any point in the file, in a way similar to the C library functions fseek() and lseek(), or the Lseek INT 21 systems call in MS-DOS.

The following example demonstrates the operation of DosChg-FilePtr(), using a modification of the rfile.c example. Here the file pointer is set to a point in the middle of a file, and the file is read and displayed from that point on. The program requires two command-line arguments: the name of the file, and the offset within the file to start reading. It then displays the file from this offset forward. Here's an example, using the kubla.txt file generated earlier:

```
C>ptrfile kubla.txt 96
New pointer location is 96
Through caverns measureless to man
  Down to a sunless sea.
```

Here we ask to see the kubla.txt file from character 96 onward. This position happens to be at the start of the last two lines, so that's all that is displayed.

The listing is very much like rfile.c, except for the inclusion of the DosChgFilePtr() function.

```
/* ptrfile.c */
/* places read/write pointer in middle of file */
/* reads balance of file and displays it */
#define INCL_DOS
#include <os2.h>
#include <stdlib.h>      /* for atol() */
```

(continued)

```
#define ATTR 0            /* normal file */
#define OPENFLAG 0x01     /* fail if no file, or open it */
#define OPENMODE 0x0040   /* acc=read-only, share=deny none */
#define BUFLEN 40         /* size of input buffer */
#define ERROR_OPEN_FAILED 110  /* explicit open failure */
#define MOVE_TYPE 0       /* start from beginning of file */

main(argc, argv)
int argc;
char *argv[];
{
   char buffer[BUFLEN+1];   /* buffer for text */
   unsigned short handle;   /* file handle from DosOpen */
   unsigned action;         /* action taken by DosOpen */
   unsigned long size=0;    /* no minimum size of file */
   unsigned length;         /* length of keyboard line */
   unsigned BytesRead;      /* bytes read by DosRead */
   long distance;       /* number of bytes to move pointer */
   unsigned long newptr;    /* new pointer location */
   unsigned rc;             /* return code */

   if( argc != 3 )
      { printf("Syntex: ptrfile fname position\n");
                                           exit(1); }

                       /* open file */
   if( rc=DosOpen(argv[1], &handle, &action, size,
                     ATTR, OPENFLAG, OPENMODE, 0L) )
      if( rc = ERROR_OPEN_FAILED )
         { printf("Can't find that file"); exit(1); }
      else
         { printf("DosOpen error=%u\n", rc); exit(1); }

                       /* convert arg to long int */
   distance = atol( argv[2] );
                       /* move file pointer */
   if( rc=DosChgFilePtr( handle, distance, MOVE_TYPE,
                                           &newptr ) )
      { printf("DosChgFilePtr error=%u\n", rc); exit(1); }
                       /* print new pointer location */
   printf("New pointer location is %ld\n", newptr );
   do  {                  /* read and display line of text */
```

(continued)

```
        if( rc=DosRead(handle, buffer, BUFLEN, &BytesRead ) )
           { printf("DosRead error=%d\n", rc); exit(1); }
                           /* display line of text */
        buffer[BytesRead] = 0;      /* put '\0' to end string */
        printf( "%s", buffer );   /* print string */
     } while( BytesRead==BUFLEN );   /* EOF when buffer not
                                          full */


   DosClose(handle);
   exit(0);
}
```

The DosChgFilePtr() function takes four arguments.

DosChgFilePtr — Change file pointer
```
DosChgFilePtr(Handle, Distance, MoveType, ANewPointer);
unsigned short Handle;        /* handle of file */
long Distance;                /* number of bytes to move */
unsigned MoveType;            /* method of moving pointer */
unsigned long far *ANewPointer;  /* address for new
                                     pointer */
```

The first argument is, not surprisingly, the handle of the file whose pointer we want to move. The second is the distance, in bytes, to move the pointer. This is an integer of type **long**, to accommodate large files. It is also a signed quantity, so the direction to move the pointer can be either forward or, if the value is negative, backward. The third argument specifies the starting location from which the pointer will be moved. This argument can have the following values:

Value	Start move at
0	Beginning of file
1	Current location
2	End of file

The final argument is the address where the new pointer, as calculated by the function, is returned. If the MoveType is set to 0 (the beginning of the file), then on return **NewPointer** should be set to the same value specified in **Distance** (moving 50 bytes from zero puts the pointer at byte 50). If MoveType is set to 2, indicating starting at the end of the file, and distance is set to 0, then **NewPointer** will return the file size.

Changing File Size

The API function DosNewSize() can change the size of the file. Here's an example which changes the size of any arbitrary file. The filename and the new size are furnished by the user as arguments on the command line.

Suppose you use DIR and find a file test.txt has a size of 1000 bytes. Here's how newsize.c would change it to 2000 bytes:

`C>newsize test.txt 2000`

Now DIR shows the file with the new size.

This function is most often used within a program that conducts random reads and writes within a file, and needs to increase the file size without explicitly writing material at the end of the file.

```
/* newsize.c */
/* changes size of existing file */
#define INCL_DOS
#include <os2.h>
#include <stdlib.h>      /* for atol */
#define SIZE 0L          /* no minimum size of file */
#define ATTR 0           /* normal file */
#define FLAG 0x01        /* fail if no file, or open it */
#define MODE 0x4042      /* acc=read/write, share=deny none */
main(argc,argv)
int argc;
char *argv[];
{
    unsigned short handle;   /* file handle from DosOpen */
    unsigned action;         /* action taken by DosOpen */
    unsigned long size;      /* new size of file */
    unsigned rc;             /* return code */

    if( argc != 3)
       { printf("Syntax: newsize filename size"); exit(1); }
    size = atol( argv[2] );

                            /* open file */
    rc = DosOpen( argv[1], &handle, &action, SIZE, ATTR,
                                    FLAG, MODE, 0L );
    if( rc ) {
       if( rc==32 )
          printf("Can't open file: sharing violation");
```

(continued)

```
      else if( rc==5 )
         printf("Can't open file: access denied");
      else if( rc==110 )
         printf("Can't open file: doesn't exist");
      else
         printf("DosOpen error=%u", rc);
      exit(1);
   }
                           /* resize file */
   if( rc=DosNewSize( handle, size ) )
      { printf("DosNewSize error=%u",rc); exit(1); }
   DosClose( handle );      /* close file */
   exit(0);
}
```

The DosNewSize() function needs to know only the handle of the file to be resized, and the size to be assigned.

DosNewSize — Change a file's size

```
DosNewSize(Handle, NewSize);
unsigned short Handle;   /* handle of file to resize */
unsigned long NewSize;   /* new size of file, in bytes */
```

You can make files both larger and smaller. The new part of a file whose size has been increased will contain garbage. Information at the end of a file is lost if the file is made smaller. DosNewSize() can't operate on a read-only file. To prepare a read-only file for resizing with DosNewSize(), use DosSetFileMode() to change a file's attributes (discussed in the last chapter).

Resetting a File Buffer

In some cases it may be desirable to ensure a file buffer is flushed—that is, written to the disk—without closing it. The API function DosBufReset() accomplishes this task.

DosBufReset — Reset file buffer

```
DosBufReset(Handle);
unsigned short Handle;   /* handle of file to reset */
```

It requires only one parameter: the handle of the file whose buffers should be reset. The function writes any unwritten data from the buffer to the disk, and also updates the directory entry for the file as if the file had been closed.

Duplicating a File Handle

Some situations may require an opened file be referenced by a handle different from the one with which it was originally opened. To obtain an additional handle, use API function DosDupHandle().

DosDupHandle — Duplicate file handle

```
DosDupHandle(OldHandle, ANewHandle);
unsigned short Handle;              /* existing file handle */
unsigned short far *ANewHandle; /* address for new handle */
```

The existing (that is, open) file handle is placed in **OldHandle**, and the function returns the duplicate handle in the address specified by **ANewHandle**. The original handle is normally closed. If a value of -1 is placed in **ANewHandle** then the function creates a new file handle value without closing the old one, and writes it over the -1.

We won't demonstrate this function here, but it becomes useful in Chapter 11, when we need to redirect the output of a pipe.

Summary

In this chapter we examined the API functions for performing disk I/O. We saw how DosOpen() opens files, and how its various parameters specify such characteristics as whether the file is readable or writeable, and whether it can be shared with other processes. We discussed DosWrite() and DosRead() for writing and reading files and DosClose() for closing them.

Various API functions query and set information about a file. DosQFileInfo() returns, among other information, the date and time a file was last written to and its size. DosQHandType() tells whether a handle belongs to a file or a device, and DosQFHandState() determines the access and sharing modes of a file. To change the maximum number of usable file handles, DosSetMaxFH() is appropriate.

You can use DosChgFilePtr() to move the file pointer to any point in the file and access the contents randomly rather than sequentially. Use DosNewSize() to change the size of an existing file and DosBufReset() to flush file buffers to disk. You can duplicate file handles with DosDupHandle().

In the next chapter we'll put what we've learned about file I/O to work in multitasking situations.

FILES AND MULTITASKING

Chapter 9

- Simultaneous reading and analyzing
- Coordination with a semaphore
- Coordination with DosReadAsync()
- Multiple semaphores and DosMuxSemWait()
- Simultaneous reading and display
- Coordinating file access
- File locking

Chapter 9

Now that we know how to read and write data files, let's see what benefits can be derived from using file I/O in a multitasking environment.

In earlier chapters we saw example programs that performed calculations with one thread while simultaneously reading data from the keyboard with another. Can the same sort of multitasking be carried out with disk I/O? The disk transfers data much more quickly than the keyboard. However, there is still time available, when a disk read or write is taking place, for the CPU to carry out other activities. In this chapter we'll examine some of the techniques used to make such multitasking possible. Significant speed increase in a program's operation can be obtained by performing disk I/O and other activities at the same time.

The first section of this chapter looks at a situation where data is being read from a series of disk files and analyzed. Analysis and reading take place at the same time, using different threads. Several approaches to this problem are examined.

You can use similar approaches to perform other sorts of activities, besides data analysis, at the same time as file I/O. A program could read or write to a disk file, and at the same time communicate with a modem, send information to a printer, read or write to another disk file, display information, and so forth.

In our data analysis programs we assume that the order in which the files are read and analyzed is not important. This is appropriate in many situations and simplifies program design. In other situations, however, the order in which data is read and processed is important. An example is a program that uses multiple threads to display the contents of a disk file on the screen. We examine this case in the second section.

The final section of the chapter explores the situation where several processes attempt to access the same file at the same time.

Reading and Analyzing Simultaneously

Let's assume a program needs to read data from a series of disk files, and analyze it. This data could be anything: the payroll for a small company, telemetry data from a rocket launch, demographic data for a sales forecast, or stock prices for calculating the value of a portfolio. In all these cases the possibility exists of performing analysis on one data file at the same time another file is being read from the disk. How does one design a program to carry out this form of multitasking?

One of the problems that must be dealt with is the coordination of the I/O task and the analysis task. In this section we examine several approaches to the problem. We see examples where no coordination is used, and where coordination is carried out using semaphores in various ways.

Creating Data Files

To show how to use multitasking to analyze data, we first need some data files to analyze. In the following examples we use eight files, each containing 10,000 integer values. The program listed below creates data files of this size which are filled with a constant value.

```c
/* makedata.c */
/* fills file with constant supplied by user */
#define INCL_DOS
#include <os2.h>
#define ATTR 0              /* normal file */
#define OPENFLAG 0x0012     /* truncate old or create file */
#define OPENMODE 0x0012     /* acc=rd/wrt share=deny all */
#define BUFSIZE 10000L      /* size of buffer in integers */
#define CHARSIZE (unsigned long)sizeof(buff)  /* in chars */

int buff[BUFSIZE];          /* data buffer */

main(argc, argv)
int argc;
char *argv[];
{
    int konst;              /* constant to fill file */
    unsigned short handle;  /* file handle from DosOpen */
    unsigned action;        /* action taken by DosOpen */
    unsigned BytesWritten;  /* bytes written by DosWrite */
    int n;                  /* loop counter */
     if( argc != 3 )
       { printf("Syntax: makedata filename constant");
                                                    exit(1); }

                            /* fill buffer with constant */
    konst = atoi( argv[2] );
    for( n=0; n<BUFSIZE; n++ )
       buff[n] = konst;
                            /* open file */
    DosOpen( argv[1], &handle, &action, CHARSIZE,
                    ATTR, OPENFLAG, OPENMODE, 0L );
                            /* write to file */
    DosWrite( handle, (char far *)buff, CHARSIZE,
                                        &BytesWritten );

    DosClose(handle);       /* close file */
    exit(0);
}
```

We should note that in this program, and those following in this chapter, we've removed the error-analysis code from the calls to the API functions. We do so to make the programs shorter and ensure the details of their operation are not obscured by unnecessary code. However, there are the usual pitfalls to this approach. When you write your own programs you should include statements to examine the return code from all DOS API functions and report any non-zero values. Otherwise when things go wrong within a DOS function you will have no indication there is a problem. This can make the debugging process much more difficult.

The makefile.c program takes as command-line arguments the name of the file to be created and the constant it is to be filled with. Our analysis programs assume the files are named SRC0.DAT, SRC1.DAT, up to SRC7.DAT. They also assume SRC0.DAT is filled with 0s, SRC1.DAT is filled with 1s, and so on. This is not very exciting data, but we're trying to keep the focus on the program structure, not on complex data analysis. To create these files, invoke the makefile.c program like this:

```
C>makefile src0.dat 0
C>makefile src1.dat 1
C>makefile src2.dat 2
- - - - - - - - - -
C>makefile src7.dat 7
```

We assume you've created these eight files and placed them in the same directory in which you'll be running the example programs. (The dashed line indicates that, for brevity, we've omitted the intervening commands.)

The Single-tasking Approach

Let's look first at how we analyze these files using the old fashioned single-tasking approach. We call this example seridata.c, since it performs the read and analysis tasks serially, rather than simultaneously.

```
/* seridata.c */
/* analyze data from disk files */
#define INCL_DOS
#include <os2.h>
#define ATTR 0           /* normal file */
#define OPENFLAG 0x01    /* fail if no file, or open it */
#define OPENMODE 0x0040  /* share=deny none, acc=read-only */
#define BUFSIZE 10000L   /* size of buffer in integers */
```

(continued)

```c
#define CHARSIZE (unsigned long)sizeof(buff)  /* in chars */
#define NAME_LEN 13      /* length of file name */
#define NUMFILES 8       /* number of files to analyse */
int buff[BUFSIZE];       /* data buffer */
                         /* file name buffer */
char files[NUMFILES][NAME_LEN] = { "SRC0.DAT", "SRC1.DAT",
                                   "SRC2.DAT", "SRC3.DAT",
                                   "SRC4.DAT", "SRC5.DAT",
                                   "SRC6.DAT", "SRC7.DAT"
                                                         };
main()
{
    int j, n;                /* loop counters */
    long total;              /* sum of all data items */
    unsigned short handle;   /* handle of source file */
    unsigned action;         /* action taken by DosOpen */
    unsigned BytesRead;      /* bytes read by DosRead */

    for(n=0, total=0; n<NUMFILES; n++) {  /* for each file */
                            /* open source file */
        DosOpen(files[n], &handle, &action, CHARSIZE,
                          ATTR, OPENFLAG, OPENMODE, 0L);
                            /* read file */
        DosRead(handle, (char far *)buff, CHARSIZE,
                                            &BytesRead );
        DosClose(handle);    /* close file */

                            /* analyze data */
        for(j=0; j<BUFSIZE; j++) {      /* each data item */
            total += buff[j];           /* add to total */
            if( buff[j] != n )
                printf("Bad data: file %d\n", buff[j], n, j);
        }
    }
                            /* display results */
    printf("Total of all data items is %ld\n", total);
    exit(0);
}
```

There should be no surprises in this program. It steps through the files one at a time, taking the name of the next file to read from the list called **files**. (In a real-world situation such file names are likely to be input by the user or read from a separate file.) The analysis consists of two parts. First, every integer in the file is checked to be sure it is the same as the file number. Thus all entries in SRC3.DAT, the file to be read when the file index **n** has a value of 3, should be 3. Second, all the data items in all the files are added together and the sum is printed out at the end of the program. Since each file contains 10,000 integers, the sum should be 0 plus 10,000 plus 20,000 and so on up to 70,000, for a total of 280,000. Seeing this number printed out verifies the program has read and "analyzed" all the data correctly.

Now let's see how to speed up the operation of the program using multitasking. Here, instead of a single thread, we use two threads running simultaneously. While one thread is reading, the other is analyzing. The problem is then to coordinate these activities so they take place at appropriate times. We examine four different approaches: no coordination, using a simple semaphore to coordinate the reads using an asynchronous read with DosReadAsync(), and using DosMuxSemWait().

Double Buffering

To read data from one file and analyze data from another at the same time requires more than one data buffer. If a single buffer were used, the analysis task would be trying to work with data that was changing during the analysis, as the reading task wrote over it. The solution is to use two (or sometimes more than two) buffers alternately. First, one buffer is filled from the disk, at the same time the other is being analyzed. Then the roles of the buffers switch, and the analysis task starts to work on the buffer just filled with data, while the read task writes over the data just analyzed.

The use of two buffers is a common feature of the techniques described in this chapter.

No Coordination

It is perfectly possible to run two threads simultaneously, each reading files and analyzing them, with no coordination between the threads. So long as each thread knows what files to work on, and uses a separate buffer from the other, they can go on their merry way. However, when the two processes are not synchronized, reading and analysis may get out of synch, so both threads are reading at the same time, and both threads are analyzing at the same time. The program will run under these circumstances, since the two threads can use the CPU at the same time, and the operating system makes it possible for several different files to be accessed at the same time. However, efficiency is increased by performing CPU-intensive analysis at the same time the disk read is taking place, so failure to coordinate the two threads will not result in the maximum increase in speed.

Coordination with a Single Semaphore

Using a single semaphore we can ensure that one thread is reading while the other is analyzing. In the example below each of two threads reads data into a buffer and analyzes it. Each thread is responsible for its own buffer. Thread 0 reads files 0, 2, 4 and 6 into buffer 0, while thread 1 reads files 1, 3, 5 and 7 into buffer 1.

Since both threads do the same thing (although to different buffers), we can use the same code for each. We've already seen an example of this in the horsrace.c program in Chapter 5. When the main program starts the threads, it passes the parameter 0 to the first thread and the parameter 1 to the second thread, using the stack as described in Chapter 5.

```
/* semdata.c */
/* analyzes data from disk files */
/* uses different thread for each buffer (sharing code) */
#define INCL_DOS
#include <os2.h>
#include <malloc.h>        /* for malloc() */
#define STACK_SIZE 512    /* size of stack for new thread */
#define ATTR 0            /* normal file */
#define OPENFLAG 0x01     /* fail if no file, or open it */
#define OPENMODE 0x0040   /* share=deny none, acc=read-only */
#define BUFSIZE 10000L    /* size of buffer in integers */
#define CHARSIZE (unsigned long)sizeof(buff[0])  /* in chars
                                                    */
#define NUMFILES 8        /* number of files to analyse */
#define NAME_LEN 13       /* length of each file name */
#define WAIT -1L          /* wait forever on semaphores */

unsigned long total;      /* sum of all data items */
int buff[2][BUFSIZE];     /* two data buffers */
unsigned long ReadSem=0;  /* control access to disk read */

                          /* file name buffer */
char files[NUMFILES][NAME_LEN] = { "SRC0.DAT", "SRC1.DAT",
                                   "SRC2.DAT", "SRC3.DAT",
                                   "SRC4.DAT", "SRC5.DAT",
                                   "SRC6.DAT", "SRC7.DAT"
                                                          };

main()     /* starts separate buff[0] and buff[1] threads */
{
    int far *stkptr;      /* note: must be type int for args */
    void far dobuff();    /* definition of thread */
    unsigned thrID;       /* space for thread ID number */
    int j;                /* loop counter for two threads */
```

(continued)

```
                                    /* start two threads */
        for( j=0; j<2; j++)  {
           stkptr = (int far *)malloc(STACK_SIZE) + STACK_SIZE;
           *--stkptr = j;        /* specify buffer number */
           DosCreateThread(dobuff, &thrID, (char far *)stkptr);
        }
        DosExit(0,0);            /* exit this thread */
    }


    /* dobuff() */
    /* thread to read and analyze a buffer */
    /* same code used for two incarnations of this thread */
    void far dobuff( buffdex )
    int buffdex;                 /* 0=buff[0], 1=buff[1] */
    {
        char far *pbuff;         /* pointer to buffer */
        unsigned short handle;   /* handle of source file */
        unsigned action;         /* action taken by DosOpen */
        unsigned BytesRead;      /* bytes read by DosRead */
        int n, j;                /* loop indices */

        for( n=buffdex; n < NUMFILES; n+=2 )  {
                                 /* set ptr to start of buffer */
           pbuff = (char far *)buff[buffdex];
                                 /* wait for read semaphore */
           DosSemRequest( &ReadSem, WAIT );
                                 /* open file */
           DosOpen( files[n], &handle, &action, CHARSIZE,
                             ATTR, OPENFLAG, OPENMODE, 0L );
                                 /* read file */
           DosRead( handle, pbuff, CHARSIZE, &BytesRead );
           DosClose( handle ); /* close file handle */
                                 /* clear read semaphore */
           DosSemClear( &ReadSem );


                                 /* analyze data */
           for(j=0; j<BUFSIZE; j++)  {  /* each data item */
              total += *( (int far *)pbuff + j );
              if( *((int far *)pbuff+j) != n )
                 printf("Bad data=file %d\n", n );
           }
        }
        if( buffdex==0 )         /* if last file for buff[0] */
           DosExit(0,0);         /* exit this thread */
        else {                   /* if last file for buff[1] */
           printf("Total of all data items is %ld\n", total);
           exit(0);              /* exit all threads */
        }
    }
```

The buffers are installed in an array with two dimensions, so they can be distinguished with a subscript, the number, 0 or 1, which is passed as a parameter to the thread. This parameter is also used as the initial value for the loop variable **n**, so in each thread **n** takes on the values of the files to be read (0, 2, 4, and 6 for thread 0; 1, 3, 5, 7 for thread 1).

We use semaphore **ReadSem** to coordinate access to the disk drive, and use DosSemRequest() and DosSemClear() to provide mutually exclusive access, as described in Chapter 6. This provides the coordination necessary to ensure the threads alternate reading and analysis.

Each thread reads and analyzes its four files. When done, thread 0 exits itself. Thread 1 prints out the results and terminates the program.

Figure 9-1 shows the relationship between the two threads and the semaphore in the form of a timing diagram. Remember that each thread is responsible for both reading and analysis in its own buffer.

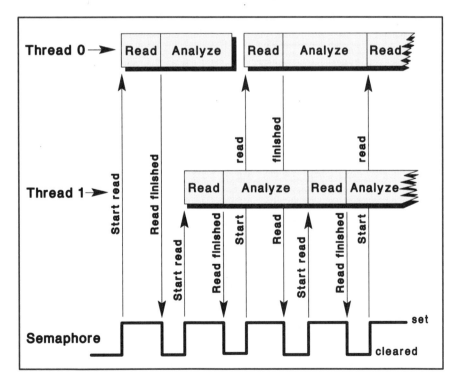

Figure 9-1
Timing Diagram of semdata.c

Notice how the reading of one buffer takes place simultaneously with the analysis of the other. Each time a thread starts a read, it sets the semaphore. When it's done, it clears it, and the other thread starts its read. If one thread, say thread 0, finishes its analysis before thread 1 finishes its read, then thread 0 must wait until thread 1 is done with the disk drive before it can start reading the next file.

It is possible for the reads to get out of order using this approach. It might happen, for example, that thread 0 starts up and reads and analyzes files 0 and 2 before thread 1 gets its first time slice and reads file 1. In this example no harm is done, since it is not important for the files to be read or analyzed in order. Where the order of reading is important, other measures are necessary, as we'll see in the second part of the chapter.

The Speed Advantage

What sort of speed advantage can we expect from designing multitasking into our data-analysis program? In theory, in the optimum situation, the speed of the program could be doubled. This supposes reading and analysis each take exactly the same length of time, for example 50 milliseconds for the read and 50 milliseconds for analysis. When this is the case one thread does not waste time after the analysis is done, waiting for the disk drive to become available. By contrast, if there is a wide disparity between reading and analysis time, the time saving cannot be very great. For instance, if the disk read takes 1 millisecond, and the analysis takes 100 milliseconds, multitasking can only improve the program's overall speed by one percent.

Whether reading and analysis take roughly the same time is dependent on many factors, such as the size of the files, the speed of the disk drive, whether the disk drive is buffered, the speed of the CPU, and the number of other processes that might be using the CPU or the drive at the same time. The programmer can control only some of these factors.

Another factor is that in most current computer systems the disk steals cycles from the CPU during read or write activity. How many cycles it steals in a particular time period is a function of the disk drive's speed and the particular hardware configuration. Even if the reading and analysis times are equal, an efficiency increase of 100 percent over the singletasking approach is impossible to realize because the analysis time is lengthened by the stolen cycles from the read process. In future computers the use of separate processors to handle different activities such as input/output may lead to a closer approach to the optimum. However, even with current machines it is possible to see improvements of more than 30 percent using some form of multitasking.

Asynchronous Input/Output

Let's look at another approach to performing disk reading and CPU analysis at the same time. This approach makes use of a new API function: DosReadAsync(). This function works very much like DosRead(). The difference is that it returns as soon as the read is *started*, not when it has completed the reading operation, as DosRead() does. This means the thread that issued the call to DosReadAsync() can go on about other business as soon as the call is issued. To indicate when the read is done, DosReadAsync() clears a semaphore. The thread can then wait on the semaphore before performing another read into the same buffer. It is up to the program to set the semaphore before invoking the function.

DosReadAsync — Read asynchronously from file

```
DosReadAsync(Handle, ASem, ARetCode, Buff, BeffLen,
                                             ABytesRead);
unsigned short Handle;      /* file handle */
unsigned long far *ASem;    /* address of RAM semaphore */
unsigned far *ARetCode;     /* address for return code */
void far *Buff;             /* input buffer */
unsigned BuffLen;           /* number of bytes to be read */
unsigned far *ABytesRead;   /* address for bytes actually
                               read */
```

DosReadAsync() takes six arguments. The **Handle**, **Buff**, **Buff-Len**, and **ABytesRead** parameters are similar to those used in DosRead(). The **ASem** parameter is the address of the RAM semaphore the function clears when the read is complete. **ARetCode** is the address of a word where the system returns errors from the read operation.

The following example performs the same analysis on the eight data files as semdata.c did. However, because it uses DosReadAsync(), it does not need to use multiple threads. It starts the read, goes on immediately to analyze the data from the previous read (if any), and then waits on a semaphore before starting the next read. It uses two buffers as before, with each one protected by its own semaphore.

```
/* syncdata.c */
/* reads and analyzes files in two buffers simultaneously */
/* uses DosReadAsync() */
#define INCL_DOS
#include <os2.h>
#define BUFSIZE 10000    /* size of buffers in integers */
#define CHARSIZE (unsigned long)sizeof(buff[0]) /* in bytes */
#define NUMFILES 8       /* number of files to analyze */
```
(continued)

```
#define NAME_LEN 13      /* length of file name */
#define ATTR 0           /* normal file */
#define OPENFLAG 0x01    /* fail if no file, or open it */
#define OPENMODE 0x0040  /* share=deny none, acc=read-only */
#define WAIT -1L         /* wait until semaphore cleared */

int buff[2][BUFSIZE];        /* two data buffers */
unsigned long sem[2];        /* two RAM semaphores */
char files[NUMFILES][NAME_LEN] = { "SRC0.DAT", "SRC1.DAT",
                                   "SRC2.DAT", "SRC3.DAT",
                                   "SRC4.DAT", "SRC5.DAT",
                                   "SRC6.DAT", "SRC7.DAT" };
main()
   {
   unsigned short handle;   /* file handle */
   unsigned action;         /* action taken by open */
   unsigned BytesRead;      /* bytes actually read */
   int toggle;              /* select buff0 or buff1 */
   unsigned n, j;           /* loop counters */
   unsigned long total;     /* sum of all data items */
   unsigned rcAsync;        /* return code for async read */

   sem[0] = 0;              /* clear semaphores */
   sem[1] = 0;
   toggle = 0;              /* start with buff[0] */

                           /* for each file to be read */
   for( n=0; n <= NUMFILES; n++ )   {

      if(n != NUMFILES)  {  /* except for last cycle, */
                            /* open file n */
         DosOpen( files[n], &handle, &action, CHARSIZE,
                     ATTR, OPENFLAG, OPENMODE, 0L );
                            /* set semaphore */
         DosSemSet( &sem[toggle] );
                      /* start reading file into buffer */
         DosReadAsync( handle, &sem[toggle], &rcAsync,
                     buff[toggle], CHARSIZE, &BytesRead );
      } /* end if */
                            /* flip the switch */
      toggle = toggle ? 0 : 1;

      if( n != 0 )  {     /* except for first cycle, */
                          /* wait on the *other* semaphore */
         DosSemWait( &sem[toggle], WAIT );
                          /* analyze the *other* buffer */
         for( j=0; j<BUFSIZE; j++ )  {
            total += buff[toggle][j];
            if( buff[toggle][j] != n-1 )
               printf("Bad data: file %d char %d\n", n-1, j );
```

(continued)

```
        }
    } /* end if */
} /* end n for loop */
                    /* print results */
printf("Total of all data items is %lu\n", total );
exit(0);
}
```

Note that each time through the loop the program is analyzing the data from the *previous* read. The variable **toggle** is used to keep track of which buffer is being used. The program reads into one buffer, for example, and then flips the toggle to analyze the contents of the *other* buffer, which contains the previously-read file.

When the first file (SRC0.DAT) is being read there is no previous file to analyze, so when **n** is 0 the analysis part of the program is skipped. Also, when the last file is being analyzed, there is no next file to read, so when **n** becomes equal to the number of files the reading part of the program is skipped. Figure 9-2 shows a flowchart of the program's operation, and Figure 9-3 shows a timing diagram.

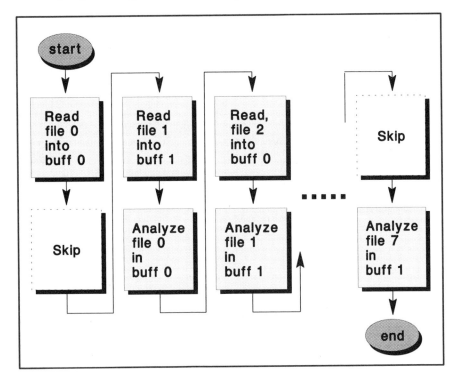

Figure 9-2
Flowchart of syncdata.c

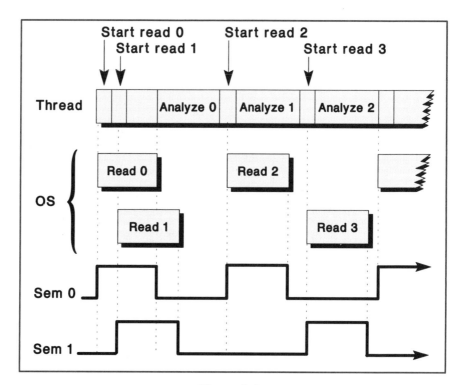

Figure 9-3
Timing Diagram of syncdata.c

A write function, DosWriteAsync(), works in the same way as DosReadAsync(). Once it starts the write operation, it returns control to the program while the system continues to write to the file. When the write operation is complete, the function clears a semaphore.

DosWriteAsync — Write asynchronously to file

```
DosWriteAsync(Handle, ASem, ARetCode, Buff, BeffLen,
                                            ABytesWrit);
unsigned short Handle;      /* file handle */
unsigned long far *ASem;    /* address of RAM semaphore */
unsigned far *ARetCode;     /* address for return code */
void far *Buff;             /* output buffer */
unsigned BuffLen;           /* number of bytes to be written */
unsigned far *ABytesWrit;   /* address for bytes written */
```

The parameters used by this function are similar to those used by DosReadAsync(). If the number of bytes actually written, reported in the **ABytesWrit** argument, does not agree with that requested in **BuffLen**, the disk may be full.

When using DosReadAsync() or DosWriteAsync(), remember not to close the file immediately after issuing the call, since this will abort the I/O operation in mid-stream. No operations may be performed on the file or on the buffer until the function reports it is finished, by clearing the semaphore.

Coordination with DosMuxSemWait()

In the semdata.c program each of two threads was responsible for its own buffer, reading files into the buffer and analyzing them. Our next example also uses two threads, but their responsibilities are divided differently. Here, one thread specializes in reading, and the other in analysis. Each thread alternates between the two buffers: the read thread fills buffer 0 with data while the analysis thread analyzes buffer 1; then they switch buffers, and the read thread fills buffer 1 while the analysis thread analyzes buffer 0.

To coordinate the I/O and analysis operations in this program we make use of the DosMuxSemWait() function, discussed in Chapter 5. This function permits a thread to wait on the clearing of either of two (or more) semaphores. In our program the read thread uses this function to wait until *either* of the two buffers is empty, while the analysis thread waits for either buffer to be full.

The need to set up the list of semaphores required by DosMuxSem-Wait() makes this listing somewhat longer, but in operation the program is not much more complicated than semdata.c or syncdata.c. The main program starts a separate thread to analyze the data, and calls a function within the same thread to perform the disk reads.

Four semaphores are used, two for each buffer. **E0** and **E1** are cleared by the analysis thread to indicate that buffer 0 and buffer 1 respectively have been analyzed (emptied). The read thread waits on these semaphores before placing data from the disk into the buffers. Semaphores **F0** and **F1** are cleared by the read thread to indicate the buffers have been filled with data. The analysis thread waits on these semaphores before starting the analysis process.

Note that it is the *clearing* of a semaphore that indicates the beginning of a particular state. The clearing of a full semaphore indicates a buffer is full, and the clearing of an empty semaphore indicates a buffer is empty. This may seem opposite to the intuitive idea of how things should work, but all the semaphore API functions wait for a semaphore to be *cleared*, not set.

```
/* paradata.c */
/* analyzes data from disk files */
/* uses separate threads for reading and analysis */
#define INCL_DOS
#include <os2.h>
#include <malloc.h>        /* for malloc() */
#define STACK_SIZE 512      /* size of stack for new thread */
#define ATTR 0              /* normal file */
#define OPENFLAG 0x01       /* fail if no file, or open it */
#define OPENMODE 0x0042     /* acc=read/write, share=deny
                               none */
#define BUFSIZE 10000L      /* size of buffer in integers */
#define CHARSIZE (unsigned long)sizeof(buff0) /* in chars */
#define NUMFILES 8          /* number of files to analyse */
#define NAME_LEN 13         /* length of each file name */

int buff0[BUFSIZE];        /* first data buffer */
int buff1[BUFSIZE];        /* second data buffer */
unsigned long E0 = 0L;      /* reading semaphores */
unsigned long E1 = 0L;
unsigned long F0 = 0L;      /* analysis semaphores */
unsigned long F1 = 0L;

struct MuxList {            /* DosMuxSemWait list structure */
   unsigned SemCount;      /*    number of semaphores */
   unsigned res1;          /*    reserved; must be 0 */
   void far *ps1;          /*    pointer to semaphore 1 */
   unsigned res2;          /*    reserved; must be 0 */
   void far *ps2;          /*    pointer to semaphore 2 */
};
                           /* file name buffer */
char files[NUMFILES][NAME_LEN] = { "SRC0.DAT",  "SRC1.DAT",
                                   "SRC2.DAT",  "SRC3.DAT",
                                   "SRC4.DAT",  "SRC5.DAT",
                                   "SRC6.DAT",  "SRC7.DAT"
                                                           };

main()                 /* starts read and analysis threads */
{
   char far *stkptr;      /* stack pointer for new thread */
   void far analyze();    /* definition of new thread */
   void read();           /* definition of read function */
   unsigned threadID;     /* space for thread ID number */
   unsigned rc;           /* return code */
```

(continued)

```
    DosSemSet ( &F0 );        /* set analysis semaphores */
    DosSemSet ( &F1 );
                             /* start thread for analyzing data */
    stkptr = (char far *)malloc(STACK_SIZE) + STACK_SIZE;
    DosCreateThread(analyze, &threadID, stkptr);
    read();                  /* call routine to read data */
}                            /* no return from read() */

/* read() */
/* reads data from file and puts results in buff0 or buff1
   */
void read()
{
    struct MuxList list;     /* structure for DosMuxSemWait */
    unsigned index;          /* index for read semaphores */
    char far *pbuff;         /* pointer to buffers */
    unsigned short handle;   /* handle of source file */
    unsigned action;         /* action taken by DosOpen */
    unsigned BytesRead;      /* bytes read by DosRead */
    int n;                   /* loop counter */

    list.SemCount = 2;     /* DosMuxSemWait read list */
    list.res1 = 0;
    list.ps1  = &E0;
    list.res2 = 0;
    list.ps2  = &E1;
                             /* read files into buff0 or buff1 */
    for(n=0; n<NUMFILES; n++)  {
                             /* open source file */
       DosOpen(files[n], &handle, &action, CHARSIZE,
                          ATTR, OPENFLAG, OPENMODE, 0L);
                             /* wait on semaphores E0 or E1 */
       DosMuxSemWait(&index, &list, -1L);
       if( index == 0 )  {            /* if event was E0 */
          pbuff = (char far *)buff0;  /*    use buffer 0 */
          DosSemSet ( &E0 );          /*    set E0 */
       } else  {                      /* else it was E1 */
          pbuff = (char far *)buff1;  /*    use buffer 1 */
          DosSemSet ( &E1 );          /*    set E1 */
       }
```

(continued)

```
                            /* read file */
        DosRead(handle, pbuff, CHARSIZE, &BytesRead );
        if( index == 0 )                    /* if event was E0 */
           DosSemClear( &F0 );              /*     clear F0 */
        else                                /* else it was E1 */
           DosSemClear( &F1 );              /*     clear F1 */
        DosClose(handle);
    } /* end of for loop */
    DosExit(0,0);                           /* exit this thread */
}


/* analyze() */
/* separate thread: analyze data from buff0 or buff1 */
void far analyze()
{
    struct MuxList list;     /* structure for DosMuxSemWait */
    unsigned index;          /* index for analyze semaphores */
    char far *pbuff;         /* pointer to buffers */
    int rc;                  /* return code */
    int n, j;                /* loop counters */
    long total = 0;          /* sum of all data items */
    list.SemCount = 2;       /* DosMuxSemWait analyze list */
    list.res1 = 0;
    list.ps1  = &F0;
    list.res2 = 0;
    list.ps2  = &F1;
    /* analyze any available buffer, until all files done */
    for(n=0; n<NUMFILES; n++)  {
                            /* wait on semaphores F0 or F1 */
      DosMuxSemWait( &index, &list, -1L );
      if( index == 0 )  {                   /* if event was E0 */
         pbuff = (char far *)buff0;         /*    use buffer 0 */
         DosSemSet( &F0 );                  /*    set F0 */
      } else  {                             /* else it was E1 */
         pbuff = (char far *)buff1;         /*    use buffer 1 */
         DosSemSet( &F1 );                  /*    set F1 */
      }
                      /* analyze data */
      for(j=0; j<BUFSIZE; j++)  {   /* each data item */
         total += *( (int far *)pbuff + j );
         if( *((int far *)pbuff+j) != n )  {
            printf("Bad data=: file %d\n", n );
         }
      }
```

(continued)

```
        if( index == 0 )                     /* if event was F0 */
            DosSemClear( &E0 );              /*    clear E0 */
        else                                 /* else it was F1 */
            DosSemClear( &E1 );              /*    clear E1 */
    }  /* end of n for */
                                /* display results */
    printf("Total of all data items is %ld\n", total);
    exit(0);                    /* exit all threads */
}
```

The read thread opens a file, then waits on both semaphores **E0** and **E1**. Initially both these semaphores are clear, so reading begins immediately. After both buffers are full, the read routine waits for one or the other buffer to be analyzed before reading again. Before filling a buffer, the read thread sets **E0** or **E1** so it will not read into this same buffer again until the contents have been analyzed. Once the read is complete, the read thread clears **F0** or **F1** to signal the analysis thread that a buffer is full and ready to be analyzed.

The analysis thread waits on both **F0** and **F1**. Initially both these semaphores are set, so no analysis takes place until a semaphore is cleared by the read thread. Once one of the semaphores is cleared, the analysis thread sets either **F0** or **F1** as appropriate, so it will not analyze this buffer again until it is refilled. When the buffer is analyzed, either **E0** or **E1** is cleared, indicating the buffer is empty and the read thread can fill it. Figure 9-4 shows a flowchart of the program.

Reading and Displaying at the Same Time

In the data analysis programs described above the order in which the files were analyzed was not important. By contrast, our next example is a program that uses multitasking to display the contents of a text file. Here only a single file is being read, and the order in which it is read and displayed is critical. The program is similar in operation to the TYPE command in DOS. The user furnishes the filename as a command-line argument.

When reading from a floppy drive on a particular system this program provided a 33 percent speed increase over a similar program that did not take advantage of multitasking. When using the single-tasking approach the display can be seen to pause when the disk is being read. This pause is eliminated with multitasking, since each read operation is performed at the same time as the previous display. The speed increase is dependent on many factors and is less marked with faster disk drives.

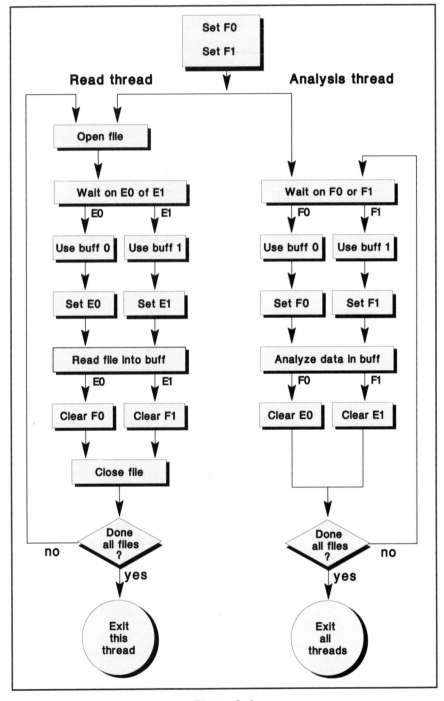

Figure 9-4
Flowchart of paradata.c

As in previous programs, there are two data buffers. The main program in readisp.c starts two threads, **reader()** and **display()**. The **reader()** thread reads from the disk file alternately into the two buffers, while **display()** alternately writes the contents of the buffers to the screen.

As in paradata.c, there are four semaphores, two for each buffer. For simplicity each pair of semaphores is set up as an array: **FullSem[0]** and **FullSem[1]** are cleared when their respective buffers are full, and **EmptySem[0]** and **EmptySem[1]** are cleared when their respective buffers are empty.

The read routine waits for a buffer to be empty, then reads data into it. Once the read is complete, the routine clears the appropriate full semaphore so the buffer can be displayed. The display routine waits for a buffer to be full, then displays it on the screen. Once the display is complete, this routine clears the appropriate empty semaphore so the buffer can be filled again by the read routine.

```
/* readisp.c */
/* reads text from disk files and displays it */
/* uses different threads for reading and display */
#define INCL_DOS
#define INCL_SUB
#include <os2.h>
#include <malloc.h>      /* for malloc() */
#define STACK_SIZE 512   /* size of stack for new threads */
#define ATTR 0           /* normal file */
#define OPENFLAG 0x01    /* fail if no file, or open it */
#define OPENMODE 0x0040  /* share=deny none, acc=read-only */
#define BUFSIZE 512L     /* size of buffers in bytes */
#define WAIT -1L         /* wait forever on semaphores */
#define HANDLE 0         /* vio handle always 0 */
char buff[2][BUFSIZE];   /* two data buffers */
                         /* cleared when reading done */
unsigned long FullSem[2] = { 0, 0 };
                         /* cleared when display done */
unsigned long EmptySem[2] = { 0, 0 };
unsigned short handle;   /* handle of source file */
unsigned action;         /* action taken by DosOpen */
unsigned BytesRead[2];   /* bytes read (for two buffers) */
```

(continued)

```
main(argc, argv)          /* starts two threads */
int argc;
char *argv[];
{
   char far *stkptr;      /* stack pointer */
   void far reader();     /* declare reading thread */
   void far display();    /* declare display thread */
   unsigned thrID;        /* space for thread ID number */

   if( argc != 2 )
      { printf("Syntax: readisp filename"); exit(1); }

   DosSemSet( &FullSem[0] );     /* buffers are */
   DosSemSet( &FullSem[1] );     /* initially empty */

                       /* open file */
   DosOpen( argv[1], &handle, &action, BUFSIZE,
                     ATTR, OPENFLAG, OPENMODE, 0L );

                   /* start read thread */
   stkptr = (char far *)malloc(STACK_SIZE) + STACK_SIZE;
   DosCreateThread(reader, &thrID, stkptr);

                   /* start display thread */
   stkptr = (char far *)malloc(STACK_SIZE) + STACK_SIZE;
   DosCreateThread(display, &thrID, stkptr);

   DosExit(0,0);       /* exit this thread */
}

/* reader() */
/* thread to read two buffers alternately */
void far reader()
{
   int toggle = 1;     /* 0=buff[0], 1=buff[1] */

   do {                /* switch to other buffer */
      toggle = ( toggle ) ? 0 : 1;
                       /* wait for display to empty buffer */
      DosSemRequest( &EmptySem[toggle], WAIT );
                       /* read from file */
      DosRead(handle, buff[toggle], BUFSIZE,
                                    &BytesRead[toggle]);
```

(continued)

```
                              /* mark buffer full, for display() */
        DosSemClear( &FullSem[toggle] );
                              /* EOF when buffer not filled */
     } while( BytesRead[toggle] == BUFSIZE );
     DosClose( handle );   /* close file */
     DosExit(0,0);         /* exit this thread */
  }

  /* display */
  /* thread to display two buffers alternately */
  void far display()
  {
     int toggle = 1;        /* 0=buff[0], 1=buff[1] */
     unsigned bytes;        /* local byte count */

     do  {                  /* switch to other buffer */
        toggle = ( toggle ) ? 0 : 1;
                              /* wait for full buffer */
        DosSemRequest( &FullSem[toggle], WAIT );
                              /* save count before next read */
        bytes = BytesRead[toggle];
                              /* display data */
        VioWrtTTy( buff[toggle], bytes, HANDLE );
                              /* mark buffer empty, for read() */
        DosSemClear( &EmptySem[toggle] );
                              /* quit when this is last buffer */
     } while( bytes == BUFSIZE );
     exit(0);                /* exit all threads */
  }
```

As in syncdata.c, a toggle is used in each thread to switch back and forth between the two buffers. This, and the use of separate full and empty semaphores for each buffer, keep the reading and display processes from getting out of order. It's also necessary to use two separate variables, one for each buffer, to record the number of bytes actually read. (This value will be less than the buffer size on the last read.) Using two separate variables permits the appropriate value to be passed from the read thread to the display thread. The display thread must save this value in a local variable; otherwise it is trashed by the read thread when it reads in the next buffer. These variables are implemented as an array of two elements.   Figure 9-5 shows a flowchart of the program.

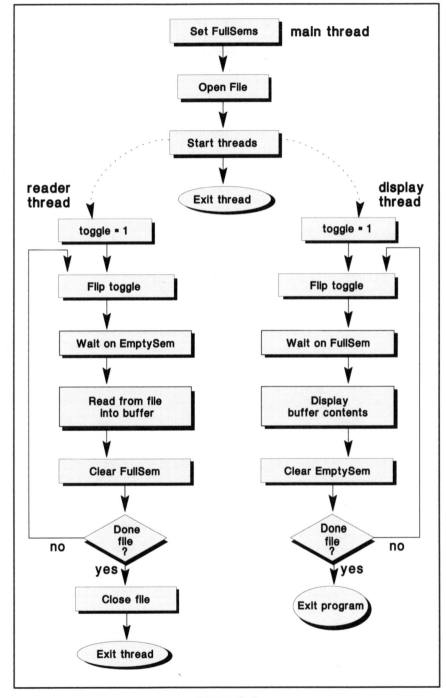

Figure 9-5
Flowchart of readisp.c

If reading into one buffer takes longer than displaying the other, both threads wait until the read is complete. If the display takes longer than reading, both threads wait until the display is complete. Figure 9-6 shows these relationships in a timing diagram.

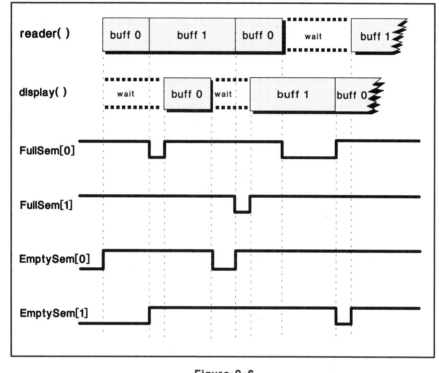

Figure 9-6
Timing Diagram of syncdata.c

When to Do What

We've looked at several different ways to use multitasking to speed up disk reads. Which approach to employ in a particular situation depends on many factors. The most realistic advice we can give is to experiment. Operating with the hardware on which your program will typically run, try several different approaches and see which one provides the best speed increase over the singletasking approach. In some situations the speed increase derived from multitasking is not worth the added complexity of implementing it. But in many cases, significant performance increases can be obtained.

Sharing Files Between Processes

As we see from the examples above, the system has no objection to different threads attempting to read different disk files at the same time. It is also possible for different threads to read from—or write to—the *same* disk file simultaneously. Since all the threads in a process own the same resources, the system assumes they all have equal rights to access a file one of them has opened. Thus coordinating access to a file by several threads is up to the programmer.

The situation is somewhat different when two different *processes* (as opposed to threads) attempt to access the same file at the same time. Here various aspects of the files themselves, such as the sharing mode and access mode, become significant.

Why would different processes need to access a file simultaneously? Perhaps a user is running two different instances of a word processing program. The program uses an initialization file to set various parameters, and both instances of the program need to be able to read the file, possibly at the same time. Or imagine an integrated application incorporating a spreadsheet and word processor. Perhaps the word processor needs to read a file to place data into a letter, while at the same time the spreadsheet is reading the file into its work area. How can such activities be coordinated?

Mutually-exclusive Access

Let's examine a pair of processes that attempt to access the same file. The first process, prw.c, creates the child and then opens the file FILE.TXT. It then gets input from the keyboard and writes it to the file, much as the wfile.c example did in the last chapter.

The child program, chrw.c, sleeps briefly until it is sure the parent has opened the file. As it attempts to open the file, the open fails: the parent has opened the file with the deny-all value in the SharingMode bit field. The child remains in a loop, trying to open the file, while the user is typing input to the parent, prw.c. As it cycles in the loop the child emits a series of beeps, indicating it is trying to open the file.

When the user types [Enter] at the start of a text line, indicating input completion, the parent process closes the file. The child is now able to open the file, so the beeping stops and the child prints out the contents of the file. In this example the parent and child cannot access the file at the same time: they have mutually exclusive access.

Here is the listing of the parent program:

```c
/* prw.c */
/* writes to disk, child then reads from disk and prints */
/* data is comes from keyboard */
#define INCL_DOS
#include <os2.h>
#include <string.h>        /* for strcat(), etc. */
#define ATTR 0             /* normal file */
#define OPENFLAG 0x12      /* truncate old or create file */
#define OPENMODE 0x4012    /* share=deny all, acc=rd/wrt */

#define NOPTR (char far *)0L  /* pointer to 0 */
#define OBLEN 32              /* length of object name buffer */
#define ASYNCH 1             /* child is asynchronous */

main()
{
   char string[80];         /* buffer for keyboard text */
   unsigned short handle;   /* file handle from DosOpen */
   unsigned action;         /* action taken by DosOpen */
   unsigned long size=0;    /* no minimum size of file */
   unsigned length;         /* length of keyboard line */
   unsigned BytesWritten;   /* bytes written by DosWrite */
   char objbuff[OBLEN];     /* buffer for DosExecPgm */
   struct _RESULTCODES childID;  /* result codes buffer */
   unsigned rc;             /* return code */

                            /* create child */
   if( rc=DosExecPgm( objbuff, OBLEN, ASYNCH,
                   NOPTR, NOPTR, &childID, "CHRW.EXE") )
      { printf("DosExecPgm error=%u\n", rc); exit(1); }

                            /* open file */
   if( rc=DosOpen("FILE.TXT", &handle, &action, size,
               ATTR, OPENFLAG, OPENMODE, 0L) )
      { printf("DosOpen error=%u\n", rc); exit(1); }

                            /* get input from keyboard */
   printf("Enter lines of text.\n");
   printf("To terminate, start line with [Enter].\n");
   do {
      gets(string);
      strcat(string, "\r\n");
      length = strlen(string);
```

(continued)

```
                                   /* write to file */
        if( rc=DosWrite( handle, string, length,
                                            &BytesWritten ) )
            {printf("DosWrite error=%d\n", rc); exit(1); }
    } while( length > 2 );

    printf("Parent will now close file and exit\n");
    DosClose( handle );
    exit(0);
}
```

The child process, chrw.c, is similar to the rfile.c example in the last chapter, except that it sits in a loop waiting for the file FILE.TXT to be available. The code 32, ERROR_SHARING_VIOLATION is returned when a process cannot access a file because another process is using it.

```
/* chrw.c */
/* child process of prw.c */
/* reads text file from disk and displays it */
#define INCL_DOS
#include <os2.h>
#define ATTR 0              /* normal file */
#define OPENFLAG 0x01       /* fail if no file, or open it */
#define OPENMODE 0x4042     /* share=deny none,
                               acc=read/write */
#define BUFLEN 40           /* size of data buffer */
#define ERROR_SHARING_VIOLATION 32  /* returned by
                                       DosOpen() */
main()
{
    unsigned rc;            /* return code */
    char buffer[BUFLEN];    /* buffer for text */
    unsigned short handle;  /* file handle from DosOpen */
    unsigned action;        /* action taken by DosOpen */
    unsigned long size=0;   /* no minimum size of file */
    unsigned length;        /* length of keyboard line */
    unsigned BytesRead;     /* bytes read by DosRead */

    DosSleep( 2000L );      /* wait for parent to open file */

    printf("\nChild will beep while attempting to open
                                            file\n");
```

(continued)

```
do  {                            /* beep until file opens */
   DosBeep( 300, 20 );           /* 300 Hz, 20 msecs */
   DosSleep( 200L );             /* 200 msecs */
   rc=DosOpen("FILE.TXT", &handle, &action, size,
                          ATTR, OPENFLAG, OPENMODE, 0L);
}  while( rc == ERROR_SHARING_VIOLATION );
if( rc )
   { printf("DosOpen error=%u\n", rc); exit(1); }
printf("\nChild has opened file\n");

do  {                            /* read file and display it */
   if( rc=DosRead(handle, buffer, BUFLEN, &BytesRead ) )
      { printf("DosRead error=%u\n", rc); exit(1); }
   buffer[BytesRead] = 0;   /* put '\0' to end string */
   printf("%s", buffer);    /* print it */
} while( BytesRead==BUFLEN );   /* EOF when buffer not
                                   full */

printf("Child closing file and exiting\n");
DosClose(handle);
exit(0);
}
```

Here's an example of the interaction between the two programs when the user enters a stanza from Henry Wadsworth Longfellow's poem, *The Song of Hiawatha.* (The dashed line indicates material from the child's repetition of the poem that was deleted for brevity.)

```
C>prw
Enter lines of text
To terminate, start line with [Enter].
Child will beep while attempting to open file
   Ye who love a nation's legends,
   Love the ballads of a people,
   That like voices from afar off
   Call to us to pause and listen,
   Speak in tones so plain and childlike,
   Scarcely can the ear distinguish
   Whether they are sung or spoken;-
   Listen to this Indian Legend,
   To this song of Hiawatha!
Parent will now close file and exit
Child has opened file
   Ye who love a nation's legends,
   - - - - - - - - - - - -
   To this song of Hiawatha!
Child closing file and exiting
```

As the user types, the child program beeps. Figure 9-7 shows the time relationship of the parent and child processes.

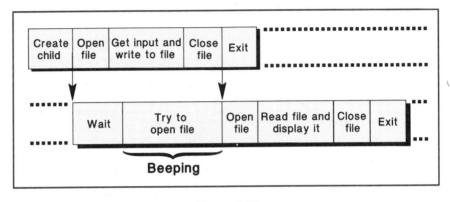

Figure 9-7
Time Relationship of prw.c and chrw.c

In this example the DosOpen() function is used as a means of communicating information about the file from one process to another. Specifically, the child process uses DosOpen() to discover when the file is closed by the parent. This use of DosOpen() is an important capability when multiple processes must interact with the file system.

Sharing and Access

In the example just described one process opened the file with the sharing mode set to deny-all, while the other process attempted to open it with read-write access. This combination (deny-all and read-write) will fail, providing mutually exclusive access to the file. However, there are other combinations of sharing mode and access mode that result in multiple processes being able to access the same file at the same time.

Figure 9-8 shows the relationship of the sharing mode used by one process to open a file, and the access mode requested by a second process when it attempts to open the same file.

		Second process Access mode		
		Read-only	Write-only	Read/Write
First process – Sharing mode	Deny read/write	FAIL	FAIL	FAIL
	Deny write	OK	FAIL	FAIL
	Deny read	FAIL	OK	FAIL
	Deny none	OK	OK	OK

Figure 9-8
Sharing Mode and Access Mode

Simultaneous Access

As an example where two processes can successfully open a file at the same time, let's consider the case where a parent and a child read the same file simultaneously.

```
/* prr.c */
/* reads from file at same time as child chrr.c */
#define INCL_DOS
#include <os2.h>
#define ATTR 0          /* normal file */
#define OPENFLAG 0x01   /* fail if no file, or open */
#define OPENMODE 0x0040 /* share=deny none, acc=read-only */
#define BUFLEN 40       /* length of file buffer */
#define NOPTR (char far *)0L  /* pointer to 0 */
#define ASYNCH 1        /* child is asynchronous */
```

(continued)

```
main()
{
    unsigned short handle; /* file handle from DosOpen */
    unsigned action;       /* action taken by DosOpen */
    unsigned long size=0;  /* no minimum size of file */
    char objbuff[BUFLEN];  /* buffer for DosExecPgm */
    struct _RESULTCODES childID;  /* result codes buffer */
    char buffer[BUFLEN+1]; /* buffer for file input */
    unsigned BytesRead;    /* bytes read by DosRead */

                           /* create child */
    DosExecPgm( objbuff, BUFLEN, ASYNCH,
                    NOPTR, NOPTR, &childID, "CHRR.EXE");
                           /* open file */
    DosOpen("FILE.TXT", &handle, &action, size,
                ATTR, OPENFLAG, OPENMODE, 0L);
    do {                       /* read file and display it */
        DosRead(handle, buffer, BUFLEN, &BytesRead );
        buffer[BytesRead] = 0;     /* put '\0' to end string */
        printf("%s", buffer);      /* print it */
    } while( BytesRead==BUFLEN );  /* EOF when buffer not
                                      full */
                           /* close file and exit */
    DosClose( handle );
    exit(0);
}
```

The parent opens the file with the sharing mode set to deny-none, allowing the child to open it while it remains open by the parent.

```
/* chrr.c */
/* child process of prr.c */
/* reads text file from disk and displays it */
#define INCL_DOS
#include <os2.h>
#define ATTR 0          /* normal file */
#define OPENFLAG 0x01   /* fail if no file, or open it */
#define OPENMODE 0x0040 /* share=deny none, acc=read-only */
#define BUFLEN 40       /* size of input buffer */
```

(continued)

```
main()
{
   char buffer[BUFLEN+1];  /* buffer for text */
   unsigned short handle;  /* file handle from DosOpen */
   unsigned action;        /* action taken by DosOpen */
   unsigned long size=0;   /* no minimum size of file */
   unsigned BytesRead;     /* bytes read by DosRead */

   DosOpen("FILE.TXT", &handle, &action, size,
                       ATTR, OPENFLAG, OPENMODE, 0L);
   do  {                        /* read file and display it */
      DosRead(handle, buffer, BUFLEN, &BytesRead );
      buffer[BytesRead] = '\0'; /* put '\0' to end string */
      printf( "%s", buffer );   /* print line */
   } while( BytesRead==BUFLEN );  /* EOF when buffer not
                                      full */
                           /* close file and exit */
   DosClose(handle);
   exit(0);
}
```

Both processes access the file as read-only, so the file can be have either the read-only or the read/write attribute.

When the program is run, and FILE.TXT contains a substantial amount of text, the two outputs are intermixed on the screen. This is not in itself a desirable result, but it does demonstrate that the two processes can read the same file at the same time. In a more realistic situation, instead of both trying to display the file on the same screen, the processes would be analyzing data from the file or performing some other operation.

Locking Files

We've seen how one process can keep other processes from accessing an entire file, by opening it with a restrictive sharing or access mode. But suppose a process wants to protect only *part* of a file, while permitting other processes to access the remainder of the file.

For this situation OS/2 makes available a function called DosFile-Locks() which permits a process to lock part of a file. The unlocked parts of the file are still accessible, but the locked part cannot be accessed until the process that locked it unlocks it.

This might be useful in a file containing a large database. One process could lock a record while updating it, but other processes would continue to have access to the other records.

DosFileLocks() is used to lock a section of file, to unlock it, and—by attempting to lock it—to test if a section is locked by another process.

DosFileLocks — Lock and unlock files

```
DosFileLocks(Handle, UnlockRange, LockRange);
unsigned short Handle;    /* file handle */
long far *UnlockRange;    /* range to be unlocked */
long far *LockRange;      /* range to be locked *
```

This function takes three arguments: the file handle, and two ranges: one for a section of file to be unlocked, and one for a section to be locked. Each of the two ranges consists of two long integers: the first is the offset into the file, in bytes, where the range begins, and the second is the length of the range in bytes. If a NULL pointer is used for either **UnlockRange** or **LockRange** then the corresponding activity—unlocking or locking—is not carried out. The ranges can be represented in C by two structures. The structure looks like this:

```
struct RANGE  {
    long lFileOffset;      /* start of locked section, in
                              bytes */
    long lRangelength;     /* length of locked section, in
                              bytes */
};
```

If any process, other than the lock owner, attempts to access a locked section of a file, or to lock or unlock a locked section, the result is code 33, ERROR_LOCK_VIOLATION.

In the example below, one process, plock.c, opens an already-existing file, and then locks part of it, from byte 50 to byte 100. The parent plock.c process then spins off a child process, chlock.c. The parent then sleeps for five seconds and unlocks the file.

As soon as it is born, the child process, chlock.c, reads and displays the initial unlocked part of the file (the first 50 bytes). It has no trouble doing this, since this part of the file is not locked. The child knows the next section of the file (bytes 50 to 100) may be locked, so it attempts to lock this part of the file.

This attempt fails until the parent process unlocks the locked section, at which point the child's lock succeeds, indicating it can now access the locked section. The child then goes on to read and display the locked section and the balance of the file.

```c
/* plock.c */
/* locks file, starts child chlock.c, which */
/* attemps to unlock file */
#define INCL_DOS
#include <os2.h>
#define ATTR 0              /* normal file */
#define OPENFLAG 0x01       /* fail if no file, or open it */
#define OPENMODE 0x4042     /* share=deny none, acc=rd/wrt */
#define NOPTR (char far *)0L  /* null far pointer */
#define OBLEN 32            /* length of object name buffer */
#define ASYNCH 1            /* child is asynchronous */

struct range   {            /* structure for DosFileLocks() */
   unsigned long offset;    /* offset from start of file */
   unsigned long length;    /* length of range to lock */
};

long LockRange[] = { 50, 100 };    /* both ranges start at
                                      50, */
long UnLockRange[] = { 50, 100 }; /*    end at 100 bytes */

main()
{
   unsigned short handle; /* file handle from DosOpen */
   unsigned action;         /* action taken by DosOpen */
   unsigned long size=0;    /* no minimum size of file */
   char objbuff[OBLEN];     /* buffer for DosExecPgm */
   struct _RESULTCODES childID;   /* result codes buffer */

                           /* open file */
   printf("Parent opening file\n");
   DosOpen("FILE.TXT", &handle, &action, size,
              ATTR, OPENFLAG, OPENMODE, 0L);
                           /* lock part of file */
   printf("Parent locking file\n");
   DosFileLocks( handle, NOPTR, LockRange );
                           /* create child */
   printf("Parent creating child\n");
   DosExecPgm( objbuff, OBLEN, ASYNCH,
                     NOPTR, NOPTR, &childID, "CHLOCK.EXE");
   DosSleep( 5000L );    /* delay */
                           /* unlock file */
   printf("Parent unlocking file\n");
   DosFileLocks( handle, UnLockRange, NOPTR );
   DosSleep( 2000L );    /* delay */
   printf("Parent closing file and exiting\n");
   DosClose( handle );
   exit(0);
}
```

Here's the child process. It reads from the file and displays its contents in much the same way rfile.c did, except before attempting to read it, it checks to see if the section from byte 50 to byte 100 is locked.

```
/* chlock.c */
/* child process of plock.c */
/* waits for unlocked file, then reads text and displays it
   */
#define INCL_DOS
#define INCL_SUB
#include <os2.h>
#define ATTR 0              /* normal file */
#define OPENFLAG 0x01       /* fail if no file, or open it */
#define OPENMODE 0x4042     /* share=deny none,
                               acc=read/write */
#define BUFLEN 51           /* size of data buffer */
#define NOPTR (unsigned far *)0L  /* null pointer */
#define ERROR_LOCK_VIOLATION 33  /* try unlock locked file */

long LockRange[2] = { 50, 100 };    /* both ranges start at
                                       50, */
long UnLockRange[2] = { 50, 100 };  /*    are 100 bytes
                                          long */

main()
{
   char buffer[BUFLEN];    /* buffer for text */
   unsigned short handle;  /* file handle from DosOpen */
   unsigned action;        /* action taken by DosOpen */
   unsigned long size=0;   /* no minimum size of file */
   unsigned BytesRead;     /* bytes read by DosRead */
   unsigned rc;            /* return code */

                          /* open file, read unlocked part */
   DosOpen("FILE.TXT", &handle, &action, size,
                          ATTR, OPENFLAG, OPENMODE, 0L);
   printf("Child reading initial unlocked section of
                                          file\n");
   DosRead(handle, buffer, BUFLEN-1, &BytesRead );
   buffer[BytesRead] = 0;
   printf("%s", buffer);
                     /* attempt to lock file */
   printf("\nChild will beep while attempting to lock
                                          file\n");
```

(continued)

```
do  {                    /* beep until file can be locked */
   DosBeep( 200, 20 );     /* 200 Hz, 20 msecs */
   DosSleep( 200L );    ·  /* 200 msecs */
   rc = DosFileLocks( handle, NOPTR, LockRange );
} while( rc == ERROR_LOCK_VIOLATION );
printf("\nChild process has locked file\n");

do  {                    /* read and display balance of file */
   DosRead(handle, buffer, BUFLEN, &BytesRead );
   buffer[BytesRead] = 0;
   printf("%s", buffer);
} while( BytesRead==BUFLEN );
   printf("Child closing file and exiting\n");
DosClose(handle);     /* close releases lock */
exit(0);              /* exit all threads */
}
```

Here's what happens when the file the two processes are operating on, FILE.TXT, contains the excerpt from *Hiawatha* seen earlier:

```
Parent opening file
Parent locking file
Parent creating child
Child reading initial unlocked section of file
  Ye who love a nation's legends,
  Love the bal
Child will beep while attempting to lock file
Parent unlocking file
Parent closing file and exiting
Child process has locked file
  lads of a people,
  That like voices from afar off
  Call to us to pause and listen,
  Speak in tones so plain and childlike,
  Scarcely can the ear distinguish
  Whether they are sung or spoken;-
  Listen to this Indian Legend,
  To this song of Hiawatha!
Child closing file and exiting
```

The locked section of file starts in the middle of the second line of the poem. The child can read up to this point, but cannot access the locked section until the parent, after a delay, releases it. While the child attempts to lock the file it beeps to let us know what it's doing. Figure 9-9 shows the relationship of plock.c and chlock.c over time.

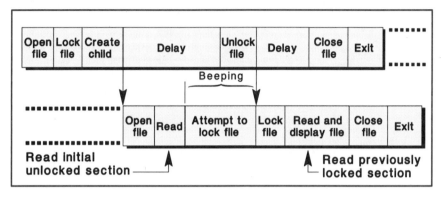

Figure 9-9
Time Relationship of plock.c and chlock.c

Summary

In this chapter we explored a variety of ways to speed up program execution by performing disk I/O at the same time as other activities. We examined how to coordinate a reading thread and a data analysis thread using a semaphore for mutual exclusion, with the asynchronous I/O function DosReadAsync(), and with multiple semaphores using DosMuxSemWait(). We also looked at how to use semaphores to coordinate the simultaneous reading and display of a disk file on the screen.

In the last section of the chapter we explored what happens when separate processes try to access the same file. The DosOpen() function and its parameters can provide mutually exclusive access, or permit several processes to access a file simultaneously. The DosFileLocks() function permits a process to deny access to only part of a file.

MEMORY

Chapter 10

Chapter 10

Many API functions exist in OS/2 to handle the allocation of memory. Why is memory allocation necessary? What do these functions accomplish, and how do they work? What special problems arise with memory allocation in a multitasking situation? How can appropriate use of memory make for a more efficient application, and also increase the efficiency of other applications in the system? In this chapter we explore the answers to these questions.

We'll examine the allocation of normal memory segments (those of 65536 bytes or less), and of huge segments (those that can be larger than 65536 bytes). We'll see how to access the memory in a segment after it's been created, and what the limits are on the number and size of segments. The size of a segment can be changed after it's been allocated, and a segment can be divided into separate areas for different purposes; we'll look at both these capabilities. We'll also see how to create segments that are discardable by the system. Finally we'll see how the system can be fooled into thinking a data segment is a code segment, so an application can store and execute "homemade" code.

This chapter concentrates on memory accessed by a single process. In the next chapter we'll explore the sharing of memory by several different processes.

Why Allocate Memory?

In many simple C programs, such as examples in earlier chapters of this book, there is no need to explicitly allocate memory. The C compiler takes care of providing a code segment to hold the executable code for the program, a data segment to hold global and static variables and constants, and a stack segment for automatic variables (and other items normally invisible to the programmer, such as function return addresses). Up to this point, we did not need to worry about memory allocation.

However, even in programs running on single-tasking systems such as MS-DOS, it is often desirable to allocate memory. For instance, in a database program the number of data records to be stored in memory may not be known in advance. Rather than declare a very large array to hold as many items as will fit in memory, a C programmer typically uses a function like malloc() to obtain the memory for each record, when it is needed. When memory for a record is no longer needed, it is released with a function like free(). This means that no memory is wasted, and that the number of data items stored can grow to fill the entire memory, even when the program does not know this size in advance.

In a multitasking environment the need for dynamic memory allocation is even more critical. Why? Because wasted memory hurts not only the program wasting it, but all the other programs running in the system as well. Like real-world commodities such as oil and magnesium, memory is a limited global resource, which should be handled as efficiently as possible by all concerned. To use memory efficiently, OS/2 programs need to dynamically allocate and free memory segments as necessary during program execution.

Differences Between MS-DOS and OS/2

Although memory allocation is a common practice in MS-DOS, there are some additional considerations involved in using memory in OS/2. This section briefly examines some of these.

We should note that in our discussion of memory management in this chapter we will frequently use the term "OS/2" to mean the *protected mode* of OS/2. We'll contrast this with the simpler memory management situation in MS-DOS. Of course OS/2 is also able to operate in *real mode* in the compatibility box; in this mode its memory management is the same as MS-DOS.

Who Controls Memory?

In a traditional single-tasking environment the application program itself controls memory allocation. The program can safely assume it has access to all the memory in the machine, and it takes what it needs. In a multitasking system such as OS/2, on the other hand, the operating system controls access to memory. The application may request memory, but may not receive it immediately. It may have to wait for a segment to be swapped in from the disk, or even for another program to terminate, before the desired memory is available. This may affect timing and other considerations in program design.

Access to Physical Addresses

An application in MS-DOS can access physical addresses (the actual hardware addresses of the memory chips). If an application knows, for instance, that the system keeps certain data in physical address 0040:0010, it can set up a pointer to this location—or any other location—and read it. In OS/2 this is not the case. An application can access only those memory segments the system has assigned to it. C programmers should be careful that the values used to construct pointers are obtained directly from the system. Trying to access memory not in a program's authorized data space leads to "protection fault" errors and causes the application to abort.

Even the physical addresses where a program and its data are loaded may change, if the program is swapped in and out of memory. However, as we'll see these address changes are invisible to the application because of the addressing scheme used in 80286 protected mode.

Memory Size

The memory in a single-tasking system does not grow or shrink. If an application finds 512K of RAM, then no amount of wishing will increase this limit. The application must either work within the limit, or inform the user there is insufficient memory and terminate.

Knowing how much memory is available is quite a different story in OS/2. The system may be running different applications, each with several different processes and threads executing simultaneously. Each of these entities may request or free memory at any time, and new processes may be started, so the pool of available memory is constantly changing. An application can get only a rough idea of how much memory is free at any given moment.

However, knowing the amount of available memory is not so critical in OS/2. If there is not enough RAM, the system can treat part of the disk as memory, so an application's memory space (or that of all the running applications together) can be larger than physical RAM.

During the course of this chapter we'll see how memory is allocated, how applications can access this memory, and how applications can request, and receive, more memory than is physically available in the system.

Memory and Hardware

In OS/2 memory allocation is determined by the hardware addressing scheme of the 80286 (or 80386) microprocessor. We therefore examine the operation of the chip before going on to investigate the API functions that deal with memory. This provides the background necessary to understand why API functions are designed as they are.

Registers Don't Hold Physical Addresses

The random access memory of a typical IBM-compatible computer—whether an XT, AT or PS/2 class—can be thought of as a series of bytes, numbered sequentially from 0 to the highest limit of memory. (For example, from 0 to 2,097,151 in a 2-Megabyte machine.) These numbers are called *physical addresses*, since they have a one-to-one correspondence with the actual physical memory locations. (Another common name is "absolute addresses".)

Unfortunately, the registers used to hold addresses in the 8086 and 80286 microprocessors are only 16 bits wide. Thus these registers can only hold addresses in the range from 0 to 65535 (2^{16}). This defines what is called a *segment:* : an area of memory with a maximum size of 65536 bytes. The segment is a fundamental architectural feature of Intel chips.

To specify a range of addresses larger than a segment, combinations of different registers must be used. The way this is done depends on the specific chip.

8086 Addressing Scheme

The 8086 uses four extra registers to extend the addressing range beyond one segment: the CS, DS, SS and ES registers. (The mnemonics stand for Code Segment, Data Segment, Stack Segment, and Extra Segment.) Each physical address is derived from two parts: the segment address, which is a value placed in one of these four segment registers, and the offset address, which specifies how far into the segment the address is located.

To calculate the physical address, the contents of the segment register is shifted left four bits (the same as multiplying it by 16) and added to the offset address. This provides a 20-bit address, enough to address 1 megabyte (1,048,576 or 2^{20} bytes). The scheme is shown in Figure 10-1.

Some of this megabyte is taken up with ROM and video display memory; the result is the infamous 640K limit on PC and XT class machines.

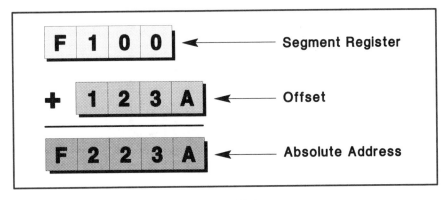

Figure 10-1
8086 Memory Addressing

80286 Addressing Scheme

The 80286, used in AT class machines and some PS/2 models, employs a different addressing method when in the protected mode. (The 80386 uses a similar approach.) Segment registers are used as before, but instead of being added to the offset address, as in the 8086, the number in the segment register is treated as an index into a table called a *descriptor table*. Because the number in the segment register is no longer an address, it is called a *selector* rather than a segment address: it selects one of the entries in the descriptor table.

To calculate a physical address, the processor takes the selector from the segment register, goes to the indicated entry in the descriptor table, finds the base address of the segment, and adds the offset to this base address. Figure 10-2 shows the 80286 memory addressing scheme.

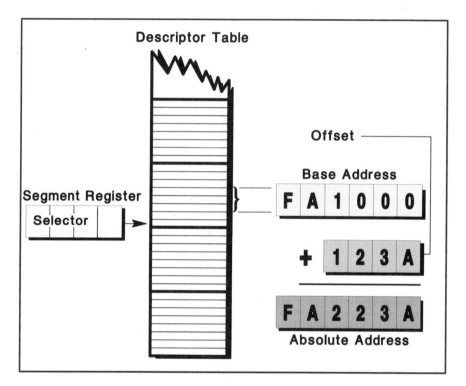

Figure 10-2
80286 Memory Addressing

The descriptor uses three bytes, or 24 bits, to specify the base address of the segment; so physical addresses up to 16,777,216 bytes (2^{24}) or 16 megabytes can be addressed.

Descriptors

There are two kinds of descriptor tables in the 80286: global and local. Each process has access to its own Local Descriptor table (LDT). Also, all processes can access a single Global Descriptor table (GDT). Which of these two tables is being accessed is indicated by a bit in the selector. Two other bits indicate the priority of the process that created the address. Thus there are 13 bits left to index into the descriptor table. Thirteen bits can specify 8192 possible values, so this is the maximum size of the descriptor tables.

Thus a 32-bit address value in OS/2 contains different kinds of information than a 32-point address in MS-DOS. Figure 10-3 shows how a 32-bit address is composed of a 16-bit selector and a 16-bit offset.

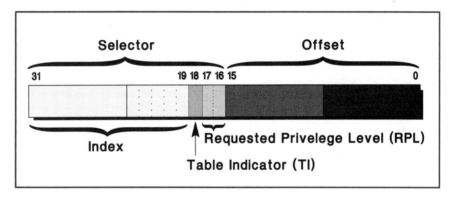

Figure 10-3
32-Bit Memory Address

Each entry in the descriptor table consists of eight bytes. This eight-byte descriptor specifies the base address of the segment, the size of the segment, and a variety of other information. There is a bit to indicate if the segment is present; that is, loaded into memory (as opposed to being on the disk). Another bit indicates if the segment has been accessed since being loaded. Three other bits indicate if the segment is code or data, if it is readable or writable, and if it is conforming. The remaining two bits specify the privilege level of the segment. Figure 10-4 shows how the descriptor is laid out.

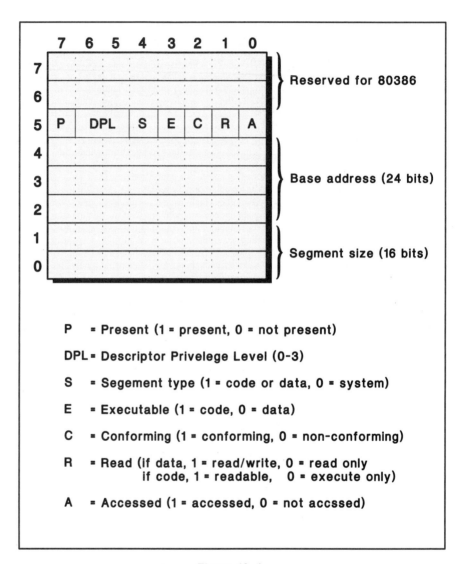

Figure 10-4
Segment Descriptor

The System Controls Base Addresses

The key to memory management in OS/2 lies in the fact that a 32-bit address, consisting of a selector and an offset, is not a physical address, but must be translated into a physical address using the descriptor table. Let's see why this is important.

During the course of its execution a program may calculate a variety of different addresses. For instance, imagine a pointer to an array. The program finds the address of the array, and places it in a variable for future use. Suppose at this point the program is swapped out of memory, and when it is swapped back in finds itself (and its array) at a different physical address in memory. Does this mean that the value in the pointer variable is now wrong?

One might think the selector part of this address would need to be modified, but in fact (and this is the key) *only the entry in the descriptor table* pointed to by the selector needs to be changed. This change is invisible to the application, since the 32-bit pointer remains the same, and the application cannot access the descriptor tables. This allows the application, and any data it accesses, to be moved around at will without affecting the operation of the program. The operating system simply changes the entries in the descriptor table to reflect the changing location of the segments.

Memory Protection

Besides facilitating memory swapping, the addressing system of the 80286 makes it possible for each application to be protected from others running in the same machine. Since a program's only access to memory is (usually) through its own Local Descriptor Table, it only has knowledge of segments with entries in this table. It also cannot modify the table itself; only the operating system can do this. Thus it is almost impossible for an application to inadvertently access the code or data in another program.

The 16-bit segment-size entry in the descriptor is an important part of the protection process. This entry can be a number up to 65535, but is often smaller. Whenever a memory access is made by an application, the 80286 checks to see if the offset is less than the segment size specified in the descriptor. If the offset is too large, a *protection fault* results and the system shuts down the offending application and returns an error message to the user.

The other bits in the descriptor table also play a part in protecting programs from each other (and from themselves). When an application accesses a variable (or starts to jump to another location in memory), the processor checks the privilege level of the segment against that of the process trying to access it. If the process has too low a privilege level, access is denied.

If the descriptor has the bit set indicating the segment is a code segment, then it cannot be written to; on the other hand, a data segment cannot be executed. (Data segments can also be specified to be writable or not, and code segments can be readable or not.)

In the examples to follow we see how the API functions provided for memory management make use of this underlying hardware architecture.

Dynamic Memory Management

The *access bit* in the descriptor table plays an important role in OS/2 memory management. When the system finds there is not enough memory to satisfy a running application, it swaps an existing segment out to the disk so it has room enough to create a new segment or read one in from the disk. How does the system decide which segment to remove from RAM?

The hardware sets the access bit automatically each time any byte in a segment is accessed. The system keeps a queue (list) of memory segments. Every time slice, when the system regains control from an application, it examines the access bit in the descriptor for each segment. If the access bit is set, the system moves that segment to the top of the queue. When the queue has been rearranged the system clears the access bit in all the tables.

Thus, as the system runs, the segments accessed the most often rise to the top of the queue; those accessed least often sink to the bottom. When the system needs to discard a segment, or swap it out to disk, it selects one from the bottom of the queue. This is called an LRU memory management scheme, an acronym for Least Recently Used.

Virtual Memory

In theory, a process running in the protected mode in a 80286 system can access 8192 entries in each of two descriptor tables, a total of 16384 segments. Each segment holds up to 65536 bytes, so the total memory a process can access is 1,073,741,824 bytes, or one gigabyte.

However, as we saw earlier, the hardware uses an addressing scheme which relies on 24-bit segment base registers, permiting physical access to only 16 megabytes.

The memory which a process appears to be able to access is called *virtual memory*, while the memory the hardware can physically access is called *physical memory*. While physical memory is indeed limited to 16 megabytes (or however much is actually installed in the machine), an application can act as if it is accessing memory far beyond this limit. Where does the extra memory come from?

The answer is that the operating system may keep memory segments in places other than RAM memory. In practice this means the hard disk. If an application requests memory not physically in RAM, OS/2 discovers this is true by reading the *present bit* in the segment selector. It then swaps the segment in from the disk. We'll see how this works in an actual example later in this chapter.

Now let's leave our general discussion and examine the specifics of memory allocation using the OS/2 API functions.

Simple Segment Allocation

Our first example demonstrates the most commonly used memory allocation functions: DosAllocSeg(). This function requests the system to make available a memory segment of a certain size, for use by the application. The segment can be used for storing and retrieving data for any purpose needed by the application. The segment can be no larger than 65536 bytes.

The example program allocates a segment, fills all the bytes in the segment with a constant, checks each byte by reading it back out, and finally frees the segment.

```c
/* easyseg.c */
/* shows usage of DosAllocSeg() and DosFreeSeg() */
#define INCL_DOS
#include <os2.h>
#define SEG_SIZE 65535  /* length of segment (maximum) */
#define SEG_FLAGS 0     /* not shareable, not discardable */
main()
{
   unsigned short Selector;   /* selector of segment */
   char far *SegPtr;          /* pointer to offset in seg */
   unsigned bindex;           /* index into segment */
   unsigned rc;               /* return variable */

                              /* allocate segment */
   if( rc=DosAllocSeg( SEG_SIZE, &Selector, SEG_FLAGS) )
      { printf("DosAllocSeg error=%u\n",rc); exit(1); }

                              /* create pointer to segment */
   SegPtr = (char far *)( (unsigned long)Selector << 16 );

                                    /* fill segment */
   for(bindex=0; bindex < SEG_SIZE; bindex++)
      *(SegPtr + bindex) = '\xAA';
                                    /* check segment */
   for(bindex=0; bindex < SEG_SIZE; bindex++)
      if( *(SegPtr + bindex) != '\xAA' )
         printf("Error: byte number %u\n", bindex );

                              /* free segment */
   if( rc=DosFreeSeg( Selector ) )
      { printf("DosFreeSeg error=%u\n",rc); exit(1); }
   exit(0);                          /* exit */
}
```

The DosAllocSeg() function takes three parameters. The first is the size of the segment desired. Since a segment can be no larger than 65536 bytes, the largest number that can be used here is 65535 (FFFF hex). A value of 0 is used to specify the maximum segment size of 65536 bytes.

The second parameter is the address where the system returns the selector for the segment. As discussed above, this selector consists mostly of an index into the local descriptor table, which contains entries describing the segment.

DosAllocSeg — Allocates a memory segment

```
DosAllocSeg(SegSize, ASelector, Flags);
unsigned SegSize;                    /* size of segment */
unsigned short far *ASelector;       /* address for seg
                                        selector */
unsigned Flags;                      /* access flags */
```

The third parameter is a word containing three 1-bit flags, as shown in Figure 10-5.

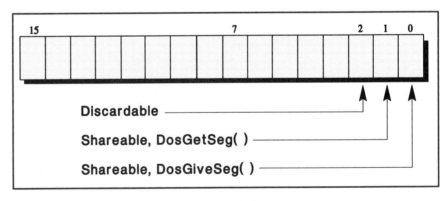

Figure 10-5
Allocation Flags

Bit 0 in the flag word is set if the segment is shareable through the DosGiveSeg() function, and bit 1 is set if the segment is shareable through DosGetSeg(). We'll examine the topic of shared segments in the next chapter, but for the time being these bits are set to zero. Bit 2 is set to indicate the segment can be discarded by the system when memory gets low. We'll look at this possibility later in the chapter; for now this bit is also set to zero.

Constructing a Pointer to the Segment

The DosAllocSeg() function provides the selector part of the segment address. To access locations within the segment it is necessary to construct a 32-bit **far** pointer to the starting address of the segment. The desired offset into the segment is then added to this base pointer to access any address in the segment.

In the program we construct the base pointer by typecasting the 16-bit selector into a 32-bit unsigned long integer, and then shifting this value left 16 bits into the left-most half of the long integer, in this line:

```
SegPtr = (char far *)( (unsigned long)Selector << 16 );
```

If there were an offset value we could add it at this point, but we want the base address of the segment, so the offset is 0. The resulting value must be cast to a **far** pointer. In our program we want to access individual bytes, so it's a **far** pointer to **char**, but it could be a pointer to **int** or other types as well (we'll see examples of other types later).

Microsoft C provides other methods for creating the **far** pointer from the selector. The C library functions FP_SEG() and FP_OFF() can be used. These functions require the include file DOS.H, and, in the program shown above, would be used like this:

```
FP_SEG(SegPtr) = Selector;    /* set selector part of
                                 pointer */
FP_OFF(SegPtr) = 0;           /* set offset part of pointer
                                 */
```

These statements would set the two halves of **SegPtr** to the appropriate values. The header files provided by Microsoft C for OS/2 C provide yet another way to do this calculation, using macros. However, for clarity we'll construct them "by hand" using the left shift operator.

Accessing Individual Segment Addresses

Accessing the contents of any offset address in the segment is easily done using the **far** pointer just constructed. In the example we use the pointer to place a value in each byte of the segment, and also to read these values back out. Pointer arithmetic moves the pointer through the segment as the value of **index** changes.

Freeing the Segment

When an application is through with a segment it can release it using DosFreeSeg(). This function takes only one parameter, the selector to the segment obtained by DosAllocSeg().

DosFreeSeg — Frees a memory segment

```
DosFreeSeg(Selector);
unsigned short Selector;    /* segment selector */
```

This function removes the segment descriptor from the descriptor table and releases the memory occupied by the segment.

When a program terminates, the segments it was using (if they are not shared by other processes) are automatically freed. Thus in the example shown it is not strictly necessary to free the segment, since the system will free it anyway. However, if a program is through using a segment, but will continue to run, it is important to free the segment so that more memory is made available to other processes in the system. Liberal use of DosFreeSeg() is part of the "good neighbor" policy in a multitasking system.

Using C Library Functions with Segments

Here's an example which uses C library functions to access a segment. The user is prompted to type a series of phrases, which are placed in the data segment using the strcpy() function. After each string is entered, the program reports the amount of free memory remaining in the segment. The strings are then read out again using printf().

```
/* strseg.c */
/* gets strings from keyboard, puts them in segment */
/* compile with -AL option, for far pointers in strcpy() */
#define INCL_DOS
#include <os2.h>
#include <stdio.h>          /* for gets() etc. */
#include <string.h>         /* for strcpy() */
#define SEG_LENGTH 100      /* length of segment */
#define SEG_FLAGS 0         /* not shareable, not discardable */
#define LINE_LENGTH 80      /* maximum length of input string */
#define MAX_LINES 20        /* max number of input strings */
```

(continued)

```
main()
{
    char string[LINE_LENGTH];    /* buffer for input string */
    unsigned short Selector;     /* selector of segment */
    unsigned free = SEG_LENGTH;  /* bytes remaining in seg */
    char *SegPtr;                    /* pointer to offset in seg */
    char *LineList[MAX_LINES];   /* list of line offsets */
    unsigned linenum = 0;        /* index of current line */
    int slength;                 /* length of input string */
    int j;                       /* loop counter */
    unsigned rc;                 /* return variable */
                                 /* allocate segment */
    if( rc=DosAllocSeg( SEG_LENGTH, &Selector, SEG_FLAGS) )
        { printf("DosAllocSeg error=%u\n",rc); exit(1); }

                            /* create pointer to segment */
    SegPtr = (char *)( (unsigned long)Selector << 16 );
                            /* print prompts */
    printf("Enter text strings, no more than 80
                                        characters\n");
    printf("Terminate with empty line\n");
    while(TRUE)  {              /* get string, find length */
        slength=strlen( gets(string) );
        if( slength < 1 )       /* if only [Enter] */
            break;              /* go print contents */
        if( slength < free )  {        /* if there's room */
            LineList[linenum++] = SegPtr; /* put pointer in
                                            list */
            strcpy( SegPtr, string );  /* put string in seg */
            SegPtr += slength+1;       /* update seg pointer */
            free -= slength+1;         /* update free bytes */
        printf("  Bytes free = %u\n", free);
        } else  {
            printf("Not enough room in segment\n");
            break;
        }
    } /* end while */
                            /* print out lines from seg */
    printf("\nContents of segment is:\n");
    for(j=0; j<linenum; j++)       /* for each line */
        printf("%s\n",LineList[j]); /* print pointer to
                                    string */

    if( rc=DosFreeSeg(Selector) )  /* free segment */
        { printf("DosFreeSeg error=%u\n",rc), exit(1); }
    exit(0);                        /* exit */
}
```

Here's a sample session, in which the user types in parts of a well-known phrase. Each line is stored in the memory segment allocated earlier in the program. When the user hits [Enter] at the start of a line, the program prints out the contents of the segment.

```
Enter text strings, no more than 80 characters
Terminate with empty line
Now is the time
   Bytes free = 84
for all good men to come
   Bytes free = 59
to the aid of
   Bytes free = 45
their party.
   Bytes free = 32

Contents of segment is:
Now is the time
for all good men to come
to the aid of
their party.
```

It is essential this program be compiled using the -AL option. This invokes the large memory model, which uses **far** pointers for data access. In the previous example we could use the small memory model and specify **far** pointers explicitly to access the segment. Here we need the large model so the library routine which contains strcpy() uses **far** pointers. As a corollary, it is no longer necessary to explicitly set the data type of our pointers to **far**—they are this class by default.

The offset to each string is stored in an array as the strings are received from the user. These values are then taken from the array to print out the strings at the end of the program.

Allocating Multiple Segments

So far we have allocated only one segment in each program. It is possible to allocate many more segments, although (as we'll see) there is a limit to how many can be allocated by a given process. Multiple segments could be used to hold a number of data items, such as structures, of the same type. In a database program, for example, the record for each employee or each inventory item could occupy its own segment. Or, different segments can hold entirely different types of data.

Our next example permits the user to specify, using command-line arguments, both the size and the number of segments to be allocated. The program then ensures everything is working correctly by filling every byte of every segment with a value, and reading the values out again to see that they are correct.

```
/* manyseg.c */
/* allocates many segments; size and number from command
   line */
#define INCL_DOS
#include <os2.h>
#define SEG_FLAGS 0      /* not shareable, not discardable */
#define MAX_SEGS 10000   /* length of selector list */

unsigned SegList[MAX_SEGS];    /* table of seg selectors */

main(argc, argv)
int argc;
char *argv[];
{
    char far *SegPtr;            /* pointer to offset in seg */
    unsigned short Selector;     /* selector of segment */
    unsigned SegSize;            /* size of each segment */
    unsigned NumSegs;            /* number of segments */
    unsigned seg;                /* segment index */
    unsigned byte;               /* byte index */
    unsigned rc;                 /* return variable */

    if( argc != 3 )
       { printf("Syntax: C>manyseg size number\n");
                                                    exit(1); }
    SegSize = atoi( argv[1] );
    NumSegs = atoi( argv[2] );
    if(NumSegs > MAX_SEGS)
       { printf("Size of selector list exceeded.\n");
                                                    exit(1); }

                        /* allocate each segment */
    for(seg=0; seg<NumSegs; seg++)  {
       printf("Allocating segment %u\n", seg);
       if( rc=DosAllocSeg( SegSize, &Selector, SEG_FLAGS ) )
          { printf("DosAllocSeg error=%u\n", rc); exit(1); }
       SegList[seg] = Selector;   /* put selector on list */
    }
```

(continued)

```
                           /* fill every byte in every segment */
        for(seg=0; seg<NumSegs; seg++)  {
          printf("Filling segment %u\n", seg);
          SegPtr = (char far *)( (unsigned long)SegList[seg]<<16
                                                              );
          for(byte=0; byte < SegSize; byte++)
            *SegPtr++ = (char)( byte+seg );
        }
                           /* check every byte in every segment */
        for(seg=0; seg<NumSegs; seg++)  {
          printf("Checking segment %u\n", seg);
          SegPtr = (char far *)( (unsigned long)SegList[seg]<<16
                                                              );
          for(byte=0; byte < SegSize; byte++)
            if( *SegPtr++ != (char)( byte+seg ) ) /* show
                                                     errors */
              printf("Error: seg %u, byte %u\n", seg, byte);
        }
                           /* free each segment */
        for(seg=0; seg<NumSegs; seg++)
          if( rc=DosFreeSeg( SegList[seg] ) )
             { printf("DosFreeSeg error=%u\n", rc); exit(1); }
        exit(0);
}
```

Using this program we can experiment with the limits imposed by OS/2 on the number of memory segments allocated, and on the total amount of memory they occupy.

There is no problem in specifying a small number of reasonably-sized segments. Here we allocate four 1000-byte segments:

```
C>manyseg 1000 4
Allocating segment 0
Allocating segment 1
Allocating segment 2
Allocating segment 3
Filling segment 0
Filling segment 1
Filling segment 2
Filling segment 3
Checking segment 0
Checking segment 1
Checking segment 2
Checking segment 3
```

The segments are all allocated, then filled, and finally their contents are read back out again and checked. The value placed in each byte is the sum of the byte number and segment number, so we guarantee the program does not produce a false positive result by reading back a byte from the wrong location in a segment, or from the same location in the wrong segment. (Only the lower half of this sum is used; the high half is discarded when the quantity is cast to **char**.)

Limited Number of Segments

What happens if you specify a really large number of segments? For instance, try typing

```
C>manyseg 10 5000
```

The program allocates segments up to a certain point; then there is a return code from DosAllocSeg():

```
- - - - - - - - - - - -
Allocating segment 1911
Allocating segment 1912
DosAllocSeg error=8
```

This error is defined as ERROR_NOT_ENOUGH_MEMORY, but in fact the problem is not that we've run out of memory, but that there is no more room in the descriptor table to hold another segment. Although there are 8192 possible entries in the table, not all these are available to the application. The number available depends on (among other factors) whether **memman** in the CONFIG.SYS file is set to **swap** and **move** or not. At least in the current version of OS/2 it seems safe to ask for up to 1900 segments when swapping and moving are activated.

Exploring Virtual Memory

The manyseg.c program can be used to explore one of OS/2's most powerful features: *virtual memory*. Virtual memory is the memory seen by an application. As we discussed earlier in the chapter, this can be larger than the amount of physical memory actually available in the system. To show the difference, let's try using manyseg.c in the same way with two different versions of the CONFIG.SYS file.

First, edit the CONFIG.SYS file so it contains the line:

```
memman=noswap, nomove
```

Now, (after rebooting to activate the new CONFIG.SYS) invoke the manyseg.c program. Set the size and number of segments so they exceed the total memory of the machine. This may take a little experimentation. In a 2-megabyte machine, with no other processes running, we find we can ask for about 20 segments of 65535 bytes each before we run out of memory. We want to ask for a few segments more than this, so we'll try 22. If you have more memory installed, you'll need to use a larger number; less memory (or other processes running) will require a smaller number. Type:

```
C>manyseg 65535 22
```

The system allocates segments until it runs out of memory, and then returns an error message. You might see, for example,

```
- - - - - - - - - - -
Allocating segment 19
Allocating segment 20
DosAllocSeg error=8
```

Here we find there is no more memory after 1.3 megabytes are allocated (the system itself is using the remainder of our 2 megabytes). The next request returns code 8; this time the message ERROR_NOT_ENOUGH_MEMORY is appropriate.

Turning on Virtual Memory Capability

If you now change the **memman** command to **swap, move** you'll see a different phenomenon. Edit the CONFIG.SYS file to include these changes, and then invoke the program the same way:

```
C>manyseg 65535 22
```

When the available memory has been filled, instead of an error message, you'll see your disk-drive light go on.

```
- - - - - - - - - - -
Allocating segment 19
Allocating segment 20     /* disk drive light goes on here */
Allocating segment 21     /* and here */
```

What's happening? The system needs to allocate another segment, but there's no space in RAM. It therefore swaps an existing segment out to disk, to make room in memory. The same thing happens until all the segments are allocated.

Once they are allocated the segments are filled and checked. During this process some segments are already in memory; accessing them does not require a disk access. Other segments will need to be swapped in from disk to be accessed, causing the disk drive light to go on. You can follow the process by watching the screen and the disk drive light. Figure 10-6 shows how segments which can't fit in RAM are stored on the disk.

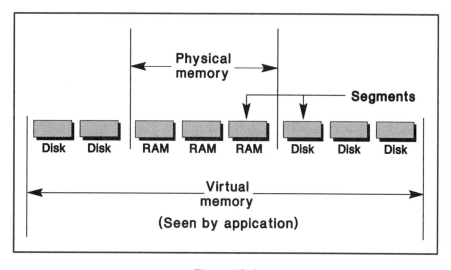

Figure 10-6
Virtual Memory

This is an astonishing accomplishment on the part of the operating system. It has succeeded in increasing the effective size of the system memory, and the application is not even aware that the memory it is addressing may not be immediately available in RAM. Virtual memory capability simplifies the design of programs, since it is no longer necessary to worry if the size of memory will be exceeded. If it is, the operating system will provide more.

Of course, there is a price to pay for this power. You probably have noticed that (not surprisingly) the allocation process slows down markedly when segments must be swapped out to disk. If in a particular application it is critical that every memory access be made in minimum time, you should be careful not to let the application use more memory than exists on the physical system. In most cases, however, an occasional disk access does not unacceptably slow down the system.

We've seen that a single application can over-commit memory (use more than is physically available). It is also possible for a combination of different applications running together in the system to jointly over-commit memory. This is a more likely situation. In either case the system handles memory allocation invisibly to the applications. However, an application may be slowed down at unexpected moments.

The SWAPPER.DAT File

Where do the segments go when they are swapped to disk? The operating system creates a special file to hold them. The file, called SWAPPER.DAT, is ordinarily in the root directory. This file has some unusual characteristics. First, it can grow until it fills all the available space on the disk. Second, it can't be erased in the usual way. This may seem like a problem, but in fact the swap file will probably not grow larger than a megabyte or so. Also, you can erase it by changing its access rights, as we'll learn in the chapter on files. If you have a system with the dual-boot option (both MS-DOS and OS/2 installed) you can also erase it by booting up MS-DOS and using its erase command.

Exploring Memory Allocation

Here's a short program that uses another API function, DosMem-Avail(), to explore memory usage. This function returns the largest block of available memory.

```
/* segmem.c */
/* shows memory use during segment allocation */
#define INCL_DOS
#include <os2.h>
#define SEG_FLAGS 0        /* not shareable, not discardable */
main(argc, argv)
int argc;
char *argv[];
{
    unsigned short Selector;    /* selector of segment */
    unsigned SegSize;           /* size of each segment */
    unsigned NumSegs;           /* number of segments */
    unsigned seg;               /* segment index */
    unsigned long OldMem;       /* orig memory available */
    unsigned long NewMem;       /* new memory available */
    unsigned rc;                /* return variable */

    if( argc != 3 )
       { printf("Syntax: C>segmem segsize numsegs\n");
                                              exit(1); }
    SegSize = atoi( argv[1] );
    NumSegs = atoi( argv[2] );
                      /* display initial available memory */
    DosMemAvail( &OldMem );
    printf("Initial free memory=%lu\n", OldMem );
```

(continued)

```
                                /* for each segment */
        for(seg=0; seg<NumSegs; seg++)  {
                                /* allocate segment */
            if( rc=DosAllocSeg( SegSize, &Selector, SEG_FLAGS ) )
                { printf("DosAllocSeg error=%u\n", rc); exit(1); }
                                /* display remaining memory */
            DosMemAvail( &NewMem );
            printf("Seg=%u: Free=%lu, diff=%ld\n",
                                    seg, NewMem, OldMem-NewMem );
            OldMem = NewMem;
        }
        exit(0);
    }
```

The largest block of free memory is not necessarily the total memory available. If the real mode box is not being used (because the CONFIG.SYS file contains the command **protectonly=yes**), or is set to less than 640K, then there are two areas of memory available: one in the real mode area below 640K, and one in high memory above the high part of OS/2. The DosMemAvail() function returns the largest of these two areas.

DosMemAvail — Finds size of largest block of free memory
```
DosMemAvail(ASize);
unsigned long far *ASize;  /* address for size of block */
```

This function takes a single parameter: the address of an unsigned long integer where the size (in bytes) can be placed.

Like manyseg.c, the program takes the size and number of the segments to be allocated as parameters on the command line. It then prints out the largest block of memory initially available. Finally it loops through the segments, allocating a segment, and printing the size of the largest free memory block and the difference between this size and the last one.

Here's the result when too much memory is requested (that is, **memman** is set to **noswap**, **nomove**), and **protectonly=yes**.

```
C>segmem 65535 25
Initial free=953888
Seg=0: Free=888320, diff=65568
Seg=1: Free=822752, diff=65568
Seg=2: Free=757184, diff=65568
Seg=3: Free=691616, diff=65568
Seg=4: Free=626048, diff=65568
```

(continued)

```
Seg=5:  Free=560480,  diff=65568
Seg=6:  Free=537600,  diff=22880
Seg=7:  Free=537600,  diff=0
Seg=8:  Free=537600,  diff=0
Seg=9:  Free=537600,  diff=0
Seg=10: Free=537600,  diff=0
Seg=11: Free=537600,  diff=0
Seg=12: Free=537600,  diff=0
Seg=13: Free=537600,  diff=0
Seg=14: Free=472032,  diff=65568
Seg=15: Free=406464,  diff=65568
Seg=16: Free=340896,  diff=65568
Seg=17: Free=275328,  diff=65568
Seg=18: Free=209760,  diff=65568
Seg=19: Free=144192,  diff=65568
Seg=20: Free=78624,  diff=65568 Seg=21: Free=35936,
                                        diff=42688

DosAllocSeg error=8
```

Looking at the numbers we can see how the system allocates memory. It starts off filling high memory and reporting the remaining block size of high memory. When the largest block available in high memory becomes smaller than that in low memory, the function starts to report the low memory size, even though it is the size of the high memory that is changing. When high memory is gone the system begins to eat away at low memory until there is no longer enough for the next segment; it then returns the well-known error code 8.

Huge Objects

The huge memory model and the **huge** keyword give the C programmer the ability to create arrays and other data constructions which are larger than the one-segment 65536-byte limit. An application can access the elements of such an array contiguously, without worrying about what segment they are in. For instance, if a program contains the declaration

```
char huge HugeArray[123000];
```

then references to elements of the array can be made even if they exceed the 65536-byte limit on segment size. For instance:

```
value = HugeArray[99000];
```

The ability to create **huge** arrays is convenient if you need to process large amounts of data. Of course, there is a price to pay, in that it takes longer to access an element in a huge array. This is because the compiler must perform extra arithmetic to calculate the address of an element in a huge array. This arithmetic is somewhat more complicated in protected mode OS/2 programs than it is in MS-DOS, because the segment part of a 32-bit address is no longer an address, but an index to a descriptor table.

Huge amounts of memory can be allocated dynamically from C programs using the C library function halloc().

Creating Huge Objects with API Functions

It is also possible to use API functions to allocate huge sections of memory. Actually, the C compiler calls these functions itself to handle huge objects, so it is instructive to see what they do. Using the API functions might also be more efficient in some cases than the corresponding C library functions.

In OS/2, a section of memory larger than one segment is called an *object*. An object is composed of a number of 65536-byte segments, plus a smaller segment if one is needed to complete an odd-sized object. A typical use for a huge object is to hold an array larger than 65536 bytes. Figure 10-7 shows such an object spread out over a number of segments.

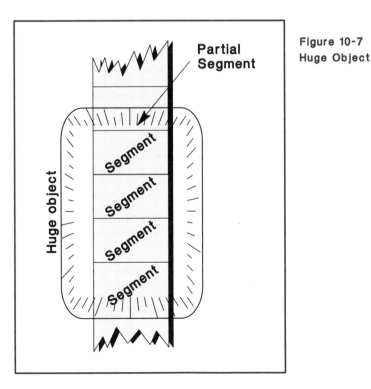

Partial
Segment

Huge object

Segment
Segment
Segment
Segment

Figure 10-7
Huge Object

Here's a program that can create almost any size array. The size of the array, in bytes, is specified by a command-line argument. The program allocates a huge object to hold the array, fills every byte, then reads all the bytes back out to verify that everything works as it should.

```
/* huge.c */
/* allocates huge object with DosAllocHuge() */
#define INCL_DOS
#include <os2.h>
#include <stdlib.h>          /* needed for atol() */
#define NO_SHARE 0           /* object will not be shared */
#define MAXNUMSEG 0          /* object will not grow */
main(argc, argv)
int argc;
char *argv[];
{
    unsigned NumSegs;        /* number of 65536 segments */
    unsigned Remain;         /* bytes in last segment */
    unsigned short Selector;   /* selector of huge object */
    char huge *SegPtr;       /* pointer to huge object */
    unsigned long HugeSize; /* total size of huge object */
    unsigned long index;     /* index into huge object */
    unsigned rc;             /* return code */

                             /* find sizes */
    if( argc != 2 )
       { printf("Syntax: C>huge size\n"); exit(1); }
    HugeSize = atol( argv[1] );
    NumSegs = HugeSize / 65536; /* find number of segments */
    Remain = HugeSize % 65536;  /* find bytes in last seg */
    printf("%u segments, last seg=%u bytes\n", NumSegs,
                                                    Remain );

                    /* allocate huge object */
    if( rc=DosAllocHuge( NumSegs, Remain, &Selector,
                                NO_SHARE, MAXNUMSEG ) )
       { printf("DosAllocHuge error=%u\n",rc); exit(1); }

                    /* derive pointer to huge object */
    SegPtr = (char huge *)( (unsigned long)Selector << 16);

                    /* fill every byte in huge object */
    printf("Filling %lu bytes\n", HugeSize );
    for(index=0; index<HugeSize; index++)
       *(SegPtr+index) = (char)index;
```

(continued)

```
                              /* check every byte in huge object */
        printf("Checking %lu bytes\n", HugeSize );
        for(index=0; index<HugeSize; index++)
          if( *(SegPtr+index) != (char)index )
            printf("Error: byte=%lu\n", index);

                              /* free huge object */
        if( rc=DosFreeSeg( Selector ) )
          { printf("DosFreeSeg error=%u\n",rc); exit(1); }
        exit(0);
      }
```

The API function used to allocate the huge object is DosAlloc-Huge().

DosAllocHuge — Allocate huge memory object

```
DosAllocHuge(NumSegs, LastSeg, ASelector, Share,
                                                MaxNumSegs);
unsigned NumSegs;              /* number of 65536-byte segments */
unsigned LastSeg;              /* bytes in last segment */
unsigned short far *ASelector;  /* address for huge
                                        selector */
unsigned MaxNumSegs;          /* max segs if object grows */
unsigned Share;               /* sharing and discardability flag
```

This function takes five parameters. The first is the number of 65536-byte segments necessary to hold the object. The second is the size of the segment necessary to hold any remaining bytes. (A value of 0 for **LastSeg** means there will be no odd-size segment.) Thus if the object to be allocated is 200,000 bytes long, three 65536-byte segments, plus one 3392-byte segment, are required to hold it. The program performs two kinds of division to derive these values from the total size.

The third parameter is the base address where the system places the selector of the huge object. Notice this is the selector to the entire huge object. Thus to free the object, as we do at the end of the program, only one call to DosFreeSeg(), using this selector, is necessary.

The selector of the huge object is also the selector of the first individual segment belonging to the object. The selectors of the other segments can also be obtained, as we'll see later.

It is possible to expand an existing object using the DosRe-AllocHuge() function. The fourth parameter in DosAllocHuge(), **MaxNumSegs**, specifies the maximum size the object will reach if it is expanded. If we don't plan to expand the object, we inform the system with a value of 0. DosAllocHuge() reserves as many contiguous selectors in the Local Descriptor table as are necessary to hold the number of segments specified in the **MaxNumSegs** parameter.

Bit fields in the fifth parameter indicates whether the object is shareable with other processes or not, and if it is discardable. This is the same arrangement as for DosAllocSeg(), and is shown in Figure 10-5. Bit 0 indicates the object is shareable with DosGiveSeg(), bit 1 indicates the object is shareable with DosGetSeg(), and bit 2 indicates the object is discardable.

Here's a sample session with the program:

```
C>huge 800000
12 segments, last seg=13568 bytes
Filling 800000 bytes
Checking 800000 bytes
```

You can try out the program using different array sizes. Sizes similar to the example may take a few seconds to execute.

One startling experiment you can perform is the creation of a single array larger than available memory. You must have **memman** set to **swap, move**. Then specify an array size that somewhat exceeds physical RAM. After the segments that will fit in memory have been filled, you'll see the disk drive light go on as the system swaps in segments from the disk to hold the remaining array elements.

32-bit Address Arithmetic

Once a huge object is allocated, the fact that it is composed of different segments becomes transparent to the C program, which steps its pointer through the array without paying the least attention to segment boundaries. However, the system is working hard to create the appropriate addresses. For a hint of what's happening, we can modify the program to print out the 32-bit pointers to some of the array elements. The following revised section of code does this, but only at a segment boundary, so we don't need to watch 65536 addresses scroll by:

```
                        /* fill every byte in huge object */
printf("Filling %lu bytes\n", HugeSize );
for(byte=0; byte<HugeSize; byte++)  {
   *(SegPtr+byte) = (char)byte;
   if( byte>65531 && byte<65540 )
      printf("%lx: %d\n", SegPtr+byte, *(SegPtr+byte) );
}
```

If you modify huge.c to incorporate this section of code, and invoke the resulting program with a size greater than 65536, you'll see the following kind of interaction:

```
C>huge3 70000
1 segments, last seg=4464 bytes
Segment pointer is 5f0000
Filling 70000 bytes
5ffffc: -4
5ffffd: -3
5ffffe: -2
5fffff: -1
6f0000: 0
6f0001: 1
6f0002: 2
6f0003: 3
Checking 70000 bytes
```

The printout shows the address of each array element and its contents. Notice how, at the segment boundary where the offset part of the address goes from FFFF (65535) to 0, the selector part of the address changes from 5F to 6F, instead of to 60 as one might expect. The low order bits of the selector, which are not part of the index, are not disturbed. The compiler has created the appropriate arithmetic to cause this to happen. We'll investigate this further in a moment.

Huge Integer Array

We created an array of type **char** in the above example, but of course it's just as easy to create arrays of other data types. The next example is the program rewritten to use an integer array. Again, the size of the array is specified by the user; this time, however, the size is the number of integers, not bytes. We've also, for variety, used array notation rather than pointer notation, to access the elements of the array.

```
/* huge2.c */
/* allocates huge object with DosAllocHuge() */
/* uses integer array */
#define INCL_DOS
#include <os2.h>
#include <stdlib.h>          /* needed for atol() */
#define NO_SHARE 0           /* segment will not be shared */
#define MAXNUMSEG 0          /* segment will not grow */
#define FAC sizeof(int)      /* number of bytes in int */
```

(continued)

```
main(argc, argv)
int argc;
char *argv[];
{
    unsigned NumSegs;          /* number of 65536 segments */
    unsigned Remain;           /* bytes in last segment */
    unsigned short Selector;   /* selector of huge segment */
    int huge *SegPtr;          /* pointer to huge segment */
    unsigned long HugeSize;    /* total size of huge segment */
    unsigned long index;       /* index into huge segment */
    unsigned rc;               /* return code */

                               /* find sizes */
    if( argc != 2 )
        { printf("Syntax: C>huge integers\n"); exit(1); }
    HugeSize = FAC * atol( argv[1] );   /* total size in bytes
                                                             */
    NumSegs = HugeSize / 65536; /* find number of segments */
    Remain = HugeSize % 65536;  /* find bytes in last seg */
    printf("%u segments, last seg=%u bytes\n", NumSegs,
                                                        Remain );

                               /* allocate huge segment */
    if( rc=DosAllocHuge( NumSegs, Remain, &Selector,
                                NO_SHARE, MAXNUMSEG ) )
        { printf("DosAllocHuge error=%u\n",rc); exit(1); }

                               /* derive pointer to huge segment */
    SegPtr = (int huge *)( (unsigned long)Selector << 16);

                               /* fill integers in huge seg */
    printf("Filling %lu integers\n", HugeSize/FAC );
    for(index=0; index < HugeSize/FAC; index++)
        SegPtr[index] = (int)index;

                               /* check integers in huge seg */
    printf("Checking %lu integers\n", HugeSize/FAC );
    for(index=0; index<HugeSize/FAC; index++)
        if( SegPtr[index] != (int)index )
            printf("Error: index=%lu\n", index);

                               /* free huge segment */
    if( rc=DosFreeSeg( Selector ) )
        { printf("DosFreeSeg error=%u\n",rc); exit(1); }
    exit(0);
}
```

Here we use a factor **FAC**, the number of bytes in an integer, at various spots in the program to change loop limits, and other items, from bytes to integers.

Selectors of Segments in Huge Object

In some situations it may be desirable for an application to access separately the individual segments comprising a large object. OS/2 makes available an API function that permits an application to figure out the values of the selectors of any segment in a huge object. This function is DosGetHugeShift().

DosGetHugeShift — Get shift count for huge objects

```
DosGetHugeShift(AShiftCount);
unsigned far *AShiftCount;      /* address for shift count */
```

The function takes only one parameter: the address where the shift count is placed. Two steps are then needed to transform this shift count into the selectors of the various segments. First, the number 1 is shifted left the number of times specified in the shift count. This creates an increment. Second, the resulting increment is added to the selector returned by DosAllocHuge(). Repeatedly adding the increment to the selector produces the selectors of all the segments.

The following example program uses this technique to derive the 32-bit pointers to all of the segments in a huge object.

```c
/* hugeshif.c */
/* derives pointers to segments in huge object */
#define INCL_DOS
#include <os2.h>
#define SIZE 0                 /* no bytes in last segment */
#define NO_SHARE 0             /* segment will not be shared */
#define MAXNUMSEG 0            /* segment will not grow */
#define MAXBYTES (unsigned) 65535
main(argc, argv)
int argc;
char *argv[];
{
    unsigned NumSegs;          /* number of 65536 segments */
    unsigned short Selector;   /* selector of huge object */
    unsigned NewSel;           /* selector of segments */
    unsigned ShiftCount;       /* from DosGetHugeShift() */
    unsigned increment;        /* to add to Selector */
    unsigned seg, rc;          /* index and return code */
    char huge *SegPtr;         /* pointer to segments */
```

(continued)

```
if( argc != 2 )
    { printf("Syntax: C>huge numsegs\n"); exit(1); }
NumSegs = atoi( argv[1] );
                            /* get the segment */
if( rc=DosAllocHuge( NumSegs, SIZE, &Selector,
                                NO_SHARE, MAXNUMSEG ) )
    { printf("DosAllocHuge error=%u\n",rc); exit(1); }


                        /* get the shift count */
if( rc=DosGetHugeShift( &ShiftCount ) )
    { printf("DosGetHugeShift error=%u",rc); exit(1); }

                        /* calculate increment */
increment = 0x01 << ShiftCount;
printf("Increment is %x\n", increment );

                        /* calculate pointers */
for(seg=0; seg<NumSegs; seg++)  {
    NewSel = Selector + seg*increment;
    SegPtr = (char huge *)( (unsigned long)NewSel << 16);
    printf("Pointer to seg %u is %lx\n", seg, SegPtr );
}
                        /* free huge segment */
if( rc=DosFreeSeg( Selector ) )
    { printf("DosFreeSeg error=%u\n",rc); exit(1); }
exit(0);
}
```

The program is invoked with one command-line argument: the number of segments to be allocated to a huge object. Here's the output when a seven-segment object is requested:

```
C>hugeshif 7
Increment is 10
Pointer to seg 0 is 5f0000
Pointer to seg 1 is 6f0000
Pointer to seg 2 is 7f0000
Pointer to seg 3 is 8f0000
Pointer to seg 4 is 9f0000
Pointer to seg 5 is af0000
Pointer to seg 6 is bf0000
```

The increment is 10 hex, so we can see the shift count is 4 (1 shifted four bits left is 10 hex). The increment is added successively to the selector of the huge object, to produce the pointers to all the segments used for the object.

The shift count is specific to the particular version of OS/2 being used. In the current release it is 4, but it might change in future versions.

Using the Shift Count for Segment Arithmetic

While the C compiler automatically performs the necessary segment arithmetic on huge array elements, there may be other situations where a C program may need to do its own segment arithmetic, and assembly programs will always need to do their own segment address arithmetic.

The fact that the selector for each segment differs by a constant from the selectors of adjacent segments is very helpful in performing such segment arithmetic. To calculate the address of any given segment, one need only take the increment (obtained by shifting 1 left **bitcount** times), multiply it by the number of the segment (from 0 up to however many segments there are), and add the selector of the base segment. The address of an element within the segment is then obtained by adding its offset. In other words,

```
address = SegBase + (SegNum * Increment) + Offset;
```

This is similar to the address arithmetic performed on huge objects in MS-DOS, except that in that case the segments are actually contiguous in memory, so their segment addresses always differ by 1000 hex (their physical addresses differ by 10000 hex, or 65536 decimal).

Changing Segment Size

It is possible to change the size of a segment after it has been allocated. This is clearly a useful capability. For instance, an application might create a segment of a certain size, and then later find that the user wishes to input more data than the segment can hold. Instead of issuing an out-of-memory message to the user, the application can simply enlarge the segment.

Here's an example that demonstrates this situation. The program stores integers in a segment which it allocates with an initial size of 10 bytes, enough to hold five data items. What happens if the user tries to input more than five integers? Instead of complaining that the segment is full, the program enlarges it, using the DosReAllocSeg() function.

```
/* realloc.c */
/* demonstrates DosReAllocSeg(): changes segment's size */
#define INCL_DOS
#include <os2.h>
#define SEG_FLAGS 0     /* not shareable, not discardable */
#define ISIZE 10        /* initial segment size (bytes) */
#define FAC sizeof(int) /* bytes in an integer */

main()
{
   int far *SegPtr;             /* pointer to seg start */
   int value;                   /* value to be stored */
   unsigned short Selector;     /* selector of segment */
   unsigned SegSize = ISIZE;    /* seg size in bytes */
   unsigned DataSize = 0;       /* how many integers input */
   unsigned j;                  /* index for integers */
   char string[80];             /* input buffer */
   unsigned rc;                 /* return code */

                  /* allocate segment */
   if( rc=DosAllocSeg( SegSize, &Selector, SEG_FLAGS ) )
      { printf("DosAllocSeg error=%u\n",rc); exit(1); }

                  /* find segment pointer */
   SegPtr = (int far *)( (unsigned long)Selector << 16 );

   while(TRUE)  {      /* loop until null entry */
      printf("\nEnter an integer: ");
      if ( strcmp(gets(string),"") == 0 )  /* if null string
                                           */
         break;                            /*    exit loop */
      value = atoi(string);                /* get value */
                  /* put value in segment */
      *( SegPtr+DataSize++ ) = value;

                  /* print out all values */
      for(j=0; j<DataSize; j++)
         printf("%u: %d\n", j, *(SegPtr+j) );

                  /* if segment too small, enlarge it */
      if( DataSize*FAC >= SegSize )  {
         SegSize += ISIZE;
         printf("Enlarging segment to %u bytes\n",
                                           SegSize );
         if( rc=DosReallocSeg( SegSize, Selector ) )
            { printf("DosReAllocSeg error=%u\n",rc);
                                           exit(1); }
      }
   }  /* end while */
```

(continued)

```
                         /* free segment */
    if( rc=DosFreeSeg( Selector ) )
       { printf("DosFreeSeg error=%u\n",rc); exit(1); }
    exit(0);
}
```

Here's part of a sample session, shown after several integers have already been input. The program prints out all the values in the segment after each integer is input. When the segment is full, the program informs the user and enlarges it; the user can then input more values. Here, once the segment holds five integers, it is full. If another integer is to be stored the segment must be enlarged, in this case to 20 bytes, so it can hold up to 10 integers.

```
- - - - - - - - - -
Enter an integer: 13
0: 10
1: 11
2: 12
3: 13

Enter an integer: 14
0: 10
1: 11
2: 12
3: 13
4: 14
Enlarging segment to 20 bytes

Enter an integer: 15
0: 10
1: 11
2: 12
3: 13
4: 14
5: 15
- - - - - - - - - -
```

The program automatically reallocates the segment, expanding it as necessary to hold however much input the user supplies. Expanding the segment does not corrupt the data already placed in it, as the program demonstrates by printing out the entire segment contents after each input.

The function used to change the size of an existing segment is DosReAllocSeg().

DosReAllocSeg() — Changes size of existing segment

```
DosReAllocSeg(NewSize, Selector);
unsigned NewSize;          /* new size requested, in bytes */
unsigned short Selector;   /* selector of segment */
```

This function takes two parameters: the new size being requested; and the selector, originally obtained from DosAllocSeg(), of the segment to be changed. Unless they are shared, segments can be either increased or decreased in size. Shared segments can only be increased.

DosReAllocSeg() helps make memory use more efficient by eliminating the necessity to allocate excessively large segments. If the amount of data a segment is called upon to hold is not known in advance, a small segment can be allocated initially, thus making a minimum demand on RAM. Then, if it becomes necessary to store more data, the segment can be expanded as needed. This keeps the size of the segment at a minimum.

Expanding Huge Segments

A huge object can be expanded or shrunk just as a normal segment can, but the DosReAllocHuge() function must be used instead of DosReAllocSeg().

DosReAllocHuge() — Changes size of huge object

```
DosReAllocHuge(NewSize, Selector);
unsigned NumSegs;          /* number of 65536-byte segments */
unsigned LastSeg;          /* number of bytes in last segment */
unsigned short Selector;   /* selector of segment */
```

In this function the new size of the object is specified with two arguments, as in DosAllocHuge(): the number of 65536-byte segments, and the number of bytes left over in the last, odd-size segment. (If this is zero there will be no odd-size segment). The third argument to the function is the selector obtained from DosAllocHuge().

The maximum memory size requested by this function must not exceed that of the **MaxNumSegs** argument originally specified in the call to DosAllocHuge().

Suballocating Blocks in Segments

Allocating a segment is, comparatively speaking, time-consuming. The system must find a suitably sized area of memory, set up the necessary entries in a process's descriptor tables, and perform other housekeeping tasks. If a program is allocating and freeing memory very often this overhead is large. To ease this problem OS/2 makes available a way to allocate small sections of memory within an existing segment. These subdivisions are called blocks.

There are two steps involved in creating these blocks (assuming a segment has already been allocated): initializing the segment for suballocation, and allocating the individual blocks.

Initializing a Segment for Suballocation

First, a section of the segment is set aside to hold blocks. This section can hold several smaller blocks or one large one. It can occupy only a small part of the segment, or almost all of it. The maximum space that can be suballocated is the original segment size minus 8 bytes. Figure 10-8 shows a segment suballocated into several blocks.

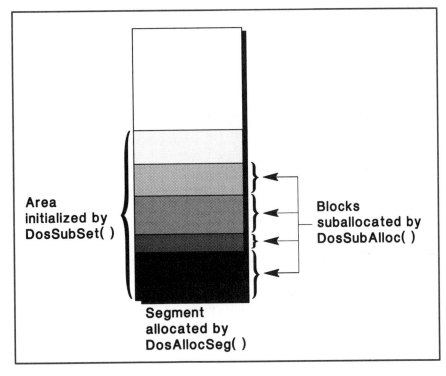

Figure 10-8
Suballocation of Segment

The function that sets aside part of the segment for suballocation is DosSubSet().

DosSubSet — Initialize for suballocation, or change size

```
DosSubSet(Selector, Flag, Size);
unsigned short Selector;   /* segment to be suballocated */
unsigned Flag;             /* 1=initialize seg, 0=expand area */
unsigned Size;             /* size of block to suballocate */
```

This function takes as input arguments the selector of the segment to be initialized, a flag, and the size of the area in the segment to be suballocated.

DosSubSet() can actually perform two different actions; which of the two is determined by the flag in the second parameter. If the flag is set to 1, the function sets aside an area within the segment for suballocation, as described. If the flag is set to 0, the function changes the size of an existing suballocated area. In this case the **Size** parameter specifies the new size to be suballocated. This must be greater than the previous suballocated size, and less than the size of the segment.

Suballocating Blocks within a Segment

Once a section of a segment is initialized for suballocation with DosSubSet(), it can be divided up into blocks. The API function that handles this is DosSubAlloc().

DosSubAlloc — Suballocate blocks within a segment

```
DosSubAlloc(Selector, ABlockOffset, Size);
unsigned short Selector; /* segment to be suballocated */
unsigned far *ABlockOffset; /* address for block offset */
unsigned Size;              /* size of block to suballocate */
```

This function must be given the selector of the segment being suballocated, and the size of the block within the suballocated area. The size of the block to be suballocated cannot exceed the size specified in DosSubSet().

The function returns the offset into the segment where the block begins. Knowing this offset, and the size of the block, the program can then use the block as desired for data storage and retrieval. If you try to use DosSubAlloc() to allocate more memory than that set aside for suballocation with DosSubSet(), you'll get return code 311, ERROR_DOSSUB_NOMEM.

Here's an example program that permits different sizes and numbers of blocks to be suballocated from a segment. The initial size of the segment is fixed at 30,000, and the part of the segment to be suballocated is set to 10,000. The block size and number of blocks are specified as command-line arguments.

```c
/* manysub.c */
/* demonstrates suballocation of blocks within segment */
#define INCL_DOS
#include <os2.h>
#define SEG_FLAGS 0        /* not shareable, not discardable */
#define SEG_SIZE 30000     /* size of initial segment */
#define SUB_SIZE 10000     /* part of seg to be suballocated */
#define SIZE 1000          /* size of block pointer list */
#define INIT_SEG 1         /* initialize segment */
unsigned OffsetList[SIZE]; /* list of block offsets */

main(argc,argv)
int argc;
char *argv[];
{
    unsigned short Selector;  /* selector of segment */
    unsigned BlocOffset;   /* offset of block into seg */
    unsigned BlocSize;     /* size of blocks to suballocate */
    unsigned NumBlocs;     /* number of blocks to suballocate */
    unsigned bloc;         /* block index */
    unsigned index;        /* byte index into block */
    char far *BlocPtr;     /* pointer to start of block */
    unsigned rc;           /* return code */

    if( argc != 3 )
        { printf("Syntax: C>suballoc size number"); exit(1); }
    BlocSize = atoi( argv[1] );
    NumBlocs = atoi( argv[2] );
                           /* get initial segment */
    if( rc=DosAllocSeg( SEG_SIZE, &Selector, SEG_FLAGS ) )
        { printf("DosAllocSeg error=%u",rc); exit(1); }

                        /* initialize seg for suballocation */
    if( rc=DosSubSet( Selector, INIT_SEG, SUB_SIZE ) )
        { printf("DosSubSet error=%u",rc); exit(1); }

                        /* suballocate and fill each block */
    for( bloc=0; bloc < NumBlocs; bloc++ )  {
```

(continued)

```
                         /* suballocate block */
        if( rc=DosSubAlloc( Selector, &BlocOffset, BlocSize
                                                      ) )
           { printf("DosSubAlloc error=%u",rc); exit(1); }
        printf("Block %u, offset=%x, ", bloc, BlocOffset );
        OffsetList[bloc] = BlocOffset;

                          /* create pointer to block */
        BlocPtr = (char far *)( (unsigned long)Selector
                                                    << 16 )
              + BlocOffset;

                          /* fill block */
        printf("pointer=%lx.  Filling block.\n", BlocPtr );
        for( index=0; index<BlocSize; index++ )
           *(BlocPtr + index) = (char)( index+bloc );
     }
                          /* check each block */
     for( bloc=0; bloc < NumBlocs; bloc++ )   {
        printf("Checking block %u\n", bloc );
        BlocPtr = (char far *)( (unsigned long)Selector
                                                    << 16 )
              + OffsetList[bloc];
        for( index=0; index<BlocSize; index++ )
           if( *(BlocPtr + index) != (char)( index+bloc ) )
              printf("Error: bloc=%u, byte=%u\n", bloc,
                                                  index );
     }
                          /* free each block */
     for( bloc=0; bloc < NumBlocs; bloc++ )
        if( rc=DosSubFree(Selector, OffsetList[bloc],
                                               BlocSize) )
           { printf("DosSubFree error=%u",rc); exit(1); }

                          /* free segment */
     if( rc=DosFreeSeg( Selector ) )
        { printf("DosFreeSeg error=%u",rc); exit(1); }
     exit(0);
  }
```

The program first allocates a segment in the usual way with Dos-AllocSeg(). It then uses DosSubSet() to specify an area of this segment for suballocation. Next it enters a loop where each of the blocks specified is created and filled with data. The blocks are created with DosSubAlloc(), and the offset for each block, returned by this function, is stored in an array for later use. A pointer to the block is created by shifting the selector for the original segment left and adding the block offset. Each block thus has its own unique base pointer. Using this pointer, each block is then filled with a number (the sum of the block number and byte number).

Once the blocks are all filled, they are all checked to make sure the data is where it should be.

When each block is no longer needed it is freed using Dos-SubFree().

DosSubFree — Free memory block within segment

```
DosSubFree(Selector, BlockOffset, BlockSize);
unsigned short Selector;    /* selector of segment */
unsigned BlockOffset;       /* offset of block to be freed */
unsigned BlockSize;         /* size of block to freed */
```

This function needs to know the selector of the segment from which the block has been suballocated, the offset of the block into the segment, and the size of the block. If you try to free more memory than has been suballocated, you'll get error 312, ERROR_DOSSUB_OVERLAP.

Here's a sample session in which the program is asked to suballocate four 512-byte blocks.

```
C>manysub 512 4
Block 0, offset=8, pointer=5f0008.  Filling block.
Block 1, offset=208, pointer=5f0208.  Filling block.
Block 2, offset=408, pointer=5f0408.  Filling block.
Block 3, offset=608, pointer=5f0608.  Filling block.
Checking block 0
Checking block 1
Checking block 2
Checking block 3
```

Notice that the first offset starts at 8, not at 0. This is why the size of the area to be suballocated cannot be more than 8 less than the size of the segment. Subsequent blocks are placed adjacent to one another.

Discarding and Locking Segments

When segments are allocated with DosAllocSeg() or DosAllocHuge(), they can be made *discardable* by setting bit 2 in the flags parameter. So far we have used a flag of 0, so none of the segments we have created have been discardable. What is a discardable segment?

If the operating system runs out of memory, it normally finds a segment which is not being used and swaps it out to the disk. Then when the segment is needed again it is swapped back in. Its contents are not changed. If the segment is discardable, on the other hand, and the memory space it occupies is needed, the system simply writes over it without saving it to disk. This is faster, since no disk access is necessary to procure the additional memory space. However, the contents of the segment are lost.

Discardable segments are appropriate in situations where the application needs to store data only briefly, or where the application can quickly regenerate the data. For example, if an application read in a record from a disk file and extracted some data items from the record, the space holding the record might be discardable at this point. Rather than freeing the segment, which might be used again to hold another record, the application could allow the operating system to discard it. Then the system could use the space if necessary, and leave it alone if not. Data for bit-mapped graphic displays might also be discardable, since in many cases such displays can be quickly redrawn.

An application which owns a discardable segment must be prepared to deal with the fact that the segment may have been discarded. It needs a way to know whether the segment has been discarded, and it must be able to regenerate lost data when necessary. The application also needs a way to keep the segment from being discarded during those periods when it is actively being used.

The DosLockSeg() function is used both to find out if a segment has been discarded, and to prevent its being discarded while it is being accessed.

DosLockSeg — Lock discardable memory segment

```
DosLockSeg(Selector);
unsigned short Selector;   /* selector of segment to be
                              locked */
```

If this function is called for a segment which has been created, but has subsequently been discarded, it returns an error code. This is how the application can tell if a segment has been discarded. If the function returns successfully, it locks the segment so it cannot be discarded.

Once the application has finished working with the segment, it can make it discardable again by issuing the DosUnLockSeg() function. Like DosLockSeg(), this function takes only one parameter, the selector of the segment to be locked.

DosUnlockSeg — Unlock discardable memory segment

```
DosUnlockSeg(Selector);
unsigned short Selector;      /* selector of segment to
                                 unlock */
```

Note that the functions DosAllocSeg() and DosReAllocSeg() both automatically lock a segment. Thus segments are normally locked unless the application overtly unlocks them.

Here's an example program that allocates a segment, unlocks it, and then waits for the user to press a key. If the user simply presses a key at this point, the program locks the segment, fills it, checks that the data read out is accurate, and then unlocks the segment.

However, assume instead the user switches to another screen group and fills up memory using another application, say manyseg.c, with enough segments to overcommit memory (as described earlier). In this case the unlocked discardable segment allocated by lock.c is discarded by the system to make room for the segments generated by manyseg.c. Now if the user switches back to the lock.c session and presses any key, the program applies DosLockSeg() to a discarded segment. This causes DosLockSeg() to return with error code 157, indicating the segment has been discarded. At this point a real application could regenerate any data that had been in the segment.

```
/* lock.c */
/* demonstrates segment locking */
#define INCL_DOS
#include <os2.h>
#define SEG_FLAGS 4       /* discardable, not shareable */
#define SEG_SIZE 65535    /* size of segment */

main()
{
    char far *SegPtr;            /* pointer to offset in seg */
    unsigned short Selector;     /* selector of segment */
    unsigned byte;               /* byte index */
    unsigned rc;                 /* return variable */

                                 /* allocate segment */
    printf("Allocating segment\n");
    if( rc=DosAllocSeg( SEG_SIZE, &Selector, SEG_FLAGS ) )
        { printf("DosAllocSeg error=%d\n",rc); exit(1); }
                                 /* find segment pointer */
    SegPtr = (char far *)( (unsigned long)Selector << 16 );
```

(continued)

```
                              /* unlock segment */
        if( rc=DosUnlockSeg( Selector ) )
           { printf("DosUnLockSeg error=%u\n",rc); exit(1); }

        while( !kbhit() )       /* wait here until keypress */
           ;
                              /* lock segment */
        if( rc=DosLockSeg( Selector ) )
           { printf("DosLockSeg error=%u\n",rc); exit(1); }

                              /* fill every byte in segment */
        printf("Filling Segment\n");
        for(byte=0; byte < SEG_SIZE; byte++)
           *(SegPtr+byte) = (char)byte;

                              /* check every byte in segment */
        printf("Checking Segment\n");
        for(byte=0; byte < SEG_SIZE; byte++)
           if( *(SegPtr+byte) != (char)byte )   /* show
                                                    errors */
              printf("Error: byte=%lu\n", byte);

                              /* unlock segment */
        if( rc=DosUnlockSeg( Selector ) )
           { printf("DosUnLockSeg error=%u\n",rc); exit(1); }

                              /* free segment */
        if( rc=DosFreeSeg( Selector ) )
           { printf("DosFreeSeg error=%u\n", rc); exit(1); }
        exit(0);
}
```

Code Segment Aliasing

You may recall that one of the bits in the segment descriptor specifies whether a segment is code or data. A data segment cannot be executed, and a code segment cannot be written to. These restrictions, while they no doubt prevent many unpleasant occurrences, pose a problem for an application that needs to create code and then execute it. Examples are programs that create part of their own code "on the fly" in order to optimize their operation (self-modifying code). Also, some in-memory language compilers generate their own executable code.

OS/2 provides a way around this dilemma: segment aliasing. The idea here is to create an additional descriptor: one with the same characteristics as for the data segment, but with the code/data bit set to **code**. The function which handles this is DosCreateCSAlias().

DosCreateCSAlias — Create code segment alias

```
DosCreateCSAlias(DataSelector, ACodeSelector);
unsigned short DataSelector;     /* data segment selector */
unsigned short far *ACodeSelector;  /* address for code
                                           sel */
```

The program gives this function the selector of the data segment to be aliased, and receives back the selector of a code segment. This is really the same segment, but with different access rights. Now the data selector is used to place code in the segment, and the code selector used to execute it.

The example program places a short section of machine language code in the segment. This code simply adds together two arguments passed from the main program, and returns the sum. (There are more convenient ways to add two numbers, but they do not demonstrate DosCreateCSAlias() nearly so well.)

A code segment alias is created for the segment, using DosCreateCSAlias(). The resulting selector is turned into a pointer, which points to the machine-language function. This pointer is then used to call the function from the C program.

It is not our intention to explain the assembly code in any detail. Briefly, the function first saves the base pointer by pushing it onto the stack. It then loads the contents of the stack pointer into the base pointer, so the contents of the stack can be conveniently referenced. The two arguments, passed from the call to the function, are found in the stack at locations BP+6 and BP+8, respectively. One is loaded into the AX register, and the second is added to it. The original values of the stack pointer and the base pointer are then restored, and the function returns. The return value is the sum, which is passed via the AX register.

```
/* codeseg.c */
/* demonstrates DosCreateCSAlias() function */
/* compile with -AL option, for far pointers in memcpy() */
#define INCL_DOS
#include <os2.h>
#include <memory.h>     /* for memcpy() */
#include <stdio.h>      /* for printf(), etc */
#define SEG_FLAGS 0     /* not shareable, not discardable */

/* array consisting of machine-language instructions */
```

(continued)

```
unsigned char AdderCode[] = {
    0x55,                   /* push bp */
    0x8b, 0xec,             /* mov  bp,sp */
    0x8b, 0x46, 0x06,       /* mov  ax,[bp+6] */
    0x03, 0x46, 0x08,       /* add  ax,[bp+8] */
    0x8b, 0xe5,             /* mov  sp,bp */
    0x5d,                   /* pop  bp */
    0xcb,                   /* retf */
};

main()
{
    char *SegPtr;               /* pointer to data segment */
    unsigned short DataSel;     /* selector for data segment */
    unsigned short CodeSel;     /* selector for code segment */
    int (*PtrAdder)(int,int);   /* pointer to function */
    int num1, num2;             /* numbers to sum */
    int sum;                    /* sum returned by function */
    unsigned rc;                /* return code */

                            /* get numbers to sum */
    printf("Enter two integers: ");
    scanf("%d %d", &num1, &num2);

                            /* allocate data segment */
    if( rc=DosAllocSeg(sizeof(AdderCode), &DataSel,
                                          SEG_FLAGS) )
        { printf("DosAllocSeg error=%u",rc); exit(1); }
                            /* create pointer to data segment */
    SegPtr = (char *)( (unsigned long)DataSel << 16 );

                            /* copy code into segment */
    memcpy( SegPtr, AdderCode, sizeof(AdderCode) );
                            /* get code segment alias */
    if( rc=DosCreateCSAlias( DataSel, &CodeSel ) )
        { printf("DosCreateCSAlias error=%u",rc); exit(1); }
                            /* create pointer to code alias */
    PtrAdder = (int (*)() )( (unsigned long)CodeSel << 16 );

                            /* call machine-language function */
    sum = (*PtrAdder)( num1, num2 );
    printf("Sum is %d\n", sum );

                            /* free the code alias */
    if( rc=DosFreeSeg( CodeSel ) )
        { printf("DosFreeSeg error=%u",rc); exit(1); }
                            /* free the data segment */
    if( rc=DosFreeSeg( DataSel ) )
        { printf("DosFreeSeg error=%u",rc); exit(1); }
}
```

The machine language instructions are placed in the segment using memcpy(). This means that the program must be compiled as a **large** model program, so that the **far** pointer version of memcpy() will be used.

Here's a sample interaction:

```
C>codeseg
Enter two integers: 5 6
Sum is 11
```

The pointer for the code segment alias is derived from the selector obtained from DosCreateCSAlias(). Note that this pointer must be typecast as a pointer to a function returning a value of type **int**. When the function is called, it is as the contents of this pointer, with two numbers input by the user as arguments. It returns the sum, which is then printed out.

Summary

This chapter has focussed on memory allocation functions. We first examined how the protected mode of the 80286 generates memory addresses, and saw that a 32-bit address consists of an offset into a segment, and an index which points to a descriptor table. The descriptor table contains an entry describing the base address, size, and access rights of the segment. This indirect addressing makes possible such OS/2 features as segment swapping and memory protection.

The simplest API function for allocating memory is DosAllocSeg(). An application may allocate many segments. If the total physical memory space is exceeded by the segments requested, the system may obtain additional space by swapping other segments, (those least recently used), to disk.

A huge segment—one larger than 65536 bytes—may be created with DosAllocHuge(). A segment's size may be changed with DosReAllocSeg(); a huge segment may be changed with DosReAllocHuge(). A segment may be subdivided into blocks for different data areas using DosSubSet() and DosSubAlloc(). Finally, a data segment may be made executable using DosCreateCSAlias().

In the next chapter we'll learn more about memory allocation when we investigate shared memory.

INTERPROCESS
COMMUNICATION

Chapter 11

Chapter 11

There are three major ways processes can communicate with one another: shared memory, pipes, and queues. In this chapter we'll explore these three techniques.

Semaphores and signals are sometimes considered to belong to the category of interprocess communication (IPC). However, both semaphores and signals communicate a state, rather than a body of data, and are more appropriately categorized as interprocess coordination. The types of IPC we will be talking about in this chapter involve substantial amounts of data: from dozens to thousands of bytes.

A fourth type of IPC, named pipes, may be available in future versions of OS/2, but is not currently implemented.

The techniques we will be discussing here apply to communication between processes. They are not usually used between threads (although some of them can be) since global data areas within a process provide a fast and convenient means of inter-thread communication. Processes, on the other hand, are far more isolated from one another. Once a parent creates a child process, there are few natural links between them. During creation, the parent can pass the child command-line and environmental variables, but from then on there must be special ways for the parent and child to communicate. Communication is even more difficult between processes that are not parents or children of each other. Mechanisms designed specifically for communication between processes are therefore necessary.

We start off with a brief comparison of the different methods of interprocess communication, and then go on to specific examples.

When To Use What

Why are there three different ways for processes to communicate with each other? Each technique is applicable in different situations.

Shared Memory

Shared memory is the simplest and fastest way to transfer data. We saw in the chapter on memory how a process can allocate a segment. If a process allocates a shared segment, then another process can also access the segment, and information can be exchanged.

Shared memory has great flexibility, since the data can be arranged within the segment in any way agreed on by the two processes. For example, a shared memory segment could be used to hold the contents of the cells in a spreadsheet application. Various processes within the application, such as those used for input to the spreadsheet, calculation, output, graphics, printing, and so forth, could then access the data as needed. Using shared memory, any process can randomly access any byte in an entire memory segment.

Shared memory has no built-in synchronization, so processes may need to coordinate their activities (often with system semaphores) to preserve the integrity of the data. However, because of its speed and simplicity, shared memory is the most-used means of interprocess communication.

Pipes

Pipes are most commonly used when data is redirected from the standard input and output devices. Pipes permit a process, rather than the computer user, to redirect data going to another process. This permits greater flexibility in the use of the redirection facility.

Pipes communicate a linear stream of bytes and use standard file functions such as DosRead() and DosWrite() to read and write data. In fact, pipes behave very much like files.

Pipes are slower than shared memory, since the information being passed must be copied into the pipe. Pipes are also restricted to 65K of data, since they must fit in a single segment. As the name suggests, one can think of pipes as conduits carrying streams of bytes: they operate on a FIFO (first-in-first-out) basis.

Queues

Queues are the most versatile means of interprocess communication. They can handle data of any length, since they are not limited to a single segment. Data in the queue can be read in several different ways: FIFO, LIFO (last-in-first-out), or according to the priority of the message.

In queues, data is shared by passing an address, rather than by copying the data itself, as pipes do. This makes a queue fast. A queue is the method of choice when large amounts of data must be transferred quickly.

Queues are used in situations where one process reads data from several other processes. An example is a scientific data analysis application that uses different processes to collect data from different experiments. These processes would all send the data, via the queue, to an analysis process. The analysis process could then read data from the different collection processes, in whatever order was appropriate.

Another example is a software utility package that serves a variety of other processes in the system. For instance, a spelling checker might be called by several instances of a word processor and by a database editor at roughly the same time. The requests for service could be placed in a queue, where they could be read and acted on by the checker.

Queues are somewhat more difficult to set up than the other means of interprocess communication, and require more planning to be properly integrated into a system. Since queues use shared segments, the segments must be created and managed, and access to them must be coordinated. Thus a queue is not a natural choice for the transfer of a few small messages.

Files as Interprocess Communication

It is perfectly feasible to use a disk file as a means of IPC. One process writes data to the disk, and another reads it. However, disk transfers are much slower than the interprocess communication methods discussed in this chapter, all of which use RAM to transfer data. Also, disk files lack the capabilities of the OS/2 IPC techniques, such as the random access quality of shared memory or the ordering and coordination mechanism of queues.

In the sections that follow we look at shared memory, pipes, and queues in turn.

Shared Memory

There are two main approaches to sharing memory between processes. The first approach uses DosAllocShrSeg() to create a shared segment and give it a name. Once this named segment is created, any other process that knows its name can access it. One might call this the "open" approach to sharing memory. An analogy is a bulletin board. Anyone who knows where the board is can walk up and read the messages tacked on the board, and anyone can post a message for others to read. This is the easier method to implement, and the most commonly used. We refer to it as *named* shared memory, but it is also called "global" shared memory, since any process that knows the name of the segment can access it.

The second system for sharing memory uses DosAllocSeg(). One process uses this function to allocate a segment in almost the same way it would allocate a non-shared segment. This process owns the segment, and has complete control over access to it by other processes. If another process wants to access the segment, the segment's owner must know the process ID of the requesting process (the "recipient"). The owner then uses this ID to obtain a special selector, which it passes to the recipient, enabling the recipient to access the segment. This could be called the "closed" approach to sharing a segment. The image here might be a security guard granting you access to a restricted area only after checking your badge.

We'll call this process *private* shared memory. It is also called "giveaway" or "local" shared memory, since one process gives away access to the shared segment, and the segment is known only to certain processes.

Private shared memory is most commonly used in queues. It can also be used between two processes when the integrity of the data is of primary importance. In a networking situation, for example, it might be important for the owner of a segment to permit access to only those processes with a correct password.

Figure 11-1 shows these two approaches to shared memory.

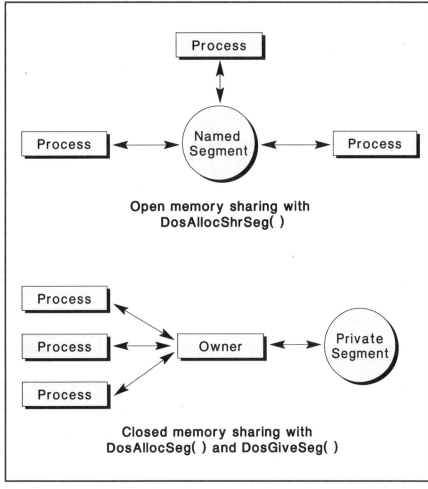

Figure 11-1
Open and Closed Memory Sharing

In this section we'll look at these two approaches in turn.

Named Shared Memory: DosAllocShrSeg()

In named shared memory, one process creates the segment using DosAllocShrSeg(). This function is very much like DosAllocSeg().

However, DosAllocShrSeg(), in addition to allocating a segment, also gives the segment a name. This name looks like a file name. It starts with the subdirectory name \SHAREMEM\. The programmer then adds a name of choice; the result is something like \SHAREMEM\DATA.SEG. This name is the key by which other processes can access the segment, using DosGetShrSeg().

Our example consists of two processes. A parent, pshare.c, creates the segment and gives it the name \SHAREMEM\SEG1.DAT. The segment takes the form of a structure, with three data items. The parent places data in the segment, and executes the child process. It then sleeps for a second to give the child time to access the segment. Finally it frees the segment and exits. Here's the parent process:

```
/* pshare.c */
/* shares memory using DosAllocShrSeg() */
/* to be used with chshare.c child process */
#define INCL_DOS
#include <os2.h>
#define LENGTH 40              /* length of object buffer */
#define FLAGS 1               /* asynchronous, no trace */
#define ARGS 0L               /* no command-line arguments */
#define ENVS 0L               /* no environmental variables */
                              /* size of shared segment */
#define SEG_SIZE sizeof(struct SharedData)
main()
{
   char fbuf[LENGTH];        /* buffer for fail-object */
   struct _RESULTCODES ChildID; /* defined in bsedos.h */
   unsigned short Selector;  /* selector for shared seg */
   unsigned rc;              /* return code */
   struct SharedData {       /* contents of shared memory */
      char DataOne;
      int DataTwo;
      long DataThree;
   }
   struct SharedData far *fptr;    /* ptr to shared seg */

                                /* get segment */
   if( rc=DosAllocShrSeg( SEG_SIZE,
                "\\SHAREMEM\\SEG1.DAT", &Selector ) )
      { printf("DosAllocShrSeg error=%u\n",rc); exit(1); }

                                /* make pointer to seg */
   fptr=(struct SharedData far *)((unsigned
                            long)Selector<<16);
```

(continued)

```
    fptr->DataOne = 'a';            /* put data in segment */
    fptr->DataTwo = 300;
    fptr->DataThree = 999000;
                                    /* start the child */
    if( rc=DosExecPgm( fbuf, LENGTH, FLAGS, ARGS, ENVS,
                             &ChildID, "CHSHARE.EXE" ) )
        { printf("DosExecPgm error=%u\n",rc); exit(1); }

    DosSleep(1000L); /* give child time to receive message */

    if( rc=DosFreeSeg( Selector ) )     /* free segment */
        { printf("DosFreeSeg error=%u\n",rc); exit(1); }
    exit(0);
}
```

DosAllocShrSeg() takes three parameters. The first is the size of the segment to be allocated, and the second is the name to be given the segment. As discussed, this name must include the subdirectory name \SHAREMEM\. (The backslashes are represented in C by double backslashes, since this character is the escape character.) The third argument is the address where the function will return the selector to the segment.

DosAllocShrSeg — Allocates a shared segment

```
DosAllocShrSeg(Size, Name, ASelector);
unsigned Size;                  /* size of segment in bytes */
char far *Name;                 /* ASCIIZ segment name */
unsigned short far *ASelector;  /* address for selector */
```

The child process accesses the shared segment using its name, prints out the data it finds there, frees the segment, and exits. Here's the listing for the child:

```
/* chshare.c */
/* child process of pshare.c */
/* gets data from shared segment and prints it out */
#define INCL_DOS
#include <os2.h>
main()
{
    struct SharedData { /* data structure of shared memory */
        char DataOne;
        int DataTwo;
        long DataThree;
    }
```

```
        struct SharedData far *fptr;    /* pointer to shared
                                           memory */
        unsigned short Selector;        /* segment selector */
        unsigned rc;                    /* return code */

                                        /* access segment */
        if( rc=DosGetShrSeg( "\\SHAREMEM\\SEG1.DAT", &Selector
                                                              ) )
           { printf("DosGetShrSeg error=%u",rc); exit(1); }

                                   /* create pointer to segment */
        fptr=(struct SharedData far *)((unsigned
                                             long)Selector<<16);

                                   /* get data from segment */
        printf("DataOne = %c\n", fptr->DataOne );
        printf("DataTwo = %d\n", fptr->DataTwo );
        printf("DataThree = %ld\n", fptr->DataThree );

        if( rc=DosFreeSeg(Selector) ) /* free segment */
           { printf("DosFreeSeg error=%u",rc); exit(1); }
        exit(0);
    }
```

Here's the output when the example is executed:

```
DataOne = a
DataTwo = 300
DataThree = 999000
```

Of course this data structure could be any kind of data an application needed: a more complex structure, an array, or whatever.

The child accesses the segment using DosGetShrSeg(). This function takes two parameters: the name of the segment, and the address where the selector to the segment can be returned. Note this is not the same selector other processes use to access the segment. Each process's selector to a segment is different, since each process has its own Local Descriptor Table. The LDT contains the list of segments that a process can access, with selectors unique to that particular process.

DosGetShrSeg() — Access an existing shared segment

```
DosGetShrSeg(Name, ASelector)
char far *Name;                 /* ASCIIZ segment name */
unsigned short far *ASelector;  /* address for selector */
```

Freeing a Shared Segment

The operating system keeps a directory of shared segments. The entry for each segment includes a count. Each time a process accesses the segment, either with DosAllocShrSeg() or with DosGetShrSeg(), this count is incremented. Each time a process frees the segment with DosFreeSeg(), the count is decremented. When the count goes to 0, the system deallocates the segment and removes it from the directory.

It is thus important that any process accessing a shared segment issue a DosFreeSeg() when it is through with the segment. If a process fails to do this, the system doesn't know when a segment is no longer needed. That segment then remains in memory, taking up space the system could put to better use.

Coordinating Repeated Access to Shared Memory

In the example of pshare.c and chshare.c, coordination was achieved with a delay and only one group of data was transferred through the shared memory segment. This is not a very realistic way to coordinate access to the segment. In the next example we show how multiple data items can be transferred using a more sophisticated coordination method.

We saw in Chapter 10 how two semaphores—one to indicate an empty buffer and one to indicate full—are used to coordinate several processes reading and writing to a file. We can use a similar approach to coordinate the transfer of multiple data items into and out of shared memory.

In our example, the parent process sends four lines of text to the child, using a shared memory segment. The parent waits on the empty semaphore, places a line of text in the segment, and then clears the full semaphore to indicate that the segment has data in it. The parent also prints out the line of text it has just placed in shared memory.

Here's the listing of the parent process. For clarity we have removed the error checking code; the usual warnings apply. Both parent and child must be compiled with the large memory model, since they use the C library routine strcpy(), which requires **far** pointers.

```
/* pshstr.c */
/* to be used with chshstr.c child process */
/* to be compiled with large memory model -AL */
#define INCL_DOS
#include <os2.h>
#define LENGTH 40              /* length of object buffer */
#define FLAGS 1                /* asynchronous, no trace */
#define ARGS 0L                /* no command-line arguments */
```

```
#define ENVS 0L                /* no environmental variables */
#define SEG_SIZE 80            /* long enough for one line */
#define LINES 4                /* number of lines of text */
#define WAIT -1L               /* semaphore wait for clear */
#define NO_EX 1                /* sem not exclusively owned */

char *msg[LINES] = { "This is a message",
                     "from the parent",
                     "to the child",
                     "using shared memory."   };
main()
{
   char fbuf[LENGTH];          /* buffer for fail-object */
   struct _RESULTCODES ChildID;  /* defined in bsedos.h */
   unsigned short Selector;    /* selector for shared seg */
   char far *fptr;             /* pointer to shared seg */
   void far *FullSem;          /* full semaphore handle */
   void far *EmptySem;         /* empty semaphore handle */
   int j;                      /* index to lines */

                               /* create system semaphores */
   DosCreateSem( NO_EX, &FullSem, "\\SEM\\S1" );
   DosCreateSem( NO_EX, &EmptySem, "\\SEM\\S2" );
   DosSemClear( EmptySem );  /* buffer is empty */
   DosSemSet( FullSem );     /* and not full */

                               /* allocate segment */
   DosAllocShrSeg(SEG_SIZE, "\\SHAREMEM\\SEG1.DAT",
                                        &Selector);
                               /* create pointer to segment */
   fptr = (char far *)( (unsigned long)Selector << 16 );

                               /* start the child */
   DosExecPgm( fbuf, LENGTH, FLAGS, ARGS, ENVS,
                                &ChildID, "CHSHSTR.EXE" );

   for( j=0; j<LINES; j++ ) { /* for each line in msg */
      DosSemRequest( EmptySem, WAIT ); /* wait for empty
                                           seg */
      strcpy( fptr, msg[j] );  /* put string in seg */
      printf("Parent sending: %s\n", fptr );
      DosSemClear( FullSem );  /* set segment full */
   }
   DosCloseSem( FullSem );     /* close full semaphore */
   DosCloseSem( EmptySem );    /* close empty semaphore */
   DosFreeSeg( Selector );     /* free segment */
   exit(0);
}
```

The child waits on the full semaphore, reads and displays the text from the segment, and then clears the empty semaphore to indicate the segment is empty and ready for more data. The interaction between parent and child continues until all lines of the message are transmitted.

```
/* chshstr.c */
/* child process of pshstr.c, receives strings from parent
   */
/* compile with large memory model -AL */
#define INCL_DOS
#include <os2.h>
#define LINES 4              /* number of lines of text */
#define WAIT -1L             /* wait for sem to clear */

main()
{
   void far *FullSem;        /* handle for full sem */
   void far *EmptySem;       /* handle for empty sem */
   unsigned short Selector;  /* selector for segment */
   char far *fptr;           /* pointer to shared memory */
   int j;                    /* line index */

                             /* open system semaphores */
   DosOpenSem( &FullSem, "\\SEM\\S1" );
   DosOpenSem( &EmptySem, "\\SEM\\S2" );
                             /* access segment */
   DosGetShrSeg( "\\SHAREMEM\\SEG1.DAT", &Selector );
                             /* create pointer to segment */
   fptr = (char far *)( (unsigned long)Selector << 16 );

   for( j=0; j<LINES; j++ )  {   /* for each line in msg */
      DosSemRequest( FullSem, WAIT );   /* wait for full */
      printf("Child received: %s\n", fptr); /* print line */
      DosSemClear( EmptySem );          /* set seg empty */
   }
   DosFreeSeg( Selector );       /* free segment and exit */
   exit(0);
}
```

When pshstr.c is invoked the result looks like this:

```
C>pshstr
Parent sending: This is a message
Child received: This is a message
Parent sending: from the parent
Child received: from the parent
Parent sending: to the child
Child received: to the child
Parent sending: using shared memory.
Child received: using shared memory.
```

Similar coordination could of course be used to transmit other data types and constructions.

Private Shared Memory: DosGiveSeg()

The second way to share memory is through private shared memory. As we noted, this approach is most commonly employed with queues; we'll see an example later. However, private memory sharing is also a more secure means of communication between processes. Because access must be specifically granted by the owner of a segment to any other process, the chances of unauthorized meddling with the data are minimized.

Unfortunately, an example to demonstrate this approach must be rather complex. To share a private segment, one process allocates a segment with DosAllocSeg(). This is similar to using the same function to create an ordinary non-shared segment, except that a bit is set in the function's allocation flags argument to indicate that the segment will be shared.

Now, if another process wants to access this segment, a byzantine series of negotiations must ensue between the owner of the segment and the recipient (the process desiring access). First the owner must know the process ID of the recipient. This is no problem if the recipient is a child of the owner, but if it is an unrelated process it must communicate the process ID to the owner via a different shared segment, or by some other means. In our example we assume the recipient is a child of the owner.

Once the owner knows the process ID of the recipient, it uses the ID as an argument for the DosGiveSeg() function. This function returns a selector which can be used by the recipient (not the owner) to access the segment. Now the problem is to communicate this selector from the owner back to the recipient. This could be effected with a named shared memory segment, a pipe, or a queue. Since we already know how to share memory with named segments, we'll use this approach.

Thus our example processes share two different segments. We call the first ID segment. It is a named shared segment created with DosAllocShrSeg(), and is used only to pass the recipient's selector from the owner to the recipient. The second segment is the private segment, created by the owner with DosAllocSeg(). We use this segment to pass the actual data between the processes. Figure 11-2 shows the communication necessary between owner and recipient in order to share a segment.

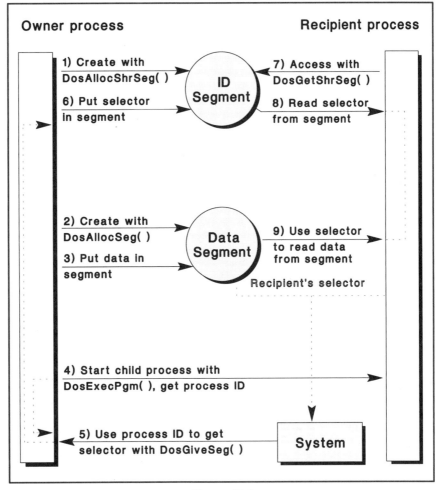

Figure 11-2
Sharing Memory with DosGiveSeg( )

In an actual application one process would likely control certain
data and several recipients (clients) would desire access to the data.
A single named shared segment would be set up for the initial communication between the owner and all the clients, while each client
would have its own private segment to share the actual data with the
owner. In our example there is only one client.

Here's the listing for the process that owns the segment (the
parent process):

```c
/* pgive.c */
/* shares memory using DosGiveSeg() */
/* to be used with chgive.c child process */
#define INCL_DOS
#include <os2.h>
#define LENGTH 40              /* length of object buffer */
#define EXEC_FLAGS 1           /* asynchronous, no trace */
#define ARGS 0L                /* no command-line arguments */
#define ENVS 0L                /* no environmental variables */
                               /* size of segments */
#define DATA_SEG_SIZE sizeof(struct Data)
#define ID_SEG_SIZE sizeof(unsigned)
#define DATA_FLAGS 1           /* shareable with DosGiveSeg */
main()
{
   char fbuf[LENGTH];          /* buffer for fail-object */
   struct _RESULTCODES ChildID; /* defined in bsedos.h */
   unsigned short DataSel;     /* data segment selector */
   unsigned short IDSel;       /* ID segment selector */
   unsigned short ChildSel;    /* child segment selector */
   unsigned rc;                /* return code */
   struct Data {               /* contents of data segment */
      char DataOne;
      int DataTwo;
      long DataThree;
   }
   struct Data far *DataPtr;   /* pointer to data seg */
   unsigned far *IDptr;        /* pointer to ID seg */

                               /* allocate ID segment */
   if( rc=DosAllocShrSeg( ID_SEG_SIZE,
                          "\\SHAREMEM\\ID.DAT", &IDSel ) )
      { printf("DosAllocShrSeg error=%u\n",rc); exit(1); }
                               /* make pointer to ID seg */
   IDptr = (unsigned far *)( (unsigned long)IDSel << 16 );

                               /* allocate data segment */
   if( rc=DosAllocSeg( DATA_SEG_SIZE, &DataSel,
                                      DATA_FLAGS ) )
```

(continued)

```
            { printf("DosAllocSeg error=%u\n",rc); exit(1); }
                                    /* make pointer to data seg */
        DataPtr = (struct Data far *)((unsigned long)DataSel
                                                        << 16);

        DataPtr->DataOne = 'a';  /* put data in data segment */
        DataPtr->DataTwo = 300;
        DataPtr->DataThree = 999000;
                                    /* start child process */
        if( rc=DosExecPgm( fbuf, LENGTH, EXEC_FLAGS, ARGS, ENVS,
                                    &ChildID, "CHGIVE.EXE" ) )
            { printf("DosExecPgm error=%u\n",rc); exit(1); }

                                    /* get child's selector */
        if( rc=DosGiveSeg(DataSel, ChildID.codeTerminate,
                                                    &ChildSel) )
            { printf("DosGiveSeg error=%u\n",rc); exit(1); }
        *IDptr = ChildSel;          /* put it in ID segment */

        DosSleep(1000L);    /* give child time to receive data */

        if( rc=DosFreeSeg( IDSel ) )        /* free ID segment */
            { printf("DosFreeSeg error=%u\n",rc); exit(1); }
        if( rc=DosFreeSeg( DataSel ) )    /* free data segment */
            { printf("DosFreeSeg error=%u\n",rc); exit(1); }
        exit(0);
    }
```

The program first allocates the ID segment with DosAllocShrSeg(), and derives a pointer to the segment.

We saw how DosAllocSeg() was used in Chapter 7. In the current example we set the flags parameter to 1, thus turning on bit 0, "shareable with DosGiveSeg()." We use this function to allocate the data segment, and fill this segment with our customary three items of data. Next we start the child process that will be the recipient of the segment. This returns the process ID of the child, which we can then use as an argument to DosGiveSeg() to obtain the child's selector to the segment.

DosGiveSeg — Give segment access to another process

```
DosGiveSeg(OwnerSel, RecipientID, ARecipientSel);
unsigned short OwnerSel;            /* owner's selector */
unsigned RecipientID;               /* recipient's ID number */
unsigned short far *ARecipientSel;  /* address for r's
                                            selector */
```

The DosGiveSeg() function needs to know the owner's selector to the segment and the process ID of the recipient; these are the first two parameters. The third parameter is the address where the recipient's selector will be placed.

Once the owner obtains this selector, it places it in the shared ID memory segment for access by the recipient. It then waits for the recipient to execute, frees both ID and data segments, and exits.

When the recipient comes into existence it first accesses the shared ID segment to get the selector of the data segment. It uses this selector to create a pointer to the data segment, and accesses the data in the segment. Finally it frees both segments and exits.

```c
/* chgive.c */
/* child process of pgive.c */
/* gets data from shared segment and prints it out */
#define INCL_DOS
#include <os2.h>
main()
{
    unsigned short IDSel;      /* selector of ID segment */
    unsigned short DataSel;    /* selector of data segment */
    unsigned rc;               /* return code */
    struct Data {              /* structure of data seg */
        char DataOne;
        int DataTwo;
        long DataThree;
    };
    unsigned far *IDPtr;       /* pointer to ID segment */
    struct Data far *DataPtr;  /* pointer to data segment */

                               /* access ID segment */
    if( rc=DosGetShrSeg( "\\SHAREMEM\\ID.DAT", &IDSel ) )
        { printf("DosGetShrSeg error=%u",rc); exit(1); }
                               /* make pointer to ID seg */
    IDPtr = (unsigned far *)( (unsigned long)IDSel << 16 );

    DataSel = *IDPtr;          /* get data selector */

                               /* make pointer to data seg */
    DataPtr = (struct Data far *)((unsigned long)DataSel
                                                    << 16);

                               /* get data from segment */
    printf("DataOne = %c\n", DataPtr->DataOne );
    printf("DataTwo = %d\n", DataPtr->DataTwo );
    printf("DataThree = %ld\n", DataPtr->DataThree );
```

(continued)

```
                            /* free ID segment */
    if( rc=DosFreeSeg( IDSel ) )
        { printf("DosFreeSeg error=%u",rc); exit(1); }
                            /* free data segment */
    if( rc=DosFreeSeg( DataSel ) )
        { printf("DosFreeSeg error=%u",rc); exit(1); }
    exit(0);
}
```

There is no need for a function (such as DosGetShrSeg()) in the recipient process to explicitly access the data segment, since this process obtains the selector to the data segment directly from the owning process, via the shared ID segment.

Pipes

Pipes are most commonly used to add flexibility to the redirection mechanism. However, they can also be used without redirection, between any two processes. We'll examine this second case first, since it is simpler, and then go on to see how pipes facilitate the redirection mechanism.

Pipes provide a means for one process to send data to another, much as if it were sending a file. The data, which consists of a stream of bytes, flows from one process, through the pipe, to the other process. The pipe provides coordination for the data transfer.

The DosMakePipe() Function

As with files pipes, are accessed using handles. In fact the same functions, DosRead() and DosWrite(), are used to read and write to both files and pipes.

Pipes are not named entities like files, and they do not need to be opened to obtain their handles. A single function, DosMakePipe(), is used to create the pipe and to return the handles to it. One handle is used by the process writing to the pipe, and the other by the process reading from it.

DosMakePipe — Create a pipe

```
DosMakePipe(AReadHandle, AWriteHandle, PipeSize);
unsigned short far *AReadHandle;    /* address for read
                                       handle */
unsigned short far *AWriteHandle;   /* address for write
                                       handle */
unsigned PipeSize;                  /* size of pipe in bytes */
```

The first two arguments to DosMakePipe() are the addresses where the read and write handles are returned by the function. The **PipeSize** argument is the size of the pipe in bytes. The pipe can be as small as you like, but cannot exceed 64K minus a header of 32 bytes—a maximum of 65504 bytes. The size of the pipe can be larger or smaller than the amount of data you intend to send.

A pipe is actually a circular buffer, maintained in memory by the system. Figure 11-3 shows the buffer.

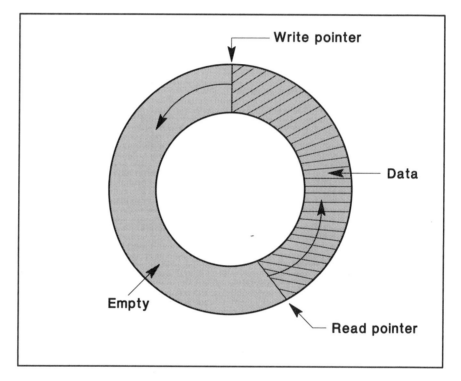

Figure 11-3
Circular Buffer Used for Pipe

A write pointer marks the place the next byte will be written, and a read pointer marks where the next byte will be read. These pointers move around the buffer in the same direction. If a write process fills up the buffer (the write pointer catches up with the read pointer), the write function is suspended until another process reads some data—at least a byte—from the pipe. Conversely, if the pipe is empty (the read pointer catches up with the write pointer), the read process is suspended until the write process has written some data into it. Thus the pipe is self-regulating: a process need not worry writing too much data or reading non-existent data.

Supplying a File Handle to Other Processes

As we've seen, DosMakePipe() returns to the creating process both the read and write handles to the pipe. This brings up a problem. Suppose the process that created the pipe wants to send data to another process. The writer process has the write handle, but the reader process does not have the read handle.

So once a process has created a pipe, the first order of business is to communicate the appropriate handle to the recipient. The handle can be sent using a command-line argument in the DosExec-Pgm() function, or using some other form of interprocess communication. In the our example we pass the handle in a shared memory segment.

Transferring Text Through a Pipe

Here's a program consisting of two processes: one to read lines of text from the keyboard, and another to display the lines on the screen. A pipe is used to send the text from one process to another. The process p_pipe.c gets the text from the user. This process creates a child process, ch_pipe.c, which displays the text.

```c
/* p_pipe.c */
/* sends strings typed at keyboard to child, using pipes */
#define INCL_DOS
#include <os2.h>
#define PIPESIZE 80            /* size of pipe buffer */
#define SEGSIZE sizeof(unsigned)    /* seg is 1 int long */
#define SEGNAME "\\SHAREMEM\\SEG1.DAT" /* shared seg name */
#define LENGTH 30              /* length of object name buff */
#define FLAGS 1               /* asynchronously, no trace */
#define ARGS 0L               /* no command-line arguments */
#define ENVS 0L               /* no environmental variables */
main()
{
    char fbuf[LENGTH];             /* name of fail-object */
    struct _RESULTCODES childID; /* ID of child process */
    unsigned short Selector;      /* selector for shared seg */
    unsigned far *fptr;           /* pointer to shared memory */
    char String[PIPESIZE];        /* buffer for data strings */
    unsigned short ReadHandle;   /* pipe's read handle */
    unsigned short WriteHandle;   /* pipe's write handle */
    unsigned Strlen;              /* bytes read from keyboard */
    unsigned WriLen;              /* bytes to write down pipe */
    unsigned Written;             /* bytes actually written */
    unsigned rc;                  /* return code */
```

(continued)

```
                               /* make pipe, get handles */
    if( rc=DosMakePipe( &ReadHandle, &WriteHandle,
                                              PIPESIZE ) )
       { printf("DosMakePipe error=%u\n", rc); exit(1); }


                               /* get shared segment */
    if( rc=DosAllocShrSeg(SEGSIZE, SEGNAME, &Selector) )
         { printf("DosAllocShrSeg error=%u\n", rc); exit(1); }
                               /* create pointer to segment */
    fptr = (unsigned far *)( (unsigned long)Selector << 16 );
    *fptr = ReadHandle;        /* put handle in segment */


                               /* start the child */
    if( rc=DosExecPgm( fbuf, LENGTH, FLAGS, ARGS, ENVS,
                               &childID, "CH_PIPE.EXE" ) )
         { printf("DosExecPgm error=%u", rc); exit(1); }

    do  {                      /* read string from kbd */
       printf("\nType string: ");
       Strlen = WriLen = strlen( gets(String) );
       if( Strlen == 0 )  {  /* if zero-length string, */
          strcpy(String, "."); /*    send a period */
          WriLen = 1;
       }                       /* write string to pipe */
       if( rc=DosWrite( WriteHandle, String, WriLen,
                                         &Written ) )
          { printf("DosWrite error=%u", rc); exit(1); }
       DosSleep( 500L );       /* wait for child to print */
    } while( Strlen > 0 );     /* quit on zero-length string */

    DosFreeSeg(Selector);      /* free segment */
    DosClose(ReadHandle);      /* close handles */
    DosClose(WriteHandle);
    exit(0);
}
```

We discussed the technique of creating a named shared segment in the first section of this chapter. Here the named segment is only one integer long, since it needs only hold the pipe's read handle. The parent places this handle in the segment where it can be accessed by the child, and then starts the child with DosExecPgm(). The parent then repeatedly reads lines of text typed by the user at the keyboard, and sends them down the pipe using the pipe's write handle and DosWrite(). The user terminates the program by typing [Enter] at the beginning of a line.

Here's the listing for the child process:

```c
/* ch_pipe.c */
/* child process of p_pipe.c */
/* gets text data from pipe and displays it */
#define INCL_DOS
#define INCL_SUB
#include <os2.h>
#define STRLEN 80                       /* length of data buffer */
main()
{
    char String[STRLEN];            /* buffer for strings */
    unsigned BytesRead;             /* bytes read from pipe */
    unsigned short Selector;        /* selector for segment */
    unsigned far *fptr;             /* pointer to segment */
    unsigned short ReadHandle;      /* handle to pipe */
    unsigned rc;                    /* return code */

                                    /* access segment */
    if( rc=DosGetShrSeg( "\\SHAREMEM\\SEG1.DAT",
                                            &Selector ) )
        { printf("DosGetShrSeg error=%u", rc); exit(1); }
                                    /* create pointer to seg */
    fptr = (unsigned far *)( (unsigned long)Selector << 16 );
    ReadHandle = *fptr;            /* get handle from segment */

    while( TRUE )  {               /* read string from pipe */
        if( rc=DosRead(ReadHandle, String, STRLEN,
                                        &BytesRead) )
            { printf("DosRead error=%u", rc); exit(1); }
        if(BytesRead==1 && String[0]=='.')   /* if line
                                            starts */
            break;                /* with period, exit */
        VioWrtTTy( "     Child: ", 13, 0 );
        VioWrtTTy( String, BytesRead, 0 );  /* display
                                            string */
    }
    exit(0);
}
```

The child obtains the read handle from the shared segment, and uses it to access the pipe with DosRead(). The strings are then displayed using VioWrtTTy(). Here's a sample session, with a quote from James Russell Lowell, a 19th century critic:

```
C>p_pipe
Type string: The foolish and
      Child: The foolish and
Type string: the dead alone
      Child: the dead alone
Type string: never change their opinions.
      Child: never change their opinions.
Type string:
C>
```

The user types each line in response to the prompt, and the child receives each line from the pipe and echoes it. When the user enters a blank line both parent and child terminate.

Sub-dividing the Message: The output of ch_pipe.c is divided into separate lines of text only by the interaction of the parent and child. The parent displays its prompt, and receives the typed input from the user, between each line of output from the child. If this did not happen, the output from the child would form one continuous stream of text, without newlines. Thus the timing of the two processes acts as a delimiter for the text output from the child.

Ordinarily, however, when lines of text are transmitted via a pipe, it is necessary to separate them explicitly with newlines, just as it is when a file is transmitted. A similar sort of delimiter must be supplied in any situation where data is divided into groups or records.

Ending the Message: Some method must be agreed on between the sender and receiver to indicate the end of transmission down a pipe. In this example the user indicates the end of the text by typing [Enter] at the beginning of a line, and the parent terminates when it sees a zero-length line. However, the child must also know transmission is over. Sending nothing at all down the pipe doesn't work, since the child waits forever in the DosRead() statement.

In this case, to signal the end of the message, the parent sends a period as a one-character string. When the child sees this, it exits. You could use a variety of techniques to end the transmission. The processes could agree on a fixed number of items to be sent, or, as we'll see later, the writer can send an EOF to the reader by closing the pipe.

If there is a danger that the writer process will not alert the reader when transmission is over, the reader might need to use a second thread to monitor a time-out function. If nothing is received from the pipe after a certain time interval, the time-out occurs and the reader can assume the writer has become incapacitated.

Pipe Size: The size of the pipe in p_pipe.c has been made the same as the input buffer: large enough to hold one line on the screen.

The user should not type more characters than this before pressing [Enter]. One line of text at a time is written to the pipe and then read from it before the next line is written, so the pipe is never filled to capacity.

In most programs that use pipes, however, the pipe is full sometimes and empty other times. The pipe mechanism ensures the reader does not read from an empty pipe and the writer does not write to a full one. Thus the size of the pipe is not critical; almost any size pipe will work. However, a pipe that is too small is inefficient because both the writing process and the reading process must frequently suspend their operation when the pipe is full or empty. A pipe that is too large wastes memory. A balance should be found between the most efficient size for fast data transfer and conserving memory.

Pipes Used in Redirection

Pipes are normally used for redirection, so let's review this mechanism to see where pipes fit in. Redirection is typically used to fool a program into believing it is reading from the keyboard and writing to the screen, when really it is reading and writing to disk files or other programs.

Command-line Redirection: For example, imagine a program that reads a stream of characters and changes any lowercase characters it encounters to uppercase. We'll call this program chredi.c. Here's the listing:

```
/* chredi.c */
/* can be used as child process of predi.c, or stand-alone
   */
/* reads from stdin, converts to uppercase, outputs to
   stdout */
#define INCL_DOS
#include <os2.h>
#include <stdio.h>                    /* for EOF */
#include <ctype.h>                    /* for toupper() */
main()
{
   int ch;

   printf("Child starting\n");
   while( (ch=getchar()) != EOF )  /* read from stdin */
      putchar( toupper(ch) );      /* convert to uppercase */
   printf("Child exiting\n");      /* display on stdout */
   exit(0);
}
```

Such a program is called a *filter* because a stream of data flows through it and is transformed in some way.

The simplest way to use chredi.c is to call it up and type something on the keyboard. What you type, whether it is in lowercase or uppercase, is echoed to the screen in uppercase when you press [Enter]. Enter [Ctrl] [Z], which sends the EOF character 0x1A, to terminate the program.

```
C>chredi
I'M TYPING THIS
IN LOWER CASE
Child exiting
C>
```

The child prints a sign-off message when it is done.

The second way to use chredi.c involves redirection on the command line. Using redirection we can feed a file into chredi.c, and it will be converted to uppercase:

```
C>chredi <source.txt
THIS IS THE CONTENTS
OF SOURCE.TXT, WHICH IS
IN LOWERCASE
Child exiting
C>
```

Similarly, we could redirect the up-shifted output from the program into a file, and use the pipe operator to read output from or send output to other programs. MS-DOS and Unix users are familiar with these operations. More ambitious applications might, in the same way, sort the incoming text, reformat it, search it for particular words, substitute "Mr John Jones" for every instance of a "$" character, or perform some other useful transformation.

Whether we invoke chredi.c directly, or use redirection, the program is always reading from stdin and writing to stdout. Redirection simply changes these handles so they point to files or other programs instead of the keyboard and screen.

Invoking Redirection from Other Processes: Suppose now that another process, instead of the user, wants to make use of chredi.c to convert a stream of text to uppercase. Ordinarily chredi.c reads from stdin. How can it be encouraged to read output generated by another program?

Pipes provide just the mechanism we need. If a parent process uses DosExecPgm() to start chredi.c as a child, it can create a pipe and send data through the pipe to chredi.c.

Figure 11-4 shows chredi.c receiving input directly from the keyboard, from a file using redirection, and from another process using a pipe.

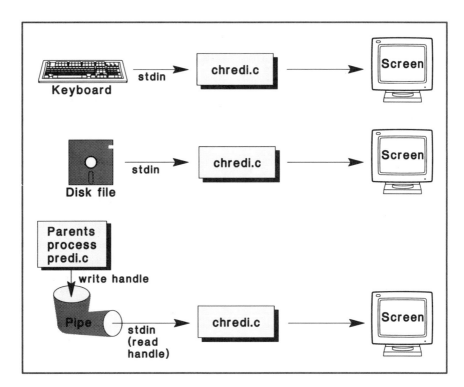

Figure 11-4
Redirection Using a Pipe

Changing Handles: The child process chredi.c reads data from the stdin handle, which is normally connected to the keyboard. To send the child information from a pipe, the parent must change the stdin handle so it points to the pipe rather than the keyboard. This involves several steps.

First, to disconnect it from the keyboard, the stdin handle (with the fixed value 0) must be closed. Then a new handle is given the value of stdin, and the read handle from the pipe is duplicated to this new handle. Now when the child reads data from stdin it actually comes from the pipe rather than the keyboard.

The parent program signals the end of transmission to the child by closing the write handle of the pipe with DosClose(). Ordinarily, a handle is inherited by a child, so that no EOF is sent to the child when the parent closes the handle, since it is still held open by the child. To cause the EOF to be sent, we must make the pipe's write handle non-inheritable by the child. Thus, before creating the child, the parent changes the appropriate bit in the file handle state word for the pipe's write handle, to make it non-inheritable.

In our example, the parent process sends a five-line quotation from Leonardo Da Vinci down the pipe, and the child displays it, converted to uppercase.

```c
/* predi.c */
/* sends strings to child process using pipes */
/* uses standard file handles */
#define INCL_DOS
#include <os2.h>
#define PIPESIZE 10         /* size of pipe buffer */
#define LENGTH 30           /* length of object name buff */
#define FLAGS 1             /* asynchronously, no trace */
#define ARGS 0L             /* no command-line arguments */
#define ENVS 0L             /* no environmental variables */
#define STDIN 0             /* standard input handle */
char *String[] = {  "Experience does not ever err,\n",
                    "it is only your judgement\n",
                    "that errs in promising itself\n",
                    "results which are not caused\n",
                    "by your experience.\n"   };
main()
{
    char fbuf[LENGTH];              /* name of fail-object */
    struct _RESULTCODES childID;    /* ID of child process */
    unsigned short ReadHandle;      /* pipe's read handle */
    unsigned short WriteHandle;     /* pipe's write handle */
    unsigned short NewStdin;        /* new stdin handle */
    unsigned HandState;             /* file handle state */
    unsigned Strlen;            /* length of string to write */
    unsigned Written;               /* bytes actually written */
    int j;                          /* string index */
    unsigned rc;                    /* return code */

    printf("Parent starting\n");
                                    /* make pipe, get handles */
    if( rc=DosMakePipe( &ReadHandle, &WriteHandle, PIPESIZE
                                                            ) )
        { printf("DosMakePipe error=%u\n", rc); exit(1); }
```

(continued)

```
DosClose( STDIN );        /* close normal stdin */
NewStdin = STDIN;         /* make stdin the same */
                          /*    as ReadHandle */
DosDupHandle( ReadHandle, &NewStdin );

                          /* make handle non-inheritable */
if( rc=DosQFHandState( WriteHandle, &HandState ) )
   { printf("DosQFHandState error=%u\n", rc); exit(1); }
HandState &= 0x7F88;      /* remove non-settable bits */
HandState |= 0x0080;      /* set non-inheritance bit */
if( rc=DosSetFHandState( WriteHandle, HandState ) )
   { printf("DosSetFHandState error=%d\n", rc); exit(1);
                                                          }

                          /* start the child */
if( rc=DosExecPgm ( fbuf, LENGTH, FLAGS, ARGS, ENVS,
                             &childID, "CHREDI.EXE" ) )
   { printf("DosExecPgm error=%u\n", rc); exit(1); }

for( j=0; j<5; j++ )   { /* write strings to pipe */
   Strlen = strlen( String[j] );
   if( rc=DosWrite(WriteHandle, String[j], Strlen,
                                            &Written) )
      { printf("DosWrite error=%u", rc); exit(1); }
}
DosClose(ReadHandle);     /* close handles, exit */
DosClose(WriteHandle);
printf("--Parent exiting\n");
exit(0);
}
```

Here's what the output from chredi.c looks like when predi.c is invoked:

```
C>predi
Parent starting
Child starting
EXPERIENCE DOES NOT EVER ERR,
IT IS ONLY YOUR JUDGEMENT
THAT ERRS IN PROMISING ITSELF
RESULTS WHICH ARE NOT CAUSED
BY --Parent exiting
YOUR EXPERIENCE.
Child exiting
```

As you can see, the parent exits before the child has completely emptied the pipe.

Since standard handles are used, there is no need for the pipe creator to pass a handle to the child process. Programming the child could hardly be simpler, and the same program can be used to receive data directly from the keyboard, from a file or another program via redirection on the command line, or from another program using a pipe.

You can use a similar approach to attach a pipe to the output of chredi.c (or to any other program). Thus a process can use DosExec-Pgm() to start a filter program, send it data, and receive the output.

Queues

The queue is the most versatile, and the most complex, of OS/2's IPC facilities. Essentially a queue is a method for organizing and allowing access to a group of shared memory segments. These shared segments constitute the items on a list. Since each segment can hold up to 64K bytes, and a queue can hold about 4000 such segments, the amount of data in a queue is limited only by the size of RAM (plus the swap space on the disk, if virtual memory is used).

Notice that, unlike a pipe, the queue itself does not actually transfer any data. The data to be exchanged is placed in shared segments where it can be accessed by the communicating processes. The queue merely provides the ordering and controlling mechanism to access the shared segments.

One Reader, Many Writers

A single process creates and thereafter "owns" a queue. Ordinarily, the owner is the only process that can read items from the queue. Other processes place items in the queue, where they remain until the owner decides to read them. Thus a queue is completely asynchronous: there can be a delay of any length between writing an item to a queue, and reading it. Many different messages may accumulate in the queue before the owner reads them. The owner has several options as to the order in which messages will be read. They can be read on a first-in-first-out basis (FIFO), on a last-in-first-out basis (LIFO), or according to priorities included with the messages by their senders. In addition, the queue owner may examine items without reading them, to see which one it wants to read next; it can then read that particular item. Figure 11-5 shows the relationship of a queue to the processes that access it.

The analogy often used to describe a queue is that of a mailbox. A mailbox belongs to one person, but many people can send mail to it. Once a letter arrives in the mailbox, it can be removed and read immediately, or the owner can decide to read it later, so that many

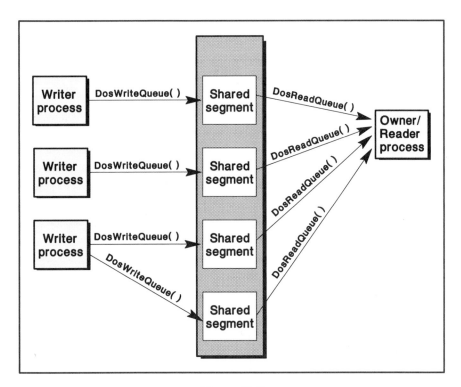

Figure 11-5
Processsess Accessing a Queue

letters accumulate in the box. Also, the mailbox owner can read the letters in a variety of different orders, just as a queue owner can.

Note the differences between queues and pipes. The pipe can hold a maximum of 64K, and the data in a pipe must be read in the same order it was placed in the pipe. Messages must also be copied into a pipe, as if they were being written to a file. A queue passes only the pointer to a shared memory segment enabling more efficient transfer of a large amount of data.

On the other hand, a pipe may be able to hold a larger number of short messages, since it can hold as many messages as will fit in 64K, while a queue is currently limited by the system to about 4000 messages.

Transferring a Single Message

In the example that follows we use a queue to transfer a single line of text from one process to another. Normally queues use multiple writers, but this example demonstrates the essentials of setting up a queue with a minimum number of processes.

The queue's owner, readq.c, is the parent process of a child that writes to the queue. The owner sets up the queue, and waits for the child to send a message, which the owner then reads. The child process, writeq.c, accesses the queue and writes the message to it.

In more detail, the reader (the queue's owner) creates the queue with DosCreateQueue(), allocates a shared memory segment with DosAllocShrSeg(), and starts the child process with DosExecPgm(). The owner then reads the contents of the queue—the message sent by the writer process—with DosReadQueue() and displays it. Finally the reader frees the shared segment with DosFreeSeg(), and closes the queue with DosCloseQueue(). Here's the listing of this reader process:

```
/* readq.c */
/* creates queue, and reads string from child process */
#define INCL_DOS
#define INCL_SUB
#include <os2.h>
#define OBJLEN 30          /* length of failed object name */
#define FLAGS 1            /* async child, no trace */
#define ARGS 0L            /* no command-line arguments */
#define ENVS 0L            /* no environmental variables */
#define PRIORITY 0         /* FIFO queue */
#define ECODE 0            /* read first element in queue */
#define WAIT (char)0       /* wait for arriving data */
#define SEMHANDLE 0L       /* ignored when WAIT/NOWAIT=0 */
#define SEGSIZE 80         /* size of shared memory seg */
main()
{
    char fbuf[OBJLEN];         /* failed object buffer */
    struct _RESULTCODES childID;  /* result codes buffer */
    unsigned short QHandle; /* place to store queue handle */
    unsigned long PID_Data; /* PID and data ID from writer */
    unsigned length=0;      /* # of bytes of data received */
    unsigned long Addr;       /* address of arriving data */
    unsigned char EPriority;  /* priority of queue element */
    unsigned short Selector; /* selector to shared segment */
    char data;                /* received data */

                              /* create queue */
    DosCreateQueue(&QHandle, PRIORITY, "\\QUEUES\\Q1");

                              /* create shared segment */
    DosAllocShrSeg( SEGSIZE, "\\SHAREMEM\\S1", &Selector );
```

(continued)

```
                                    /* start child */
        DosExecPgm( fbuf, OBJLEN, FLAGS, ARGS, ENVS,
                                    &childID, "WRITEQ.EXE" );

                                    /* read data from queue */
        DosReadQueue( QHandle, &PID_Data, &length, &Addr,
                        ECODE, WAIT, &EPriority, SEMHANDLE );

                                    /* display data */
        VioWrtTTy( "\n\rParent received: ", 19, 0 );
        VioWrtTTy( (char far *)Addr, length, 0 );

        DosFreeSeg( Selector );    /* clean up and exit */
        DosCloseQueue( QHandle );
        exit(0);
}
```

Notice that the reader process never uses the selector returned from DosAllocSeg(). This function is executed only to provide access to the segment; the actual address used to read the data, **Addr**, is supplied by the DosReadQueue() function.

The writer (the child process) references the shared segment with DosGetShrSeg(), opens the queue with DosOpenQueue(), accesses the shared segment with a pointer, inserts the data to be transmitted into the segment, and writes to the queue with DosWriteQueue(). Then the writer frees the segment with DosFreeSeg() and closes the queue with DosCloseQueue(). Here's the listing of the writer process:

```
/* writeq.c */
/* child process of readq.c */
/* puts record in queue for parent to read */
#define INCL_DOS
#define INCL_SUB
#include <os2.h>
#define REQUEST 0                /* queue ID data, not used */
#define EPRIORITY 0              /* all elements equal */
#define STRLEN (strlen(msg))    /* length of message */
char msg[] = "Greetings, parent!  I am the child.";
```

(continued)

```
main()
{
    unsigned OwnerPID;          /* PID of queue owner */
    unsigned short QHandle;     /* queue handle */
    unsigned short Selector;    /* selector to shared memory */
    char far *fptr;             /* pointer to shared memory */
    int j;                      /* index string copy */
                                /* open shared segment */
    DosGetShrSeg( "\\SHAREMEM\\S1", &Selector );
                                /* open queue */
    DosOpenQueue( &OwnerPID, &QHandle, "\\QUEUES\\Q1" );
                                /* create pointer to mem */
    fptr = (char far *)( (unsigned long)Selector << 16 );

    for( j=0; j<STRLEN; j++ ) /* place line of data in seg */
      *(fptr+j) = *(msg+j);
    VioWrtTTy("Child sending: ", 15, 0);  /* display text
                                             line */
    VioWrtTTy(fptr, STRLEN, 0);
                                /* write to queue */
    DosWriteQueue(QHandle, REQUEST, STRLEN,  fptr,
                                             EPRIORITY);

    DosFreeSeg( Selector );      /* clean up and exit */
    DosCloseQueue( QHandle );
    exit(0);
}
```

When readq.c is invoked, the child first displays the message it is about to send. Then the parent displays what it has received: hopefully this is the same message.

```
C>readq
Child sending: Greetings, parent! I am the child.
Parent received: Greetings, parent!  I am the child.
C>
```

Let's look at the various queue-oriented API functions used in this example. We'll examine the queue owner, readq.c, first.

DosCreateQueue()

The queue is created using DosCreateQueue(). The process issuing this function becomes the owner of the queue. Only the owner may read or remove items from the queue, although, if there are multiple threads in the owner process, they each have the same access to the queue as the thread that created it.

> ## DosCreateQueue — Create queue
>
> ```
> DosCreateQueue(AQHandle, Priority, QName;
> unsigned short far *AQHandle;   /* address for queue handle
>                                 */
> unsigned Priority;              /* order to access elements */
> char far *QName;                /* name of queue */
> ```

The first parameter is the address where the system returns the handle of the queue. This handle is used for subsequent accesses to the queue, such as reading from it with DosReadQueue() and closing it with DosCloseQueue(). The queue handle is similar to the handles used for disk file access, but is not in the same sequence as file handles.

The second parameter determines the order in which messages are read from the queue, assuming there is more than one waiting to be read. Here are the three possibilities:

Value	Message ordering
0	FIFO (first-in-first-out)
1	LIFO (last-in-first-out)
2	Priority of each message specified by sender

If the Priority option is chosen, each writer process determines the priority of its message using a parameter in DosWriteQueue(). Our present example uses FIFO ordering, but toward the end of this section we'll discuss how to implement LIFO and priority ordering.

The third parameter in DosCreateQueue() is the name of the queue. As was true with named shared memory, this is a pathname that must include a special directory name: for queues this is \QUEUES. Thus if a particular queue is called Q2.DAT, the complete pathname would be \QUEUES\Q2.DAT. (In C, double backslashes must be used.)

Allocating the Shared Segments

One process needs to allocate a shared segment with DosAllocShrSeg(), and the other process needs to access the segment with DosGetShrSeg(). In this example the reader allocates the segment, but it is common for writers to allocate the segment, since they know how much data they need to transfer, and can size the segment accordingly.

Whichever process allocates the segment, the other process must either wait until the segment is allocated, or be prepared to receive a return code of 2, ERROR_FILE_NOT_FOUND, from Dos-

GetShrSeg(). In the example the reader allocates the segment before creating the writer with DosExecPgm(), so the problem does not arise.

The DosReadQueue() Function

A message placed in a queue (or more exactly in a shared memory segment administered by a queue) is read with DosReadQueue(). It may appear that this function requires an alarming number of parameters, but they all have important roles to play.

DosReadQueue — Read message from queue

```
DosReadQueue(QHandle, AReq, ALen, AAddr, Code, Wait, APrio,
Sem);
unsigned short QHandle;    /* queue handle */
unsigned long far *AReq;   /* address for value from writer
                              */
unsigned far *ALen;        /* address for length of msg */
unsigned long far *AAddr;  /* address for pointer to msg */
unsigned Code;             /* number of particular element */
unsigned char Wait;        /* 0=wait for message, 1=no wait */
unsigned char far *APrio;  /* address for priority */
void far * long Sem;       /* semaphore handle (if no wait) */
```

The first parameter, **Qhandle**, is the handle obtained from Dos-CreateQueue() or DosOpenQueue(). This identifies which queue is being read.

The second argument, **AReg**, is the address where the system will place a value that is actually two parameters, each occupying half of the long integer. The right half is the ID of the process that sent the message. This ID is useful information to the process receiving the data (in the mailbox analogy it is the return address). The second half of this argument is a special value given to DosWriteQueue() by the writer. This parameter provides a single integer variable to use for communicating special information between writer and reader, in any way mutually agreed on by both processes. The system simply passes this value from one process to another, without disturbing it. In the mailbox analogy this parameter corresponds to a single number scrawled on the outside of the envelope. It might be used, for example, to signal the last message of a series.

ALen, the third parameter, is the address where the length, in bytes, of the incoming message is placed. In the example we've used this value as a parameter in the VioWrtTTy() function to print out the message.

The forth parameter, **AAddr**, is the address where the pointer to the shared segment is placed. Note that the reader does not obtain this address from the selector to the shared memory segment, but from DosReadQueue().

The fifth parameter, **Code**, is used to override the normal order in which the messages are to be read. Normally this parameter is set to zero, to indicate the next message in sequence should be read. However, if the function DosPeekQueue() is used to examine a message without removing it from the queue, then this parameter can be set to the value returned by DosPeekQueue() so that a particular message can be read in random order. In our example we don't use this parameter.

Wait, the sixth parameter, is used to tell the system what action to take if there is no message ready for reading (if the queue is empty). If this argument is set to 0, the DosReadQueue() function is blocked until an item arrives to be read. If the argument is set to 1, the thread continues on past the DosReadQueue() even if the queue is empty. In this case a system semaphore (see the eighth argument) is used to indicate to the thread when a message has arrived in the queue.

The **APrio** argument, number seven on the list, is used to return the priority of the incoming message. This value only has meaning if a priority ordering is being used for the queue elements, as specified in the DosCreateQueue() function. In our example we don't read this value, since we're using a simple FIFO ordering.

The eighth and (finally) the last argument to DosReadQueue() is **Sem**, the handle of a semaphore that signals the arrival of a message in the queue. This argument is only meaningful if the **Wait** argument has been set to 1 to indicate that the function will not wait on an empty queue. Since our example does wait, the system ignores this parameter. Either a RAM or system semaphore may be used when this argument is active.

Note that DosReadQueue() actually removes an item from the queue as it reads it. Once this function has read a particular item, the item is gone and cannot be accessed again via the queue mechanism. (The function DosPeekQueue(), which we'll look at later, takes a less drastic approach.)

Accessing the Queue Element

The main role of DosReadQueue() is to return the address and the length of the message placed in the queue. Once the queue owner in our example learns these values, it can access the data in the shared segment, and use VioWrtTTy() to print out the message it finds there. The queue owner then frees the shared segment, and closes the queue using DosCloseQueue().

The DosCloseQueue() Function

By using DosCloseQueue() the owner of a queue removes the queue from the system. Further attempts to access the queue after the owner has closed it elicit error codes.

```
                  DosCloseQueue — Close queue
DosCloseQueue(QHandle);
unsigned short QHandle;   /* handle of queue to be closed */
```

When a process that does not own the queue issues DosClose-Queue(), that process's access to the queue is terminated, but other processes can continue to access the queue normally; the queue itself is unaffected.

Writing to the Queue

Now let's examine the functions used in the process that writes to the queue: writeq.c in our example.

Before a process can write to a queue it must have access to a shared memory segment in which it will place the message to be communicated. Since in our example the queue owner has already allocated memory with DosAllocShrSeg(), the queue writer needs only to access it with DosGetShrSeg(). This returns a selector, which is then made into a pointer, as described in the first section of this chapter under shared memory.

While the reader accesses a queue message using an address obtained from DosReadQueue(), the writer accesses it using this pointer to the shared segment. The pointer is then given to DosWrite-Queue() so this function knows where the message is and can communicate its location to the reader.

Opening the Queue

Those processes that do not own a queue obtain access to it using DosOpenQueue().

```
                  DosOpenQueue — Open queue
DosOpenQueue(AOwnerPID, AQHandle, QName);
unsigned far *AOwnerPID;        /* address for owner ID */
unsigned short far *AQHandle;   /* address for queue handle
                                   */
char far *QName;                /* ASCII queue name */
```

When this function is executed the system returns the process ID of the queue's owner in **AOwnerPID.** In our example we don't make use of this ID. We use the queue handle returned in **AQHandle** for all subsequent accesses to the queue.

To obtain these two pieces of information, the function needs to be given the name of the queue (**QName**), expressed as an ASCIIZ string. As noted earlier in the discussion of DosCreateQueue(), this pathname must start with the directory name QUEUES.

Once the queue is open, and the writing process places the message to be transmitted in the shared memory segment, the segment is placed in the queue with DosWriteQueue().

```
                   DosWriteQueue — Write to Queue

DosWriteQueue(QHandle, Request, Length, Addr, Priority);
unsigned short QHandle;      /* queue handle */
unsigned Request;            /* private data for reader */
unsigned Length;             /* length of message */
unsigned char far *Addr;     /* address of message */
unsigned Priority;           /* priority of message */
```

The process calling DosWriteQueue() provides all five parameters to the function; nothing is returned. First is the handle of the queue, **QHandle**, obtained from DosOpenQueue(). Second is the special one-integer piece of data, **Request**, that may be sent to the reader and accessed via DosReadQueue(). This argument is optional; in our example we don't use it. Third is the length, **Length**, of the message; and fourth is its address, **Addr**. Finally comes the **Priority** argument, which is used only if the queue was created with priority ordering in DosCreateQueue. When this is true, each message sent to the queue by DosWriteQueue() can have its own priority. The range is from 0 to 15, with low numbers indicating low priority. We don't use priority in this example, so this parameter is ignored.

Once the message is written to the queue, the writer can free the shared segment, and close the queue. As we noted earlier, when a process that does not own the queue closes it, only that process's ability to access the queue is terminated. The owner and other processes access it as before.

Multiple Writers

Ordinarily more than one writer can place data in the queue. Our next example makes use of three writer processes and one reader. The parent process, rqmult.c, creates three different shared memory segments, and starts three child processes. Its purpose is to read one message from each of its children. To know how many messages to read, this reader process makes use of a new function, DosQueryQueue().

```c
/* rqmult.c */
/* creates queue, reads data from several child processes */
#define INCL_DOS
#define INCL_SUB
#include <os2.h>
#define OBJLEN 30           /* length of failed object name */
#define PRIORITY 0          /* FIFO queue */
#define ECODE 0             /* read first element in queue */
#define NOWAIT (char)0      /* wait for arriving data */
#define SEMHANDLE (long)0   /* ignored when NOWAIT=0 */
#define SEGSIZE 80          /* size of each segment */
#define FLAGS 1             /* async child, no trace */
#define ARGS 0L             /* no command-line arguments */
#define ENVS 0L             /* no environmental variables */
main()
{
    unsigned short QHandle; /* place to store queue handle */
    unsigned long PID_Data; /* PID and data ID from writer */
    unsigned length=0;      /* # of bytes of data received */
    unsigned long Addr;     /* address of segment */
    unsigned char EPriority;  /* priority of queue element */
    unsigned short Select1; /* selector to shared seg1 */
    unsigned short Select2; /* selector to shared seg2 */
    unsigned short Select3; /* selector to shared seg3 */
    char fbuf[OBJLEN];      /* failed object buffer */
    struct _RESULTCODES childID;  /* result codes buffer */
    unsigned NumMsgs;       /* number of msgs in queue */
    unsigned AsciiNum;      /* number in ASCII for display */
    int count;              /* loop variable */

                            /* create queue */
    DosCreateQueue( &QHandle, PRIORITY, "\\QUEUES\\Q1" );

                            /* create shared segments */
    DosAllocShrSeg( SEGSIZE, "\\SHAREMEM\\S1", &Select1 );
    DosAllocShrSeg( SEGSIZE, "\\SHAREMEM\\S2", &Select2 );
    DosAllocShrSeg( SEGSIZE, "\\SHAREMEM\\S3", &Select3 );

                            /* start children */
    DosExecPgm( fbuf, OBJLEN, FLAGS, ARGS, ENVS,
                            &childID, "WQMULT1.EXE" );
    DosExecPgm( fbuf, OBJLEN, FLAGS, ARGS, ENVS,
                            &childID, "WQMULT2.EXE" );
    DosExecPgm( fbuf, OBJLEN, FLAGS, ARGS, ENVS,
                            &childID, "WQMULT3.EXE" );
    DosSleep(4000L);        /* wait for all children */
```

(continued)

```
                                     /* display number of msgs */
      DosQueryQueue( QHandle, &NumMsgs ); /* get number */
      AsciiNum = NumMsgs + 48;    /* convert to ASCII */
      VioWrtTTy( "Number of messages received: ", 29, 0 );
      VioWrtTTy( (char far *)&AsciiNum, 1, 0 );

      for(count=0; count<NumMsgs; count++)  {  /* for each
                                                   child */

                                   /* read data from queue */
         DosReadQueue( QHandle, &PID_Data, &length, &Addr,
                   ECODE, NOWAIT, &EPriority, SEMHANDLE );
                                   /* display data */
         VioWrtTTy("\r\nParent received: ", 19, 0);
         VioWrtTTy( (char far *)Addr, length, 0 );
      }
      DosFreeSeg( Select1 );          /* clean up and exit */
      DosFreeSeg( Select2 );
      DosFreeSeg( Select3 );
      DosCloseQueue( QHandle );
      exit(0);
   }
```

The three children (the writers) are similar. We'll list the first one:

```
/* wqmult1.c */
/* child process of rqmult.c */
/* puts string in queue for parent to read */
#define INCL_DOS
#include <os2.h>
#define REQUEST 0                   /* not used */
#define STRLEN strlen(msg)          /* length of message */
#define EPRIORITY 0                 /* all elements equal */
char msg[] = "This is child number one";

main()
{
   unsigned OwnerPID;        /* PID of queue owner */
   unsigned short QHandle;   /* queue handle */
   unsigned short Selector;  /* selector to shared memory */
   char far *fptr;           /* pointer to shared memory */
   int j;                    /* index to chars in text */
```

(continued)

```
    DosSleep(1000L);               /* let parent finish */
                                   /* open shared segment */
    DosGetShrSeg( "\\SHAREMEM\\S1", &Selector );

                                   /* open queue */
    DosOpenQueue( &OwnerPID, &QHandle, "\\QUEUES\\Q1" );

                                   /* create pointer to mem */
    fptr = (char far *)( (unsigned long)Selector << 16 );

    for( j=0; j<STRLEN; j++ ) /* place line of text in seg */
       *(fptr+j) = *(msg+j);
                                   /* send buffer to queue */
    printf("Child 1 writing to queue\n");
    DosWriteQueue( QHandle, REQUEST, STRLEN, fptr,
                                           EPRIORITY );

    DosFreeSeg( Selector );    /* clean up and exit */
    DosCloseQueue( QHandle );
    exit(0);
}
```

There are several differences (besides the program title) between the three writers. To transform wqmult1.c into wqmult2.c and wqmult3.c:

> 1) Make the appropriate changes in the message sent to the reader:
>
> ```
> char msg[] + "This is child number two";
> ```
>
> 2) Change the delay to 2000L for wqmult2.c, and 3000L for wqmult3.c:
>
> ```
> DosSleep( 2000L )
> ```
>
> 3) Change the segment name:
>
> ```
> DosGetShrSeg( "\\SHAREMEM\\S2", &Selector );
> ```
>
> 4) Change the message the child itself prints:
>
> ```
> printf("Child 2 writing to queue\n");
> ```

As writeq.c did, each of the three writer processes places a single line of text in its own shared memory segment.

To establish the order in which the messages are sent, each of the writers waits for a different length of time before sending its message. The wqmult1.c process waits one second, wqmult2.c waits two seconds, and wqmult3.c waits three seconds. The reader process waits four seconds before reading any of the messages. (Ordinarily system semaphores are used to achieve coordination between the reader and the writers; we'll discuss this at the end of the chapter.)

Since we have specified FIFO ordering, using the priority argument in DosCreateQueue(), we would expect the reader process to read and display the messages in the same order in which they are sent. This is indeed what happens, as we see from the program's output when the reader process is invoked:

```
Child 1 writing to queue
Child 2 writing to queue
Child 3 writing to queue
Number of messages received: 3
This is child number one
This is child number two
This is child number three
```

First, at one-second intervals, the children (the writer processes) announce they are writing to the queue. Then the reader wakes up and checks the queue using DosQueryQueue(). This function returns the number of items in the queue, and this number is used as a loop variable to determine how many times to read the queue. Reading and display are carried out as in previous examples. Because the priority is FIFO, the messages are displayed in the same order they were sent.

Checking for Messages

The DosQueryQueue() function provides a way for a process to find out how many messages are currently waiting, unread, in the queue.

> ### DosQueryQueue — Query size of queue
>
> ```
> DosQueryQueue(QHandle, ANumber);
> unsigned short QHandle;   /* queue handle */
> unsigned far *ANumber;  /* address for number of elements */
> ```

This function has two parameters: the queue handle, and the address where the system can return the number of items in the queue.

Different Priorities

So far in our queue examples we've used FIFO priority. However, it's easy to experiment with different priorities. For instance, to change the last example to LIFO priority, all we need do is change one parameter in rqmult.c: the value of the Priority argument to Dos-CreateQueue(). Change the #define statement that specifies this value to:

```
#define PRIORITY 1          /* LIFO queue */
```

Now when we run the program, the output will look like this:

```
C>rqmult
Child 1 writing to queue
Child 2 writing to queue
Child 3 writing to queue
Number of messages received: 3
This is child number three
This is child number two
This is child number one
```

The parent reads the messages in the reverse order in which they were placed in the queue. Figure 11-6 shows the different priorities.

The third way to organize the message priority is to assign each message its own priority value. We can try this out in the rqmult.c example by making a few changes.

First, the Priority argument to DosCreateQueue() in rqmult.c is changed to 2:

```
#define PRIORITY 2               /* priority queue */
```

Then, in each writer process, the value of the EPriority argument to DosWriteQueue() is changed to the particular priority the process wants to use for its message.

For example, change the value in wqmult1.c like this:

```
#define EPRIORITY 5              /* lowest priority */
```

And in wqmult2.c like this:

```
#define EPRIORITY 15             /* highest priority */
```

And finally in wqmult3.c like this:

```
#define EPRIORITY 10             /* middle priority */
```

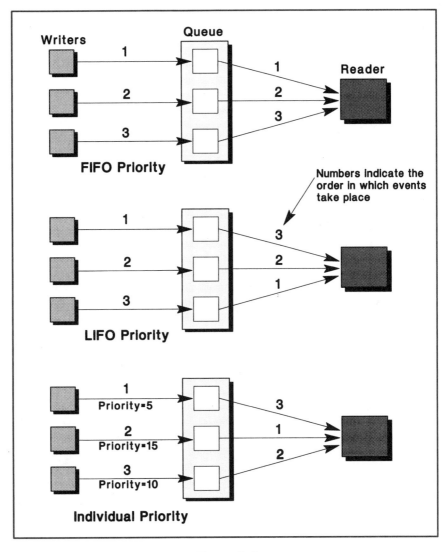

Figure 11-6
Queue Priorities

When we run the program we find that rqmult.c reads the messages in order of increasing priority:

```
C>rqmult
Child 1 writing to queue
Child 2 writing to queue
Child 3 writing to queue
Number of messages received: 3
This is child number two
This is child number three
This is child number one
```

These three ways of handling priority should take care of most situations. If not, there is a further refinement that can be used when reading queue items.

Peeking at a Queue

Sometimes it may be desirable for a process to examine the items in a queue before actually reading them and thereby removing them from the queue. DosPeekQueue() performs this action.

DosPeekQueue — Read queue without removing elements

```
DosPeekQueue(QHand, AReq, ALen, AAddr, ACode, Wait, APrio,
Sem);
unsigned short QHand;        /* queue handle */
unsigned long far *AReq;     /* address for PID and private
                                code */
unsigned far *ALen;       /* address for length of message */
unsigned long far *AAddr;   /* address for pointer to
                                message */
unsigned far *ACode;         /* address for element number */
unsigned Wait;               /* 1=wait for msg, 0=no wait */
unsigned char far *APrio;   /* address for priority */
void far *Sem;              /* semaphore handle, if wait=1 */
```

Most of the parameters are the same as those in DosReadQueue(). The exception is **ACode**, which in DosReadQueue() was the variable **Code**. In DosPeekQueue() it is the address of the variable, so the function can return a value as well as receive one.

If the program sets **ACode** to 0, then DosPeekQueue() accesses the first element in the queue. However, it returns the code of the variable just "peeked." If the program decides to actually read this same queue element (as opposed to peeking at it), this code value is used as input to the **Code** parameter in DosReadQueue().

If a program peeks a particular element in a queue and then leaves the value in **ACode** intact and executes DosPeekQueue() again, the *next* element in the queue is peeked. This allows the program to step through the queue looking for particular elements.

Queues and Private Shared Memory

In the queue examples so far, the queue elements have been *named* shared memory segments. This is the simplest approach, but it suffers from the drawbacks inherent in named shared memory. Any process that knows the name of the segment can access it, thus potentially interfering with communication between the queue reader and writer. Also, both processes must know the name of the segment in advance (or go to the trouble of communicating an entire string).

A more secure approach, and often a more convenient one, is to use *private* shared memory segments as queue elements.

Private shared memory is much simpler to use in a queue than as a stand-alone shared segment. No special mechanism is needed to pass the process ID of the queue owner to the queue writer; the ID is obtained automatically when the writer opens the queue. Also, the queue owner does not need to allocate a segment or issue Dos-GetShrSeg().

Here are the steps taken by the queue writer (in our example the child process of the queue owner) to place a message in the queue:

1) Allocate a segment using DosAllocSeg(), with the allocation flag set to "shareable with DosGiveSeg()."

2) Open the queue with DosOpenQueue(). This returns the queue owner's PID.

3) Use this ID in DosGiveSeg(); this will return the owner's selector to the segment.

4) Insert data into the shared segment using the pointer obtained from the *owner's* selector.

5) Put this segment into the queue with DosWriteQueue(), again using the pointer from the owner's selector.

The queue owner (the parent process) has comparatively little to do:

1) Create the queue with DosCreateQueue().

2) Get the address of the shared segment using DosReadQueue().

3) Read data from shared segment using this address.

Here's the listing for the parent program:

```
/* rgive.c */
/* creates queue, children pass data in private segments */
#define INCL_DOS
#define INCL_SUB
#include <os2.h>
#define OBJLEN 30           /* length of failed object name */
#define PRIORITY 0          /* FIFO queue */
#define ECODE 0             /* read first element in queue */
#define NOWAIT (char)0      /* wait for arriving data */
#define SEMHANDLE (long)0   /* ignored when NOWAIT=0 */
#define FLAGS 1             /* async child, no trace */
#define ARGS 0L             /* no command-line arguments */
#define ENVS 0L             /* no environmental variables */
main()
{
    unsigned short QHandle; /* place to store queue handle */
    unsigned short Selector; /* selector of shared segment */
    unsigned long PID_Data; /* PID and data ID from writer */
    unsigned length=0;      /* # of bytes of data received */
    unsigned long Addr;     /* address of structure */
    unsigned char EPriority; /* priority of queue element */
    char fbuf[OBJLEN];      /* failed object buffer */
    struct _RESULTCODES childID;  /* result codes buffer */
    unsigned NumMsgs;       /* number of msgs in queue */
    unsigned AsciiNum;      /* number in ASCII for display */
    int count;             /* loop variable */

                            /* create queue */
    DosCreateQueue( &QHandle, PRIORITY, "\\QUEUES\\Q1" );

                            /* start children */
    DosExecPgm( fbuf, OBJLEN, FLAGS, ARGS, ENVS,
                            &childID, "WGIVE1.EXE" );
    DosExecPgm( fbuf, OBJLEN, FLAGS, ARGS, ENVS,
                            &childID, "WGIVE2.EXE" );
    DosExecPgm( fbuf, OBJLEN, FLAGS, ARGS, ENVS,
                            &childID, "WGIVE3.EXE" );

    DosSleep(4000L);            /* wait for all children */

                            /* display number of msgs */
    DosQueryQueue( QHandle, &NumMsgs ); /* get number */
    AsciiNum = NumMsgs + '0';    /* convert to ASCII */
    VioWrtTTy( "Number of messages received: ", 29, 0 );
    VioWrtTTy( (char far *)&AsciiNum, 1, 0 );
```

(continued)

```
        for(count=0; count<NumMsgs; count++)  {  /* for each
                                                      child */

                                /* read data from queue */
        DosReadQueue( QHandle, &PID_Data, &length, &Addr,
                    ECODE, NOWAIT, &EPriority, SEMHANDLE );

                                /* display data */
        VioWrtTTy("\r\nParent received: ", 19, 0);
        VioWrtTTy( (char far *)Addr, length, 0 );
        Selector = Addr >> 16;      /* construct selector */
        DosFreeSeg( Selector );     /* free shared segment */
        }
    DosCloseQueue( QHandle );    /* free queue */
    exit(0);
}
```

Here's the listing for the first child (writer) process. As in wqmult.c, the three children are the same except for the messages they send to the queue owner, the time delays they use, and the printf() statements that display what they're doing.

```
/* wgive1.c */
/* child process of rqmult.c */
/* puts string in queue for parent to read; uses
   DosGiveSeg() */
#define INCL_DOS
#include <os2.h>
#define REQUEST 0           /* DosWriteQueue; not used */
#define STRLEN strlen(msg)  /* length of message */
#define EPRIORITY 0         /* all elements equal */
#define ALLOCFLAG 1         /* shareable with DosGiveSeg */
char msg[] = "This is child number one";

main()
{
    unsigned OwnerPID;          /* PID of queue owner */
    unsigned short QHandle;     /* queue handle */
    unsigned short Selector;    /* selector to shared memory */
    unsigned short OwnerSel;    /* owner's selector */
    char far *fptr;             /* pointer to shared memory */
    int j;                      /* index to chars in text */

    DosSleep(1000L);                /* let parent finish */
                                    /* open shared segment */
    DosAllocSeg( STRLEN, &Selector, ALLOCFLAG );
```

```
                                    /* open queue */
        DosOpenQueue( &OwnerPID, &QHandle, "\\QUEUES\\Q1" );

                                       /* give queue owner access */
                                       /* to shared segment */
        DosGiveSeg( Selector, OwnerPID, &OwnerSel );

                                       /* create pointer to mem */
                                       /* using owner's selector */
        fptr = (char far *)( (unsigned long)OwnerSel << 16 );

        for( j=0; j<STRLEN; j++ ) /* place line of text in seg */
           *(fptr+j) = *(msg+j);
                                       /* send buffer to queue */
        printf("Child 1 writing to queue\n");
        DosWriteQueue( QHandle, REQUEST, STRLEN, fptr,
                                                   EPRIORITY );

        DosFreeSeg( Selector );   /* clean up and exit */
        DosCloseQueue( QHandle );
        exit(0);
    }
```

The output of this program looks like that from the earlier example:

```
Child 1 writing to queue
Child 2 writing to queue
Child 3 writing to queue
Number of messages received: 3
Parent received: This is child number one
Parent received: This is child number two
Parent received: This is child number three
```

Suballocation and Queues

Another approach to creating shared memory for queues is to use only one shared segment for several different writers. The writers can obtain blocks in the segment using DosSubAlloc(), and communicate the addresses of these blocks to the reader with DosWriteQueue().

The amount of data that can be in the queue at any time is clearly restricted by this approach, since one segment can hold only 64K bytes. Also, suballocation works best when the blocks to be sub-allocated are roughly the same size; this avoids memory fragmentation. If the messages in your queue are short and of similar lengths, this is a worthwhile approach, since suballocation is faster than allocating an entire segment.

Timing Considerations

In the examples above we have in a number of places used timing delays, generated by DosSleep(), to facilitate coordination between processes. We chose this approach because it is simple to implement and does not obscure the operation being discussed. However, using timing delays is inappropriate in a serious application. Delays are subject to failure when applications in other sessions change the timing between processes. In any case, they are inefficient.

In most cases, coordination between processes engaged in interprocess communication should be handled by system semaphores. Readers and writers of queues should use semaphores to ensure the queue owner does not attempt to read a segment before it has been written, and that a queue writer does not write into a segment in the process of being read by the queue owner.

Summary

This chapter has focused on the interprocess communication techniques of shared memory, pipes, and queues.

A memory segment can be shared between processes in two ways. A named shared segment is allocated by one process with DosAllocShrSeg(), and accessed by other processes with DosGetShrSeg(). Alternatively, a process can allocate a segment using DosAllocSeg() with the sharing bit set, and, after considerable initialization, accessed by other processes using a selector provided by DosGiveSeg().

A pipe is created with DosMakePipe(), which returns read and write handles to the pipe. With these handles the pipe can be accessed much as a file would be, using DosRead(), DosWrite(), DosClose(), and similar file-oriented functions. Pipes are typically used to connect processes to other processes using redirection.

Queues are the most complex system of IPC. One process creates a queue with DosCreateQueue(); this process owns the queue and is the only process that can read from it. Reading is accomplished with DosReadQueue(). Other processes may access the queue with DosOpenQueue(), and write to it with DosWriteQueue(). The owner can peek into the queue (read without removing the item) with DosPeekQueue(), and remove the queue altogether with DosCloseQueue(). The number of messages in the queue can be ascertained with DosQueryQueue.

MONITORS
AND SIGNALS

Chapter 12

Chapter 12

This chapter covers two topics. The first is device monitors, which give an application such powers as intercepting keystrokes intended for other programs. The second is signals, which permit special handling of external events such as a user pressing the [Ctrl] [c] keys.

These topics have a common element in that certain keys may cause special effects in applications that are prepared to deal with them. However, device monitors and signals have quite different purposes and mechanisms, and their juxtaposition in this chapter is mostly due to the difficulty of finding a more appropriate home for the relatively short discussion of signals.

Device Monitors

Device monitors enable an application in OS/2 to perform many of the roles that were handled by TSR ("Terminate and Stay Resident") programs in MS-DOS. Let's recall briefly what TSRs do, and what their drawbacks are.

"Terminate and Stay Resident" Programs

In the MS-DOS world, TSRs have achieved wide popularity. Such programs are installed in memory, but remain inactive until certain conditions are met. Often the condition that brings a TSR to life is the pressing of a certain key or key combination. Until this "hot-key" is pressed, other programs run normally, as if the TSR were not there. When the hot-key is pressed the TSR comes to life, instantly placing a calculator, note pad, phone book, or some other useful utility on the screen. When the user is through with the utility, the TSR becomes inactive again, and the original program is restored to its former state. Another type of TSR always operates in the background. Such an application might, for example, translate certain keystrokes into other keystrokes: the keystroke "macro expander."

Although TSRs in MS-DOS are convenient for the user, in effect allowing instant switching from one application to another, they also present problems. This is especially true when more than one TSR is loaded at the same time. Often a combination of TSRs has to be installed in a certain order to work correctly, and some TSRs are incompatible with each other no matter how they are installed. Special programs have even been created just to organize TSRs and resolve conflicts between them. These problems arise because MS-DOS was not originally designed to handle TSRs. That TSRs work as well as they do is more a tribute to the ingeniousness of applications programmers than the designers of MS-DOS.

Another problem is that loading a few TSRs can quickly deplete the scarce memory resources of an MS-DOS system. Even if the TSRs are compatible with one another, there may not be room for all of them at the same time a foreground program is running.

Also, programming a TSR is not particularly simple. The interrupt vector that points to the keystroke routine must be altered by the TSR, and various other steps must be taken, all of which require an intimate knowledge of the system software. Some languages, such as Turbo C, now include extensions that reduce the necessity of writing parts of a TSR in assembly language. Nevertheless, creating a TSR is still not a simple operation.

The OS/2 Approach to TSRs

In OS/2 the technique of intercepting hot-keys has been organized much more simply and cleanly than it was in MS-DOS. An application no longer has to deal with messy details about keyboard interrupts. In fact, applications are forbidden to access interrupts, so a new mechanism has been created: the *device monitor*. The device monitor is, in effect, an extension to a device driver. Using system calls, an application can install a device monitor and arrange communication with it, thus providing itself with access to the data coming from or going to a device via the device driver.

In OS/2, device monitors apply only to character-oriented devices; they do not work with block-oriented peripherals such as disk drives. Of the character devices, device monitors can at present be used with the keyboard, the mouse, and the printer. A typical application needs to monitor data generated by the keyboard, so this is what we'll concentrate on in this chapter.

Monitors and Multitasking

Notice that no special mechanism is necessary in OS/2 to emulate the action of the "Terminate and stay resident" systems call in MS-DOS (the notorious INT 27). Simply running a program with DETACH places it in the background, in effect giving it the status of a TSR program. That is, it is loaded into memory, but is invisible to the user. Thus part of the complexity of MS-DOS TSRs disappears in OS/2, because it is handled naturally by the operating system.

Moreover, in OS/2 the monitor application is actually running concurrently with the foreground application. In MS-DOS it is dormant, and can only be awakened by interrupts caused by the keyboard device handler.

The other tricky job performed by TSRs is gaining access to the stream of keystrokes, so that the application knows when to come to life; this is the task performed by device monitors in OS/2.

Data Path Taken by Keystrokes

Normally, keystrokes are generated in the hardware of the keyboard, pass from there to the keyboard device driver, and from there to a distributor routine which routes them to the foreground application requesting them. When a device monitor is installed, the keystrokes are sent to the monitor before being sent on to the foreground application. If several monitors are installed, the keystroke passes through each of them in turn, as shown in Figure 12-1.

The information concerning each keystroke is referred to as a keystroke *packet*. It is this information that is sent along the route of keystroke data flow. This keystroke packet contains a surprising amount of information; we'll look at it in detail later.

Organization of a Monitor Application

There are several different aspects to creating a device monitor application. We'll briefly review them here, show a simple application, and then examine the steps in more detail. Finally we'll show device monitors that have greater capabilities.

A monitor application first sets up a monitor and a communications path to it. Then the application (or one of its threads) typically sits in a loop reading the keystroke packets as they arrive from the monitor. Most packets will be of no interest to the application, and are passed on as quickly as possible down the chain to other applications. If the desired hot-key is detected, however, the application then takes appropriate action such as placing a calculator or appointment list on the screen.

Thus the application has several options with respect to the keystroke packets that reach it. A keystroke can be consumed (read and discarded), it can be passed on unchanged, or it can be transformed into another keystroke or group of keystrokes before being sent on. A keyboard macro application, for example, would use the latter approach to translate a single keystroke into a series of characters, such as a frequently typed phrase.

Monitor Setup: There are several steps to setting up the monitor. First it must be "opened" with the API call DosMonOpen(). This function returns a handle to the device being monitored. This handle is specific to the device; other processes in the same screen group, that open monitors to the same device, will receive the same handle.

Next the ID of the screen group whose keystrokes are to be monitored must be obtained. Since the monitor application will typically run in the background, using DETACH, it will be in a separate screen group; so obtaining the ID of the current screen group will not help. However, the ID of the current *foreground* screen group can be found using DosGetInfoSeg().

The ID of this foreground screen group, and the handle from DosMonOpen(), are used as arguments to DosMonReg(). This API function sets up two buffers to be used as communication areas between the device driver and the device monitor. Although these buffers reside in the monitor application's data space, they should not be touched by the application itself; they are used only by the system.

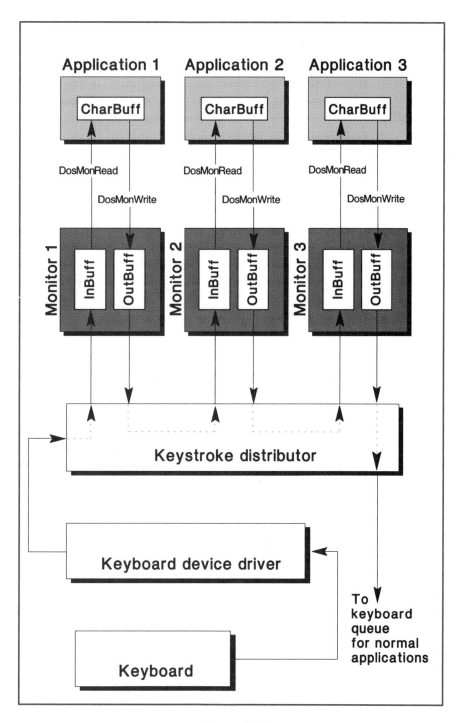

Figure 12-1
Keystroke Data Flow

When the monitor is successfully installed, it is often desirable to pop up a temporary window to inform the user of this fact. When the monitor application is run in the background with DETACH, a popup window is the only way to assure the user that the application has installed itself successfully and is on the watch for keystrokes.

Reading and Writing Data Packets

Once the application has set up the monitor, it typically sits in a loop, reading keystrokes, passing most of them on, and taking action on a few. The API call used to read the keystrokes is DosMonRead(). This function places the incoming data packet in a special buffer (different from those set up by the DosMonReg() call described above) where it can be examined by the application.

Notice that the application is not "busy-waiting" (using unnecessary machine cycles) when it is cycling in the loop reading keystroke packets. If no key has been pressed, the application blocks on the DosMonRead() call, and control is returned to the operating system until a keystroke packet arrives. The application unblocks and comes to life only when a key is pressed, so the number of machine cycles involved in the monitoring process is very small.

A function similar to DosMonRead(), DosMonWrite(), is used to write the same keystroke (or other keystrokes) back out to the monitor chain. Figure 12-2 shows the process in the form of a flowchart.

Removing the Monitor

A monitor application should include code to remove the monitor from the chain and terminate itself. This is usually accomplished with a hot-key (different from the key used to activate the monitor). The API function that removes the monitor is DosMonClose(). It flushes any data remaining in the monitor buffers, and removes the monitor from the data path.

Before exiting, it is useful for the application to pop up another window, this time informing the user that the monitor has been successfully removed.

A Simple Monitor Application

The following program, monf1.c, is a simple monitor application. It's purpose is to place a message on the screen each time the [F1] key is pressed. This is not the kind of action that a power-user is desperate for, but it does demonstrate the basics of monitors. It can be easily expanded to perform a more useful task, such as displaying an ASCII table or other reference.

The example is run as a background process, using the command:

```
C>detach monf1
```

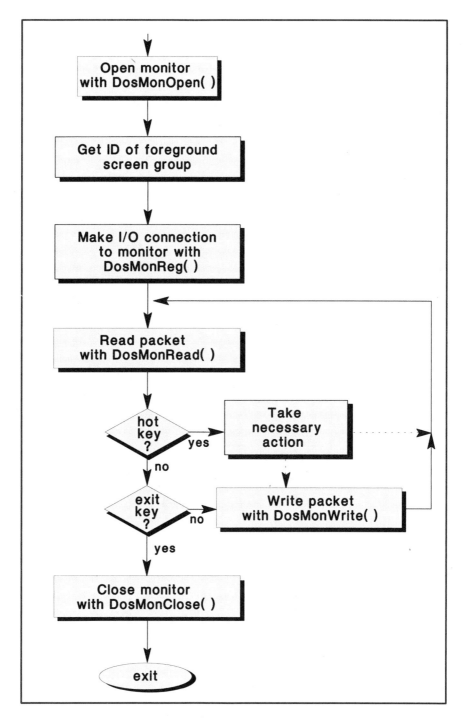

Figure 12-2
Flowchart of Keystroke Monitor Application

When it is first started, monf1.c displays a popup window informing the user that it is installed. Then it vanishes into the background, where it waits in a loop, monitoring all keystrokes in its screen group. Most keystrokes are passed on unaltered, but if it sees the [F1] key, it displays a message in a popup window. When the user presses the [Esc] key, the program removes the monitor and exits, again telling the user it is doing so in a popup window.

```c
/* monf1.c */
/* keyboard monitor responds to [F1] key */
/* run with "detach monf1" */
#include "kbdmon.h"          /* structure definitions */
#define INCL_DOS
#define INCL_SUB
#include <os2.h>
#define NOPREF 0             /* anywhere in chain is OK */
#define VIOHANDLE 0          /* for VioPopUp(): always 0 */
#define WAIT 0               /* monitor waits for input */
#define F1 59                /* ext code for [F1] key */
#define ESC 27               /* ascii code for [Esc] key */
#define RELEASE 0x40         /* KbdDDflags key release bit */
main()
{
    unsigned short KbdHandle;   /* keyboard monitor handle */
    unsigned ID;                /* current screengroup ID */
    struct _GINFOSEG far *globptr;  /* pointer to global
                                       seg */
    struct KeyPacket CharBuff;  /* buffer for keystrokes */
    struct MonBuff InBuff;      /* buffer for registration */
    struct MonBuff OutBuff;     /* buffer for registration */
    unsigned short global_seg, local_seg; /* seg addresses */
    unsigned WaitFlag = 0x01;   /* VioPopUp() waits for
                                   screen */
    unsigned ByteCnt;           /* for DosMonRead() */

                                /* open keyboard monitor */
    DosMonOpen( "KBD$", &KbdHandle );

                                /* get ID of current sceen grp */
    DosGetInfoSeg(&global_seg, &local_seg);
    globptr = (struct _GINFOSEG far *) ( (long)global_seg <<
                                                        16 );

    ID = globptr->sgCurrent;

                                /* put length of buffers into */
                                /*   first word of buffers */
    InBuff.length = (unsigned)sizeof(struct MonBuff);
    OutBuff.length = (unsigned)sizeof(struct MonBuff);
```

(continued)

```
DosMonReg( KbdHandle,   /* register monitor buffers */
           (unsigned char *)&InBuff,
           (unsigned char *)&OutBuff,
           NOPREF, ID );
                         /* print sign-on message */
VioPopUp( &WaitFlag, VIOHANDLE );
printf("MONF1 is installed\n");
DosSleep( 1500L );
VioEndPopUp( VIOHANDLE );

while(TRUE)   {
                         /* read packet into buffer */
   ByteCnt = sizeof(CharBuff);
   DosMonRead( (unsigned char *)&InBuff,
               WAIT,
               (unsigned char *)&CharBuff,
               &ByteCnt );
                         /* check packet for [F1] key */
   if( CharBuff.CharRec.Ascii == 0  &&
       CharBuff.CharRec.Scan == F1  &&
       ! (CharBuff.KbdDDflags & RELEASE)  )    {
                         /* print acknowlegement message */
      VioPopUp( &WaitFlag, VIOHANDLE );
      printf("The [F1] key was pressed\n");
      DosSleep( 1500L );
      VioEndPopUp( VIOHANDLE );
   }
                         /* if [Esc] key, exit */
   else if( CharBuff.CharRec.Ascii == ESC)
      break;             /* don't send packet on */

                         /* for all other characters, */
   else                  /*    send packet on */
   DosMonWrite( (unsigned char *)&OutBuff,
                (unsigned char *)&CharBuff, ByteCnt);
} /* end while */

DosMonClose( KbdHandle );   /* close monitor */
                            /* printf sign-off message */
VioPopUp( &WaitFlag, VIOHANDLE );
printf("MONF1 is un-installed\n");
DosSleep( 1500L );
VioEndPopUp( VIOHANDLE );
exit(0);
}
```

The structure of the program is similar to that shown in the flow-chart.

The kbdmon.h Header File

The program **#includes** a header file called kbdmon.h. This file contains the definitions of various structures that will be used in the program. Here's the listing of the header file:

```
/* structures for keyboard monitor */

struct CharRecord {   /* structure of Character Record */
    unsigned char Ascii;       /* ascii value of character */
    unsigned char Scan;        /* scan code of character */
    unsigned char DBCSstatus;  /* language support */
    unsigned char DBCSshift;   /* language support */
    unsigned int  ShiftState;  /* shift state */
    unsigned long Time;        /* time of keystroke in ms */
};

struct KeyPacket {    /* structure of Kbd data packet */
    unsigned char     MonFlags;       /* dispatch flags */
    unsigned char     Orig_scan_code; /* original scan code
                                         */
    struct CharRecord CharRec;        /* (see struct above) */
    unsigned          KbdDDflags;     /* device driver flags */
};

struct MonBuff {     /* input and output buffer structure */
    unsigned  length;       /* length of MonBuff */
    unsigned char buffer[128];   /* used by system */
};
```

The **MonBuff** definition is used to define the **InBuff** and **OutBuff** structures where the keystroke distributor places and reads the keystroke packets for the monitor. The structure of these two buffers consists of two parts: an initial word in which the application must store the length of the structure (including this word), and a buffer for the data. This buffer must be at least 20 bytes longer than the internal device driver buffer. The documentation is currently somewhat ambiguous about this figure, with recommendations from 64 to 128 bytes. Either figure seems to work; in the kbdmon.h file the buffers are made 128 bytes long.

Two structures, **KeyPacket** and **CharRecord** (which is an element of **KeyPacket**), define the data packet that carries the information about each keystroke. Let's look at these structures in detail. (A more exhaustive description can be found in the <u>OS/2 Device Drivers Guide</u>.)

The Keystroke Packet

The structure **KeyPacket** consists of four members. The first member is an **unsigned char** (byte) called **MonFlags**. The rightmost two bits of this byte, bits 0 and 1, are not used in keystroke monitors and can be ignored. Bit 2, if set, indicates that the entire data packet is being used to flush the keystroke path. If a device monitor application encounters a packet with this bit set, it should flush any internal buffers, and send the packet on without changing it. Applications that normally send on all but specific keystrokes should have no trouble with flush packets. Bits 3 through 7 of the **MonFlags** byte are not used by the application, and should normally be sent on unaltered. However, if the application is inserting a new packet in the data stream, these bits should be set to 0.

The second member of **KeyPacket** is **Orig_scan_code**. This character represents the unaltered scan code read by the keyboard before alterations by the device driver. (The scan code is a unique position-dependant code for each keyboard key.) This field should normally be passed unaltered along the chain, but (as with the upper five bits of the **MonFlags** byte) it should be set to 0 if the application is adding a new packet to the data stream. The **MonFlags** and **Orig_scan_code** bytes are sometimes considered to be part of a *Monitor Flags* word as shown in Figure 12-3.

The third member of **KeyPacket** is the structure **CharRecord**. We'll return to this in a moment. The forth and last member of **KeyPacket** is **KbdDDFlags** (for KeyBoarD Device Driver Flags). This word has several fields as shown in Figure 12-4.

Bits 0 to 5 of the **KbdDDFlags** word are used to indicate that the device driver is to take some special action. If no action is to be taken, they are set to 0. Application-generated packets must also set this field to 0. Examples of codes that initiate special actions are 05h, which is the [Ctrl] [Alt] [Del] key sequence that causes a warm boot; 09h, which is the [Ctrl] [s] key combination that causes a pause in scrolling; 0Ah, which is sent by any key as a wakeup following a pause; and 12h, which indicates the [Ctrl] [c] key sequence used to terminate a program. We don't use this bit field in our examples.

Bit 6 of **KbdDDFlags** is set to indicate that a key has been released. We make use of this bit to determine when extended key codes (such as function and cursor keys) have been completed. Bit 7 indicates that the scan code of the packet that preceded the current one is a secondary key prefix; bit 8 indicates that the character is a typamatic repeat of a toggle key, and bit 9 indicates that the previous keystroke was an accent key. We don't make use of bits 7, 8, and 9.

Bits 10 through 13 should be passed on unaltered by the application. If the application generates a packet, these bits should be set

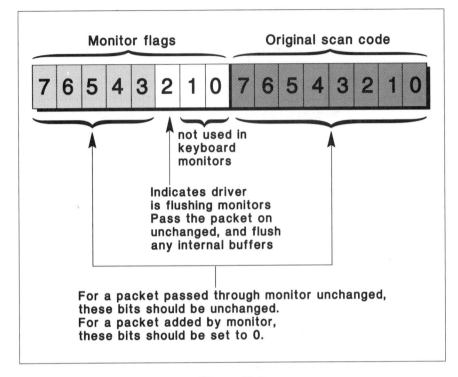

Figure 12-3
Monitor Flags Word

to 0. Bits 14 and 15 are available for monitor applications to communicate among themselves, using whatever protocol they agree on. The operating system never alters these bits.

Operation of the monf1.c Program

Now that we know something about the structure of the data packet used to contain keystroke information, let's look at the details of the monf1.c program.

The DosMonOpen() Function: The program first gets a handle to the device monitor with DosMonOpen().

```
                    DosMonOpen — Open device monitor
DosMonOpen(DevName, AHandle);
char far *DevName;              /* ASCIIZ device name */
unsigned short far *AHandle;   /* address for device handle
                                  */
```

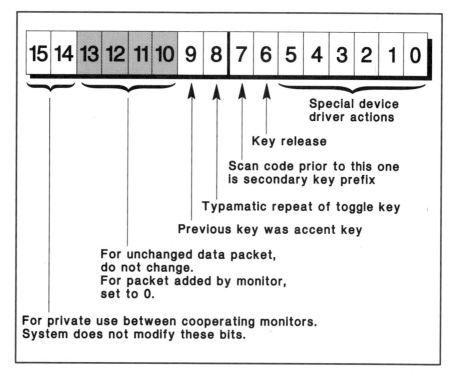

**Figure 12-4
KbdDDFlag Word**

This function requires the name of the device to be monitored, such as "KBD$", "MOU", or "LPT1", and returns the monitor handle to the device. Only one call to DosMonOpen() is necessary for any given device. Additional monitors may be registered by the same process using the same handle.

The Foreground Screengroup ID: The next function, DosMon-Reg(), requires the ID of the foreground screen group. This is obtained from a structure called the Global Information Segment. This structure is maintained by the system, and is available to all processes. Another set of structures keeps track of information for individual processes. These are the Local Information Segments and each is accessible only from the current process. These structures are defined in BSEDOS.H. Here's what they look like:

```
struct _GINFOSEG   {       /* Global Info Segment */
   unsigned long time;
   unsigned long msecs;
   unsigned char hour;
   unsigned char minutes;
   unsigned char seconds;
   unsigned char hundredths;
   unsigned int  timezone;
   unsigned int  cusecTimerInterval;
   unsigned char day;
   unsigned char month;
   unsigned int  year;
   unsigned char weekday;
   unsigned char uchMajorVersion;
   unsigned char uchMinorVersion;
   unsigned char chRevisionLetter;
   unsigned char sgCurrent;
   unsigned char sgMax;
   unsigned char cHugeShift;
   unsigned char fProtectModeOnly;
   unsigned int  pidForeground;
   unsigned char fDynamicSched;
   unsigned char csecMaxwait;
   unsigned int  cmsecMinSlice;
   unsigned int  cmsecMaxSlice;
   unsigned int  bootdrive;
   unsigned char amecRAS[32];
 };

struct _LINFOSEG  {            /* Local Info Segment */
   unsigned int  pidCurrent;
   unsigned int  pidParent;
   unsigned int  prtyCurrent;
   unsigned int  tidCurrent;
   unsigned int  sgCurrent;
   unsigned int  sgSub;
   unsigned int  fForground;
};
```

The API function DosGetInfoSeg() returns the segment selectors for these structures.

DosGetInfoSeg — Gets selectors for information segments

```
DosGetInfoSeg(AGloSegSel, ALocSegSel);
unsigned short far *AGloSegSel;   /* address for global seg
                                     sel */
unsigned short far *ALocSegSel;   /* address for local seg
                                     sel */
```

Once the segment selector is obtained it must be converted to a pointer by shifting it left 16 bits.

There is wealth of information in these structures, but at the moment we are only interested in the ID of the foreground screen group, which is represented by the variable **sgCurrent** in the _GIN-FOSEG structure.

The buffers used by DosMonRead() and DosMonWrite() must contain, as their first word, their own length in bytes. After obtaining the foreground screen group ID, the program places these length values in the buffers.

The DosMonReg() Function: To tell the system where the buffers are, and to cause the monitor to be installed, the application executes DosMonReg().

DosMonReg — Registers buffers for device monitor

```
DosMonReg(Handle, InBuff, OutBuff, PosFlag, Index);
unsigned short Handle;        /* device handle */
unsigned char far *InBuff;    /* address of input buffer */
unsigned char far *OutBuff;   /* address of ouput buffer */
unsigned PosFlag;             /* 0=no pref, 1=front, 2=back */
unsigned Index;               /* ID of screengroup */
```

The **Handle** argument is the value returned from DosMonOpen(). **InBuff** and **OutBuff** are the special data areas provided by the application for the monitor. The application should not attempt to interfere with these buffers. The **PosFlag** argument gives the application the chance to influence the location of the monitor in the chain. A value of 0 specifies no preference. A value of 1 specifies the front of the chain: in other words, the monitor will be first to intercept the keystrokes. A value of 2 specifies the end of the chain: the monitor will be last to intercept the keystrokes. Different kinds of monitors will have different preferences.

If another monitor application has already chosen the front position, the next monitor to specify the front option will be placed second from the front, the next will be placed in third position, and so on. Similarly, the second application to choose the last position will be placed second from last, and so on.

For keyboard monitors, the **Index** argument is the ID of the screengroup to be monitored. This is usually the current foreground screengroup (not the screengroup of the application, which is typically running in background mode with DETACH, in a special background screengroup).

As the final part of the installation section, the program pops up a window that says the monitor is installed.

The DosMonRead() Function: In the background, the program waits in a loop, where it reads keystroke packets with DosMonRead().

```
DosMonRead — Reads packet from monitor stream

DosMonRead(InBuff, WaitFlag, CharBuff, AByteCnt);
unsigned char far *InBuff;       /* address of input buffer */
unsigned WaitFlag;               /* 0=wait, 1=no wait */
unsigned char far *CharBuff;     /* buffer accessible to app */
unsigned far *AByteCnt;          /* Address for byte count */
```

In the DosMonRead() function, **InBuff** is the monitor input buffer, accessible only to the system. **WaitFlag** is normally set to 0 to indicate that the function should wait until the next packet is received. When set to 1 the function will not wait if no packet is available. **CharBuff** is the buffer into which the keystroke data packet will be placed by the monitor. Here it can be examined by the application to determine which keystroke it represents. **AByteCnt** should be set to the number of bytes in the **CharBuff** buffer. The function will reset it to the bytes actually read, so it must be reset before every use of DosMonRead().

Analyzing Keystroke Packets: Only a few parts of each keystroke packet need to be checked. In the case of normal ASCII characters, only the field **CharBuff.CharRed.Ascii** must be examined; but if we're looking for a keystroke that results from an extended code (a two-byte code whose first byte is 0, as produced by function and cursor keys), then several other fields must be analyzed. The ASCII code of such characters may be 0, but the scan code will have a unique value for the appropriate key. Also, to avoid responding twice to the same keypress, we check the RELEASE bit in the **KbdDDFlags** word.

The DosMonWrite() Function: Keystrokes are written back into the monitor data stream using DosMonWrite().

DosMonWrite — Writes packet to monitor stream

```
DosMonWrite(InBuff, CharBuff, AByteCnt);
unsigned char far *OutBuff;    /* address of input buffer */
unsigned char far *CharBuff;   /* buffer accessible to app */
unsigned ByteCnt;              /* byte count */
```

The **OutBuff** argument to DosMonWrite() is the buffer that will be used by the system. **CharBuff** is filled in by the application with the appropriate data packet. **ByteCnt** is filled in with the value obtained from DosMonRead().

Most keystroke packets are written back unaltered into the data stream. That is, DosMonRead() transfers the data from **InBuff** to the application's buffer **CharBuff**, and the application does not change it in any way before writing from **CharBuff** back out to **OutBuff** with DosMonWrite(). However, this is often not true of the hot-key itself. In the example, the [F1] key is not passed along; it causes the program to place its popup message on the screen. The [Esc] key is also not passed along; when it is discovered the program terminates. Consuming a packet in this way is simply a matter of failing to execute the DosMonWrite().

Note that, since the [Esc] key is used as a terminator, the program will terminate whenever the [Ctrl] [Esc] key combination is pressed to switch to another screen group; this is probably an undesirable characteristic in real monitor applications.

When the program terminates, the monitor is removed from the data stream with DosMonClose().

DosMonClose — Removes monitor

```
DosMonClose(Handle);
unsigned short Handle;    /* monitor handle of device to
                             close */
```

This function needs only the **Handle** that was originally obtained from DosMonOpen().

Compiling Glitch: Be careful when developing monitor programs. If you inadvertently leave a previous version of the application running in the background, then the compiler won't be able to access the .EXE file. One of the earliest parts of a monitor application to be developed should be the code that removes the monitor from the system and terminates the program. If the program is running in the background and won't recognize a hot-key to terminate itself, you may need to reboot to get rid of it.

Adding Packets to the Data Stream: montime.c

We've seen how keystroke packets can be sent on unchanged, and how they can be consumed by a monitor application. How do we create and send a completely new packet?

Our next example prints the time on the screen in response to a hot-key. You might use it, for example, if you were writing a report with a word processor, and needed to fill in the current time at many places in the report. Instead of consulting your watch and typing in the time, you would simply press [Alt] [t]. (A similar approach could be used to obtain the date.)

The program runs entirely in the background (except for sign-on and sign-off messages). When the user presses the [Alt] [t] keys the program reads the time data from the structure already used by Dos-GetInfoSeg(). It constructs a string from the values for hours, minutes, and seconds, and sends the individual characters of this string down the monitor chain with DosMonWrite(), in the form 12:27:24.

```c
/* montime.c */
/* keyboard monitor prints time when [Alt] [t] is pressed */
/* run with "detach montime" */
#include "kbdmon.h"           /* for structure definitions */
#define INCL_DOS
#define INCL_SUB
#include <os2.h>
#include <string.h>           /* for strcat(), strcpy() */
#include <stdlib.h>           /* for itoa() */
#define NOPREF 0              /* anywhere in chain is OK */
#define VIOHANDLE 0           /* for VioPopUp(): always 0 */
#define WAIT 0                /* monitor waits for input */
#define ALT_T 20              /* ext code for [Alt][t] keys */
#define F10 68                /* ascii code for [F10] key */
#define RELEASE 0x40          /* KbdDDflags key release bit */

main()
{
    char Temp[10];                    /* string for itoa() */
    char Mtime[30];                   /* string to hold time */
    unsigned short KbdHandle;         /* keyboard monitor handle */
    unsigned ID;                      /* current screengroup ID */
    struct _GINFOSEG far *globptr;    /* pointer to global seg
                                         */
    struct KeyPacket CharBuff;        /* buffer for keystrokes */
    struct MonBuff InBuff;            /* used for registration */
    struct MonBuff OutBuff;           /* used for registration */
```

(continued)

```
unsigned short global_seg, local_seg; /* seg addresses */
unsigned WaitFlag = 0x01;    /* VioPopUp() waits for
                                    screen */
unsigned ByteCnt;            /* for DosMonRead() */
int j;                       /* character index */


                             /* open keyboard monitor */
DosMonOpen( "KBD$", &KbdHandle );

                        /* get current screen group ID */
DosGetInfoSeg(&global_seg, &local_seg);
globptr = (struct _GINFOSEG far *) ( (long)global_seg <<
                                                  16 );
ID = globptr->sgCurrent;

                        /* put length of buffers in */
                        /*     first word of buffers */
InBuff.length = (unsigned)sizeof(struct MonBuff);
OutBuff.length = (unsigned)sizeof(struct MonBuff);
DosMonReg( KbdHandle,    /* register monitor buffers */
         (unsigned char *)&InBuff,
         (unsigned char *)&OutBuff,
         NOPREF, ID );
                        /* print sign-on message */
VioPopUp( &WaitFlag, VIOHANDLE );
printf("MONTIME is installed\n");
DosSleep( 1500L );
VioEndPopUp( VIOHANDLE );

while(TRUE)  {
                        /* read packet into buffer */
   ByteCnt = sizeof(CharBuff);
   DosMonRead( (unsigned char *)&InBuff,
            WAIT,
            (unsigned char *)&CharBuff,
            &ByteCnt );
                        /* check for [Alt] [t] keys */
   if( CharBuff.CharRec.Ascii == 0  &&
      CharBuff.CharRec.Scan == ALT_T  &&
      ! (CharBuff.KbdDDflags & RELEASE)  )   {

                        /* get time */
      itoa( (int)globptr->hour, Temp, 10);
      strcpy( Mtime, Temp );
      strcat( Mtime, ":");
      itoa( (int)globptr->minutes, Temp, 10);
```

(continued)

```
                strcat( Mtime, Temp );
                strcat( Mtime, ":");
                itoa( (int)globptr->seconds, Temp, 10);
                strcat( Mtime, Temp );
                                        /* print time */
                CharBuff.MonFlags = 0;
                CharBuff.Orig_scan_code = 0;
                CharBuff.CharRec.Scan = 0;
                CharBuff.KbdDDflags = 0;
                for( j=0; j<strlen(Mtime); j++)  {
                    CharBuff.CharRec.Ascii = Mtime[j];
                    DosMonWrite( (unsigned char *)&OutBuff,
                                (unsigned char *)&CharBuff,
                                                        ByteCnt);
                }   /* end for */
            }   /* end if */
                                        /* if [F10] key, exit loop */
            else if( CharBuff.CharRec.Ascii == 0    &&
                    CharBuff.CharRec.Scan  == F10   &&
                    ! (CharBuff.KbdDDflags & RELEASE)  )
                break;

            else                        /* pass other packets along */
                DosMonWrite( (unsigned char *)&OutBuff,
                            (unsigned char *)&CharBuff, ByteCnt);
        }
        DosMonClose( KbdHandle );
        VioPopUp( &WaitFlag, VIOHANDLE );
        printf("MONTIME is un-installed\n");
        DosSleep( 1500L );
        VioEndPopUp( VIOHANDLE );
        exit(0);
    }
```

The new keystroke packet is created by filling in the appropriate parts of the **CharBuff** structure. **MonFlags**, **Orig_scan_code**, the **Scan** part of **CharRec**, and **KbdDDFlags** should all be set to 0. The only part of the packet that needs to change from one character to the next is the **Ascii** field of **CharRec**. The various characters of the time string are placed here and DosMonWrite() is called, in a loop, to send them off one by one.

Accessing the Screen from a Monitor Application

In some applications it's important for a monitor application to access the foreground screen and its contents. For example, when a spelling checker is awakened by a hot-key, it might need to see which word the cursor is currently pointing to, so it can check that word's spelling. A context-sensitive help process would work the same way.

How can a monitor application examine the screen? In background mode it does not have access to the screen at all, while if it executes a normal popup, the original screen is replaced by the popup window. Fortunately, the VioPopUp() function provides an option that solves this problem. If bit 1 of the **OptionFlags** argument to VioPopUp() is set, then the screen will not be cleared and the cursor position will not be changed when the pop-up occurs. (For this to work the screen must be in an 80 by 25 text mode.)

Here's a monitor program, monword.c, that accesses whatever word the cursor is positioned on when the [F1] key is pressed. For simplicity the example does not include a 90,000 word dictionary to check the spelling of the word. Instead it simply displays another popup window that demonstrates that it knows what the word is, in the form:

```
The word is aardvark
```

The monword.c program installs itself in the same way as the earlier monitor examples. When it detects the [F1] key it executes a non-destructive popup window, giving it access to the screen without changing the original screen contents. Then it finds the cursor position with VioGetCurPos().

```
/* monword.c */
/* keyboard monitor reads word from screen */
/* run with "C>detach monword" */
#include "kbdmon.h"              /* structure definitions */
#define INCL_DOS
#define INCL_SUB
#include <os2.h>
#define NOPREF 0                 /* anywhere in chain is OK */
#define VIOHANDLE 0              /* for VioPopUp(): always 0 */
#define WAIT 0                   /* monitor waits for input */
#define F1 59                    /* ext code for [F1] key */
#define F10 68                   /* ext code for [F10] key */
#define ESC 27                   /* ascii code for [Esc] key */
#define RELEASE 0x40             /* KbdDDflags key release bit */
main()
{
    unsigned short KbdHandle;    /* keyboard monitor handle */
    unsigned ID;                 /* current screengroup ID */
    struct _GINFOSEG far *globptr; /* pointer to GlobalSeg */
    struct KeyPacket CharBuff;   /* buffer for keystrokes */
    struct MonBuff InBuff;       /* buffer for registration */
    struct MonBuff OutBuff;      /* buffer for registration */
```

(continued)

```
            unsigned short global_seg, local_seg; /* seg addresses */
            unsigned WaitFlag = 0x01; /* VioPopUp() waits for screen
                                           */
            unsigned NoClear =  0x03; /* VioPopUp() wait, no clear */
            unsigned ByteCnt;          /* for DosMonRead() */
            char buff[80];             /* buffer for screen word */
            unsigned len;              /* length of buffer contents */
            unsigned row;              /* row of cursor position */
            unsigned col;              /* column of cursor position */
            int j;                     /* character index in buff */

                                       /* open keyboard monitor */
            DosMonOpen( "KBD$", &KbdHandle );

                                       /* get ID of current sceen grp */
            DosGetInfoSeg(&global_seg, &local_seg);
            globptr = (struct _GINFOSEG far *)( (long)global_seg <<
                                                          16 );

            ID = globptr->sgCurrent;

                                       /* put length of buffers into */
                                       /*    first word of buffers */
            InBuff.length = (unsigned)sizeof(struct MonBuff);
            OutBuff.length = (unsigned)sizeof(struct MonBuff);
            DosMonReg( KbdHandle,    /* register monitor buffers */
                    (unsigned char *)&InBuff,
                    (unsigned char *)&OutBuff,
                    NOPREF, ID );
                                       /* print sign-on message */
            VioPopUp( &WaitFlag, VIOHANDLE );
            printf("MONWORD is installed\n");
            DosSleep( 1500L );
            VioEndPopUp( VIOHANDLE );

            while(TRUE)  {
                                       /* read packet into buffer */
               ByteCnt = sizeof(CharBuff);
               DosMonRead( (unsigned char *)&InBuff,
                        WAIT,
                        (unsigned char *)&CharBuff,
                        &ByteCnt );
                                       /* check packet for [F1] key */
               if( CharBuff.CharRec.Ascii == 0  &&
                  CharBuff.CharRec.Scan == F1  &&
                  ! (CharBuff.KbdDDflags & RELEASE)  )   {
                                       /* pop up, don't clear screen */
                  VioPopUp( &NoClear, VIOHANDLE );
                                       /* get cursor position */
                  VioGetCurPos( &row, &col, VIOHANDLE );
```

(continued)

```
                                /* go right until blank */
        for( j=0; ; j++, col++ )  {
          len = 1;
          VioReadCharStr( buff+j, &len, row, col,
                                          VIOHANDLE );
          if( *(buff+j) == ' ' )
             break;
        }  /* end for */
        VioEndPopUp( VIOHANDLE );

                                /* use popup to show word */
        VioPopUp( &WaitFlag, VIOHANDLE );
        VioWrtTTy("The word is ", 12, VIOHANDLE );
        VioWrtTTy( buff, j, VIOHANDLE );
        DosSleep( 3000L );
        VioEndPopUp( VIOHANDLE );
      }  /* end if */

                                  /* if [F10] key, quit */
      else if( CharBuff.CharRec.Ascii == 0    &&
               CharBuff.CharRec.Scan == F10 &&
               ! (CharBuff.KbdDDflags & RELEASE)   )
        break;                   /* don't send packet on */

      else                      /* send packet on */
        DosMonWrite( (unsigned char *)&OutBuff,
                     (unsigned char *)&CharBuff, ByteCnt);
    }  /* end while */
    DosMonClose( KbdHandle );   /* close monitor */
                                /* printf sign-off message */
    VioPopUp( &WaitFlag, VIOHANDLE );
    printf("MONWORD is un-installed\n");
    DosSleep( 1500L );
    VioEndPopUp( VIOHANDLE );
    exit(0);
}
```

The program assumes that the cursor is positioned on the first letter of the word to be examined, so it moves right, examining the letters in the word with VioReadCharStr(). It stores each letter in **buff**, and looks for a space. Once it finds the space, it considers that it has found the complete word. A more sophisticated program would not assume the cursor was positioned at the start of the word, and would deal with words at the ends of the text line, which this program doesn't.

The program uses a normal destructive popup window to display the word it found, and then returns to background mode. Pressing [F10] removes the monitor and terminates the program.

Dangers and Responsibilities

Device monitors add a great deal of flexibility to OS/2, but they also bring responsibilities. A monitor application actually becomes a part of the device driver it is monitoring, so defects in the programming of a monitor can cause problems as severe as bugs in device drivers. For example, a monitor's failure to pass on the keystrokes sent to it can cause the entire system to hang. Thus considerable care must be used in designing the monitor.

To avoid degrading the system's response to keystrokes, a monitor must pass on the keystroke packets as quickly as possible. If there are many monitors active at the same time, each one will degrade keyboard performance to some extent, so each must be as efficient as possible.

The thread that handles DosMonRead() and DosMonWrite() should not be permitted to suffer any interruptions, such as waiting for a semaphore or being shut down by a critical section. It is often best to use one thread exclusively for reading and writing monitor data. Analysis of the data packets, and actions taken, can be handled by another thread. The read/write thread can be given a higher priority than the other threads in the program to assure its rapid response.

Signals

What happens to a running application when a user types the [Ctrl] [c] key combination? Ordinarily the process will be terminated, and control will return to the operating system. However, in many—perhaps most—applications, this response is unsatisfactory. Some applications may use [Ctrl] [c] for their own purposes: for cursor control (as in WordStar), or to move from one mode in the application to another (to bring up the main menu, for example). Other applications will terminate on [Ctrl] [c], but need to take specific actions before they do so, such as completing disk writes, closing files, or taking the necessary steps to shut down a telecommunications link.

Kinds of Signals

For these reasons applications need a way to intercept [Ctrl] [c] and similar key combinations. The mechanism provided in OS/2 for this purpose is the *signal*. There are actually six signals in OS/2, as shown in the following table:

Signal	Mnemonic	Value	Default action
[Ctrl] [c]	SIG_CTRLC	1	Terminate process
Broken pipe	SIG_BROKENPIPE	2	none
Terminate	SIG_KILLPROCESS	3	Terminate process
[Ctrl] [Break]	SIG_CTRLBREAK	4	Terminate process
Flag A	SIG_PFLG_A	5	none
Flag B	SIG_PFLG_B	6	none
Flag C	SIG_PFLG_C	7	none

The SIG_CTRLC and SIG_CTRLBREAK signals are generated from the keyboard. The SIG_KILLPROCESS signal is generated when one process kills another using DosKillProcess(). Unless intercepted, these three signals will cause a process to terminate. The SIG_BROKENPIPE signal is generated when two processes are communicating via a pipe, and the process reading from the pipe ends before the writer is finished. The three flag signals are a generalization of the signal concept that permits one process to notify another that a critical event has occurred; the two processes must agree in advance on the meaning of these flag signals.

Signal Handlers

Normally a signal causes the default action: program termination, or no action at all in the case of the flag signals. To change this default action, a process can designate a particular routine, called a *signal handler*, to be executed when the signal is received. The application registers the signal handler routine by passing its address to the system with the DosSetSigHandler() function.

Now imagine that the application is executing code when the signal is received. The application will be interrupted, and control will be transferred from the code that was executing to the signal handler routine. The signal handler will take whatever steps are necessary and can then either return to the same place in the interrupted thread, or terminate the process, as shown in Figure 12-5.

Once the signal has been received, the system will not recognize further signals of the same type until the signal has been reset. This keeps the signal handler routine from being entered a second time before it has finished processing. The signal may be reset at the end of the signal handler routine.

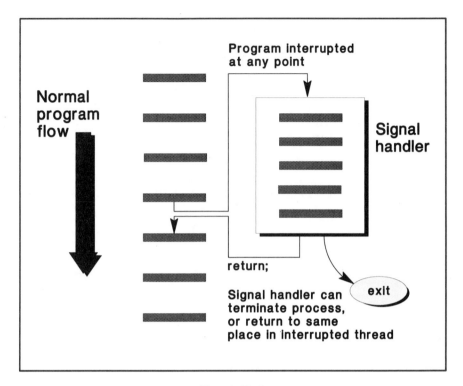

Figure 12-5
Signal Handler

Processing a Signal and Terminating

The simplest signal handler is one that, when activated by a signal, completes its task and then terminates the entire process. Here's such an example.

```
/* signal.c */
/* tests signal mechanism, using CTRL-C */
#define INCL_DOS
#include <os2.h>
#define TO_HANDLER 2        /* action: go to handler */
#define SIGNUM 1            /* signal to look for is CTRL-C */

main()
{
    void pascal far handler();      /* signal handler */
    void (pascal far *OldAddr)();   /* addr for previous
                                       handler */
    unsigned OldAction;             /* previous action */
    unsigned rc;                    /* return code */
```

(continued)

```
                              /* set CTRL-C to trap to handler */
    if( rc=DosSetSigHandler( handler, &OldAddr,
                             &OldAction, TO_HANDLER, SIGNUM) )
       { printf("DosSetSigHandler error=%u", rc); exit(1); }

    while(TRUE)  {        /* print message until signaled */
       printf("Main running...");
       DosSleep( 200L );
     }
}

/* handler() */
/* executed when CTRL-C pressed */
void pascal far handler()
{
   printf("\n\nCTRL-C is being processed\n");
   DosSleep( 4000L );   /* CTRL-C typed here has no effect */
   printf("Program terminating\n");
   exit(0);                 /* exit all threads */
}
```

The main part of the program first sets up the signal handler by passing its address, **handler**, to the system, with DosSetSigHandler(). Then it sits in a loop printing a short message. The user can now interrupt the program at any time by pressing the [Ctrl] [c] keys. When the program receives the [Ctrl] [c] signal, control immediately goes to the signal handler routine. Here's some sample output from the program:

```
Main running...Main running...Main running...Main running...
Main running...Main running...Main running...Main running...
Main running...Main running...Main running...Main running...
Main running...Main running...Main running...

CTRL-C is being processed
Program terminating
```

As you can see, the signal handler routine doesn't perform a very useful task: it simply prints a message, waits a few seconds, prints another message, and terminates the entire program. A real signal handler would presumably engage in useful activities, such as closing disk files, before terminating the program.

The DosSetSigHandler() Function

The DosSetSigHandler() function can be used in several ways, depending on the values of the arguments given it.

```
           DosSetSigHandler — Set signal handler

DosSetSigHandler(Handler, PrevHand, PrevAct, Action,
                                                  SigNum);
void (pascal far Handler)();   /* signal handler */
void (pascal far *PrevHand)();   /* previous signal
                                    handler */
unsigned far *PrevAct;         /* previous action (0 to 3) */
unsigned Action;               /* action to perform */
unsigned Signum;               /* signal number to act on */
```

The first argument is the address of the signal handler function itself. This is a **far** function of type **pascal**. The next two arguments are addresses. In the first one the system will place the address of the previous signal handler, and in the second it will place the action it took. If there was no previous signal handler, these addresses will consist of zeros.

The **Action** argument specifies what DosSetSigHandler() is to do. There are five choices:

Value	Action when signal received
0	Install the system default for the signal
1	Ignore the signal
2	Transfer control to routine specified
3	Signal error if flag signal received
4	Reset the signal

In our example we used an action of 2, which causes control to be transferred to the address specified, when the appropriate signal is received. However, as can be seen, there are other options as well. Later examples will exercise some of these options.

The **Signum** argument specifies the particular signal that is to be acted upon. The seven possibilities (such as SIG_CTRLC), and their corresponding values, were shown earlier.

Returning From a Signal Handler

In the signal.c example it was assumed that [Ctrl] [c] would cause the program to terminate; the signal handler existed simply to perform some cleanup activities before terminating the program. However, in many applications a signal handler needs to return control to the calling program, and be prepared to handle the same signal again. This would be the case if [Ctrl] [c] were interpreted as a keystroke with specific meaning for the program.

In these circumstances the signal handler must be able to return to the original place in the code where the process was operating when the signal occurred. This can be effected in C with a simple **return** statement at the end of the signal handler. This causes an IRET (return from interrupt) machine language instruction to be executed, and restores the registers to the state before the signal occurred.

Here's an example that allows the user to interrupt the program repeatedly by pressing [Ctrl] [c].

```
/* retsig.c */
/* shows return from signal handler */
#define INCL_DOS
#include <os2.h>
#define SYS_DEFAULT 0      /* action: system default */
#define IGNORE 1           /* action: ignore signal */
#define TO_HANDLER 2       /* action: go to handler */
#define RESET 4            /* action: reset signal */
#define SIGNUM 1           /* signal to look for is CTRL-C */
#define MAX 50             /* number of times to do loop */

main()
{
    void pascal far handler();       /* signal handler */
    void (pascal far *OldAddr)();    /* addr for previous
                                        handler */
    unsigned OldAction;              /* previous action */
    int j;                           /* loop index */
    unsigned rc;                     /* return code */

                              /* set CTRL-C to trap to handler */
    if( rc=DosSetSigHandler( handler, &OldAddr,
                        &OldAction, TO_HANDLER, SIGNUM) )
        { printf("DosSetSigHandler error=%u", rc); exit(1); }

    for(j=0; j<MAX; j++)  {        /* keep printing message */
        printf("%d Main running\n", j);
        DosSleep( 200L );
    }
}
```

(continued)

```
/* handler() */
/* executed when CTRL-C pressed */
void far pascal handler(arg, signum)
unsigned arg, signum;              /* must use arguments */
{
    void (pascal far *OldAddr)(); /* addr of previous handler
                                     */
    unsigned OldAction;            /* previous action */
    unsigned rc;                   /* return code */

    printf("\nSignal handler is active\n");
    DosSleep( 3000L );
                                 /* reset the same signal */
    if( rc=DosSetSigHandler( (void (pascal far *)())0L,
&OldAddr,
                               &OldAction, RESET, SIGNUM) )
        { printf("DosSetSigHandler error=%u", rc); exit(1); }

    printf("Signal handler terminating\n");
    return;
}
```

This program is similar to the last one, though somewhat more complicated. One difference is that the handler function acknowledges the two arguments passed to it by the system. The first of these arguments is only used when flags are being passed (an example of flag signals will be shown). The second argument is the number of the signal that caused the handler to be called. In this example we don't make use of either of these arguments, but space must be set aside for them, or the handler function will not be able to return to the main program without fouling up the stack and causing a system error.

Another addition to the program is the invocation of DosSetSigHandler() with the **Action** argument set to a value of 4. This causes the signal received (in this case [Ctrl] [c]) to be reset. This is necessary so that subsequent signals will be recognized.

A final point is that, since [Ctrl] [c] is always interpreted by the application as an invitation to enter the signal handler, and never to terminate the program, it is important to have some other way to return to the operating system. In the example, our failsafe system is to print our message only fifty times, and then terminate.

Here's a sample session with retsig.c:

```
0 Main running
1 Main running
2 Main running
3 Main running
Signal handler is active
Signal handler terminating
4 Main running
5 Main running
6 Main running
7 Main running
Signal handler is active
Signal handler terminating
8 Main running
9 Main running
- - - - - - - -
47 Main running
48 Main running
49 Main running
```

The signal handler will be invoked each time [Ctrl] [c] is pressed, until the 50th message is printed.

Ignoring Signals

Once it is called, a signal handler cannot be interrupted by the same signal until it resets it. However, the system will record additional signals that are generated while the signal handler is at work, and retransmit them as soon as the original signal is reset. Thus pressing [Ctrl] [c] while the signal handler is executing will not cause an immediate effect, but will cause the signal handler to be invoked a second time once it has finished processing the previous signal.

If this is not desired, DosSetSigHandler() can be issued with the **Action** argument given the value of 1, as soon as the signal handler is started. This causes incoming signals of the specified type to be ignored, that is, forgotten. Subsequently when the signal handler finishes its work and resets the signal (setting **Action** equal to 4), there will not be any leftover signals to cause an immediate call back into the signal handler.

Using Flag Signals

The SIG_CTRLC, SIG_KILLPROCESS, and SIG_CTRLBREAK signals are generated by specific events that would ordinarily cause a program to terminate. The SIG_BROKENPIPE signal is also specific to a particular event. Three other signals, the *flag* signals, are generated by other processes using the DosFlagProcess() function. These signals can be used simply for communication between processes. Since they cause another process to interrupt what it is doing, and immediately attend to the signal, they are useful when one process needs to let another know about an emergency situation.

In this example one process starts another process, waits two seconds, and then sends it the SIG_PFLG_A signal. The child process responds to the signal, and then resets it so it is ready to respond again. In fact, in this example, the parent continues to send the SIG_PFLG_A signal every two seconds, and the child responds to it each time.

```
/* psig.c */
/* starts child process, sends it flag */
#define INCL_DOS
#include <os2.h>
#define LENGTH 40      /* length of object name buffer */
#define FLAGS 1        /* asynchronously, no trace */
#define COMS 0L        /* no command-line arguments */
#define ENVS 0L        /* no environmental variables */
#define ACTION 0       /* notify entire subtree */
#define FLAGNUM 0      /* Flag A */
#define FLAGARG 99     /* argument to pass to process */
main()
{
    char fbuf[LENGTH];           /* buffer for fail-object */
    struct _RESULTCODES childID; /* defined in bsedos.h */
    unsigned rc;                 /* return code */

                                 /* start child */
    if( rc=DosExecPgm( fbuf, LENGTH, FLAGS, COMS, ENVS,
                               &childID, "CHSIG.EXE" ) )
        { printf("DosExecPgm error=%u\n",rc); exit(1); }

    while(TRUE)   {              /* signal the child */
        DosSleep( 2000L );       /* every two seconds */
```

(continued)

```
              printf("\nParent signalling child with Flag A\n");
              if( rc=DosFlagProcess( childID.codeTerminate, ACTION,
                                             FLAGNUM, FLAGARG ) )
                  { printf("DosFlagProcess error=%u\n",rc); exit(1);
                                                                     }
          }
      }
/* chsig.c */
/* receives flag signal A from parent psig.c */
#define INCL_DOS
#include <os2.h>
#define TO_HANDLER 2        /* action: go to handler */
#define RESET 4             /* action: reset current signal */
#define FLAGA 5             /* signal to look for is Flag A */

main()
{
     void pascal far handler();      /* signal handler */
     void (pascal far *OldAddr)();   /* addr of previous
                                          handler */
     unsigned OldAction;             /* previous action */
     unsigned rc;                    /* return code */

                            /* set Flag A to trap to handler */
     if( rc=DosSetSigHandler( handler, &OldAddr,
                          &OldAction, TO_HANDLER, FLAGA) )
        { printf("DosSetSigHandler error=%u",rc); exit(1); }

     while(TRUE)  {              /* keep printing message */
        printf("Child running...");
        DosSleep(200L);
      }
}

/* handler() */
/* executed when Flag A received */
void pascal far handler(arg, signum)
unsigned arg, signum;
{
     void (pascal far *OldAddr)();   /* addr of previous
                                          handler */
     unsigned OldAction;             /* previous action */
     unsigned rc;                    /* return code */

     printf("\nChild received Flag A: ");
     printf("arg=%u, signum=%u\n", arg, signum);
```

(continued)

```
                              /* reset current signal */
     if( rc=DosSetSigHandler( (void(pascal far *)())0L,
                     &OldAddr,&OldAction, RESET, FLAGA ) )
       { printf("DosSetSigHandler error=%u", rc); exit(1); }
     return;
}
```

The parent also passes an argument to the child using the signal handler as a vehicle. The argument is included in the last argument of DosFlagProcess() function in the parent process, and received as an argument to the handler function in the child process. In this case the argument is always 99. Here's an example of the interchange between processes:

```
Child running...Child running...Child running...Child running...
Child running...Child running...Child running...Child running...
Child running...Child running...
Parent signalling child with Flag A
Child received Flag A: arg=99, signum=5
Child running...Child running...Child running...Child running...
Child running...Child running...Child running...Child running...
Child running...Child running...
Parent signalling child with Flag A
Child received Flag A: arg=99, signum=5
Child running...Child running...Child running...Child running...
```

Since DosSetSigHandler() is not set up to look for the SIG_CTRLC signal, the [Ctrl] [c] key combination can be used in the normal way to terminate the program.

The DosFlagProcess() Function

The DosFlagProcess() function exists solely to set flag signals in other processes.

DosFlagProcess — Send flag signal to another process

```
DosFlagProcess(ProcessID, Action, FlagNum, Argument);
unsigned ProcessID;   /* ID of process to send flag signal
                         to */
unsigned Action;      /* 0=Entire subtree, 1=process only */
unsigned FlagNum;     /* 0=Flag A, 1=Flag B, 2=Flag C */
unsigned Argument;    /* meaning agreed on by processes */
```

The first argument in DosFlagProcess() is the ID of the process the signal is to be sent to. The second argument specifies whether this ID applies only to the indicated process, or to the entire subtree of processes generated by the indicated process. The third parameter indicates which of the three flag signals (A, B, or C) is to be sent, and the final argument can be used to communicate a one word value from the signaller process to the signalee. This value can have any meaning that both processes can agree on.

The DosHoldSignal() Function

If a process is executing a time-sensitive or otherwise critical section of code, it may be necessary to ensure that a signal does not interrupt the process in this section of code. One way to do this is with the function DosHoldSignal(). This function can be used to either enable or disable signal handling.

DosHoldSignal — Find current disk drive

```
DosHoldSignal(Action);
unsigned Action;            /* 0=enable signals, 1=disable  */
```

This function takes only one argument, a word that indicates whether signals are to be enabled or disabled. A signal occurring while signals are disabled will be recognized and acted on in the usual way once signals are again enabled.

Summary

In this chapter we first showed how device monitors can be used to give OS/2 applications the capabilities of TSRs in MS-DOS. We saw how a handle to a device is obtained with DosMonOpen(), and how special system I/O buffers for the monitor are registered with DosMonReg(). Once this initialization has taken place, device monitor applications typically wait in a loop, reading data packets with DosMonRead(), and writing them with DosMonWrite().

We examined the structure of keyboard data packets, and saw how monitors can pass these packets along unchanged, consume them, or generate new packets to send along the monitor chain. We also found how an application can examine and interact with the screen contents of the foreground process.

The second topic of this chapter was signals. Signals are generated by such key combinations as [Ctrl] [c], or can be generated by one process as a way of communicating urgent information to another process. We saw how a process can install a signal handler using DosSetSigHandler(), and how this same function can be used to perform other tasks such as resetting signals or causing them to be ignored. The DosFlagProcess() function is used to generate flag signals, which are sent from one process to another. The DosHold-Signal() function is used to disable signals altogether in critical parts of the program, and also to re-enable them.

THE MOUSE
AND GRAPHICS

Chapter 13

This chapter covers two rather disparate topics: the mouse, and direct access to the display memory. While not directly related, both topics deal with enhancing the user interface by augmenting the capabilities of the screen. Another similarity is that neither the mouse nor direct screen access will be required by all programmers. The mouse is not installed on some systems, and for reasons we'll discuss, direct access to the display may not be necessary in many applications. However, the mouse is becoming more popular, and direct access to the screen memory is the simplest way to solve many programming problems, so both topics are important in a discussion of OS/2.

The Mouse

A mouse enables the user to input positional information faster and more conveniently than is possible with the cursor keys. The motion of the mouse is connected, via software, to a pointer on the screen, so that moving the mouse moves the pointer. Buttons on the mouse can be used to signal an application when the pointer is aligned with a particular word or other screen element. For instance, if the user moves the mouse pointer to the word "Quit" on the screen and clicks a mouse button, the software may infer that it should terminate itself.

In this section we'll see how the OS/2 API functions can be used to connect the mouse to the pointer, find out where the pointer is located on the screen, learn the state of the mouse buttons, and perform other mouse-related tasks.

Mouse Preliminaries

In order to use the mouse, two device drivers must be installed in the system, and pathnames to these drivers must be included in the CONFIG.SYS file.

There are probably several mouse drivers included on your system disk. The one that is appropriate depends on which mouse you're using—bus or serial—and who manufactured it. On our system, which uses a Microsoft bus mouse, the appropriate driver is called MOUSEA04.SYS. (This driver is alleged to be for the Inport mouse, but turns out to be necessary for our bus mouse.)

Another separate device driver is necessary for the mouse pointer. On our system this driver is called POINTDD.SYS. The CONFIG.SYS file should contain lines similar to these:

```
device=c:\os2\mouse04.sys
device=c:\os2\pointdd.sys
```

When you boot your system you should see messages verifying that these drivers were successfully installed.

Mouse Basics

The functions that control the mouse are all part of the MOU subsystem: that is, a group of functions in a DLL library, like the VIO sybsystem. The mouse functions all start with the letters "Mou". Like the VIO functions, the MOU functions can be replaced with a different library of functions if desired. The Presentation Manager installs such an alternate library, which supports the API functions as before, but is tailored to work in the new environment.

The mouse can be used in either character mode, where it points to the row and column of a particular character; or in graphics mode, where it points to individual pixels. We'll concentrate on character mode applications in this chapter.

There are three essential steps in writing a program to control the mouse. First the mouse must be "opened": that is, a handle must be obtained for the mouse device. The API function MouOpen() does this. Second, assuming a system mouse pointer will be used, the pointer must be made visible; this is done with MouDrawPtr(). (This step may not be necessary in some systems.)

Finally, information about the mouse must be obtained by the application. There are several functions that do this, but the most comprehensive one is MouReadEventQue(). This function reports whether the mouse buttons have been pressed, and where the mouse is. An application (or one thread of a multithreaded application) typically sits in a loop, querying MouReadEventQue() and taking appropriate action, depending on the input from the mouse. Figure 13-1 shows these actions as a flowchart.

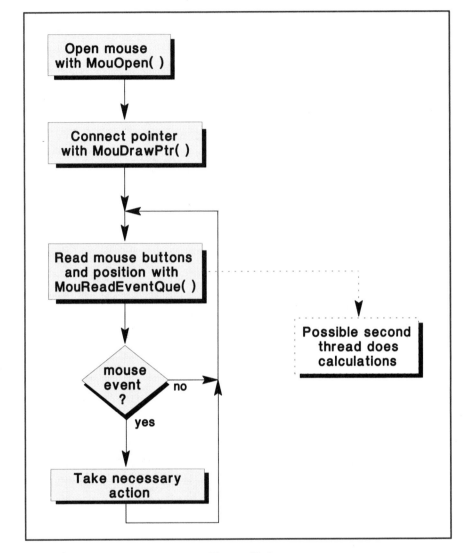

Figure 13-1
Flowchart of Mouse Operation

Let's look at a simple program that incorporates these API functions. This example simply connects the pointer to the mouse, so that the user can control the position of the pointer by moving the mouse. The only mouse event that the program looks for is the pressing of mouse button number 2. This is the right-hand button on a two-button mouse. (We'll assume a two-button mouse is being used in these examples; if you're using a three-button mouse, translate the

references to the right-hand button to mean the middle button.)
When the right-hand button is pressed, the program exits.

```c
/* event.c */
/* read event queue, move mouse pointer .*/
#define INCL_SUB
#include <os2.h>
#define BUTTON2    0x10              /* bit 4: button 2 down */

char Blank[2] = { 0x20, 0x07 };  /* space, normal attribute
                                    */
                                 /* to clear screen */
main()
{
   unsigned short MouHandle;     /* mouse handle */
   struct _MOUEVENTINFO Event;   /* mouse event info */
   unsigned ReadType = 1;        /* 0=no wait, 1=wait */
   unsigned rc;                  /* return code */
                                 /* clear screen */
   VioScrollUp( 0, 0, -1, -1, -1, Blank, 0 );

                                 /* get mouse handle */
   if( rc=MouOpen( 0L, &MouHandle ) )
     { printf("MouOpen error=%u",rc); exit(1); }

                                 /* draw standard pointer */
   if( rc=MouDrawPtr( MouHandle ) )
     { printf("MouDrawPtr error=%u",rc); exit(1); }

   while( TRUE )  {              /* wait for mouse events */

     if( rc=MouReadEventQue( &Event, &ReadType,
                                           MouHandle ) )
        { printf("MouReadEventQue error=%u",rc); exit(1); }

                         /* if right button pressed, exit */
     if( Event.fs & BUTTON2 )
        break;
   }
   MouClose( MouHandle );
   exit(0);
}
```

When executed, this program first clears the screen, and then
displays the default mouse pointer, which is a character-size block in
reverse video. Moving the mouse will cause the pointer to move. The

left mouse button will have no effect, but the right-hand one will
cause the program to terminate.

The MouOpen() Function: The MouOpen() function takes two
arguments. The first is the name of the device driver that draws the
mouse pointer. If you are using the default driver, which is ordinarily the case, this argument takes the value 0.

MouOpen — Open mouse, get handle

```
MouOpen(DriverName, AMouHandle);
char far *DriverName;         /* ASCIIZ pointer driver name */
unsigned short far *AMouHandle;  /* address for mouse
                                      handle */
```

The second argument to MouOpen() is an address where the
handle to the mouse will be returned. The handle returned from
MouOpen() is used as an input parameter to most of the other mouse
functions.

The MouDrawPtr() Function: The mouse pointer is not visible
directly after a MouOpen(). This is because the entire screen is
defined as a restricted area: one in which the pointer is hidden. To
make it visible the function MouDrawPtr() must be used.

MouDrawPtr — Make mouse pointer visible

```
MouDrawPtr(MouHandle);
unsigned short MouHandle;    /* mouse handle */
```

The only argument to MouDrawPtr() is the handle to the mouse.

MouDrawPtr() can also be used to restore the visibility of the
mouse pointer in an area where it has been hidden with MouRe-
movePtr(), a function we'll examine later.

The MouReadEventQue() Function: Central to the operation
of the mouse is finding out where it is and which of its buttons are
being pushed. The MouReadEventQue() function performs this role.

MouReadEventQue — Read data from mouse event queue

```
MouDrawPtr(ABuffer, AReadType, MouHandle);
struct _MOUEVENTINFO far *ABuffer; /* address for info
                                        buffer */
unsigned far *AReadType;    /* address for wait/no wait */
unsigned short MouHandle;   /* mouse handle */
```

This function takes three arguments. The first is the address of a structure where information about the mouse will be returned. This structure is defined in BSESUB.H as:

```
struct _MOUEVENTINFO  {
    unsigned fs;            /* event mask status word */
    unsigned long Time;     /* time in milliseconds */
    unsigned row;           /* row where mouse is located */
    unsigned col;           /* column where mouse is located */
}
```

The **fs** or "event mask" member of the **_MOUEVENTINFO** structure is divided into bitfields, as shown in Figure 13-2.

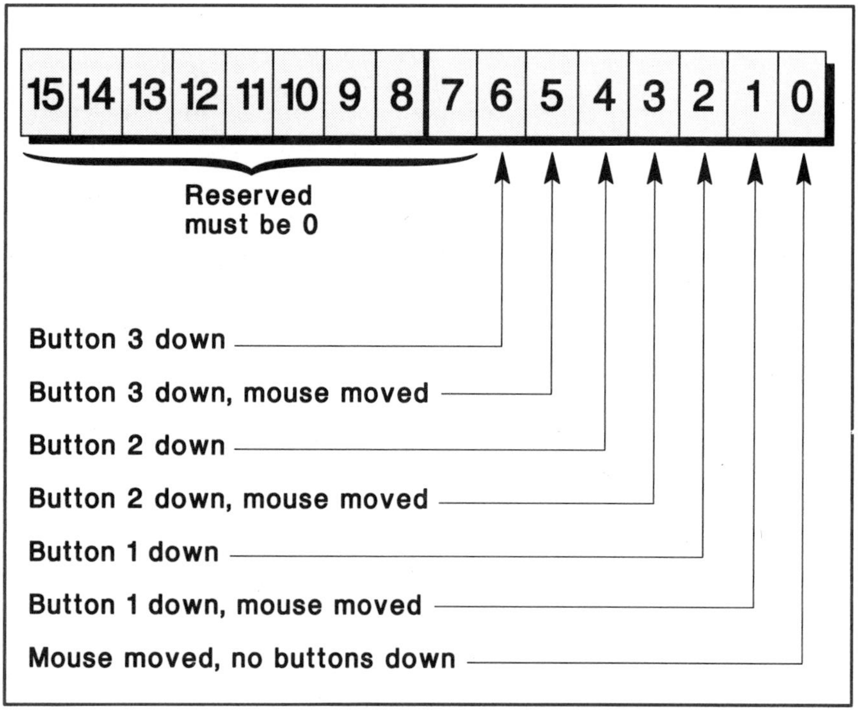

Figure 13-2
Mouse Event Mask Word

From the appropriate bitfield we can learn if the mouse has moved, and if any buttons are being pressed.

The **Time** member of the structure returns the time, in milliseconds, when the mouse event occurred. The **row** and **col** members return the location of the mouse. In the coordinate system used, the upper left-hand corner of the screen has coordinates 0, 0.

The second argument to MouReadEventQue() is called the **ReadType**. This argument is set by the application to specify whether the function should wait if no mouse event has taken place, or whether it should immediately return to the program. A value of 1 indicates wait, while 0 indicates no-wait. In our examples we will wait on this function, but if a particular thread needed to do other processing while there were no mouse events taking place, it could use the no-wait option.

The final argument to DosReadEventQue() is the mouse handle, originally obtained from MouOpen().

In the event.c example, the program sits in a **while** loop, repeatedly executing MouReadEventQue(). If there is no mouse event (if none of the buttons have been pushed and the mouse has not moved), the function will block. As soon as a mouse event takes place, the function unblocks and fills in the event structure. The program makes use of only one bit in this structure: bit 4 of the **fs** member. This bit is set if mouse button 2 (the right-hand button) is pressed and the mouse has not moved. If we wanted to ensure that we learned immediately that the button had been pressed, even if the mouse was moving, we would need to also query bit 3.

Various other functions can perform some of the data-gathering operations of MouReadEventQue(). For instance, MouGetPtrPos() can be used to determine the location of the pointer, and MouGetEventMask() obtains the event mask. These specialized functions might be more efficient when speed is important.

The MouClose() Function: When we want to stop using the mouse and remove the mouse pointer from the screen, we can execute the MouClose() function, which closes the mouse device.

MouClose — Close mouse device driver

```
MouClose(MouHandle);
unsigned short MouHandle;    /* mouse handle */
```

This function takes only one argument: the mouse handle. It is not really necessary to execute it at the end of a program, since the system will close the mouse when the program terminates. A program could use it at any point, however, to remove the mouse pointer.

Some Bells and Whistles

The event.c program is a bare bones example of mouse operation. The next example includes several embellishments. First, you may have noticed that in event.c the cursor (not to be confused with the mouse pointer) remains in view, blinking on and off. In many mouse applications this is undesirable, so we'll include code to make the cursor invisible. When we do this we must also be careful to restore the original cursor at the end of the program, since the system does not do this for us.

Second, we'll place a box, consisting of solid rectangles in reverse video, on the screen. One of the capabilities built into the standard mouse pointer is the ability to change its attribute, depending on what background it's on. On a black background the pointer consists of a white block, while on a white background it turns black, so it is always visible (the reverse of a chameleon). By drawing a white box on the screen we can demonstrate this capability. We'll also draw a line of text to demonstrate the interaction of the pointer with characters.

Third, it is sometimes important to specify the initial pointer position. In event.c we let the system specify the initial pointer position, which turned out to be the center of the screen. In the next example we'll specify a different initial position, using the MouSetPtr() API function.

```
/* event2.c */
/* read event queue, move mouse pointer */
/* clears and restores cursor */
#define INCL_DOS
#define INCL_SUB
#include <os2.h>
#define BUTTON2   0x10        /* bit 4: button 2 down */
#define UPPER     0          /* upper row of box */
#define LOWER     10         /* lower row of box */
#define LEFT      0          /* left column of box */
#define RIGHT     20         /* right column of box */

char string[] = "Test Test Test";

char Blank[2] = { 0x20, 0x07 };  /* space, normal
                                    attribute */
                                 /* to clear screen */
char Fill[2] =  { 0x20, 0x70 };  /* space, reverse
                                    attribute */
```

(continued)

```
main()
{
    unsigned short MouHandle;        /* mouse handle */
    struct _PTRLOC MouPos;           /* mouse position */
    struct _MOUEVENTINFO Event;      /* mouse event info */
    struct _VIOCURSORINFO OldCur;    /* old cursor */
    struct _VIOCURSORINFO Cursor;    /* new cursor */
    unsigned ReadType = 1;           /* 0=no wait, 1=wait */
    unsigned row;                    /* row index of filled box */
    unsigned rc;                     /* return code */
                                     /* clear screen */
    VioScrollUp( 0, 0, -1, -1, -1, Blank, 0 );

                            /* save old cursor */
    VioGetCurType( &OldCur, 0 );
    Cursor.yStart = 0;     /* make */
    Cursor.cEnd = 0;       /* the current */
    Cursor.cx = 1;         /* cursor */
    Cursor.attr = -1;      /* invisible */
    VioSetCurType( &Cursor, 0 );
                            /* get mouse handle */
    if( rc=MouOpen( 0L, &MouHandle ) )
       { printf("MouOpen error=%u",rc); exit(1); }

    MouPos.col = 40;       /* set cursor position */
    MouPos.row = 5;
    if( rc=MouSetPtrPos( &MouPos, MouHandle ) )
       { printf("MouSetPtrPos error=%u",rc); exit(1); }

                            /* draw standard pointer */
    if( rc=MouDrawPtr( MouHandle ) )
       { printf("MouDrawPtr error=%u",rc); exit(1); }

                            /* fill box with reverse video */
    for( row=UPPER; row<=LOWER; row++ )
       VioWrtNCell( Fill, RIGHT-LEFT+1, row, LEFT, 0 );
                            /* print some text */
    VioWrtCharStr( string, sizeof(string), LOWER+1, LEFT,
                                                        0 );

    while( TRUE )  {       /* wait for mouse events */

       if( rc=MouReadEventQue( &Event, &ReadType,
                                            MouHandle ) )
          { printf("MouReadEventQue error=%u",rc); exit(1); }

                            /* if right button pressed, exit */
       if( Event.fs & BUTTON2 )
          break;
    }
```

(continued)

```
MouClose( MouHandle );          /* close mouse handle */
VioSetCurType( &OldCur, 0 );    /* restore old cursor */
exit(0);
}
```

When you run this program you'll see a white box in the upper left-hand corner of the screen. Move the mouse pointer into the box; you'll see the pointer turn from white to black. Move it into the text; the text character under the pointer will appear in reverse video. The pointer automatically makes itself visible against any background. The output of the program, with the mouse pointer in the white box, is shown in Figure 13-3.

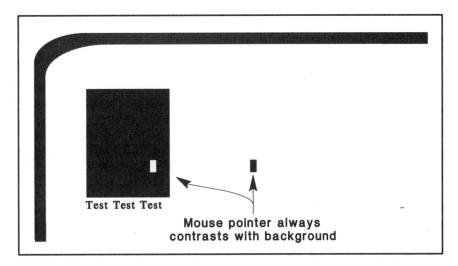

Test Test Test

Mouse pointer always
contrasts with background

Figure 13-3
Output of event2.c

The MouSetPtrPos() Function: You'll also see that the pointer starts out close to the top of the screen, rather than in the center. This is effected by the MouSetPtrPos() function.

MouSetPtrPos — Set mouse pointer position

```
MouSetPtrPos(ABuffer, MouHandle);
struct _PTRLOC far *ABuffer;   /* address of location buffer
                                  */
unsigned short MouHandle;      /* mouse handle */
```

The first argument to this function is a structure in which the coordinates of the mouse pointer can be placed. The structure is defined in BSESUB.H as:

```
struct _PTRLOC  {
    unsigned row;
    unsigned col;
}
```

As with the data returned by MouReadEventQue(), the coordinate system assumes the upper left-hand corner of the screen is 0, 0.

The second argument to MouSetPtrPos() is the usual mouse handle, obtained from MouOpen().

Hiding the Cursor: The cursor is removed from the event2.c program using the VioSetCurType() function, with the **attr** member of the **_VIOCURSORINFO** structure set to -1. Before doing this, however, the data for the original cursor is saved using VioGetCurType(). Then, at the end of the program, the old cursor is restored using Vio-SetCurType() again.

Hiding the Mouse Pointer

In some applications there may be regions of the screen in which the mouse pointer should not appear. Suppose, for example, that an application places boxes on the screen to hold warning messages. It might be inappropriate for the pointer to enter these boxes.

To hide the pointer in specific regions of the screen we can use the function MouRemovePtr(). The next example places a white (reverse video) box on the screen, and then uses this function to keep the mouse pointer from appearing anywhere within the box.

```
/* remove.c */
/* remove mouse pointer from area of screen */
#define INCL_DOS
#define INCL_SUB
#include <os2.h>
#define BUTTON2   0x10      /* bit 4: button 2 down */
#define UPPER     5         /* upper row of collision area */
#define LEFT      20        /* left col of collision area */
#define LOWER     15        /* lower row of collision area */
#define RIGHT     60        /* right col of collision area */
```

(continued)

```
char Blank[2] = { 0x20, 0x07 };    /* space, normal attribute
                                      */
                                   /*   to clear screen */
char Fill[2]  = { 0x20, 0x70 };    /* space, reverse
                                      attribute */
main()
{
    unsigned short MouHandle;        /* mouse handle */
    struct _PTRLOC MouPos;           /* mouse position */
    struct _MOUEVENTINFO Event;      /* mouse event info */
    struct _VIOCURSORINFO OldCur;    /* old cursor */
    struct _VIOCURSORINFO Cursor;    /* new cursor */
    struct _NOPTRRECT NoPtr;         /* remove pointer area */
    unsigned ReadType = 1;           /* 0=no wait, 1=wait */
    unsigned row;                    /* row for filling area */
    unsigned rc;                     /* return code */

                            /* clear screen */
    VioScrollUp( 0, 0, -1, -1, -1, Blank, 0 );

    VioGetCurType( &OldCur, 0 );   /* save old cursor */
    Cursor.yStart = 0;             /* make */
    Cursor.cEnd = 0;               /* the */
    Cursor.cx = 1;                 /* current */
    Cursor.attr = -1;              /* cursor */
    VioSetCurType( &Cursor, 0 );   /* invisible  */

                        /* get mouse handle */
    if( rc=MouOpen( 0L, &MouHandle ) )
       { printf("MouOpen error=%u",rc); exit(1); }

    MouPos.col  = 10;       /* set initial pointer position */
    MouPos.row = 10;
    if( rc=MouSetPtrPos( &MouPos, MouHandle ) )
       { printf("MouSetPtrPos error=%u",rc); exit(1); }

                        /* draw standard pointer */
    if( rc=MouDrawPtr( MouHandle ) )
       { printf("MouDrawPtr error=%u",rc); exit(1); }

                        /* draw collision area */
    for( row=UPPER; row<=LOWER; row++ )
       VioWrtNCell( Fill, RIGHT-LEFT+1, row, LEFT, 0 );
```

(continued)

```
NoPtr.row =      UPPER;  /* set collision area */
NoPtr.col =      LEFT;
NoPtr.cRow =     LOWER;
NoPtr.cCol =     RIGHT;
if( rc=MouRemovePtr( &NoPtr, MouHandle ) )
    { printf("MouRemovePtr error=%u",rc); exit(1); }

while( TRUE )   {        /* wait for mouse events */

   if( rc=MouReadEventQue( &Event, &ReadType,
                                        MouHandle ) )
       { printf("MouReadEventQue error=%u",rc); exit(1); }

                        /* if right button pressed, exit */
   if( Event.fs & BUTTON2 )
      break;
}
MouClose( MouHandle );        /* close mouse handle */
VioSetCurType( &OldCur, 0 );  /* restore old cursor */
exit(0);
}
```

When this program is executed, a large white box appears in the center of the screen. The pointer can be moved to the edges of the box, but not within it. The effect is of the pointer passing behind the box, as if the box hid it from view.

The remove.c program is similar to the previous event.2 example. The reverse video box is drawn using the VioWrtNCell() function, and the "collision area" (the region in which the pointer will be hidden) is set using the MouRemovePtr() function. Note that there is no logical connection between the box and the collision area; we must be careful in the program to ensure that their boundaries coincide.

The MouRemovePtr() Function: This function takes only two arguments.

MouRemovePtr — Remove pointer from screen area

```
MouRemovePtr(ABuffer, MouHandle);
struct _NOPTRRECT far *ABuffer;  /* address of buffer */
unsigned short MouHandle;        /* mouse handle */
```

The first argument is the address of a structure in which the coordinates of the collision area are placed. The structure, defined in BSESUB.H, looks like this:

```
struct _NOPTRRECT   {
   unsigned row;          /* top row of collision area */
   unsigned col;          /* left column of collision area */
   unsigned cRow;         /* bottom row of collision area */
   unsigned cCol;         /* right column of collision area */
};
```

The first and second members of this structure are the top row and left column of the collision area, while the third and forth members are the bottom row and right-hand column.

Better names for the elements of this structure would be upper, left, bottom, and right.

The application places appropriate values in the structure, and then calls MouRemovePtr() to define the rectangle as a collision area.

As we noted earlier, the MouDrawPtr() function can be used to restore a collision area to its normal state. Only one collision area can be in effect at any one time: that defined by the last call to MouRemovePtr().

Custom Mouse Pointers

You can attach the mouse to other objects on the screen besides the default mouse pointer. This is useful if you want to use a different kind of pointer, or if you need closer control over the pointer than that provided by the driver installed with the system.

As an example, here's a program that uses the Greek letter Omega (Ω) for a pointer. This is the simplest sort of custom pointer, since only one character need be drawn. However, multiple characters could also be used, thus increasing the size and complexity of the pointer.

To use a custom pointer we first ensure that the standard system pointer does not appear. This can be done either with MouRemovePtr(), using a collision area the size of the entire screen, or by simply not turning on the pointer with MouDrawPtr(). We use the second approach in the example.

Now that we're responsible for the pointer, we need to keep track of where the mouse is, and redraw the pointer whenever the mouse moves. Also, we need to save the background character the pointer is hiding, and restore the character when the pointer moves to another location.

As in previous examples, we use a loop in which we repeatedly execute MouReadEventQue(). Whenever the mouse has moved, indicated by bit 0 of the event mask, we restore the previously-saved character under the old position of the pointer, save the new location of the pointer, and finally draw the pointer in the new location.

```
/* pointer.c */
/* substitutes self-generated pointer for standard one */
#define INCL_DOS
#define INCL_SUB
#include <os2.h>
#define BUTTON2  0x10        /* bit 4: button 2 down */
#define MOVED    1           /* bit 0: mouse moved */
#define UPPER    0           /* upper row of box */
#define LOWER    10          /* lower row of box */
#define LEFT     0           /* left column of box */
#define RIGHT    20          /* right column of box */

char string[] = "Test Test Test";
char Blank[2] = { 0x20, 0x07 };  /* space, normal attribute
                                    */
char Fill[2] =  { 0x20, 0x70 };  /* space, reverse attribute
                                    */
char NuPtr[2] = { 0xE9, 0x07 };  /* omega, normal attribute
                                    */
char OldChar[2];                 /* old background char */

main()
{
   unsigned short MouHandle;    /* mouse handle */
   struct _MOUEVENTINFO Event;  /* mouse event info */
   unsigned ReadType = 1;       /* 0=no wait, 1=wait */
   unsigned row;                /* row index of filled box */
   unsigned OldRow;             /* old pointer row */
   unsigned OldCol;             /* old pointer column */
   unsigned len = 2;            /* cell string length */

                                /* clear screen */
   VioScrollUp( 0, 0, -1, -1, -1, Blank, 0 );

   MouOpen( 0L, &MouHandle );   /* get mouse handle */

                                /* fill box with reverse video */
   for( row=UPPER; row<=LOWER; row++ )
      VioWrtNCell( Fill, RIGHT-LEFT+1, row, LEFT, 0 );
                                /* print some text */
   VioWrtCharStr( string, sizeof(string), LOWER+1, LEFT,
                                                        0 );

   OldCol = 40;                 /* start pointer in center */
   OldRow = 12;

   while( TRUE )  {             /* wait for mouse events */

      MouReadEventQue( &Event, &ReadType, MouHandle );
```

```
                              /* if mouse has moved, */
        if( Event.fs & MOVED )   {
                              /* restore background character */
            VioWrtCellStr( OldChar, 2, OldRow, OldCol, 0 );
            OldRow = Event.row;   /* save new location */
            OldCol = Event.col;
                              /* save char in new location */
            VioReadCellStr(OldChar, &len, Event.row, Event.col,
                                                             0);
                              /* draw pointer in new location */
            VioWrtCellStr( NuPtr, 2, Event.row, Event.col, 0 );
        }
                              /* if right button pressed, exit */
        if( Event.fs & BUTTON2 )
            break;
    }
    MouClose( MouHandle );      /* close mouse handle */
    exit(0);
}
```

When you execute this program you'll see the letter omega appear instead of the standard pointer. Although it does not change its attribute depending on the background, as the standard pointer does, the omega is always visible, since it appears as a white character when it's on a black background, and as a white character in a black character-size box when it's on a white background.

It's almost as easy to draw more than one character, so your custom pointer can be as complex as you desire: it might be a spaceship, for example, or a human figure, or a running horse. By contrast, the standard pointer is always a single character.

A Drop-down Menu Example

Let's look at an example in which the mouse is used to operate a drop-down menu. This is an increasingly popular approach to creating a user interface. Typically a group of menu titles are displayed across the top of the screen. By moving the mouse pointer to one of them and pressing a button, a menu with a number of items "drops down" from the title. These items represent actions to be carried out (such as printing or saving a file) or options to be set (switching between ASCII or binary formats). The mouse can then be used to select one of the menu items.

The Presentation Manager has its own drop-down menu facility, but you may not want to use it, or you may be running in a system without the Presentation Manager.

This example first places a one word menu title at the top of the screen; in this case the word "MENU". A real application would have many different menus, but one will serve for a demonstration. When the mouse pointer is moved to the menu title, the title reflects this by changing to reverse video, or being "highlighted."

If the pointer is on the menu title and at the same time the user presses the left-hand mouse button, the menu will "drop down": that is, a list of options will be displayed under the menu title. If the pointer is now moved down this list, each item in turn will be highlighted. The user can execute one of the choices on the list by releasing the mouse button while the corresponding selection is highlighted.

In our example program there are four selections: "Print", which causes a word to be printed halfway down the screen, "Clear", which causes this word to be erased, "Beep", which sounds a tone on the speaker, and "Quit", which terminates the program. (Pressing the right-hand button has no effect in this example.)

```c
/* menu.c */
/* generates pull-down menu */
#define INCL_DOS
#define INCL_SUB
#include <os2.h>
#define BUTTON1_MOVE 0x02 /* bit 1: 1 down and cur moving */
#define BUTTON1      0x04 /* bit 2: button 1 down */
char Blank[2] = { 0x20, 0x07 };  /* space, normal attribute
                                     */
main()
{
    unsigned short MouHandle;   /* mouse handle */
    struct _MOUEVENTINFO Event;    /* mouse event info */
    unsigned ReadType = 1;      /* 0=no wait, 1=wait */
    unsigned row;               /* row index */
    unsigned char norm = 0x07; /* normal video attribute */
    unsigned char revr = 0x70; /* reverse video attribute */

                                /* clear screen */
    VioScrollUp( 0, 0, -1, -1, -1, Blank, 0 );

    MouOpen( 0L, &MouHandle ); /* get mouse handle */
    MouDrawPtr( MouHandle );   /* draw standard pointer */

                                /* print "MENU", normal attr  */
    VioWrtCharStrAtt( "MENU", 4, 0, 0, &norm, 0 );

    while( TRUE )  {
                                /* wait for mouse events */
        MouReadEventQue( &Event, &ReadType, MouHandle );
```

(continued)

```
                              /* if ptr on "MENU" */
   if( Event.col<4 && Event.row==0 )  {
                              /* hi-lite "MENU" */
      VioWrtCharStrAtt( "MENU", 4, 0, 0, &revr, 0 );
                              /* if left button down */
      if( Event.fs & BUTTON1 )  {
                              /* enter menu-item loop */

         do  {                /* read event queue again */
            MouReadEventQue( &Event, &ReadType,
                                           MouHandle );

                              /* hi-lite item pointed to */
            if( Event.row==1)
              VioWrtCharStrAtt( "Print", 5, 1, 0, &revr,
                                                 0 );
            else
              VioWrtCharStrAtt( "Print", 5, 1, 0, &norm,
                                                 0 );
            if( Event.row==2)
              VioWrtCharStrAtt( "Beep", 4, 2, 0, &revr,
                                                 0 );
            else
              VioWrtCharStrAtt( "Beep", 4, 2, 0, &norm,
                                                 0 );
            if( Event.row==3)
              VioWrtCharStrAtt( "Clear", 5, 3, 0, &revr,
                                                 0 );
            else
              VioWrtCharStrAtt( "Clear", 5, 3, 0, &norm,
                                                 0 );
            if( Event.row==4)
               VioWrtCharStrAtt( "Quit", 4, 4, 0, &revr,
                                                 0 );
            else
              VioWrtCharStrAtt( "Quit", 4, 4, 0, &norm,
                                                 0 );

                              /* end loop when button released */
         } while( Event.fs & BUTTON1 ||
                 Event.fs & BUTTON1_MOVE );
                              /* clear menu items */
         for( row=1; row<6; row++)
           VioWrtNCell( Blank, 5, row, 0, 0 );
```

(continued)

```
                              /* take action if ptr on item */
            switch( Event.row )  {
               case( 1 ):    /* print at row 12 */
                  VioWrtCharStr( "MESSAGE", 7, 12, 0, 0 );
                  break;
               case( 2 ):    /* beep the speaker */
                  DosBeep( 100, 500 );
                  break;
               case( 3 ):    /* clear row 12 */
                  VioWrtNCell( Blank, 7, 12, 0, 0 );
                  break;
               case( 4 ):    /* exit */
                  exit(0);
            }  /* end switch */
         }  /* end 2nd if */
      }  /* end 1st if */
      else
                              /* print "MENU", normal attr  */
         VioWrtCharStrAtt( "MENU", 4, 0, 0, &norm, 0 );
   }  /* end while(1) */

   MouClose( MouHandle );    /* close mouse handle */
   exit(0);
}
```

The program uses the usual loop in which MouReadEventQue()
is repeatedly executed. If the pointer is on the menu title, the title is
highlighted. If the pointer is on the title, and at the same time the left-
hand mouse button is pressed, the program drops into an inner **do**
loop in which all the menu items are displayed, and individual items
are highlighted when the pointer is placed on them. When the mouse
button is released, the action indicated by the highlighted item is
carried out, using the **switch** statement.

This program is clearly not a full-featured application, but it
does give some idea how easy it is to create a menu-driven user interface. In a more serious program there would be more menus, which
would (presumably) cause more meaningful actions to occur. Also,
borders could be drawn around the menus, and color could be used,
to make the display more attractive in color systems.

Mouse Moving and Not Moving: In menu.c we check for two
conditions in the MouReadEventQue() loop: whether button 1 is
pressed and the mouse is *not* moving, and whether button 1 is
pressed and the mouse *is* moving. Assuming that the button is
pressed, one of these conditions will always be true (but never both at
once). However, if we checked only if the button was pressed and the
mouse was not moving (bit 2), then when the mouse was moving, a

considerable time might elapse before the button-press was recognized by the program. Thus for a system to have the fastest response, both conditions must be monitored.

Mouse Glitch: On our version of OS/2, the mouse pointer suffers from an annoying bug which is revealed in the menu.c program. Suppose the pointer is sitting on a line of text, and that line is erased. The text vanishes, but when the mouse pointer is moved, the character it was hiding reappears; rising from the dead, as it were. In the example, once a menu selection is made, the menu is erased, but the one character that was under the pointer remains.

Hopefully this problem will be corrected on future versions of OS/2. If not, it will be necessary to record the mouse position, and take special action to erase the character under it as soon as it moves.

Separate Thread for the Mouse

It is often useful to create a separate thread of execution dedicated to the mouse. This thread can sit in a loop, monitoring MouReadEvent-Que(), as our examples have done. At the same time, other threads can perform other actions, such as disk access or computation; perhaps carrying out the actions chosen by the user from a menu. In this way the user enjoys a continuous fast response from the mouse, while other parts of the program are not delayed waiting for user input. This is the way the mouse is most commonly used.

Graphics

In MS-DOS most applications—especially those using graphics—find it necessary to bypass the DOS and BIOS video functions, and instead access the screen by writing directly into the display memory. This approach is much faster and offers greater flexibility than going through the MS-DOS system functions. What is the situation with regard to graphics and direct memory access in OS/2?

Remember that, as far as the video display is concerned, OS/2 is really two different systems. First there is the VIO subsystem, which is part of the OS/2 kernel, and which we have been using throughout this book. Second, there is the Presentation Manager.

The Presentation Manager offers the functions to create a complete graphics-based user interface, with drop-down menus, windows, scroll bars, and other niceties. Applications that make use of the Presentation Manager functions can draw text—and graphics—that will appear in a window on the Presentation Manager desktop. These windows can be moved and resized while the application is running. Also, by using these functions and following the appropriate guidelines, applications can employ a consistent user interface that will be easy for users to learn. Thus it is probably the case that most major graphics-oriented applications will be written to run under the Presentation Manager.

However, while Presentation Manager programming provides a rich vocabulary of functions, it is also not easy to learn, and requires considerable program overhead. Many shorter programs may not require a full-scale Presentation Manager treatment, and can be more quickly and conveniently coded to run with the VIO functions. Also, in many cases it is far easier to adapt an existing MS-DOS text-based program to work under VIO than under the Presentation Manager. So the question is, Is it possible to directly access the video memory, using only the OS/2 kernel?

The answer is yes, it is possible for an application, using VIO kernel functions, to directly address the video memory, and to draw graphics images directly to the screen.

There are two levels of direct video access: programs can write to the *logical buffer* or to the *physical buffer*. We'll look at these situations in turn.

Writing to the Logical Video Buffer

Assume that a particular character application is running, and that, without stopping it, the user switches to the session manager, or toggles directly to a program in another session. What happens to the screen image that was generated by the original application? As you have no doubt noticed, whenever you switch back to a session, that session's screen display is restored to its former condition. The system has saved it in something called the Logical Video Buffer (LVB). There is an LVB for each session, so each time you switch out of a session, its LVB is saved, and each time you switch back again, its LVB is written back to the display. In effect a number of displays all exist at the same time, but only the one belonging to the foreground program is actually visible. This works relatively seamlessly, and is essential to providing the user with a feeling of continuity when switching among programs in a multitasking system.

There is, however, a limitation: the LVB can be used only for character-mode displays, not for graphics. Why is this? Primarily the problem is one of memory space. A graphics display requires many more bytes than does a character display. Even a low-resolution CGA display can use 16K, EGA can use 256K, and VGA and other displays even more. If many programs are running simultaneously, and each requires a large buffer for its LVB, several megabytes might be necessary for the LVBs alone, leaving little room for the applications themselves. Thus the designers of OS/2 decided to restrict each LVB to character mode, which requires only a 4K buffer.

Applications can write directly to the LVB. This can provide a faster way to draw complex character images than is possible with the VIO functions, especially if a large area is to be filled in all at once. (Writing a single word or line of text is more easily handled with the ordinary VIO calls.)

Accessing the LVB: There are three steps necessary for an application to access the LVB. First it must learn where the buffer is. This is done using the VioGetBuff() function, which returns a pointer to the start of the LVB. Next, using this pointer, the application can write whatever characters it wants to the LVB. These characters do not become visible immediately, because the LVB is not the same thing as the physical screen. To transfer the contents of the LVB to the physical screen buffer, another API function must be employed: VioShowBuff(). As soon as this function is executed, whatever was previously written to the LVB is transferred to the physical screen and immediately becomes visible. This can be an effective tool for creating displays: an application can spend as long as it wants to create a complex display on the LVB; the slow process of generation will not be visible to the viewer. Then the image can be made to appear all at once with VioShowBuff().

Here's a program that uses direct access to the LVB to write a square box, full of reverse video Xs, on the screen.

```
/* logic.c */
/* demonstrates use of logical video buffer */
#define INCL_DOS
#define INCL_SUB
#include <os2.h>
#define HANDLE   0          /* vio handle, always 0 */
#define UPPER    5          /* upper row of fill area */
#define LOWER   15          /* lower row of fill area */
#define LEFT    20          /* left column of fill area */
#define RIGHT   60          /* right column of fill area */
#define COLS    80          /* columns per line */
main()
{
    unsigned long ptr;      /* pointer to logical buffer */
    unsigned len;           /* length of logical buffer */
    unsigned offset;        /* offset into logical buffer */
    int row;                /* row index */
    int col;                /* column index */
    unsigned rc;            /* return code */

                            /* get pointer to logical buffer */
    if( rc=VioGetBuf( &ptr, &len, HANDLE ) )
        { printf("VioGetBuf error=%u",rc); exit(1); }
```

```
                                      /* fill box in logical buffer */
     for( row=UPPER; row<=LOWER; row++ )      /* reverse attr */
        for( col=LEFT; col<=RIGHT; col++ )   /* capital X */
           *( (unsigned far *)ptr + col + row*COLS ) = 0x7058;

     printf("Writing completed to logical buffer.\n");
     printf("Will wait 2 secs, then update physical
                                              buffer.\n");
     DosSleep( 2000L );

     offset = 0;                    /* display logical buffer */
     if( rc=VioShowBuf( offset, len, HANDLE ) )
        { printf("VioShowBuf error=%u",rc); exit(1); }

     printf("Buffer has been updated\n");
     DosSleep( 2000L );
```

The program first fills the square area in the logical buffer with reverse video Xs. Then it prints several lines of text using the C library routine printf(). Finally it waits two seconds, and then updates the physical display with VioShowBuf(). Note that the lines of text appear on the screen immediately: this is because the routine for **printf()** (and the standard VIO functions as well), updates *both* the LVB and the physical buffer simultaneously (assuming the process is in the foreground). When, two seconds after the text is printed, the box appears on the screen, it does not write over these phrases. This is because they were written *after* the box was written to the LVB. Figure 13-4 shows the output of logic.c when the box and the text attempt to occupy the same space on the screen.

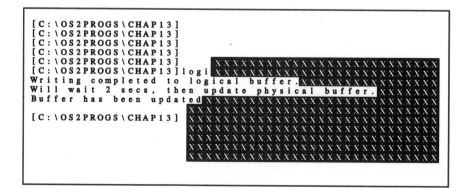

Figure 13-4
Output of logic.c

The VioGetBuf() Function: This function returns a **far** pointer to the LVB, and also the length of the LVB (4000 bytes in the case of an 80 by 25 character display).

VioGetBuf — Get pointer to logical video buffer

```
VioGetBuf(APointer, ALength, VioHandle);
unsigned long far *APointer;   /* address for buffer pointer
                                  */
unsigned far *ALength;         /* address for buffer length */
unsigned short VioHandle;      /* VIO handle, always 0 */
```

The three parameters to VioGetBuf() are the address where the pointer to the LVB will be returned, the address where the length of the LVB will be returned, and the standard VIO file handle. The pointer obtained from VioGetBuf() can be used without modification to access the LVB.

The VioShowBuf() Function: Once the LVB has been filled with the desired characters, it can be made visible using VioShowBuf(), which causes the contents of the LVB to be written to the physical video buffer.

VioShowBuf — Display logical video buffer

```
VioShowBuf(Offset, Length, VioHandle);
unsigned Offset;               /* offset into LVB */
unsigned Length;               /* length of LVB */
unsigned short VioHandle;      /* VIO handle */
```

This function takes three parameters. The first is the offset into the buffer where the updating should begin. If the entire screen is to be updated, this value is 0. Second is the length of the buffer to be updated. This is the same as the length returned from VioGetBuf(), assuming that the entire screen will be updated. The third argument is the VIO handle. In our example we update the entire screen, but it would be more efficient to update only that portion of the screen in which changes had been made.

Details of LVB Operation: Direct LVB access can be used in the background as well as the foreground. If the application is in the background when the screen is updated, the image will appear only when the application is switched to the foreground.

Direct LVB access to the display can be mixed with access using the standard VIO calls. Whichever method is appropriate for a specific operation can be used: large fill areas can be written directly to the LVB, text can be written using the VIO calls. However, care must be taken that visual anomalies don't arise because the VIO functions write to both the LVB and physical buffer simultaneously, while direct access affects only the LVB.

Writing to the Physical Video Buffer

To make graphics applications possible under VIO, and to simplify the porting of MS-DOS applications to OS/2, the designers of OS/2 made it possible for VIO applications to directly address the physical screen memory. This is an important concession, since allowing the programmer to access the physical screen leads to some potential system problems, as we'll see later.

Note that the *logical* video buffer can be directly accessed in character mode, but not in graphics mode. Thus direct access to the *physical* screen buffer is necessary if a program is to draw graphics without using the facilities of the Presentation Manager.

Disadvantages of Physical Buffer Access: There are several disadvantages to accessing the physical video buffer directly. First, a routine that accesses the buffer directly can do so for only one graphics adaptor and mode at a time. A routine that writes to the CGA display in mode 4 won't work in EGA mode 16, for example. An application must therefore have a variety of graphics routines built in, and select the correct one depending on the adaptor and display in use, or it must resign itself to working only with a specific display. Thus applications that directly access the physical display buffer are no longer device independent.

Second, while each screen group has its own logical buffer, there is only one physical buffer. When an application is switched into the background, whatever it drew on the physical screen will be lost, and the system will not be able to restore it. It is possible for the application to restore the image, as we'll see later, but this requires extra programming and may also require extra time when screen switches take place.

Applications that access the physical screen can still run under the Presentation Manager. However, each application must run in its own screen group; it cannot run in the Presentation Manager window.

Finding the Physical Buffer: Access to the physical screen buffer is obtained using the API function VioGetPhysBuf(). This function returns a selector to the start of screen memory, and gives the application permission to address this part of memory.

Locking the Screen: Since there is only one physical video display buffer in the system, it is essential that an application that is in the background not write to the buffer, since it would write over whatever information the foreground application was trying to display. To prevent such an unfortunate event, the application, before writing to the physical buffer, must check to make sure it is in the foreground. This is done with the function VioScrLock(). This function will cause an application to block if it is the background mode, and to be released when it moves to the foreground.

The VioScrLock() function not only protects the system from the application, it also helps to protect the application from the system. Imagine that an application draws half a picture, and is then interrupted by a screen switch. The screen switch will probably destroy what was written, so when the application returns and finishes the write operation, only the second half of the image will be visible. VioScrLock() is used to prevent a write operation from being interrupted in this way. The physical screen is locked with VioScrLock() before it is accessed, and unlocked with a function called (not surprisingly) VioScrUnLock() when the access is complete. While it is locked, the screen cannot be switched to the background.

The Physical Video Buffer in Character Mode: Although it is usually used for graphics, direct access to the physical video buffer can also be used in character mode. Let's look at this situation first, since it is simpler and quite similar to the technique used to access the LVB. The following example writes a box full of reverse video Xs to the physical buffer.

Run the program, and switch to another session when the image is on the screen. When you switch back again your screen will be restored. The system saves the contents of the physical buffer to the LVB just before the switch is made. (This is the case in character mode, but not with graphics.)

The example assumes that an 80 by 25 EGA text mode is in use, with a screen memory that starts at B8000 and is 4000 bytes long. You'll need to modify the input values to VioGetPhysBuf(), as discussed below, if you're using another system (such as a monochrome display).

```
/* physic.c */
/* writes characters directly to physical display buffer */
#define INCL_DOS
#define INCL_SUB
#include <os2.h>
#define HANDLE   0          /* VIO handle, always 0 */
#define WAIT     1          /* wait until screen available */
#define UPPER    10         /* upper row of box */
#define LOWER    15         /* lower row of box */
#define LEFT     0          /* left column of box */
#define RIGHT    60         /* right column of box */
#define COLS     80         /* columns on screen */
```

(continued)

```
main()
{
    struct _VIOPHYSBUF phys;  /* data for physical buffer */
    unsigned far *ptr;        /* pointer to physical buffer */
    int row;                  /* row index */
    int col;                  /* column index */
    char status;              /* status of VioScrollLock() */
    unsigned rc;              /* return code */

                              /* start of EGA memory */
    phys.pBuf = (unsigned char far *)0xB8000;
    phys.cb = 4000;           /* 25x80x2 buffer length */

                              /* get selector to phys buff */
    if( rc=VioGetPhysBuf( &phys, 0 ) )
       { printf("VioGetPhysBuf error=%u",rc); exit(1); }

                              /* make pointer to phys buff */
    ptr=(unsigned far *)( (unsigned long)phys.asel[0]<<16);

                              /* lock the screen */
    if( rc=VioScrLock( WAIT, &status, HANDLE ) )
       { printf("VioScrLock error=%u",rc); exit(1); }

                              /* draw box in physical buff */
    for( row=UPPER; row<=LOWER; row++ )
       for( col=LEFT; col<=RIGHT; col++ )
          *( ptr+col+row*COLS ) = 0x7058;

                              /* unlock screen */
    if( rc=VioScrUnLock( HANDLE ) )
       { printf("VioScrUnLock error=%u",rc); exit(1); }
    exit(0);
}
```

The VioGetPhysBuf() Function: This function is used to find the start of the physical video buffer. It takes two arguments.

```
        VioGetPhysBuf — Get selector to physical video buffer
VioGetPhysBuf(AStructure, Reserved);
struct _VIOPHYSBUF far *AStructure;    /* address of
                                          structure */
unsigned Reserved;                     /* reserved, always 0 */
```

The first argument is a pointer to a structure that is used for both input to the function and output from it. Here's the structure, as defined in BSESUB.H:

```
struct _VIOPHYSBUF {
    unsigned long pBuf;        /* starting address of buffer */
    unsigned long cb;          /* length of buffer */
    unsigned asel[1];          /* selectors returned */
    }
```

The first two elements of the structure, the starting address and length of the physical buffer, are filled in by the application. This information depends on the video mode to be used. For example, the monochrome display memory starts at B0000 hex, CGA at B8000, and EGA at A0000. Text modes are 4000 bytes long for an 80 by 25 display, but graphics modes range from 16K to more than 256K. If an application does not already know what display it is running under, it can call VioGetConfig() to determine the display and adaptor types, and VioGetMode() to determine the video mode. The starting address and buffer length can then be set appropriately. As noted above, you may need to change these values in the example program if you are using a display other than EGA text.

The third element of the structure is an array in which selectors to the physical buffer are returned. One selector is returned for each 64K segment used by the display. The first selector addresses the first segment. If the display is 64K bytes long, or less, then only this selector is needed. If the display is longer, the second selector addresses the second 64K segment, and so forth. Since this is a selector (not a pointer as was returned by VioGetBuf() for the LVB), it must be shifted left 16 bits to form a 32-bit **far** pointer before it can be used to access the buffer.

The second argument to VioGetPhysBuf() is reserved and must be 0.

The VioScrLock() Function: This function tests whether the physical screen is available, and if so, locks it, so that the application cannot be interrupted by being shifted into the background.

VioScrLock — Lock physical screen buffer

```
VioScrLock(WaitFlag, AStatus, VioHandle);
unsigned WaitFlag;            /* 0=no wait, 1=wait */
unsigned char far *AStatus;   /* 0=successful, 1=not */
unsigned short VioHandle;     /* VIO handle, always 0 */
```

The function takes three arguments. The first is a flag that specifies whether the function should wait if the physical buffer is unavailable (usually because the application is in the background). A value of 1 means that the function should block until the screen becomes available; this is the more usual option. A value of 0 means the function should not wait; this permits the thread to perform other processing while waiting for the screen.

The second argument is the address where the status of the request will be returned. This value will be 0 if the screen can be written to, and 1 if it cannot. This argument is used when the no-wait option is specified for the first argument; the thread can query it to see whether to write to the screen or do other processing. Since our application uses the wait option, we don't make use of this parameter.

The third argument to VioScrLock() is the VIO handle, which must be zero.

The programmer must be careful when using VioScrLock(). While the screen is locked, an application effectively hangs the system, by preventing the user from switching to another session. Other applications may continue to run in the background, but they can't be accessed by the user. Thus it is important that the time when the screen is locked be as short as possible.

In fact, the effects of VioScrLock() are so drastic that OS/2 provides a sort of safety valve in the event an application locks the screen for an excessively long time. If an application locks the screen, and the user presses the [Ctrl] [Esc] keys to switch to another session, OS/2 will eventually interrupt the application to permit the screen switch to take place. Currently it will wait 30 seconds before making the switch. If the application is still drawing on the screen when the switch takes place, the picture will be lost.

The VioScrUnLock() Function: Once an application has finished writing to the physical screen buffer it must release the buffer; thus re-enabling screen switching. This is accomplished with the VioScrUnLock() function.

VioScrUnLock — Unlock physical screen buffer

```
VioScrUnLock(VioHandle);
unsigned short VioHandle;    /* VIO handle, always 0 */
```

This function takes only one argument, the VIO handle, which must be 0.

What happens if, after an application has released the screen with VioScrUnLock(), the user switches to another session? In a character application such as physic.c, no harm is done since the physical buffer is saved in the LVB before a switch is made. However, in a graphics application the LVB is not available, so on return to the application from a different session the physical screen buffer is altered and the display trashed. We'll see soon how to deal with the problem of a trashed graphics display.

Writing Graphics to the Physical Video Buffer

We've explored writing characters to the physical video buffer; now let's see how to write graphics. The next example paints the screen white, waits two seconds, and then draws four lines on the screen: a black horizontal, a black vertical, a magenta diagonal, and a cyan diagonal. The program then waits three seconds and exits. When the program terminates, the system restores the previous LVB for the CMD.EXE screen, and the graphics image vanishes.

This example uses CGA graphics mode 4, which has a resolution of 320 by 200 pixels, each of which can be one of four colors. For four colors, each pixel requires two bits, so each byte can hold the information for four pixels. In CGA graphics the even scan lines occupy memory starting at B8000 hex, while the odd scan lines start at BA000 hex.

Like the last example, this program uses VioGetPhysBuf() to obtain the selector to the screen, and VioScrLock() and VioScrUn-Lock() to ensure the program is in the foreground, and to prevent screen switches while the image is being created.

Before creating the image, the program must switch into the appropriate graphics mode. The VioSetMode() function, described in Chapter 3, is used for this purpose.

```
/* graphic.c */
/* draws graphics on physical display buffer */
#define INCL_DOS
#define INCL_SUB
#include <os2.h>
#define HANDLE   0          /* vio handle, always 0 */
#define WAIT     1          /* wait until screen available */
#define CYAN     0x01       /* colors for */
#define MAGENTA  0x02       /*   cga graphics */
#define BLACK    0x00       /*    display */
#define BUFSIZE  12         /* size of _VIOMODEINFO buffer */
#define BYTES    40         /* bytes/row/2 */

unsigned char far *ptr0;   /* pointer to physical buffer */

main()
{
    struct _VIOPHYSBUF phys;   /* data for physical buffer */
    struct _VIOMODEINFO moda;  /* data for video mode */
    char status;               /* status of VioScrLock() */
    int byte;                  /* index into video buffer */
    int x;                     /* horiz coordinate */
    unsigned rc;               /* return code */
```

(continued)

```
                              /* start of EGA memory */
    phys.pBuf = (unsigned char far *)0xB8000;
    phys.cb = 16384;         /* length: 320 by 200, 4 colors */

    moda.cb = BUFSIZE;       /* change to CGA graphics mode */
    moda.fbType =    3;
    moda.color =     2;
    moda.col =      40;
    moda.row =      25;
    moda.hres =    320;
    moda.vres =    200;
    if( rc=VioSetMode( &moda, HANDLE ) )
       { printf("VioSetMode error=%u",rc); exit(1); }

                              /* get selector to phys buffer */
    if( rc=VioGetPhysBuf( &phys, 0 ) )
       { printf("VioGetPhysBuf error=%u",rc); exit(1); }

                              /* make pointer to phys buffer */
    ptr0 = (unsigned char far *)
                     ( (unsigned long)phys.asel[0]<<16 );

                              /* lock the screen */
    if( rc=VioScrLock( WAIT, &status, HANDLE ) )
       { printf("VioScrLock error=%u",rc); exit(1); }
                              /* fill screen with white */
    for( byte=0; byte<8000; byte++)  { /* for every byte */
       *(ptr0+byte) = 0xFF;            /* first mem bank */
       *(ptr0+byte+8192) = 0xFF;       /* 2nd mem bank */
    }
    DosSleep( 2000L );       /* admire fill */

    for(x=0; x<200; x++)  {    /* draw four lines */
       putpt( x, x, CYAN );             /* diagonal */
       putpt( x, 199-x, MAGENTA );      /* diagonal */
       putpt( x, 100, BLACK );          /* horizontal */
       putpt( 100, x, BLACK );          /* vertical */
    }
    DosSleep( 3000L );       /* admire lines */

                              /* unlock screen */
    if( rc=VioScrUnLock( HANDLE ) )
       { printf("VioScrUnLock error=%u",rc); exit(1); }
    exit(0);                 /* exit */
}
```

(continued)

```
/* putpt() */
/* function to draw a pixel (two bits) on the screen */
putpt(col, row, pixel)              /* given coordinates, */
int col, row;                       /* and color value */
unsigned char pixel;                /* of pixel */
{
    int addr;                       /* offset address */
    int j;                          /* shift count */
    int shift;                      /* bits to shift pixel */
    int mask = 0xFF3F;              /* mask for background */
    unsigned char temp;             /* background storage */

    addr = row*BYTES + (col>>2);    /* get offset address */
    if(row & 1)                     /* if odd row, */
        addr += 8152;               /*    add 2nd mem bank */
    pixel<<= 6;                     /* start pixel on left */
    shift = col & 0x03;             /* number to shift */

    for(j=0; j<shift; j++)  {       /* shift mask and pixel */
        mask >>= 2;                 /* right, shift times */
        pixel >>= 2;
    }                               /* get existing byte */
    temp = *(ptr0+addr) & (char)mask; /* AND off old pixel */
    *(ptr0+addr) = temp | pixel;    /* OR on new pixel */
}
```

The putpt() function places a single pixel on the screen. It is entered with the col and row coordinates of the pixel, and its color value, which is a two-bit quantity with one of the following values:

Binary	Hex	Color
00	0x00	Black
01	0x01	Cyan
10	0x02	Magenta
11	0x03	White

The main program calls this function repeatedly to draw the four lines.

The screen is filled with white by writing four pixels at a time (one byte) into the physical display buffer. Each pixel has the value 11 binary, so a byte value of 0xFF causes all four pixels to turn white at once. The loop fills both memory banks simultaneously.

Restoring Trashed Graphics Images

If a program places a graphics image on the physical screen, and then unlocks the screen with VioScrUnLock(), the image is vulnerable to being trashed whenever a screen switch takes place. If the user switches to another session, or if a background task places a popup window on the screen, the graphics image will be destroyed. As we mentioned, the system makes no attempt to save graphics images, since doing so potentially requires huge amounts of memory.

You can verify this rather somber truth by modifying the graphic.c example to draw its design and then wait until a key is struck before exiting. Run the program, and when it has created its design and unlocked the screen, but before exiting, switch to the session manager with [Ctrl] [Esc]. Then switch back to graphic.c. You'll find the screen image bears little relationship to the one originally drawn.

How can an application protect itself against having its graphics image trashed? The answer is that it can't; but it can find out when the image is about to be trashed, so that it can save it in an internal buffer. Once saved, the image can then be restored when it's safe (usually when the application again finds itself in the foreground).

The function VioSavReDrawWait() is used in a dual capacity: both to find out when the screen is about to be switched, and to find out when it's time to restore the image. This function typically runs in its own separate thread. Other threads can then continue calculating data for new screen images or performing other tasks, without being bothered with the status of the physical screen. We've used this multithread approach in our example program.

The example is much like the earlier graphic.c program. It paints the screen white, and draws four lines in different colors. However, its behavior is very different when you switch to the session manager. On return, the original image is restored exactly to its original form.

The saving and restoring is handled in the second thread, called SaveReDraw() in this example. The thread starts by executing VioSavReDrawWait(). This function blocks until notified that the screen is about to be switched. At this point the function unblocks, and the thread saves the screen image in its own buffer. Now the thread executes the same function again. This time the function will unblock when the image is ready to be restored. The thread restores it, and executes VioSavReDrawWait() again in preparation for the screen to be trashed. This wait-save-wait-restore cycle continues as long as necessary. Pressing any key terminates the program.

Figure 13-5 shows a flowchart of the program's operation.

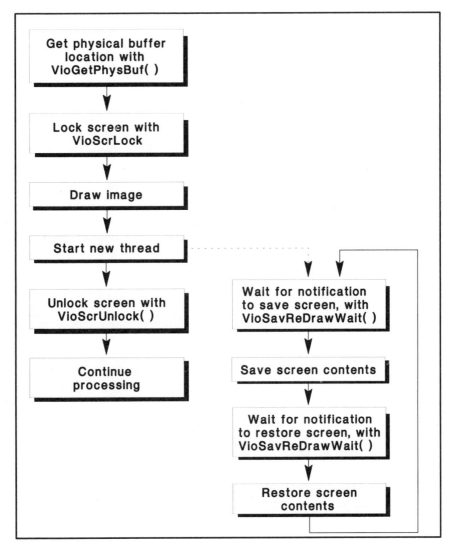

Figure 13-5
Flowchart of redraw.c

```
/* redraw.c */
/* demonstrates automatic saving of screen image */
#define INCL_DOS
#define INCL_SUB
#include <os2.h>
#include <malloc.h>        /* for malloc() */
#define HANDLE   0         /* vio handle, always 0 */
#define WAIT     1         /* wait until screen available */
#define CYAN      0x01     /* colors for */
#define MAGENTA   0x02     /*   CGA grahics */
#define BLACK     0x00     /*   display */
#define BUFSIZE  12        /* size of _VIOMODEINFO buffer */
#define BYTES    40        /* bytes per row/2 */
#define STACK_SIZE 1024    /* size of new thread's stack */

unsigned char store[16384];  /* buffer to store screen
                                 image */
unsigned char far *ptr0;   /* pointer to physical buffer */

main()
{
   struct _VIOPHYSBUF phys;  /* data for physical buffer */
   struct _VIOMODEINFO moda; /* data for video mode */
   char status;             /* status of VioScrLock() */
   int byte;                /* index into video buffer */
   int x;                   /* horiz coordinate */
   char far *stkptr;        /* stack pointer for new thread */
   void far SaveReDraw();   /* prototype for new thread */
   unsigned threadID;       /* thread ID number */
   unsigned rc;             /* return code */

                            /* start of EGA memory */
   phys.pBuf = (unsigned char far *)0xB8000;
   phys.cb = 16384;         /* length: 320 by 200, 4 colors */

   moda.cb = BUFSIZE;       /* change to CGA graphics mode */
   moda.fbType =    3;
   moda.color =     2;
   moda.col =      40;
   moda.row =      25;
   moda.hres =    320;
   moda.vres =    200;
   if( rc=VioSetMode( &moda, HANDLE ) )
      { printf("VioSetMode error=%u",rc); exit(1); }

                            /* get selector to phys buffer */
   if( rc=VioGetPhysBuf( &phys, 0 ) )
      { printf("VioGetPhysBuf error=%u",rc); exit(1); }
```

(continued)

```
                                /* make pointer to phys buffer */
    ptr0 = (unsigned char far *)
                    ( (unsigned long)phys.asel[0]<<16 );

                                /* lock the screen */
    if( rc=VioScrLock( WAIT, &status, HANDLE ) )
        { printf("VioScrLock error=%u",rc); exit(1); }
                                /* fill screen with white */
    for( byte=0; byte<8000; byte++)  { /* for every byte */
        *(ptr0+byte) = 0xFF;             /* first mem bank */
        *(ptr0+byte+8192) = 0xFF;        /* 2nd mem bank */
    }

    for(x=0; x<200; x++)  {    /* draw four lines */
        putpt( x, x, CYAN );             /* diagonal */
        putpt( x, 199-x, MAGENTA );      /* diagonal */
        putpt( x, 100, BLACK );          /* horizontal */
        putpt( 100, x, BLACK );          /* vertical */
    }
                                /* start save/redraw thread */
                                /* get stack space */
    stkptr = (char far *)malloc(STACK_SIZE) + STACK_SIZE;
                                /* start new thread */
    if( rc=DosCreateThread( SaveReDraw, &threadID, stkptr) )
        { printf("DosCreateThread error=%d\n",rc); exit(1); }

                                /* unlock screen */
    if( rc=VioScrUnLock( HANDLE ) )
        { printf("VioScrUnLock error=%u",rc); exit(1); }

    while( !kbhit() )           /* loop until key struck */
        ;
    getche();                   /* digest character */
    exit(0);                    /* exit all threads */
}

/* putpt() */
/* function to draw a pixel (two bits) on the screen */
putpt(col, row, pixel)              /* given coordinates, */
int col, row;                       /* and color value */
unsigned char pixel;                /* of pixel */
{
    int addr;                       /* offset address */
    int j;                          /* shift count */
    int shift;                      /* times to shift pixel */
    int mask = 0xFF3F;              /* mask for background */
    unsigned char temp;             /* background storage */
```

(continued)

```
      addr = row*BYTES + (col>>2);    /* get offset address */
      if(row & 1)                      /* if odd row, */
         addr += 8152;                 /*    add 2nd mem bank */
      pixel<<= 6;                      /* start pixel on left */
      shift = col & 0x03;              /* number to shift */

      for(j=0; j<shift; j++)  {        /* shift mask and pixel */
         mask >>= 2;                   /* right, shift times */
         pixel >>= 2;
      }
      temp = *(ptr0+addr) & (char)mask; /* get existing byte */
      *(ptr0+addr) = temp | pixel;      /* OR on new pixel */
}
 /* SaveReDraw() */
/* thread to handle screen save and restore */
void far SaveReDraw()
{
   struct _VIOMODEINFO moda;   /* data for video mode */
   unsigned Index = 0;         /* 0 = both save and redraw */
   unsigned Notify;            /* action code returned */
   unsigned byte;              /* index to video buffers */
   unsigned rc;                /* return code */

   while(TRUE)  {
      if( rc=VioSavRedrawWait( Index, &Notify, 0 ) )
         { printf("VioSavReDrawWait error=%u",rc); exit(1);
                                                             }

      if( Notify==0 )  {      /* if "save" */
         for( byte=0; byte<8000; byte++)  { /* for every
                                                        byte */
            store[byte] = *(ptr0+byte); /* first mem bank */
            store[byte+8192] = *(ptr0+byte+8192); /* 2nd
                                                        bank */
         }  /* end for */
      }  /* end if */
                                  /* if "restore" */
      else if( Notify==1 )  {
         moda.cb = BUFSIZE;              /* change back to */
         moda.fbType =    3;             /* CGA graphics mode */
         moda.color =     2;
         moda.col =      40;
         moda.row =      25;
         moda.hres =    320;
         moda.vres =    200;
         if( rc=VioSetMode( &moda, HANDLE ) )
             { printf("VioSetMode error=%u",rc); exit(1); }
```

(continued)

```
                                     /* restore screen image */
            for( byte=0; byte<8000; byte++)   {   /* for every
                                                          byte */
               *(ptr0+byte) = store[byte]; /* first mem bank */
               *(ptr0+byte+8192) = store[byte+8192]; /* 2nd
                                                          bank */

         }  /* end for */
      }  /* end else-if */
   }  /* end while(1) */
}
```

The VioSavReDrawWait() Function: This function takes three arguments.

```
VioSavReDrawWait — Wait for screen save or restore
VioSavReDrawWait(Indicator, ANotify, Reserved);
unsigned Indicator;        /* 0=save/redraw, 1=redraw only */
unsigned far *ANotify;     /* address for action taken */
unsigned Reserved;         /* reserved, must be 0 */
```

The first argument is set by the application. It indicates whether the application should be informed when it is time for either save or redraw, or if it should be informed only for redraw. A 0 indicates both save and redraw, while a 1 indicates redraw only. In our example we use the same call to the function to check for both save and redraw, so we set this value to 0.

The second argument is an address in which the function returns a code indicating what the application should do. The **notify** code has the following values:

Value	Action
0	Save screen buffer, registers, state bits
1	Restore screen buffer, registers, state bits

In our example we either save the screen buffer (if **notify** is 0) or restore it (if **notify** is 1).

When our application restores the image, it must first change to the CGA graphics mode it originally used to draw the image. When a screen switch takes place the system puts the screen back in text mode, so the mode information is lost, and must be restored by the application.

In some circumstances it may be necessary for an application to save the contents of registers in the graphics adaptor at the same time it saves the screen image. This enables the restoration of any state in any graphics mode. However, some of the registers in the EGA adaptor are read-only, so this system will not always work.

In our application we save each byte of the image in a buffer, and restore the display by reading these bytes back in again. Another approach, that might be faster in some circumstances, is to again execute the operations that created the image in the first place. For instance, in the example program we could have filled the screen with white and then drawn the lines to restore the image, as we did originally, rather than saving and restoring all the bytes from a buffer. Which approach is faster depends on the complexity of the image and other aspects of the program.

Summary

The first topic covered in this chapter was the mouse. The mouse device can be opened, and a handle to it returned, with MouOpen(). It is closed with MouClose(). The function MouDrawPtr() is used to establish a connection between the mouse and its pointer, and to restore a previously hidden pointer. Information about the position of the mouse and the status of its buttons can be obtained using MouReadEventQue().

The position of the mouse pointer can be set with MouSetPtrPos(), and the pointer can be hidden in all or part of the screen with MouRemovePtr(). An example program showed how the mouse can be used to activate a drop-down menu.

The second topic of this chapter was direct access to the video display buffer. Each session has its own logical display buffer (LVB), which is saved when the screen is switched. This buffer can be used only with characters, and is accessed with VioGetBuf(). Material placed in the buffer does not become visible immediately, but is transferred to the physical buffer and made visible with VioShowBuf().

The VioGetPhysBuf() function is used to access the physical video buffer, which is connected directly to the display hardware. Before placing data in this buffer the screen must be locked with VioScrLock(). This function prevents an application that is in the background from writing to the physical display, and also keeps the screen from being switched while an image is being created. VioScrUn-Lock() unlocks the screen when drawing is completed. Both graphics and character images can be written to the physical buffer.

Since the system does not save graphics images when the screen is switched, the application must do so. The application finds out when to save an image by waiting on VioSavReDrawWait(), and learns when to restore the image by waiting on the same function.

Chapter 14

Chapter 14

Certain features of OS/2 receive considerable publicity: breaking the 640K barrier, threads, interprocess communication. Another feature, *dynamic linking*, is not as highly publicized and is probably not as well understood. Yet dynamic linking represents as much of a revolutionary change as OS/2's other features. It has an important effect on the operation of the system, and will influence all serious OS/2 programmers. This chapter explores the benefits of using dynamic linking, and shows how to write dynamic link routines and call them from applications.

Briefly, dynamic linking refers to linking applications with library routines at load time, or at run time, rather than at compile time. Dynamic linking is a somewhat more complex topic than those in previous chapters. However, it is not too difficult to write simple, workable dynamic link modules, as we'll see in this chapter. As it turns out, we can write dynamic link modules entirely in C; in many cases there is no need for assembly language at all. However, we will see one example where a small assembly file gives us added capability.

Dynamic Linking: the Basics

Before we delve into dynamic linking, let's review the linking process in general, and see what it accomplishes in a traditional single-tasking operating system.

Object Files

In most systems, including MS-DOS and OS/2, compilers and assemblers do not create the final, executable code for a program. Instead, they produce an intermediate file called an object (.OBJ) file. This object file can be linked together with other object files, and with library (.LIB) files, to produce an executable (.EXE) file.

The use of this intermediate step—object files—adds flexibility to the process of creating programs. If a program consists of several source files, and one of them is changed, the other source files do not need to be recompiled or reassembled. Only the changed file must be recompiled; then all the object files are relinked. In programs with many source files this can save considerable time in the development process.

Library Files

Linking also permits the use of library files. Library files are collections of object files, that can be used by many different programs. Library files typically contain functions to perform I/O and other common tasks in a system. These library functions form an intermediate level between the functions built into the operating system, and the functions written specifically for each application. Library functions can insulate a program from changes in hardware, providing increased portability for programs. Thus if a new printer is attached to the system, only the library file that contains functions to handle the printer need be changed; the object files that call these functions don't need to be recompiled.

Static Linking

In traditional microcomputer operating systems such as MS-DOS, linking always takes place before a program is executed. The various source files of the program are compiled or assembled, the resulting object files are then linked into an executable file, and the result stored for later execution. This executable file is a complete, stand alone unit, relying only on functions built into the operating system, and on the underlying hardware, to carry out its mission. The process is shown in Figure 14-1.

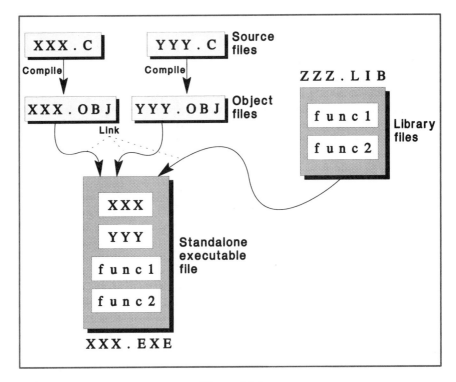

Figure 14-1
Static Linking

Linking a program at compile time is known as *static linking*. Although static linking makes possible separate compilation and the use of library files, it also has disadvantages.

The first problem is that once a program has been linked into an executable file, nothing in it can be changed without relinking the entire file. For example, if a new printer is added to the system, and a program does not already contain library functions to handle the printer, then a completely new executable file must be created by relinking the object files with new library files. This creates a problem for the software developer, who must either place code for many different printers in the program, (making it unnecessarily large) or provide many different versions of the program.

In a multiprogramming system, static linking has another disadvantage. Each executable program that uses a particular library routine must contain its own copy of the routine, even if other programs using these same library routines are in memory at the same time. There is no facility for sharing common code between different processes. This wastes memory and thus degrades the performance of the system.

Dynamic Linking

Dynamic linking solves both problems: it permits library files to be changed independent of the executable version of a program, and it permits library functions to be shared by different programs.

In dynamic linking the executable application file does not contain the code for the library routines. This code is contained in a separate file, called a dynamic link library, or DLL. The system takes care of loading the appropriate DLL file when it is needed, and making the connections between it and the application that uses it. Figure 14-2 shows how this looks.

There are actually two versions of dynamic linking: loadtime and runtime. In loadtime dynamic linking, the executable application file contains references to the functions in the DLL. When the application is loaded into memory, the system sees that there are references to these functions, loads them, and makes the connections between the application and the dynalink functions. In runtime dynamic linking, the application, during the course of execution, notifies the system that it needs to access a function in a DLL. The system then loads the DLL module into memory and provides the application with the addresses of the library functions.

Notice the advantages of dynamic linking over static linking. Since the dynalink library is entirely separate from the application, it can be changed at any time without affecting the application. If a new printer is added to the system, the dynalink function for the printer can be changed without recompiling or linking the application. The application always thinks it's talking to the same function, but the function in the DLL library can be changed at any time. Conversely, the application can be changed without altering the DLL. The pro-

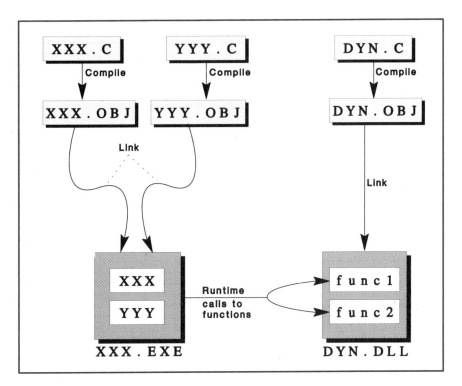

Figure 14-2
Dynamic Linking

grammer does not require access to the object files from which the DLL was created.

Also, since the operating system, rather than the linker, is responsible for making the connection between the dynalink routine and the application, it can connect the dynalink routine to more than one program at the same time. Thus several applications can share the same dynalink code.

Runtime dynamic linking carries the process even further. In loadtime linking the *system* is responsible for loading the dynalink routines and making the connections to the application. In runtime linking the *application*, using API functions, causes the dynalink routines to be loaded and connected. This means that the application can decide which dynalink library routines to load, when to load them, and when to remove them, based on changing circumstances. For instance, an application could ask the user if it was necessary to use a plotter, and load dynalink libraries for the plotter, only if and when they were required. Or the application could investigate the environment and load dynalink routines only for equipment that it found actually connected to the system.

The VIO, KBD, and MOU subsystems are examples of DLL libraries created to run specific hardware devices.

In this chapter we'll look at examples of applications that call dynamic link routines. The examples will show loadtime linking, runtime linking, accessing global and local data segments from dynamic link modules, and initializing dynalink modules.

Loadtime Dynamic Linking

In this example we'll examine an application that calls a dynalink function at loadtime. The application is very simple: it repeatedly prints a phrase on the screen. To do the printing, it calls two dynalink functions. One dynalink function prints the message in reverse video, the other prints it with the blinking attribute. Our application calls the routines alternately, with delays between each call, so it's easy to see the action of the application on the screen. After a few seconds the screen appears as shown in Figure 14-3.

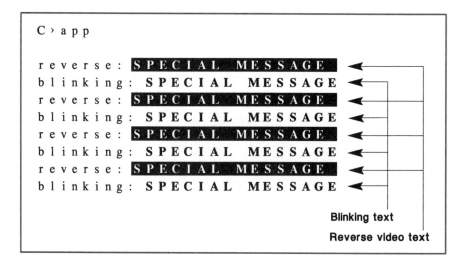

Figure 14-3
Output of the APP.C Program

Of course a real dynalink module would contain routines with more capability than this. Routines in a graphics DLL, for instance, might draw lines or circles on the screen when given appropriate coordinates, or a DLL might contain routines to control a plotter, printer, or other peripheral.

Our application is created from three source files. The first is the application program itself, APP.C. The second is the dynalink file, DYN.C. Finally, a definition file, DYN.DEF, is necessary to provide additional information to the linker. We'll look at these three files in turn, and then look at a MAKE file to put them all together.

The Application Source File

Here's the source file for the application program:

```
/* app.c */
/* application that calls routines in DLL */
#define INCL_DOS
#define INCL_SUB
#include <os2.h>

char msg[] = "SPECIAL MESSAGE";
char rev[] = "\r\nreverse: ";
char blk[] = "\r\nblinking: ";
main()
{
   void far pascal reverse( char far *, int );
   void far pascal blinking( char far *, int );

   while( !kbhit() )   {
                           /* print msg in reverse video */
      VioWrtTTy( rev, sizeof(rev), 0 );        reverse( msg,
      sizeof(msg) );         /* call DLL function */
      DosSleep(500L);
                           /* print blinking msg */
      VioWrtTTy( blk, sizeof(blk), 0 );
      blinking( msg, sizeof(msg) ); /* call DLL function */
      DosSleep(500L);
   }
   exit(0);
}
```

The program will print the message alternately in blinking and reverse video, until the user presses any key.

Notice that the calls to the dynalink routines, reverse() and blinking(), look just like calls to any other functions. The functions are declared to be of type **void far pascal** in prototypes at the beginning of the program; these prototypes are necessary. (They could go in a header file.) Both of these functions take as parameters the **far** address of the message, and the length of the message. Where are these functions located? In the dynamic link library module, which we'll look at next.

The Dynalink Library Source File

The dynamic link library (DLL) module contains the functions reverse() and blinking(). Here's the source file:

```
/* dyn.c */
/* uses DLL to print messages in reverse video and blinking
   */
#define INCL_SUB
#include <os2.h>

int _acrtused=0;                      /* avoids unwanted code */

void far pascal
reverse(msgptr, length)
char far *msgptr;                     /* pointer to message */
int length;                           /* length of message */
{
   unsigned row, col;                 /* cursor position */
   unsigned char attr = 0x70;  /* reverse video attribute */
   VioGetCurPos( &row, &col, 0 );  /* get cursor position */
                                      /* display string */
   VioWrtCharStrAtt( msgptr, length, row, col, &attr, 0 );
}

void far pascal
blinking(msgptr, length)
char far *msgptr;                     /* pointer to message */
int length;                           /* length of message */
{
   unsigned row, col;                 /* cursor position */
   unsigned char attr = 0x87;         /* blinking attribute */

   VioGetCurPos( &row, &col, 0 );  /* get cursor position */
                                      /* display string */
   VioWrtCharStrAtt( msgptr, length, row, col, &attr, 0 );
}
```

Each function uses VioGetCurPos() to find the position of the cursor, and then VioWrtCharStrAtt() to write, at the cursor position, the message whose address was passed by the application. The use of different attributes creates the reverse video or blinking effect.

A language-specific oddity in the program is the declaration of the variable **_acrtused**. This variable is created by the Microsoft C compiler so that the runtime library module CRT0 will be added to the code by the linker. In the DLL module this code is unnecessary, and by declaring the variable we can keep it from being added to the module.

The naming of the functions in the DLL deserves some thought. A typical DLL module will be accessed by many different applications. Thus it is important that the names of the functions do not conflict with those of functions in other applications or other DLLs. A good way to avoid such conflicts is to include a product-specific component in the name. If you're writing a routine for a NorthCoast brand plotter for example, you could call your functions NorCoPlot_Circle(), NorCoPlot_Line(), and so forth. The names reverse() and blinking(), used in the examples, are chosen for their simplicity; they are not idiosyncratic enough to make good function names in a serious DLL module.

In general the dynalink file looks like other files that contain functions. The way it is linked to the application is what makes it a dynalink file.

The Definition File

To create the proper connections between the application and the dynalink file, the linker must have additional information. This is provided by a *definition* (.DEF) file. Here's how the file DYN.DEF looks:

```
;dyn.def
;definition file for dyn.c

LIBRARY DYN INITINSTANCE      ;type of initialization
PROTMODE                      ;protected mode only
EXPORTS REVERSE               ;specifies entry points
        BLINKING
```

Module definition files are described in the programmer's guide. They contain statements that specify various aspects of a file: whether it is shared or not, whether it is execute only, the names and characteristics of its data segments, and so forth. The name of the .DEF file is, by default, given automatically to the .DLL file, in this case DYN.

The file shown above has three statements. The first statement, LIBRARY, specifies that the file named DYN.DLL (which will be generated from DYN.C) is a DLL file, rather than an ordinary application. The INITINSTANCE modifier specifies that the module will be initialized each time it is called by a different application, rather than only when it is loaded for the first time. (We'll explore this later.)

The second statement indicates that the module will run only in protected mode, not in the compatibility box.

The third statement specifies the names of the functions within the dynalink module that will be made available or "exported" to applications. In this case, they are the function names "reverse" and "blinking."

Now that we have the appropriate source files, how do we go about turning them into executable files? First, APP.C is compiled into the object file APP.OBJ, and DYN.C is compiled into DYN.OBJ.

The IMPLIB Utility

The next step is to turn the definition file DYN.DEF into a library file, DYN.LIB, using the IMPLIB utility. This .LIB file does not contain any actual routines, and is very short. What is its purpose?

Our final executable application file, APP.EXE, does not include the code for reverse() and blinking(). However, in order to locate and call the DLL module containing these functions, APP.EXE must contain information about them. This information is included in a special record that is attached to the APP.EXE file. This record contains the name of the dynamic link module, DYN.DLL in this case; and the names of the entry points of the routines to be accessed: reverse() and blinking(). It is the job of the IMPLIB utility to take this information from the .DEF file and create a .LIB file that can be attached by the linker to the APP.OBJ file. (As we'll see later, there's another approach to providing the application with this information.)

Finally, the CL utility is used to generate the executable application file APP.EXE by linking APP.OBJ and DYN.LIB. The Link utility generates the dynalink library file DYN.DLL from DYN.OBJ, DYN.DEF, and the system file DOSCALLS.LIB. The construction of APP.EXE and DYN.DLL is shown in Figure 14-4.

When we execute the APP.EXE file, the system sees that the calls to reverse() and blinking() refer to a DLL file, so it loads this file from the disk and makes the appropriate connections so the application can access these functions. If the DLL module is already in memory it need not be loaded again; only the connections are made.

The Make File

Since there are several source files involved in creating our application, and since various compiler and linker options need to be specified to produce the desired results, it's convenient to show the MAKE file for the application.

MAKE files are great time savers when a project involves multiple files. If you are not familiar with them you can learn more by studying the documentation provided with your programmer's toolkit.

Essentially, the MAKE file consists of pairs of lines. The first line in a pair describes dependencies: the file preceding the colon is dependent on the files following the colon. Dependent means that if the date and time of creation of the dependent files is later than that

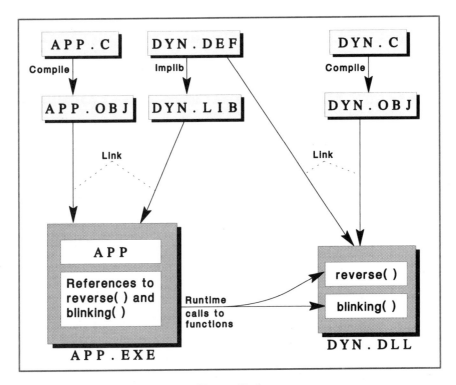

Figure 14-4
Constructing the APP.EXE and DYN.DLL Files

of the file that depends on them, then the dependent file must be regenerated, using the command in the second line. The second line, which must be indented, is a command to run a program, usually a compiler or linker, to generate the dependent file.

Thus the MAKE file provides a complete specification of which other files each file is derived from, and how it is derived.

Here's the MAKE file for this application:

```
# makedyn
# make file for app.c and dyn.c

dyn.lib: dyn.def makedyn
   implib dyn.lib dyn.def

app.obj: app.c makedyn
   cl -c -Lp -G2s -Zp app.c

dyn.obj: dyn.c makedyn
   cl -c -Lp -G2s -Zp dyn.c
```

(continued)

```
c:\dyn.dll: dyn.obj dyn.def makedyn
   link dyn,c:\dyn.dll,,doscalls.lib,dyn.def;

app.exe: app.obj dyn.lib makedyn
   cl -Lp -G2s -Zp -o app app.obj dyn.lib
```

The first entry creates the DYN.LIB file, using IMPLIB. The second and third entries compile APP.C and DYN.C into .OBJ files. The fourth entry creates the DYN.DLL file, which is placed in the root directory where the system can find it. The fifth entry creates the application itself.

The Microsoft utility CL is used to compile the .C files into .OBJ files. The -c parameter means compile only, don't link. As noted earlier in this book, the -Lp option generates a protected-mode file, -G2s enables the 80286 instruction set, -Zp specifies structure packing on 1-byte boundaries. The -o option prevents the compiler from thinking that the global variables have been defined more than once. The Link utility must be used to create the DLL file; CL can't do this. For more information on CL and Link, see the C language documentation.

For the MAKE file, just shown, to work, the pathnames of the LIB and INCLUDE subdirectories must be specified in the environment using SET commands, usually in a startup command file. The subdirectories must contain the appropriate library files, with names recognizable to the system.

Directory Structure

In this chapter we'll assume that each example occupies its own directory. All the files making up the example will go in this directory. In this way the same names can be used for the different files in several different examples. The directory for this first example is DYN1.

The only file that does not go in the example's directory is the DYN.DLL file: the dynalink module itself. To make it easy for the system to find, this file is placed in the root directory. A potential problem here is that the dynalink modules for all the examples have the same name. To avoid trouble, execute each example only when it is the last example created with MAKE. This avoids using the DYN.DLL file from one example with the .EXE file from a different example.

Loading and Executing the Application

When the application file APP.EXE is loaded into memory, the system examines the special record attached to the file and sees that there are references to functions in a dynalink module. It then finds this DLL module on the disk and loads it into memory. It puts the addresses of the functions at appropriate places in the special record, so that the application can call the functions. The application and the module remain in memory together until the function terminates. (If another application is using the DLL module, it will remain until the count of the applications using it goes to zero.) Figure 14-5 shows these steps.

Of course if the system needs memory, and swapping is enabled, any segment—including the application and the DLL—may be swapped out at any time, as described in the chapter on memory.

Avoiding IMPLIB

In the DYN1 example we used IMPLIB to create a file DYN.LIB from DYN.DEF. This DYN.LIB file was then linked to APP.OBJ to supply the application with information about the functions in the DLL module. This information can be provided in a different way. A second .DEF file can be created and linked directly to the application, eliminating the need for a .LIB file. This .DEF specifies the files to be "imported" by the application. Here's what the file would look like. We'll call this example DYN2.

```
;app.def
;definition file for app.c
PROTMODE                ;protected mode
IMPORTS DYN.REVERSE     ;file and entry point of DLL routines
        DYN.BLINKING
```

When this approach is used, the application must be linked with Link rather than CL. The MAKE file is:

```
# makedyn
# make file for app.c and dyn.c

app.obj: app.c makedyn
    cl -c -Lp -G2s -Zp app.c

dyn.obj: dyn.c makedyn
    cl -c -Lp -G2s -Zp dyn.c

c:\dyn.dll: dyn.obj dyn.def makedyn
    link dyn,c:\dyn.dll,,doscalls.lib,dyn.def;

app.exe: app.obj app.def makedyn
    link app,app,,doscalls.lib,app.def;
```

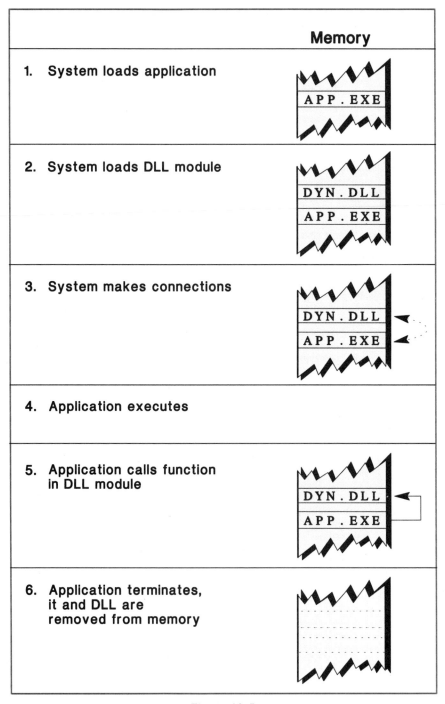

Figure 14-5
Loadtime Dynamic Linking

The app.c, dyn.c, and dyn.def files are the same as in DYN1.

Microsoft recommends the previous approach, using IMPLIB to create a .LIB file for the application. It is generally easier to use IMPLIB than to create a new .DEF file for each application.

Multiple Access to the DLL

You can arrange to call our example DLL from several instances of the application at the same time. (Use either DYN1 or DYN2.) This demonstrates how a single DLL can be accessed simultaneously by several applications. First, start up APP.EXE and leave the program running, printing its messages on the screen. Then switch to another session and invoke the program again. You can do this as often as you like. You'll have multiple instances of your application running in memory at the same time, but only one instance of the DLL. Each program calls the functions in the DLL whenever it needs to. Since these functions are reentrant, they can actually be executed simultaneously by different programs.

In this example there's no way for your application to tell that other applications are accessing the DLL at the same time. However, we'll look at an example later in this chapter where an application can find out which other applications are accessing a DLL module.

Linking at Runtime

As we've seen, loadtime dynamic linking is practically invisible to the applications programmer. Functions in a DLL can be called from the application just like other functions. The system takes care of loading the DLL and resolving the references to the functions within it. However, while programmers do not need to worry about the mechanism of this linkage, they also have little control over it. The system automatically loads the DLL file along with the application (unless the DLL is already in memory). The DLL then remains in memory until all the applications using it have terminated.

However, it may happen that an application knows more about its need for a DLL than the operating system does. Suppose a spreadsheet application needs to call a complex statistical analysis function, which is part of a DLL library. The spreadsheet program may be in memory for a long time, but it needs the function only occasionally, and then only for a short time. There is no need for the DLL routine to be kept in memory the entire time the spreadsheet is executing, as it would be using loadtime dynamic linking.

Using runtime dynamic linking, the DLL can be loaded into memory, accessed, and released, all under control of the application. This is accomplished using API functions from within the application, as shown in Figure 14-6.

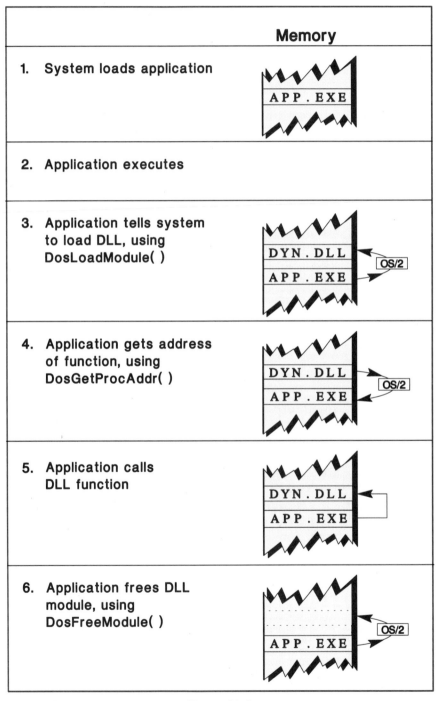

Figure 14-6
Runtime Dynamic Linking

Our next example shows this approach applied to our reverse()
and blinking() functions. We'll call the directory for this example
DYN3. The DYN.C file is unchanged from DYN1 and DYN2, but APP.C
has been rewritten to call the API dynalink library functions explicitly. Here's the source file:

```c
/* app.c */
/* application that calls routines in DLL */
/* loads DLL at run time using API calls */
#define INCL_DOS
#define INCL_SUB
#include <os2.h>
#define SIZE 32                 /* size of fail buffer */
char msg[] = "SPECIAL MESSAGE";
char rev[] = "\r\nreverse: ";
char blk[] = "\r\nblinking: ";

main()
{
    char FailBuf[SIZE];      /* fail-object name buffer */
    unsigned Handle;         /* dynalink module handle */
                             /* prototypes for functions */
    void (far pascal *Func1)(unsigned far *, int);
    void (far pascal *Func2)(unsigned far *, int);

                             /* load DLL module */
    DosLoadModule( FailBuf, SIZE, "DYN", &Handle );

                             /* get addresses of functions */
    DosGetProcAddr( Handle, "REVERSE", &Func1 );
    DosGetProcAddr( Handle, "BLINKING", &Func2 );

    while( !kbhit() )  {
                             /* print msg in reverse video */
        VioWrtTTy( rev, sizeof(rev), 0 );
        (*Func1)( (unsigned far *)msg, sizeof(msg) );
        DosSleep(500L);
                             /* print blinking msg */
        VioWrtTTy( blk, sizeof(blk), 0 );
        (*Func2)( (unsigned far *)msg, sizeof(msg) );
        DosSleep(500L);
    }                        /* free module */
    DosFreeModule( Handle ); /* (not really necessary) */
    exit(0);
}
```

This program makes use of three API functions that deal with dynamic link libraries: DosLoadModule(), DosGetProcAddr(), and DosFreeModule(). Let's look at each of these in turn.

The DosLoadModule() Function

This function causes the system to look for the DLL specified, and, if it is not already in memory, load it from the disk. Until this function is executed the system has no idea that the application has any interest in the DLL.

DosLoadModule — Load dynamic link module

```
DosLoadModule(ObjBuff, BuffLen, ModName, AModHandle);
char far *ObjBuff;            /* name of failure-object */
unsigned BuffLen;            /* length of object name buffer
                                */
char far *ModName;           /* ASCIIZ name of DLL module */
unsigned far *AModHandle;    /* address for handle of DLL
                                module */
```

This API function needs to know the name of the DLL module to be loaded. It also must know the address and length of a buffer in which the name of a file involved in the failure of the call can be placed by the system. (This is like the DosExecPgm() API.) The function returns a handle to the DLL module. This handle is used for subsequent references to the module.

The DosGetProcAddr() Function

Once the application has caused the DLL module to be loaded into memory, it needs to know the addresses of the functions within the module, so it can call them. It finds this out using the DosGetProcAddr() function.

DosGetProcAddr — Get DLL function address

```
DosGetProcAddr(ModHandle, FuncName, AFuncAddr);
unsigned ModHandle;              /* handle of DLL module */
char far *FuncName;              /* ASCIIZ name of function */
(pascal far * far *)()AFuncAddr; /* address for function */
```

Given the handle of the DLL module and the name of the function, DosGetProcAddr() returns the address of the function. This address can then be used for calls to the function, as can be seen in the APP.C file above.

The DosFreeModule() Function

When an application knows it will no longer be using a particular DLL module, it can free it using DosFreeModule().

DosFreeModule — Free DLL module

```
DosFreeModule (ModHandle);
unsigned ModHandle;      /* handle for DLL module */
```

This function takes only one parameter: the handle of the module to be freed. Once DosFreeModule() is executed, the module handle becomes invalid, as do function addresses previously obtained through DosGetProcAddr(). If you want to access the functions again, you'll need to start over with DosLoadModule().

Actually, a program's links to a DLL module are dissolved when the program terminates, so we don't need to use DosFreeModule() in this program. However, in the general case it should be used to free the DLL as soon as the application is finished with it.

The system keeps track of how many applications are accessing a particular DLL module. The DLL will be removed from memory as soon as the last program that is accessing it either terminates, or releases the module with DosFreeModule().

No .LIB File Needed

In runtime dynamic linking the program makes explicit requests to the system to load the DLL module and access its functions. The linker that creates the executable application file is not concerned that the program will, at some future time, want to make contact with a particular DLL library. Thus there is no need for the special record, which contains the DLL module name and function names, to be appended to the application .EXE file. The .LIB file is not needed, so the IMPLIB utility need not be invoked to create it. The application can be compiled and linked just as if it did not access a dynalink routine. (The DYN.DLL file still requires DYN.DEF.) Here's what the MAKE file looks like for the runtime dynamic link example:

```
# makedyn
# make file for app.c and dyn.c

app.obj: app.c makedyn
   cl -c -Lp -G2s -Zp app.c

dyn.obj: dyn.c makedyn
   cl -c -Lp -G2s -Zp dyn.c
```

(continued)

```
c:\dyn.dll: dyn.obj dyn.def makedyn
   link dyn,c:\dyn.dll,,doscalls.lib,dyn.def;

app.exe: app.obj makedyn
   cl -Lp -G2s -Zp -o app app.obj
```

Instance and Global Data

In the examples shown so far, the dynamic link module DYN.DLL had no external data (except for the variable **_acrtused**). The automatic variables **row** and **col** are created each time the function containing them is called, just as automatic variables are created in non-DLL functions. However, external variables (as opposed to local, automatic variables) are somewhat different than those in normal functions.

External data in a DLL can be either *instance* or *global*. Separate segments are generated to hold both kinds of data. There is a separate instance data segment for each application that calls the DLL. This provides a place for the DLL to record information about a specific application. By contrast, there is only one global data segment. This provides an area where the DLL can keep track of data common to all the applications.

For example, suppose the DLL is provided to handle calls to a printer. The instance data segments might be used to record what sort of formatting information each application expected, while the global data segment might record information about the printer itself. An application can, using functions in the DLL module (or pointers supplied by the DLL), access both its own specific instance data segment and the global segment. Figure 14-7 shows how this looks.

An Application Using Data Segments

Let's look at a simple application program that demonstrates instance and global data segments in a DLL. It goes in subdirectory DYN4. The DLL contains two parts: one is a routine that uses an instance data segment, and the other is a routine that uses a global data segment. These parts are created and compiled separately, then linked together to form the DLL. This provides the DLL with both instance and global data segments.

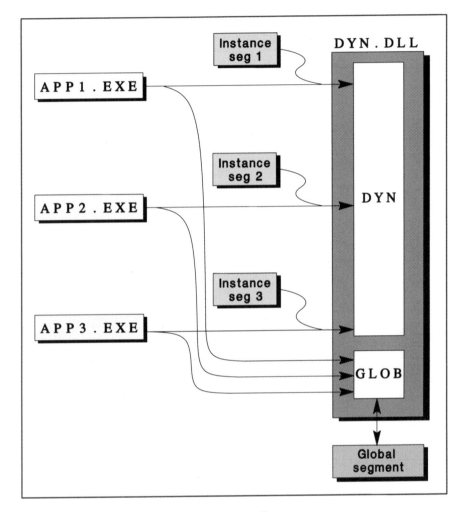

Figure 14-7
Instance and Global Data

The application in this example is invoked by the user with an arbitrary string on the command line. For instance, the first time you invoke the program you might type:

`app Joe`

Then you can switch to another session and invoke the application again, this time with:

`app Peter`

The application passes these names to the DLL. The DLL stores each name in two places. It stores it in the instance data segment (which has room for only one name per application), and it also adds it to a list of names in the global data segment.

Functions in the DLL can then be called by the application to display either the name used by a particular application, or the list of names stored by all applications. Here's a sample interaction with the application. We'll assume it's already been invoked twice in different sessions as described. Now we'll invoke it again, with the name Robert:

```
C>app Robert
Type 'g' to see all app's names,
     'l' to see this app's name,
     'q' to quit program: l
Local name: Robert

Type 'g' to see all app's names,
     'l' to see this app's name,
     'q' to quit program: g
List of names in global space:
Joe
Peter
Robert
```

By typing the appropriate letter, the application will print out either the name sent to it from the current application, or a list of names sent by all the applications connected to it. Typing 'q' terminates the program.

Source Files

Here's the source file for the application:

```
/* app.c */
/* exercises global and local DLL segments */
#define TRUE 1

main(argc, argv)
int argc;
char *argv[];
{
    void far pascal glostore( char far *, int );
    void far pascal gloshow();
    void far pascal locstore( char far *, int );
    void far pascal locshow();
```

(continued)

```
if( argc != 2 )
   { printf("Syntax: app name"); exit(1); }

                              /* store name in global space */
glostore( argv[1], strlen(argv[1]) );
                              /* store name in local space */
locstore( argv[1], strlen(argv[1]) );

while( TRUE )   {
   printf("\nType 'g' to see all app's names,\n");
   printf("      'l' to see this app's name,\n");
   printf("      'q' to quit program:\n");
   switch( getch() )   {
      case 'g':
         gloshow(); break;       /* get global names */
      case 'l':
         locshow(); break;       /* get local name */
      case 'q':
         exit(0);
   }
  }
}
```

There are four functions in the DLL. The first, glostore(), takes the name provided by the user on the command line and passed to it by the application, and adds it to the list of names in the global segment. The second, locstore(), places the name in the instance segment for the particular application. The third, gloshow(), prints out the contents of the list of names stored in the global segment, and the forth, locshow(), prints out the name stored in the instance segment.

The APP.C program calls the first two of these functions to store the name as soon as it executes. It then sits in a loop waiting for the user to type a letter. On command it then prints out either the list of names from the global segment, or the name in the instance segment, depending on whether the user types 'g' or 'l'.

The source file for the part of the DLL that uses the instance data segment is called DYN.C, as in previous examples. Here's the listing:

```
/* dyn.c */
/* stores or displays application-specific name */
#define INCL_SUB
#include <os2.h>
#define LENGTH 30                /* length of name buffer */
```

(continued)

```
static char name[LENGTH];        /* local buffer for name */
int _acrtused=0;                 /* avoids unwanted code */

void far pascal
locstore( nameptr, length )      /* stores name in local seg */
char far *nameptr;               /* pointer to name */
int length;                      /* length of name */
{
   int j;

   for(j=0; j<length; j++)       /* transfer name */
      name[j] = *nameptr++;      /* to local segment */
}

void far pascal
locshow()                        /* display local name */
{
   VioWrtTTy("Local name: ", 12, 0 );
   VioWrtTTy( name, strlen(name), 0 );
   VioWrtTTy("\r\n", 2, 0 );
}
```

This file contains two functions locstore() and locshow(), one to store the instance name, and one to display it.

The source file for the part of the DLL that uses a global segment is called GLOB.C. Here's its listing:

```
/* glob.c */
/* stores list of names in global data segment */
/* each application sends one name */
#define INCL_SUB
#include <os2.h>
#define NUMBER 20         /* number of names */
#define LENGTH 30         /* length of names */
                          /* global name array */
static char names[NUMBER][LENGTH];
unsigned count=0;         /* current number of entries */

void far pascal
glostore(nameptr, length) /* stores name in global seg */
char far *nameptr;        /* pointer to name to be stored */
int length;               /* length of name */
```

(continued)

```
{
   int j;

   for( j=0; j<length; j++ )              /* transfer string */
      names[count][j] = *(nameptr+j);  /* to global array */
   count++;                               /* number of names */
}

void far pascal
gloshow()                       /* displays list of stored names */
{
   static char head[] = "List of names in global space\r\n";
   int j;

   VioWrtTTy( head, strlen(head), 0 );
   for(j=0; j<count; j++)  {               /* display each name */
      VioWrtTTy( names[j], strlen(names[j]), 0 );
      VioWrtTTy( "\r\n", 2, 0 );
   }
}
```

Again, this file contains two functions, glostore() and gloshow(): the first adds the name passed to it from app.c to the list in the global data segment, the second displays this entire list.

Definition File

When data segments are used in a DLL module, the definition file used with the DLL must contain information about these segments. Here's the listing for DYN.DEF:

```
;dyn.def
;definition file for dyn.c

LIBRARY DYN INITINSTANCE     ;type of initialization

PROTMODE                     ;protected mode only

EXPORTS LOCSTORE             ;specifies function entry points
        LOCSHOW              ;in DLL module
        GLOSTORE
        GLOSHOW
```

(continued)

```
                                    ;non-shared and shared segments
SEGMENTS EACHPRO         CLASS 'FAR_DATA' NONSHARED
         EACHPRO_CONST  CLASS 'FAR_DATA' NONSHARED
         EACHPRO_BSS    CLASS 'FAR_DATA' NONSHARED
         ALLPROS        CLASS 'FAR_DATA' SHARED
         ALLPROS_CONST  CLASS 'FAR_DATA' SHARED
         ALLPROS_BSS    CLASS 'FAR_DATA' SHARED
```

The names of the functions to be exported are listed under EXPORTS as in previous examples. The SEGMENTS field is new. This field specifies the name of each segment. The CLASS of the segment is CODE or DATA; this can be NEAR or FAR. Thus FAR_DATA specifies a data segment referenced with **far** pointers. The NONSHARED and SHARED options specify whether the segment is to be instance or global.

Why are there so many segments? We really want to specify only two, one instance and one global: EACHPRO and ALLPROS. However, the C compiler generates additional segments with the _CONST and _BSS endings for each segment specified in the CL option. To tell the linker what do with these segments, it's necessary to include them in the definition file.

Actually, the linker automatically creates a global data segment for any DLL module that does not have segments overtly defined for it in a definition file. Thus it is not really necessary to specify the global data segment ALLPROS in the definition file; it's included only to show the contrast with the instance data segment, which does need to be specified.

The MAKE File

Here's the MAKE file that specifies how the various elements described above are put together.

```
# makedyn
# make exe files for app.c and dyn.c

dyn.lib: dyn.def makedyn              #DLL library file
    implib dyn.lib dyn.def

app.obj: app.c makedyn               #application obj file
    cl -c -Lp -G2s -Zp app.c

dyn.obj: dyn.c makedyn               #local data DLL obj file
    cl -c -Asnu -Lp -G2s -Zp -ND EACHPRO dyn.c
```

(continued)

```
glob.obj: glob.c makedyn               #global data DLL obj file
    cl -c -Asnu -Lp -G2s -Zp -ND ALLPROS glob.c

app.exe: app.obj dyn.lib makedyn       #application exe file
    cl -Lp -G2s -Zp -o app app.obj dyn.lib

c:\dyn.dll: dyn.obj glob.obj dyn.def makedyn   #DLL exe file
    link dyn+glob,c:\dyn.dll,,doscalls.lib,dyn.def;
```

The files DYN.OBJ and GLOB.OBJ are compiled by CL using somewhat different options than our earlier dynalink modules. The -ND option specifies that the file will have a data segment with a nonstandard name: EACHPRO for DYN.C and ALLPROS for GLOB.C.

Ordinarily the stack and the data share the same segment. However, when the -ND option is used, this assumption is no longer true: the contents of SS and DS segment registers are not the same. The program must therefore be compiled using the -A option to create a customized memory model. The complete option is -Asnu, where the 's' specifies the small memory model, 'n' means near data pointers, and 'u' causes different segments to be allocated for the stack and data. (Refer to the C compiler user's guide for more information on these options.)

Initialization Routines

It's possible to specify a DLL initialization routine: code that will be executed when the DLL is first loaded. Such a routine is useful when a DLL is controlling a resource (such as a plotter), and needs to initialize the resource the first time it is called. A plotter initialization routine could, for instance, send configuration codes to the plotter to adapt it to the system.

The initialization routine must be written in assembly language. However, the assembler routine does not need to do anything more than call a C language routine to do the work. Hence the same short assembly source file can be used for all programs. (Or, if you prefer, you can write the entire initialization routine in assembly language.)

The programs in this example go in the directory DYN5.

Source Files

We use the same reverse() function in the DLL as in earlier programs; it prints, in reverse video, a message passed to it. However, to save space we've eliminated the blinking function. The application file looks like this:

```
/* app.c */
/* application that calls routine in DLL */
#define INCL_DOS
#define INCL_SUB
#include <os2.h>

char msg[] = "SPECIAL MESSAGE";
char rev[] = "\r\nreverse: ";

main()
{
   void far pascal reverse( char far *, int );

   while( !kbhit() )  {
                                 /* print msg in reverse video */
      VioWrtTTy( rev, sizeof(rev), 0 );
      reverse( msg, sizeof(msg) );
      DosSleep(500L);
   }
   exit(0);
}
```

The source file for the dynalink module lacks the blinking() function, but now sports a new function, init(), which is called by the assembly language routine when the DLL is first loaded:

```
/* dyn.c */
/* uses DLL to print messages in reverse video */
/* contains initization routine, called by get.asm */
#define INCL_SUB
#include <os2.h>

char initmsg[] = "THE DLL IS INITIALIZING SOMETHING\r\n";
int _acrtused=0;                  /* avoids unwanted code */

int far pascal                    /* initialization routine */
init()
{                                 /* print message */
   VioWrtTTy( initmsg, sizeof(initmsg), 0 );
   return(1);                     /* tell get.asm all's well */
}
```

(continued)

```
void far pascal
reverse(msgptr, length)          /* print in reverse video */
char far *msgptr;                 /* pointer to message */
int length;                       /* length of message */
{
    unsigned row, col;                /* cursor position */
    unsigned char attr = 0x70;        /* reverse video */

    VioGetCurPos( &row, &col, 0 );   /* get cursor position */
                                      /* display string */
    VioWrtCharStrAtt( msgptr, length, row, col, &attr, 0 );
}
```

The init() function doesn't do much: it prints out a message to let us know when it executes. In a real application it would perform useful work.

Here's what the assembly routine that calls the init() function looks like:

```
;get.asm
;executed when dynalink module loaded
;calls C routine init() to do real work

        EXTRN    INIT:FAR              ;declare C function
        ASSUME   CS: _TEXT             ;CS register points here
_TEXT   SEGMENT  BYTE PUBLIC 'CODE'    ;code segment called
                                                          _TEXT
START   PROC     FAR                   ;specifies far return
        call     INIT                  ;calls C routine
        ret                            ;far return
START   ENDP                           ;end of procedure
_TEXT   ENDS                           ;end of segment
        END      START                 ;entry point to this code
```

Aside from establishing itself in the appropriate code segment, this routine does very little: it merely calls the init() function and then returns control to the operating system.

The DYN.DEF file is:

```
;dyn.def
;definition file for dyn.c

LIBRARY DYN INITINSTANCE        ;type of initialization
PROTMODE                        ;protected mode only
EXPORTS REVERSE                 ;specifies function entry points
```

This is similar to previous DYN.DEF files, except that the only function in the DLL that needs to be exported is reverse().

The MAKE File

How do we put all this together? Here's the MAKE file that constructs the final APP.EXE and DYN.DLL files:

```
# makedyn
# make exe files for app.c and dyn.c

dyn.lib: dyn.def makedyn                #DLL library file
    implib dyn.lib dyn.def

app.obj: app.c makedyn                  #application obj file
    cl -c -Lp -G2s -Zp app.c

dyn.obj: dyn.c makedyn                  #DLL obj file
    cl -c -Asnu -Lp -G2s -Zp dyn.c

get.obj: get.asm makedyn                #assembler obj file
    masm get.asm,,,;

c:\dyn.dll: dyn.obj dyn.def get.obj makedyn   #DLL exec file
    link dyn+get,c:\dyn.dll,,doscalls.lib,dyn.def;

app.exe: app.obj dyn.lib makedyn    #application exe file
    cl -Lp -G2s -Zp -o app app.obj dyn.lib
```

The new wrinkle here is the addition of an entry to generate an object file from GET.ASM. The Microsoft macro assembler does this. The resulting GET.OBJ file is then linked with DYN.OBJ to create the DYN.DLL module. You'll need to install the macro assembler MASM.EXE in the current directory or in a directory specified in the PATH command. You don't need to know anything about assembly language to make the example work, or even to create different DLL modules, since the assembly code's only activity is to call a C function.

Running the Program

What happens, after we've created the necessary executable files, when we execute this application?

First the single line "THE DLL IS INITIALIZING SOMETHING" appears on the screen. This indicates that, on the loading of the DLL, the assembly routine has been activated and called the init() function in the dynalink module. Once the initialization routine terminates the program starts printing the phrase "SPECIAL MESSAGE" in reverse video, at half-second intervals, in the usual way.

Summary

In this chapter we've explored the topic of dynamic linking. We've seen how to write a dynamic link module in C, and how to create an application that calls functions in the DLL. A special definition file (DYN.DEF in the examples) must be linked to the dynalink module to establish this connection. Another file must be linked to the application: either a library file derived from the first definition file, or a different definition file. Neither of these files contain the actual code of the functions to be called. They contain only the function names and the name of the DLL module that contains them.

We saw an example of a dynamic link module that was connected to the application at load time, and another example in which the application connected itself to the DLL module at run time. The runtime example made use of the API functions DosLoadModule() to load the DLL module into memory, DosGetProcAddr() to find the addresses of the functions within the module, and DosFreeModule() to release memory occupied by the DLL.

Other examples explored the use of instance and global data segments used in a dynamic link module, and an initialization routine that is activated when the DLL is first loaded.

Index

Managing OS/2
Profiting from Changing Standards

Mike Edelhart
and
David Strom

In this time of transition from DOS to OS/2, this book lets you manage both worlds so you understand:

- OS/2's capabilities and its relation to DOS
- The commands, processes, and interfaces of OS/2
- The move from DOS to OS/2, and getting up and running
- Configurations and real memory requirements
- Advanced features and troubleshooting

Plus thorough discussions of the changes and challenges for the OS/2 user, and real-world solutions to the top issues corporations face in moving to OS/2.

Ignore or misunderstand OS/2 and you'll be left in the dust. Master the possibilities now and you'll reap OS/2's benefits.

ISBN: 0-13-642893-2 • $24.95

To Order:
Call 1(800) 624-0023,
in New Jersey: 1(800) 624-0024
Visa/MC accepted

Inside the Norton Utilities™

The Official Guide.

by Rob Krumm
with an Introduction by Peter Norton

More than a million PC users depend on the Norton Utilities to make their computers reliable, efficient tools. The official guide to these best-selling programs, *Inside the Norton Utilities* shows you the most efficient way to use:

- Norton Utilities—the original
- Norton Utilities Advanced Edition—faster, and with new features
- Norton Commander—for high speed computer management
- Norton Editor—a programmer's tool in the Norton tradition

With this book you'll learn to fill the gaps in DOS's functionality. You'll explore memory and hard disk organization. You'll learn how to use the Norton Utilities, and, more importantly, how the Norton Utilities work with your data.

Inside the Norton Utilities covers formatting disks and erasing and copying files and disks. Then it shows you how to undo it all using UnErase and other Norton Utility functions. Working with Inside the Norton Utilities you'll learn how DOS stores data and gain greater control over your files. You'll stop losing data accidentally, and you'll stop disasters before they happen.

Rob Krumm runs a computer school in Walnut Creek, California. He is the author of *Getting The Most Out Of Utilities On IBM PC* and *Understanding and Using dBASE III Plus*. His columns and commentaries regularly appear in the *San Francisco Examiner* and Computer Currents.

ISBN: 0-13-467887-7 • $19.95

Inside the IBM PC

Access to Advanced Features and Programming, Revised and Expanded
by Peter Norton

The most widely recognized book about the IBM PC written by the most highly acclaimed IBM PC expert. Covers the IBM PC, XT and AT, every version of DOS from 1.1 to 3.0.

The classic work includes:

- The fundamentals of the 8088 and 80286 microprocessors, DOS and BIOS
- Programming examples to show how the machine works, in BASIC, Pascal, and Assembly Language
- How ROM is allocated
- A detailed look at disk data storage

Your only source for understanding and using the hardware and software that make up your IBM PC system.

ISBN: 0-89303-583-1 • $21.95 (book)
ISBN: 0-13-467325-5 • $39.95
(book/disk, includes 15 programs)

The Hard Disk Companion

by Peter Norton and Robert Jourdain

Head's crashed? Space fragmented? Just can't find that expense report file?

Hard disks have become an intrinsic part of msot personal computer systems, but many users don't really know how to handle them. Whether you're preparing to add a hard disk to your system or you've been using one for years, The Hard Disk Companion provides the guidance and advice you need.

- Learn to double, triple, even quadruple your hard disk's performance
- Learn about DOS commands and utilities for file recovery
- Get help determining your hard disk needs
- Follow step-by-step instructions for installation and setup

It's all here—from the pleasure of purchase to the grief of head crashes—with tips, warnings, and essential assistance you just won't find anywhere else!

ISBN: 0-13-383761-0 • $21.95

Peter Norton's Assembly Language Book for the IBM PC

by Peter Norton and John Socha

Learn to write efficient, full-scale assembly language programs that double and even triple your programs' speed. To learn techniques and enhance your knowledge, you'll build a program step-by-step.

The book is divided into three parts:

- Part 1 focuses on the mysteries of the 8088 microprocessor
- Part 2 guides you into assemby language
- Part 3 tackles the PC's more advanced features and debugging techniques

The book disk package includes a fully integrated, powerful disk for instant, hands-on experience in assembly language. The disk contains all the examples discussed in the book, and advanced professional version of the program you build.

With the expertise of Peter Norton and John Socha to guide you, you're guaranteed an experience that's both informative and practical.

ISBN: 0-13-661901-0 • $21.95 (book)
ISBN: 0-13-662149-X • $39.95 (book/disk)
Requires: IBM PC, AT, XT or compatible

Peter Norton's DOS Guide

Revised and Expanded
by Peter Norton

Here's tried and true instruction from the true-blue friend of PC users everywhere. Newly updated with coverage of DOS 3.3, this best-seller is distinguished by Norton's easy-to-follow style and honestly factual approach. Includes advice on hard disk management and discussions of batch files for DOS customization.

Topic-by-topic organization make this manual not only a lively tutorial, but also a long-lasting reference.

ISBN: 0-13-662073-6 • $19.95

The Norton Portfolio

From Brady Books

To Order: Call 1 (800) 624-0023,
in New Jersey 1 (800) 624-0024
Visa/MC accepted

Finally. A pro
for people who h

Nobody ever said programming PCs was supposed to be easy.

But does it have to be tedious and time-consuming, too?

Not any more.

Not since the arrival of the remarkable new program in the lower right-hand corner.

Which is designed to save you most of the time you're currently spending searching through the books and manuals on the shelf above.

It's one of a quintet of pop-up reference packages, called the Norton On-Line Programmer's Guides™, that actually *gather your data for you*—on OS/2 Kernel API or your favorite programming language.

Each package comes complete with a comprehensive, cross-referenced database crammed with just about everything you need to know to write applications.

Not to mention a wealth of wisdom from the Norton team of top programmers. (*PC Week* used the words "massive" and

"authoritatively detailed" to describe the information

DATA AND FEATURES

OS/2 KERNEL API (1M of data)
- Kernel API: Describes all OS/2 API services: DOSx, KBDx, MOUx and VIOx.
- Structure Tables: Lists all of the OS/2 data structures used in the Kernel API.
- Conversion Guide: DOS-to-OS/2 table shows which OS/2 calls replace DOS and ROM BIOS services.

ASSEMBLY (600K of data)
- DOS Service Calls: All INT 21h services, interrupts, error codes and more.
- ROM BIOS Calls: All ROM calls.
- Instruction Set: All 8088/86 instructions, addressing modes, flags, bytes per instruction, clock cycles and more.
- MASM: Pseudo-ops and assembler directives.

BASIC (270K each database)
- IBM BASICA, Microsoft QuickBASIC and TurboBASIC.
- Statements and Functions: Describes all statements and built-in library functions.

C (600K each database)
- Microsoft C and Turbo C: Describes the C language.
- Library Functions: Detailed descriptions of all functions.
- Preprocessor Directives: Describes commands, usage and syntax.

PASCAL—Turbo (360K of data)
- Language: Describes statements, syntax, operators, data types and records.
- Library: Describes the library procedures and functions.

FEATURES (all versions)
- Memory-resident—uses just 71K.
- Full-screen or moveable half-screen view, with pull-down menus.
- Auto lookup and searching.
- Tools for creating your own databases.
- More data: All five Norton Guides feature a variety of tables, including ASCII characters, line-drawing characters, keyboard scan codes and much more.
- Includes both OS/2 protected mode and DOS versions.

contained in the Guides. If you'd rather see for yourself, you might take a moment or two to examine the data box you just passed.)

You can, of course, find most of this information in the books and manuals on our shelf.

Designed for the IBM® PS/2® and PC families, and 100% compatibles. Available at most software

gramming tool
ate manual labor.

But Peter Norton—who's written a few books himself—figured you'd rather have it on your screen.

Instantly.

In either full-screen or moveable half-screen mode.

Popping up right next to your work. Right where you need it.

A Guides reference summary screen (shown in blue) pops up on top of the program you're working on (shown in green).

Summary data expands on command into extensive detail. And you can select from a wide variety of information.

This, you're probably thinking, is precisely the kind of thinking that produced the classic Norton Utilities.™

And you're right.

But even Peter Norton can't think of everything.

Which is why each version of the Norton Guides comes equipped with a built-in

compiler—the same compiler used to develop the databases contained in the Guides.

So you can create new databases of your own, complete with electronic indexing and cross-referencing.

No wonder *PC Week* refers to the Guides as a "set of programs that will delight programmers."

Your dealer will be delighted to give you more information. All you have to do is call. Or call Peter Norton Computing.

And ask for some guidance.

THE NORTON *On Line Programmer's* GUIDES

■ The ultimate productivity tool for programmers. ■ Puts volumes of data at your fingertips. ■ Replaces most manual searches with a few simple keystrokes. ■ Includes compiler for creating your own databases. ■ Also available for BASIC, BIOS/DOS/Assembly, C and Pascal.

Peter Norton
COMPUTING

dealers, or direct from Peter Norton Computing, Inc., 2210 Wilshire Blvd. #186, Santa Monica, CA 90403. 213-319-2000. Visa and MasterCard welcome. ©1988 Peter Norton Computing

ORDER DIRECT FROM PETER NORTON

Credit Card Orders Only: 1-800-365-1010

MCI MAIL: 226-1869   *FACSIMILE: (213) 458-2048*

PROGRAM	PRICE	QUANTITY	AMOUNT
The Norton Utilities™ 4.5 Advanced Edition AE20006	$150.		$.
The Norton Utilities™ 4.5 Standard Edition SE10006	$100.		$.
The Norton Commander™ 2.0 NC20006	$ 89.		$.
The Norton Editor™ NE20006	$ 75.		$.
The Norton Guides™:			
OS/2 GS10006	$150.		$.
BIOS/DOS/Assembly GA10005	$100.		$.
Basic GB10005	$100.		$.
C GC10005	$100.		$.
Pascal GP10005	$100.		$.
Dan Bricklin's™ Demo II DT10000	$195.		$.
California Residents: Please add sales tax (in Los Angeles County 6.5%, elsewhere 6%).			$.
Shipping and Handling (U.S. and Canada): Please add $5.00 for the first unit and $1.00 for each additional unit. Check/Money Order; U.S. Dollars drawn on U.S. Bank.			$.
Outside the U.S. and Canada: Please add $10.00 per unit Check/Money Order; U.S. Dollars drawn on U.S. Bank.			$.
		TOTAL ▶	$.

■ Please allow 4-6 weeks delivery.
■ Please attach order form with payment.
■ $500 Minimum on PO's. No C.O.D. orders.
■ Prices subject to change without notice.

VISA OR MASTERCARD NUMBER ONLY: _____ — _____ — _____ — _____

Expiration Date: _____

CHECK OR MONEY ORDER ENCLOSED ☐

NAME _____

COMPANY _____

ADDRESS _____

CITY	*STATE*
COUNTRY *ZIP*	*TELEPHONE*

VISA™

Peter Norton Computing, Inc.
2210 Wilshire Boulevard, Santa Monica, CA 90403
Telex: 6502261869

MasterCard